W9-BSI-271

**MALMARNA &
FURTHER AFIELD**
See pages 100–133

**EXCURSIONS FROM
STOCKHOLM**
See pages 140–151

LILLA VÄRTAN

DJURGÅRDEN

SALTSJÖN

DJURGARDEN
See pages 84–99

0 metres	500
0 yards	500

EYEWITNESS TRAVEL

STOCKHOLM

EYEWITNESS TRAVEL
STOCKHOLM

MAIN CONTRIBUTOR: KAJ SANDELL

DK

LONDON, NEW YORK,
MELBOURNE, MUNICH AND DELHI
www.dk.com

Produced by Streiffert Förlag AB, Stockholm
CHIEF EDITOR Bo Streiffert
PROJECT EDITOR Guy Engström
EDITORS Monica Nilsson, Guy Engström
DESIGNER Bo Streiffert
PICTURE RESEARCH Guy Engström

Dorling Kindersley Ltd
MANAGING EDITOR Anna Streiffert
ART DIRECTOR Gillian Allan

MAIN CONTRIBUTOR Kaj Sandell

CONTRIBUTORS
Lisa Carlsson, Jan & Christine Samuelson
Christina Sollenberg Britton, Stockholm Visitors Board

MAPS Stig Söderlind

PHOTOGRAPHERS Jeppe Wikström, Erik Svensson

ILLUSTRATIONS
Urban Frank, assisted by Jan Rojmar

Reproduced by PDC Tangen, Norway
Printed and bound in Malaysia by Vivar Printing Sdn. Bhd

First American Edition, 2000

12 13 14 15 10 9 8 7 6 5 4 3 2 1

Published in the United States by DK Publishing,
375 Hudson Street, New York, New York 10014

Reprinted with revisions 2001, 2004, 2007, 2010, 2012

Copyright 2000, 2012 © Dorling Kindersley Ltd, London

ALL RIGHTS RESERVED. WITHOUT LIMITING THE RIGHTS UNDER COPYRIGHT
RESERVED ABOVE, NO PART OF THIS PUBLICATION MAY BE REPRODUCED, STORED IN
A RETRIEVAL SYSTEM, OR TRANSMITTED IN ANY FORM OR BY ANY MEANS,
(ELECTRONIC, MECHANICAL, PHOTOCOPYING, RECORDING OR OTHERWISE),
WITHOUT THE PRIOR WRITTEN PERMISSION OF THE COPYRIGHT OWNER
AND THE ABOVE PUBLISHER OF THE BOOK.

Published in Great Britain by Dorling Kindersley Limited.

A CATALOGING IN PUBLICATION RECORD IS AVAILABLE
FROM THE LIBRARY OF CONGRESS.

ISBN 1542-1554
ISBN 978-0-75668-402-0

Front cover main image: Looking over Söder Mälarstrand in Stockholm

FLOORS ARE REFERRED TO THROUGHOUT IN ACCORDANCE WITH EUROPEAN USAGE; IE
THE "FIRST FLOOR" IS THE FLOOR ABOVE GROUND LEVEL.

MIX
Paper from
responsible sources
FSC
www.fsc.org   FSC™ C018179

**The information in this
Dorling Kindersley Travel Guide is checked regularly.**
Every effort has been made to ensure that this book is as up-to-date as
possible at the time of going to press. Some details, however, such as
telephone numbers, opening hours, prices, gallery hanging
arrangements and travel information are liable to change. The
publishers cannot accept responsibility for any consequences arising
from the use of this book, nor for any material on third party websites,
and cannot guarantee that any website address in this book will be
a suitable source of travel information. We value the views and
suggestions of our readers very highly. Please write to: Publisher,
DK Eyewitness Travel Guides, Dorling Kindersley, 80 Strand,
London WC2R 0RL, Great Britain, or email: travelguides@dk.com.

◁ **Dawn at Skeppsbron, on the eastern side of Gamla Stan**

CONTENTS

**Wooden sculpture on the
17th–century warship *Vasa***

INTRODUCING
STOCKHOLM

**Kaknästornet, Stockholm's tallest
building at 155 m (508 ft)**

Late winter walk along the shores of Kungsholmen

A packet of traditional round Swedish crispbread

The renovated Royal chapel at the Royal Palace

The Royal Palace in Gamla Stan

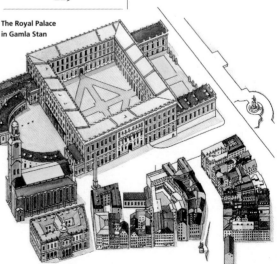

INTRODUCING
STOCKHOLM

FOUR GREAT DAYS IN STOCKHOLM

In Stockholm you are never far from water. Between them, the city's 14 islands offer a beguiling mix of culture and nature – there is something for everyone here. As well as being beautiful seen from the water, this city is also a pleasure to explore on foot, particularly around Gamla Stan's medieval lanes and

Hercules outside Drottningholm

alleys and the leafy island of Djurgården. To help you to make the most of your visit, here are ideas for four themed days out. All the sights are accessible using public transport. Prices include travel, food and admission charges. Family prices are for two adults and two children.

Looking over the Nordiska museet towards the city centre

MUSEUMS MEANDER

- **A sunken ship and Swedish history on Djurgården**
- **Lunch near Kungsträdgården park**
- **Skeppsholmen – "museum island"**

TWO ADULTS allow at least 800 kr

Morning
Start the day on the island of Djurgården at the **Vasa-museet** *(see pp92–4)*. The impressive 17th-century warship *Vasa* is worth at least 90 minutes, and try not to miss the informative video. Next door, the **Nordiska museet** *(see pp90–91)* gives a glimpse into Swedish life over the centuries. Allow 2 hours. Leaving the island over **Djurgårdsbron** *(see p88)*, turn left and a 15-minute waterside walk down Strandvägen brings you to

Kungsträdgården *(see p64)*. Around this park are plenty of places for a lunch break.

Afternoon
Refreshed, head for Skepps-holmen, passing the stately **Grand Hotel** *(see p79)* and the **Nationalmuseum** *(see pp82–3)*. Once there, you can choose between the **Moderna museet** *(see pp80–81)* and the **Arkitekturmuseet** *(see p78)*. Finish with a late *"fika"* (coffee break) in the museum café, or try the restaurant with its view over the water.

PALACES AND WATERWAYS

- **Kungliga Slottet (the Royal Palace)**
- **The city from the water**
- **Drottningholm Palace**

TWO ADULTS allow at least 380 kr

Morning
Start the day with a touch of royalty at **Kungliga Slottet** *(see pp50–53)*, the Royal Palace, in Gamla Stan. Choose any combination of tours – the Royal Apartments, the Tre Kronor Museet or Gustav III's Museum of Antiquities – which will take up most of the morning. Then, just before noon, step outside for the Changing of the Guard, complete with full horse parade over Norrmalm Bridge. Afterwards, take a gentle walk through the cobblestone streets of Gamla Stan to **Stortorget** *(see p54)* for lunch at any one of the cafés lining the square. The charming Chokladkoppen is an excellent choice, popular with tourists and locals alike. During the winter holidays, one of the oldest *Julmarknad* (Christmas Markets) is held here.

Drottningholm Palace by boat

Afternoon

After lunch it is onto the water. An hour canal cruise to **Drottningholm Palace** *(see pp146–9)*, the residence of the Swedish royal family, also provides a waterfront tour of the city on the way to the palace just outside of town. Be sure to visit the Chinese Pavilion and the beautiful summer gardens in the palace grounds. "Under the Bridges of Stockholm" is another popular canal tour, which takes two hours and passes all of the city's major landmarks. Coffee and cakes are available on board. For both tours, it is worth booking in advance during peak times *(see pp204–5)*.

The busy Stortorget square in the heart of Gamla Stan

A WALK FROM NATURE TO CULTURE

- **The mountain park of Vita Bergen**
- **Shopping and eating in trendy SoFo**
- **Old Södermalm and the Katarinahissen lift**

TWO ADULTS allow at least 300 kr

Morning

Begin on the island of Söder-malm at **Vita Bergen** *(see p130)*, a beautiful mountain park. Here you will find allotment-gardens, worker's houses from the early 18th century and the monumental **Sofia Kyrka** *(see p130)*. Then head down-hill and into trendy "SoFo" (the area south of Folkungagatan). A variety of boutiques and cafés are

located here, with Folkunga-gatan itself leading towards **Medborgarplatsen** *(see p131)*. Traditional Swedish lunch can be had at an outdoor restaurant on the square.

Afternoon

From Medborgarplatsen it is not far to **Katarina Kyrka** *(see p128)* and the characteristic 18th-century cottages of old Södermalm. For a more contemporary view of Söder, the stretch of Götgatan between Medborgarplatsen and Slussen has an eclectic mix of shops, many selling Swedish design. The area east of here is **Mosebacke** *(see p128)*. Here you will find the **Södra Teatern** *(see p176)* and a public terrace, offering amazing views of the city. A more glamorous viewing point is the cocktail bar right at the top of **Katarinahissen** lift *(see p127)*, accessible from **Slussen** *(see p126)*.

A FULL FAMILY DAY

- **A trip to the Skansen zoo and open-air park**
- **Amusements at Gröna Lund**
- **The world of Pippi Longstocking and a theatre visit at Junibacken**

FAMILY OF 4 allow at least 1,800 kr

Morning

Start the day at the world's oldest open-air museum and zoo of Scandinavian wildlife, **Skansen** *(see pp96–7)*, on the

Children having fun at Skansen, on the island of Djurgården

island of Djurgården. Here you can visit period houses preserved and transported from all over Sweden, watch traditional glass blowing, and walk through a typical Swedish town, complete with market and post office. After such a busy morning, take a well-deserved break in one of the many cafés in the grounds of the park.

Afternoon

On to **Gröna Lund** *(see p95)*, an amusement park where you can ride one of the roller coasters, float through the Tunnel of Love or relax on the Ferris wheel. Alter-natively, enter the world of celebrated children's author Astrid Lingren at **Junibacken** *(see p88)* to explore her well-loved collection of books; little ones can play in Pippi Longstocking's house, the Villa Villekulla. It also has one of Sweden's leading children's theatres.

People enjoying picnics at Nytorget in "rustic chic" SoFo

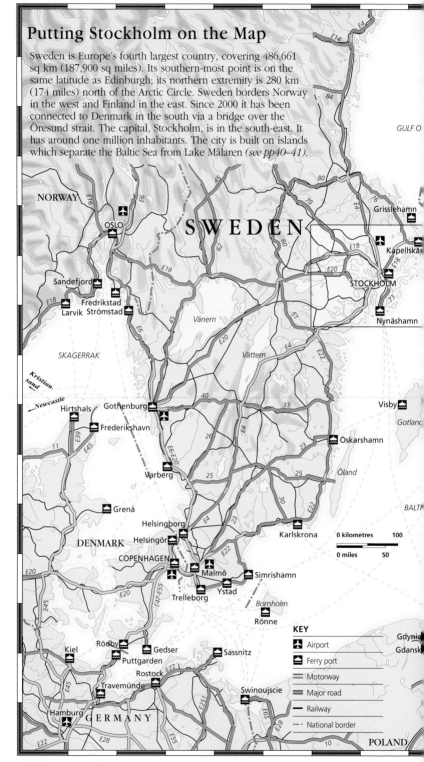

Putting Stockholm on the Map

Sweden is Europe's fourth largest country, covering 486,661 sq km (187,900 sq miles). Its southern-most point is on the same latitude as Edinburgh; its northern extremity is 280 km (174 miles) north of the Arctic Circle. Sweden borders Norway in the west and Finland in the east. Since 2000 it has been connected to Denmark in the south via a bridge over the Öresund strait. The capital, Stockholm, is in the south-east. It has around one million inhabitants. The city is built on islands which separate the Baltic Sea from Lake Mälaren *(see pp40–41)*.

GULF O

NORWAY

OSLO

SWEDEN

Grisslehamn

Kapellskä

E18

STOCKHOLM

Sandefjord

Fredrikstad

Larvik Strömstad

Vänern

Nynäshamn

SKAGERRAK

Vättern

Kristian-sand

Newcastle

Hirtshals Gothenburg

Frederikshavn

Visby

Gotland

Oskarshamn

Varberg

Öland

Grenå

BAL T

Helsingborg

Karlskrona

| 0 kilometres | 100 |

DENMARK Helsingör

| 0 miles | 50 |

COPENHAGEN

Malmö Simrishamn

Trelleborg Ystad

Bornholm

Rönne

KEY

Gdynia

Gdansk

✈	Airport
⚓	Ferry port
═══	Motorway
━━━	Major road
───	Railway
·-·-·	National border

Kiel Rödby Gedser Sassnitz

Puttgarden

Rostock

Travemünde

Swinoujscie

Hamburg **GERMANY**

POLAND

◁ **View of Stockholm from Mosebacke, painted in 1787 by Elias Martin**

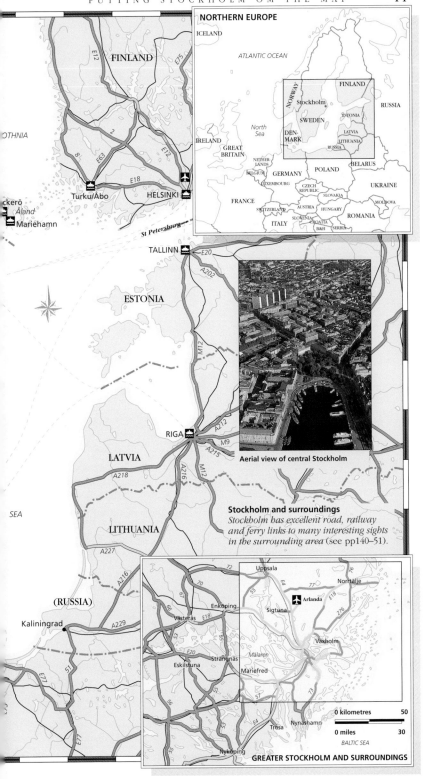

NORTHERN EUROPE

ICELAND

ATLANTIC OCEAN

FINLAND

NORWAY

Stockholm

RUSSIA

SWEDEN

ESTONIA

North Sea

LATVIA

IRELAND

DEN-MARK

LITHUANIA

RUSSIA

GREAT BRITAIN

NETHER-LANDS

BELARUS

BELGIUM

GERMANY

POLAND

UKRAINE

LUXEMBOURG

CZECH REPUBLIC

FRANCE

SWITZERLAND

AUSTRIA

SLOVAKIA

MOLDOVA

SLOVENIA

HUNGARY

ROMANIA

ITALY

CROATIA

B&H

SERBIA

E12

FINLAND

E75

E63

E12

2

OTHNIA

8

E18

Turku/Åbo

HELSINKI

ckerö

Åland

Mariehamn

St Petersburg

TALLINN — E20

A202

ESTONIA

M12

Aerial view of central Stockholm

RIGA

A212

A215

M9

LATVIA

A218

M12

A216

Stockholm and surroundings
*Stockholm has excellent road, railway
and ferry links to many interesting sights
in the surrounding area (see pp140–51).*

SEA

LITHUANIA

A227

(RUSSIA)

A216

Kaliningrad

A229

51

E77

72

Uppsala

70

E4

77

Norrtälje

67

55

E18

66

Enköping

Sigtuna

Arlanda

276

Västerås

E18

53

55

E20

Vaxholm

Eskilstuna

Strängnäs

Mälaren

Mariefred

56

73

57

0 kilometres   50

0 miles   30

Trosa   Nynäshamn

E4

BALTIC SEA

Nyköping

GREATER STOCKHOLM AND SURROUNDINGS

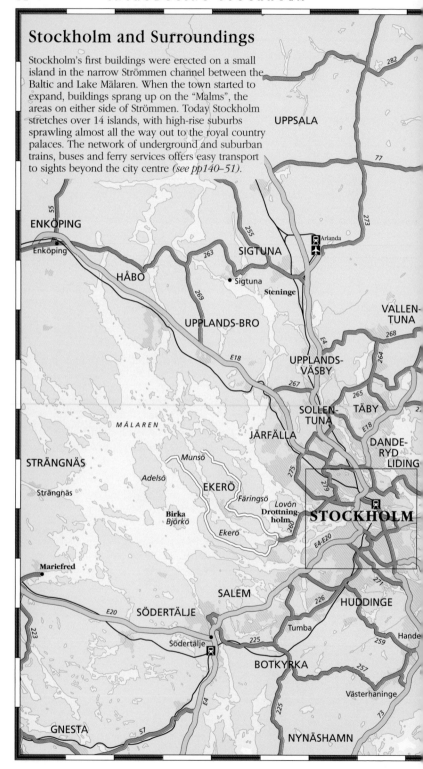

Stockholm and Surroundings

Stockholm's first buildings were erected on a small island in the narrow Strömmen channel between the Baltic and Lake Mälaren. When the town started to expand, buildings sprang up on the "Malms", the areas on either side of Strömmen. Today Stockholm stretches over 14 islands, with high-rise suburbs sprawling almost all the way out to the royal country palaces. The network of underground and suburban trains, buses and ferry services offers easy transport to sights beyond the city centre *(see pp140–51)*.

UPPSALA

ENKÖPING

Enköping

HÅBO

SIGTUNA

Sigtuna

Steninge

Arlanda

UPPLANDS-BRO

VALLEN-TUNA

UPPLANDS-VÄSBY

SOLLEN-TUNA

TÄBY

JÄRFÄLLA

DANDE-RYD

LIDING

STRÄNGNÄS

MÄLAREN

Munsö

Adelsö

EKERÖ

Färingsö

Lovön

Drottning-holm

STOCKHOLM

Strängnäs

Birka
Björkö

Ekerö

Mariefred

SALEM

SÖDERTÄLJE

HUDDINGE

Tumba

Hande

Södertälje

BOTKYRKA

Västerhaninge

GNESTA

NYNÄSHAMN

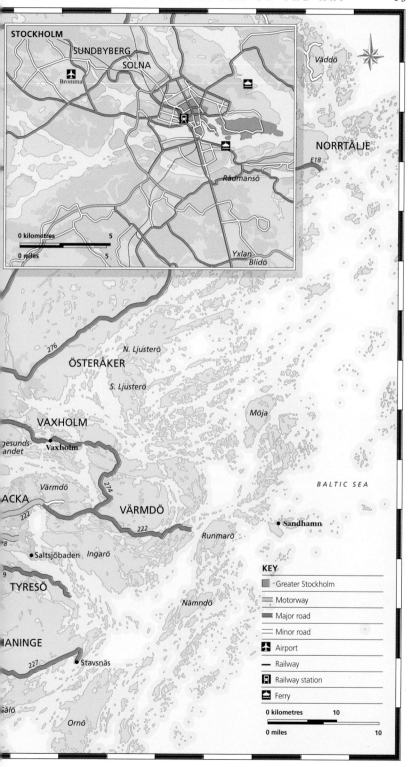

STOCKHOLM
SUNDBYBERG
SOLNA
Bromma
Väddö
NORRTÄLJE
E18
Rådmansö

0 kilometres 5
0 miles 5

Yxlan
Blidö

276
N. Ljusterö
ÖSTERÅKER
S. Ljusterö

Möja

VAXHOLM
gesunds-
andet
Vaxholm

BALTIC SEA

Värmdö
274
ACKA
VÄRMDÖ
222
222
Sandhamn

Runmarö

Saltsjöbaden Ingarö

TYRESÖ
Nämndö

HANINGE

227
Stavsnäs

ålö
Ornö

KEY

Greater Stockholm
Motorway
Major road
Minor road
Airport
Railway
Railway station
Ferry

0 kilometres 10
0 miles 10

THE HISTORY OF STOCKHOLM

*L*egends and theories about Stockholm's origins have been many and varied, and sometimes even contradictory. But they have a common factor – control over the waterways. The generally accepted founder of Stockholm is the 13th-century regent Birger Jarl who, according to the medieval Erik's Chronicle, wanted to build a fortress to protect Lake Mälaren from marauding pirates.

A thousand years ago the waters around the island now known as Gamla Stan were busy with warships, trading vessels and pirate ships using the narrow channel between the Baltic and Lake Mälaren. In those days boat was the quickest and safest method of travel.

Stockholm's oldest preserved city seal (1296)

In the first literary mention of what was to become Stockholm, the Icelandic poet and saga writer Snorre Sturlasson (1178–1241) described a barrier of piles across a waterway which he named Stocksundet, the present Norrström. The island formed by this piling became known as Stockholm. Excavations in the late 1970s revealed the remains of a large number of piles in the water dating from the 11th century. Snorre also mentioned a 12th- century castle tower which would have predated Birger Jarl's fortress, the predecessor of the present Royal Palace.

Documents show that Stockholm was already a city in 1252, four years after Birger Jarl became regent. Many towns in Sweden started to expand in the early 13th century. Stockholm was a late starter but soon caught up. A document from 1289 describes Stockholm as the biggest place in the kingdom. But it was not the capital city, because the king was always on the move. Birger Jarl's son, King Magnus Ladulås, did not regard Stockholm as his capital either. For a long time the city's importance lay in its role as a trading centre. It became an important port for the German-dominated Hanseatic League, which controlled Swedish overseas trade from the 13th century until the late 17th century.

The frontiers of the Nordic countries remained undefined for some time, but with a background of similar languages and cultures, Sweden, Norway and Denmark signed the Kalmar Union in 1397. Finland at that time was still part of Sweden. The era of union became one of conflict and violence. At the battle of Brunkeberg in Stockholm in 1471 the Danish king tried to take control of Sweden, but was defeated by the regent Sten Sture. A new Danish campaign in 1520 culminated in the notorious Stockholm Bloodbath at Stortorget *(see p54)*, when more than 80 Swedish noblemen were executed.

TIMELINE

Birger Jarl, Stockholm's founder

1008 Olof Skötkonung converts to Christianity and is baptized in Västergötland			**c.1250** Birger Jarl founds Stockholm **1350** Code of Magnus Eriksson replaces provincial laws	**1364** Albrecht of Mecklenburg chosen as Sweden's King **1397** Kalmar Union links the Nordic countries	
1000	**1100**	**1200**	**1300**	**1400**	**1500**
800–975 Vikings settle and trade at Birka *(see p144)*	**1275** Magnus Ladulås chosen as Sweden's king at Mora **1101** Three Kings' Meeting fixes Scandinavian frontiers		**1280** Ordinances of Alsnö give nobility freedom from taxation	**1349–50** Plague ravages Sweden **1471** Sten Sture the Elder defeats the Danish King Kristian at Brunkeberg	**1520** Swedish noblemen executed in Stockholm Bloodbath

◁ Painting in Storkyrkan (Stockholm's cathedral) depicting a remarkable light phenomenon seen in 1535

The newly chosen king, Gustav Vasa, making his ceremonial entry into Stockholm, Midsummer Day 1523

THE VASA ERA

One of those who managed to avoid execution in the Stockholm Bloodbath was the young nobleman Gustav Eriksson. At the end of 1520 Gustav organized an army to oust the Danish King Kristian from Sweden. Gustav was successful and on 6 June 1523 – later to become Sweden's National Day – he was named king with the title Gustav Vasa.

When Gustav Vasa took the throne he discovered a nation in financial crisis. He called on Parliament to pass a controversial law transferring the property of the Church to the State, which then became the country's most important source of economic power. Another important result of this policy was the gradual separation from Catholicism and the adoption of the Lutheran State Church.

Portrait of Erik XIV (1561)

During his reign Gustav Vasa implemented tough economic policies in order to concentrate central power in Stockholm. This effective dictatorship also resulted in the Swedish Parliament's decision in 1544 to make the monarchy hereditary.

Descendants of Gustav Vasa oversaw the rise of Sweden into one of Europe's great powers. During the reign of Gustav's son Erik XIV, there were wars against Denmark, Lübeck and Poland. His brothers dethroned him and he died in prison, probably of a pea soup poisoned by his brother Johan III. During the reign of Karl IX, the third son, Sweden waged war against Denmark and Russia.

GUSTAV II ADOLF AND KRISTINA

When the next king, Gustav II Adolf, came to power in 1611, Sweden was involved in wars against Russia, Poland and Denmark. Under his rule Sweden steadily increased its influence over the Baltic region. Stockholm started to develop into the country's political and administrative centre. In 1630 Gustav II Adolf, together with his influential chancellor Axel Oxenstierna, decided to intervene in the Thirty Years War on the

TIMELINE

Vasa dynasty's coat of arms

1523 Gustav Vasa chosen as king in Strängnäs and marches into Stockholm	**1542** Nils Dacke and supporters stage a peasant revolt in Småland	**1560** Gustav Vasa dies	**1568** Erik XIV imprisoned by his brothers at Gripsholms Slott	**1611** Gustav II Adolf comes to power
			1577 Erik XIV dies, probably poisoned	
1525		**1550**	**1575**	**1600**
1527 Reformation, Parliament confiscates Church property	**1544** Hereditary monarchy established for Gustav Vasa's male descendants	**1561** Eric XIV is crowned king and his brothers' powers curbed	**1570** Nordic Seven Years War ends	**1612** Axel Oxenstierna named State Chancellor
		1569 Johan III crowned in Stockholm	**1587** Johan III's son Sigismund chosen king of Poland	

side of the Protestants, using religious motives as a pretext. Sweden had some notable military successes during the war, but paid a heavy price for winning the bloody battle at Lützen in 1632 as the king was killed in action.

Gustav II Adolf's only child, Kristina, came to the throne at the age of six. During her reign (1633–54), life at the court was influenced by the world of science and philosophy. Kristina corresponded with leading academics and invited the French philosopher René Descartes, who died in 1650 only a few months after arriving in Stockholm. The Tre Kronor castle became the permanent royal residence. Kristina's reluctance to marry resulted in her cousin, Karl Gustav, becoming Crown Prince. Kristina abdicated and left for Rome, where she converted to Catholicism.

Karl XII with the widowed queen on his arm leaving the burning Tre Kronor fortress

the frozen waters of the Great Belt *(see p19)*. Karl XI (1660–97) secured the southern Swedish provinces, and divided the land more evenly between the crown, nobility and peasants.

While the body of Karl XI lay in state at Tre Kronor in 1697 a fire broke out which destroyed most of the building. The new monarch was the teenage Karl XII (1697–1718). He faced awesome problems when Denmark, Poland and Russia formed an alliance in 1700 with the aim of crushing the power of Sweden. Karl XII set off to battle.

Denmark and Poland were soon forced to plead for peace, but Russia resisted. A bold push towards Moscow was unsuccessful and the Swedish army suffered a devastating defeat at Poltava in 1709. This marked the beginning of the end for Sweden as a great power.

Karl XII, the most controversial Swedish monarch, returned to Sweden in 1715 after an absence of 15 years. His plans to regain Sweden's position of dominance never came to pass and he was killed in Norway in 1718.

By now, Sweden was in crisis. Crop failures and epidemics had annihilated one-third of Stockholm's population and the state's finances were drained.

Queen Kristina, fascinated by science and corresponding with leading scientists

THE CAROLIAN ERA

Karl X Gustav (1654–60) was the first of three Karls to reign. At the height of Sweden's era as a great power and in one of the most audacious episodes in the history of war, he conquered Denmark by leading his army across

---

1617 Death penalty introduced for conversion to Catholicism

1632 Gustav II Adolf killed at battle of Lützen

1633 Six-year-old Kristina becomes queen; guardians rule

1654 Kristina abdicates and Karl X Gustav crowned king

1655 Kristina converts to Catholicism and is ceremonially greeted in Rome

1697 Tre Kronor castle destroyed by fire; 15-year-old Karl XII crowned

1625   **1650**   **1675**   **1700**

1618 Thirty Years War starts in Germany

1648 Peace of Westphalia gives Sweden new territories

1658 Swedish army crosses the Great Belt and acquires new territory under Peace of Roskilde

1680 Karl XI starts the era of Carolian autocracy and limits powers of the nobility

1709 Swedish army defeated by Peter the Great at Poltava

1718 Karl XII dies

Gustav II Adolf

Sweden's Era as a Great Power

For more than a century (1611–1721) Sweden was the dominant power in northern Europe, and the Baltic was effectively a Swedish inland sea. The country was at its most powerful after the Peace of Roskilde in 1658, when Sweden acquired seven new provinces from Denmark and Norway. Outside today's frontiers the Swedish Empire covered the whole of Finland, large parts of the Baltic, and important areas of northern Germany. Over 111 years as a great power Sweden spent 72 of them at war when many treasures were brought back to the new palaces. It was also an era of cultural development and efficient government.

SWEDISH EMPIRE

■ *Sweden's empire after the Peace of Roskilde, 1658*

The Tre Kronor Castle
Built as a defensive tower in the 1180s, the Tre Kronor castle was the seat of Swedish monarchs from the 1520s and became the administrative centre of the Swedish Empire. It was named after the three crowns on the spire which burned down in 1697.

The columns of troops
ride out over the shifting ice towards Danish Lolland.

THE THIRTY YEARS WAR

A major European war raged between 1618–48, largely on German soil. Sweden entered the war in 1631 in an alliance with France. Gustav II Adolf was a fine military leader and had modernized the Swedish army which immediately had major successes at the battles of Breitenfeld (1631) and Lützen (1632), where the king, however, was killed. Later the Swedes

pressed into southern Germany and also captured and plundered Prague (1648). Some rich cultural treasures were brought back to Sweden from the war. In 1648 the Peace of Westphalia gave Sweden several important possessions in northern Germany.

The death of Gustav II Adolf at the Battle of Lützen in 1632

Stockholm in 1640
The city's transformation from a small medieval town into a capital city can be seen in the network of straight streets, similar to the present layout.

Karl XI's Triumphs
The roof painting in Karl XI's gallery at the Royal Palace (1693) by the French artist Jacques Foucquet shows in allegoric form the king's victories at Halmstad, Lund and Landskrona.

Count Carl Gustaf Wrangel *(see p56).*

King Karl X Gustav himself leads the Swedish army of 17,000 men.

The Powerful Nobility
The nobility were very influential in the Empire era and many successful soldiers were ennobled. The Banér family coat of arms from 1651 is adorned by three helmets and barons' crowns.

Bondeska Palatset
One of the leading buildings of the era (1662–73), this palace was designed by Tessin the Elder and Jean de la Vallée for the State Treasurer Gustav Bonde (see p58).

CROSSING THE GREAT BELT
When Denmark declared war on Sweden in autumn 1657, the Swedish army was in Poland. Marching west, Karl X Gustav captured the Danish mainland, but without the navy, he could not continue to Copenhagen. However, unusually severe weather froze the sea, making it possible for the soldiers to cross the ice of the Great Belt, and the Danes had to surrender.

Karl XII's Pocket Watch
The warrior king's watch-case dates from 1700. It shows the state coat of arms, as well as those of the 49 provinces that belonged to Sweden at that time.

Karl XII's Last Journey
After being hit by a fatal bullet at Fredrikshald in Norway (1718), the king's body was taken first to Swedish territory then on to Uddevalla for embalming. Painting by Gustav Cederström (1878).

Gustav III with the white armband he wore when mounting his *coup d'état* in 1772

THE AGE OF LIBERTY AND THE GUSTAVIAN ERA

A new constitution came into force in 1719 which transferred power from the monarch to parliament. As a result, Sweden developed a system of parliamentary democracy similar to that of Britain in the early 18th century.

The "Age of Liberty" coincided with the Enlightenment, with dramatic advances in culture, science and industry. The botanist Carl von Linné became one of the most famous Swedes of his time. Another was the scientist, philosopher and author Emanuel Swedenborg. The production of textiles expanded in Stockholm, and Sweden's first hospital was constructed on Kungsholmen.

Changes in the balance of power around 1770 gave the new king, Gustav III, an opportunity to strike in an attempt to regain his monarchical powers. On 19 August 1772 Gustav accompanied the guards' parade to the Royal Palace where, in front of his life-guards, he declared his intention to

mount a bloodless *coup d'état*. The guards and other military units in Stockholm swore allegiance to the king, who tied a white handkerchief round his arm as a badge and rode out into the city to be acclaimed by his people. Absolute power had been restored.

Gustav III was influenced by the Age of Enlightenment and by French culture, which had a great effect on Swedish cultural life (*see pp22–3*). But over the years opposition grew to the king's absolute powers, largely because of his costly war against Russia. In 1792 he was murdered by a nobleman, Captain Anckarström, during a masked ball at the Opera House (*see p23*).

Gustav III was succeeded by his son, Gustav IV Adolf. During his reign Sweden was dragged into the Napoleonic wars. After a war against Russia in 1808–9, Sweden lost its sovereignty over Finland, which at the time accounted for one-third of Swedish territory. The king abdicated and left Stockholm to flee the country.

THE ERA OF KARL JOHAN AND BOURGEOIS LIBERALISM

By the early 19th century the absolute powers of the monarch had been removed for all time, and the privileges

Napoleon's former marshal, Jean-Baptiste Bernadotte, as King Karl XIV Johan surrounded by his family

TIMELINE

1719 New constitution transfers power from the king to Parliament	**1741** Carl von Linné appointed professor at Uppsala	**1754** Royal family moves into Royal Palace **1780s** Immigrants are given wide religious freedom		**1790** Swedish defeat over Russia at battle of Svenskund **1792** Gustav III murdered
1720	**1740**	**1760**	**1780**	**1800**
1738 Parliamentary power is established in the Age of Liberty as the "Hat" party wins elections *Carl von Linné (1707–78)*		**1772** Gustav III crowned and mounts *coup d'état giving* the king absolute power	**1778** National costume decreed. Death penalty removed for some crimes	**1786** Swedish Academy founded

Newspaper readers outside the *Aftonbladet* office in 1841

Norwegians were reluctant to unite with Sweden, but a union between the two countries was agreed which lasted from 1814 to 1905. A long era of peace began and with it came a dramatic increase in the country's population, which grew by 1 million to 3.5 million by 1850. Many Swedes were driven into poverty because there was not enough work to go round. Mass emigration followed. From the 1850s to the 1930s about 1.5 million people left Sweden. Most of the emigrants travelled to North America in search of a better life.

of the aristocracy were undermined even more in 1809 with a new constitution that divided power between the king, the government and parliament.

With a new class structure and the effect of the French Revolution, a new middle class emerged which also wanted to be more influential. One of the best-known newspapers founded around this time was the liberal mouthpiece, *Aftonbladet*.

Difficulties in finding a suitable new monarch led eventually to the choice of one of Napoleon's marshals, Jean-Baptiste Bernadotte, who took on the more authentic Swedish name of Karl Johan. Founder of the present royal dynasty, Karl XIV Johan continued to speak French and never fully learned the Swedish language. His French wife, Queen Desideria, found Stockholm a cultural backwater compared with Paris.

In 1813 a Swedish army with Karl Johan at its head became involved in a campaign against Napoleon. The Battle of Leipzig ended in defeat for France, but more significantly Denmark had to hand over Norway to Sweden. The

Stockholm's Eldkvarn mill, destroyed by fire in 1878

FOLK MOVEMENTS AND INDUSTRIALIZATION

As Sweden was transformed from an agricultural society into an industrialized country the problems posed by the population surplus were gradually tackled. Its industrial revolution started around 1850, gathering momentum in the late 19th century, and the textile, timber and iron industries provided the main sources of employment. In 1806 the nation's first steam-driven mill, Eldkvarn, was built on the site of the present-day City Hall in Stockholm. It continued production until destroyed by fire in 1878.

Folk movements sprang up in the 19th century which still play an important role in Swedish life. A temperance movement emerged against a background of alcohol abuse – in the 1820s annual consumption of spirits was 46 litres (80 pints) per person.

1809 Sweden loses Finland and Gustav IV Adolf abdicates

1810 Parliament chooses Jean-Baptiste Bernadotte as Crown Prince

1869 Emigration to North America increases due to crop failures

1842 Primary schools established by decree in every parish

1876 L M Ericsson starts manufacture of telephones

August Strindberg

1908 Royal Dramatic Theatre opens

1820	1840	1860	1880	1900

1818 Karl XIV Johan is crowned King of Sweden and Norway

1814 Sweden gains Norway in peace treaty with Denmark

1850 Sweden has 3.5 million population, 93,000 living in Stockholm

1859 Sweden's first railway opens

1879 August Strindberg's novel *The Red Room* is published

1905 Parliament dissolves union with Norway

The Era of Gustav III

Gustav III (1771–92) is one of the most colourful figures in Swedish history. The king's great interest in art, literature and the theatre made the late 18th century a golden age for Swedish culture, and several prestigious academies were founded at this time. After a bloodless revolution in 1772 Gustav III ruled with absolute power and initiated a wide-ranging programme of reform. But his attacks on the privileges of the nobility and his adventurous and costly foreign policy made him powerful enemies. In 1792 he was murdered during a masked ball at Stockholm's Opera House.

The Swedish Academy
The academy was founded by Gustav III in 1786 to preserve the Swedish language. Members received a token depicting the king's head at every meeting.

Gustav III's Coronation, 1772
The coronation of the all-powerful monarch in Stockholm's cathedral was a magnificent ceremony, portrayed here by C G Pilo (1782). Every detail was overseen by Gustav himself, who used his flair for the dramatic in politics as well.

A courtier entertains by reading aloud.

Gustav III studies architectural designs.

COURT LIFE AT DROTTNINGHOLM
Hilleström's painting (1779) gives an insight into court life at Drottningholm, where the king resided between June and November. In the present-day Blue Salon, Gustav III and Queen Sofia Magdalena socialized with their inner circle. Behaviour was modelled on the French court and etiquette was even stricter at Drottningholm than at Versailles.

The Battle of Svenskund
Gustav III was not known as a successful warrior king, but in 1790 he led the Swedish fleet to its greatest victory ever, when it defeated Russia in a major maritime battle in the Gulf of Finland.

Life in the Inns
The city abounded with inns, frequently visited by the 70,000 inhabitants. J T Sergel's sketch shows a convivial dinner party.

Murder at the Masked Ball
In 1792 Gustav III fell victim to a conspiracy at the Opera House. He was surrounded by masked men and shot by Captain Anckarström on the crowded stage. He died of his wounds 14 days later.

Gustav III's Mask and Cocked Hat
Despite his mask, Gustav III was easy to recognize since he was wearing the badges of two orders of chivalry. The drama intrigued the whole of Europe and inspired Verdi's opera Un Ballo in Maschera.

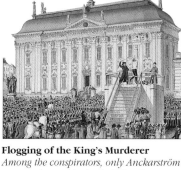

Flogging of the King's Murderer
Among the conspirators, only Anckarström was condemned to death. Before he was taken to his execution in Södermalm he was flogged on three successive days on the square in front of Riddarhuset.

Queen Sofia Magdalena does her needlework.

Bust of Catherine the Great of Russia, the king's cousin

GUSTAVIAN STYLE

The mid-18th century saw the emergence of Neo-Classicism, with the focus on antiquities and Greek ideals. Gustav III embraced this trend with great enthusiasm and supported the country's talented artists and authors. He established his own Museum of Antiquities *(see pp52–3)* with marble sculptures which he brought home from Italy. In handicrafts, the sweeping lines of Rococo elegance were replaced by the stricter forms of what has become known as Gustavian Style. Rooms at the Royal Palace were renovated with decoration and furnishings adapted to suit this style.

Chair designed in Gustavian Style

Swedish Court Costume
In 1778 Gustav III introduced a costume based on French lines to restrain fashion excesses. This is the male court costume for daily wear.

UNIVERSAL SUFFRAGE

Sweden's population reached 5 million around 1900 despite mass emigration to America. Many people moved to the towns to work in industry, and by the early 20th century Stockholm's population was about 300,000, a fourfold increase since the year 1800.

Increasing social awareness and the rise of the Social Democrat and Liberal parties in the early 20th century gave impetus to the demands for universal suffrage. Radical authors like August Strindberg became involved. A political battle ensued which was not resolved until 1921 when universal suffrage was introduced for both sexes.

Another question which was hotly debated in the 19th century was the role of the king and the extent of his powers. In his "courtyard speech" at the Royal Palace in 1914 King Gustav V called for military rearmament. This led to a constitutional crisis and the resignation of the Liberal government. After the 1917 election the king was forced to accept a government which contained republican-friendly Social Democrats, including the future prime minister, Hjalmar Branting. By then it was parliament, not the king, that decided what sort of government Sweden should have.

Branting and Gustav V in conversation, 1909

THE GROWTH OF THE WELFARE STATE

In 1936 the Social Democrats and Farmers' Party formed a coalition which developed what was to become known as the welfare state. The Social Democrat prime minister, Per Albin Hansson (1885–1946), defined the welfare state as a socially conscious society with financial security for all. Reforms introduced under this policy included unemployment benefit, paid holidays and childcare. As a result, poverty in Sweden virtually disappeared during the 1930s and 1940s.

The right of everyone to good housing was also part of welfare state policy. Under the principle of "work-home-centre" a new Stockholm suburb, Vällingby, was planned and built in the early 1950s. The idea was to transform the dormitory suburbs into thriving communities where people would both live and work. The concept was unsuccessful. It soon became apparent that the people who lived there still worked somewhere else, and vice versa. The great shortage of housing in the 1960s led to the "million" programme, which involved the building of a million homes in an extremely short time. These areas soon became known as the "new slums" despite high standards of construction.

Calls for democratic reforms in June 1917 led to riots like this one outside the parliament building in Stockholm

TIMELINE

1920	1940	1960
1914 Gustav V gives his "courtyard speech".	**1932** Suicide of industrial magnate Ivar Krueger is followed by stockmarket crash	**1940** Sweden-German agreement on transit of German military personnel	**1955** Obligatory national health insurance	**1958** Women can be ordained as priests
1921 Universal suffrage for men and women				**1967** Right-hand driving introduced

Selma Lagerlöf, winner of the Nobel Prize for Literature

1930 Rise of Functionalist style in architecture, stimulated by the Stockholm Exhibition	**1939** Sweden has coalition government and declares neutrality in World War II	**1950** First public TV broadcast in Sweden	**1964** Art exhibition Moderna Museet shows works by Andy Warhol, Roy Lichtenstein and Claes Oldenburg	**1973** Gustav VI Adolf dies and is succeeded by grandson, Carl XVI Gustaf

THE WAR YEARS

Sweden declared its neutrality during both World War I and II. Its policy of continuing to trade with nations involved in the conflict during World War I provoked a number of countries into imposing a trade blockade on Sweden. The situation became so serious that hunger riots broke out in some towns.

Neutrality stamp issued in 1942

World War II produced an even more difficult balancing exercise for Swedish neutrality, largely because its Nordic neighbours were at war. With a combination of luck and skill, Sweden remained outside the conflict, but the concessions it had to make were strongly criticized both nationally and internationally.

THE POST-WAR ERA

Although the Social Democrats dominated government from the 1930s to the 1970s the socialist and non-socialist power blocs in Swedish politics have remained fairly evenly matched since World War II.

The policy of non-alignment has not proved an obstacle to Swedish involvement on the international scene, including the United Nations. The country has offered asylum to hundreds of thousands of refugees from wars and political oppression. Prime minister Olof Palme (1927–86), probably the best-known Swedish politician abroad, was deeply involved in questions of democracy and disarmament, as well as the problems of the Third World. He was renowned for condemning undemocratic acts by dictators. Palme's assassination on the streets of Stockholm in 1986 sent a shock wave across the world, but strangely the murder has still not been solved.

Important changes took place during the closing decades of the 20th century. These included a new constitution in 1974 which removed the monarch's political powers. In 1995 Sweden joined the European Union after a referendum approved entry by only the narrowest of majorities.

Sveavägen, the site of Palme's murder, 1986

The start of the new millennium marked a change in the role of the church in Sweden, which severed its connections with the state after more than 400 years.

The last decade has seen a significant number of jobs created in high technology companies and the almost total absence of heavy industry has made Stockholm one of the world's cleanest cities. In 2010, it was granted the European Green Capital Award by the EU Commission, making Stockholm Europe's first green capital.

The centre of Vällingby, which attracted attention among city planners worldwide in the 1950s

74 The monarch loses all political powers	**1980** New constitution gives women the right of succession to the throne	**1995** Sweden joins European Union	**2000** Öresund bridge opens between Denmark and Sweden	**2007** Legendary film maker Ingmar Bergman dies	
				2010 Crown Princess Victoria marries Daniel Westling	
	1980		**2000**		**2020**
1986 Prime minister Olof Palme murdered in Stockholm				**2003** Foreign minister Anna Lindh murdered in Stockholm	
74 ABBA pop group wins Eurovision Song Contest			**2000** Swedish Church separated from the State		

Crown Princess Victoria

STOCKHOLM THROUGH THE YEAR

Stockholm's heart never misses a beat despite the vagaries of the climate. Although summer is a glorious time to visit the capital, the city shimmering in ice and snow is also an amazing experience, and numerous popular events take place throughout the year. Stockholm's countless sporting fixtures attract top-class international stars. Its many concerts, both pop and classical, indoor and outdoor, feature performers from around the world. Sweden's national festivals are celebrated in the traditional way in Stockholm and are always popular attractions for both locals and visitors alike. The capital's proximity to the surrounding countryside and water provides an extensive range of opportunities for all kinds of outdoor activities throughout the year.

Crocus, a sure sign of spring

SPRING

As in all the Nordic countries, people long for spring after the dark days of winter, and it has a big impact on life in the capital. Sun-lovers sit on the steps of Konserthuset (Concert Hall) and Kungliga Dramatiska Teatern (Royal Dramatic Theatre); people work on their boats; football competes with ice hockey for attention; spring flowers come into bud in Kungsträdgården; and the traditional *semla* cream buns go on sale to break the Lenten fast.

Semla bun

MARCH

Stockholm International Boat Show *(early Mar)*. The spring's major boat exhibition at Stockholm International Fairs in Älvsjö.
Outdoors Fair *(Mar)*. Camping, tourism, and outdoor equipment fair at Stockholm International Fairs in Älvsjö.

Spring sun-bathers at Djurgårdsbrunnsviken

Kuriosa *(early Mar)*. A fair selling antiques and collectables, held at the Sollentuna Exhibition Centre.
Garden Fair *(Mar)*. Everything for the gardener on show at Stockholm International Fairs in Älvsjö.
Stockholm Art Fair *(Mar)*. Works of art are on sale at the Sollentuna Exhibition Centre.
Spring Salon *(Jan–Mar)*. Annual art show mainly featuring new artists that takes place at Liljevalchs Konsthall (gallery) on Djurgården.

APRIL

Swedish Football Championship *(last weekend in Apr)*. Series starts at Råsunda and Söder stadiums.
Walpurgis Night at Skansen *(30 Apr)*. Traditional celebrations with massed standard bearers, folk dancing, torchlight procession, student choirs, bonfire and fireworks.
The King's Birthday *(30 Apr)*. The king is greeted at Kungliga Slottet (Royal Palace) with a military parade, and children hand over flowers and gifts.

MAY

Gröna Lund *(first week of May)*. Djurgården's amusement park opens for its 130-day season. Exciting rides and attractions include rollercoasters and a free-fall tower. There are also stages hosting music and other entertainment and plenty of places to eat. Gröna

Walpurgis Night bonfire at Evert Taubes Terrass, Riddarholmen

Lund's beautiful gardens include 30,000 pansies and 25,000 summer flowers.
Round Lidingö Race *(2nd Sat in May)*. Long-distance sailing race with hundreds of boats of all shapes and sizes.
Circus Princess *(May)*. A series of circus performances by female artists, the best of whom is chosen as the year's Circus Princess.
Archipelago Fair *(late May)*. Second-hand leisure boats for sale, purchase or exchange.
"Tjejtrampet" *(last weekend in May)*. 45-km (28-mile) cycling competition at Gärdet with 7,000 female cyclists.
Elite Race *(last weekend in May)*. Trotting competition at Solvalla with top horses from all over the world.
Theatre in Hagaparken *(late May)*. Outdoor theatre in the old palace ruins.
Kungsträdgården *(late May)*. The programme of summer entertainment in the park starts on the main stage.
Gärdet Race *(late May)*. Veteran cars in friendly competition at Gärdet.

AVERAGE DAILY HOURS OF SUNSHINE

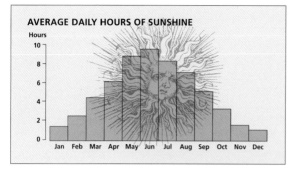

Sunshine Chart
Stockholm's climate can vary markedly from hot, sunny days followed by a cooler rainy spell during the summer to winters with freezing temperatures and snow. From mid-June to mid-July it never really gets dark. Winter days are very short, although there can still be a strong sun at times.

SUMMER

Stockholm shows its best face at this time of year. Although May can be warm, summer does not really start until early June when the schools break up. In late June the sun shines almost round the clock, and with it comes a vibrant outdoor life with picnics and street festivals. The capital gets a bit emptier at peak holiday-time in July. When the schools go back in late August, Swedes celebrate the arrival of two annual culinary delights: crayfish and fermented Baltic herring.

Traditional Midsummer celebrations at Skansen, the open-air museum

JUNE

Stockholm Marathon *(first Sat in Jun)*. One of the world's 10 biggest marathons with around 13,000 runners.
A Taste of Stockholm *(early Jun)*. Kungsträdgården becomes the world's largest outdoor restaurant.
Archipelago Boat Day *(early Jun)*. Classic steamboats assemble at Strömkajen near the Grand Hôtel for a round trip to Vaxholm.
Stockholm Grand Prix *(Jun)*. Season's second-largest racing event at Täby racecourse with an international field.
National Day *(6 Jun)*. Celebrations at Skansen take place in the presence of the royal family.
Midsummer Eve *(next to last Sat in Jun)*. A major Swedish festival celebrated at Skansen over three days. It starts at 2pm on Midsummer Eve with the traditional raising of the maypole and ring dancing.

Music at the Palace *(Jun–Aug)*. Summer concert season starts in the Hall of State and the Royal Chapel at Kungliga Slottet (Royal Palace).
Drottningholms Slottsteater *(Jun–Aug)* Season of concerts, opera and dance throughout the summer in the 18th-century court theatre.
Palace Gala *(mid-Jun)*. Concerts featuring the popular classics as well as more modern music played by international stars in the park at Ulriksdals Slott.
Boules Festival *(mid-Jun)*. Boules enthusiasts gather in Kungsträdgården.
Stockholm Jazz Fest *(mid-Jun)*. Great artists from around the world play in a fantastic outdoor setting on the beautiful island of Skeppsholmen.

JULY

Round Gotland Race *(first week in Jul)*. Major international sailing event, with start and finish at Sandhamn.

DN Gala *(Jul)*. Major international athletics competition at Stockholm Stadion.

AUGUST

Midnight Race *(early Aug)*. Night-time running that takes place over a distance of 10 km (6 miles) in Söder. The event attracts around 16,000 participants.
Philharmonikerna i det Gröna *(2nd Sun in Aug)*. Royal Philharmonic Orchestra performs free for picnicking music-lovers on the lawn by Sjöhistoriska museet.
"Tjejmilen" *(last Sun in Aug)*. About 25,000 female runners compete in a 10-km (6-mile) event at Gärdet.

Crayfish

Baltic Sea Festival *(late Aug)*. Various Swedish orchestras perform well-known classical pieces at the Berwaldhallen concert hall.
Crayfish Season *(last week in Aug)*. A time for Swedes to eat crayfish and sing "schnapps songs".

AVERAGE MONTHLY RAINFALL

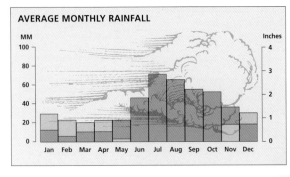

MM
100
80
60
40
20
0

Inches
4
3
2
1
0

Jan Feb Mar Apr May Jun Jul Aug Sep Oct Nov Dec

Rainfall Chart
Some years Stockholm can have very rainy summers, but in other years the weather can be dry for several weeks at a time. Heavy snowfall in winter may lie until March, but some winters have been known to be virtually free of snow.

▨ Rain (from the baseline)
☐ Snow (from the baseline)

AUTUMN

Early autumn mornings can be crisp and clear, but summer often stages a successful and lengthy last-ditch stand, and the trees explode in a cascade of colours.

Globen and other indoor arenas draw increasingly large attendances, and cultural activities in theatres and art galleries get under way again, although many outdoor events continue well into the autumn, weather permitting.

Chanterelles

SEPTEMBER

Now is the time to pick mushrooms in the forests, or apples, pears and plums in the garden. The summer cottages are shut and the boats are laid up for the winter, but there is still a lot going on in the capital.
Stockholm Beer and Whisky Festival *(last two weekends in Sep)*. Lively festival with over 500 beers, whiskies and ciders.
Stockholm Cup *(first weekend in Sep)*. Horse race at Täby course with an international field.

Elite Series *(first weekend in Sep)*. The season's first ice-hockey matches at Globen.
Swedish Army Tattoo *(first weekend in Sep, even-numbered years)*. Military bands and display groups perform at Globen.
Stockholm Race *(last weekend in Sep)*. Fun-run round the city centre starting from Stadion.
Pet Fair *(last weekend in Sep)*. Pets of all kinds on show at Soluntuna Exhibition Centre.
Traditional Fair at Skansen *(last weekend in Sep)*. Among the items on sale are textiles, woodcrafts and toys.
Lidingö Race *(end of Sep)*. The world's largest cross-country race with competitors of all ages, including elite runners, senior citizens and children.

OCTOBER

This is a busy time for theatres, cinemas, restaurants and clubs. There are fewer outdoor events, instead people head for the parks and forests for autumn strolls.
Stockholm Open *(mid-Oct)*. ATP tennis tournament at Kungliga Lawn Tennishallen.

Annual Stockholm International Horse Show at Globen

NOVEMBER

As darkness falls over the city, there is a wide selection of events to choose from.
Autumn Antiques Fair *(mid-Nov)*. Notable antiques fair with a chance of some real finds at Wasahallen.
Scandinavian Sail and Motor Boat Show *(mid-Nov)*. Exhibition at Stockholm International Fairs with everything for large motor boats or yachts.
Det Goda Köket cookery exhibition *(mid-Nov)*. Food, wine, cooking equipment and master classes at Stockholm International Fairs.
Skating Premiere *(mid-Nov)*. Skating with music starts on a rink in Kungsträdgården.
Stockholm International Film Festival *(mid-Nov)*. Ten-day event with public screenings and the presentation of awards.
Stockholm International Horse Show *(late Nov)*. World Cup competition in dressage and jumping plus entertainment at Globen.
Christmas displays *(late Nov)*. Shop windows and streets are seasonally decorated.

Profusion of autumn colours in Hagaparken

AVERAGE MONTHLY TEMPERATURE

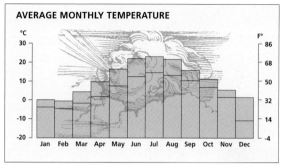

°C: 30, 20, 10, 0, -10, -20

F°: 86, 68, 50, 32, 14, -4

Jan Feb Mar Apr May Jun Jul Aug Sep Oct Nov Dec

Temperature Chart
Stockholm has a maritime climate and is much milder than might be expected. The summers are usually fairly cool, but sometimes there can be hot sunshine for several weeks running. Winter temperatures often fall below freezing, but it is rarely severely cold. The average maximum and minimum temperatures are shown.

WINTER

Winter can vary from temperatures a few degrees above freezing with slush on the streets to sparkling sunny days with the city under a dazzling white blanket of snow, ice-covered water and temperatures well below zero. Stockholmers get out their skis, skates, or toboggans, or go for long walks. There are also several cultural and sporting events.

DECEMBER

Sometimes the eagerly awaited Christmas season seems a long way off, but there is no shortage of activities in early December, when some of the year's most important events are staged.
Handicraft and Arts Exhibition *(early Dec)*. Popular arts and crafts show at Sollentuna Exhibition Centre.
Nobel Day *(10 Dec)*. The year's Nobel Prize laureates are honoured in a ceremony at Konserthuset (Concert Hall). In the evening the royal family attends a banquet at Stadshuset (City Hall).

Lucia, the "Queen of Light", with her attendants at Skansen

Lucia Celebrations *(13 Dec)*. Sweden's white-clad Lucia, the "Queen of Light", with her girl attendants and "star boys", serves the Nobel laureates early morning coffee with saffron buns and performs traditional songs. In the evening a Lucia procession winds through the city to celebrations and fireworks at Skansen. Many Swedish homes, schools and workplaces have their own Lucia.
Christmas Markets *(from early Dec)*. An array of Christmas goods on sale at traditional markets at Skansen, Rosendals Slott, Kungsträdgården, Stortorget in Gamla Stan and Drottningholms Slott.
Christmas *(24–26 Dec)*. Filled with traditions, Christmas is the most important Swedish holiday. The main event is Christmas Eve, when an abundant *smörgåsbord* is followed by gifts, often delivered by a family member disguised as Father Christmas.
Christmas Sales *(first weekday after Christmas)* Shops start their sales.
New Year *(31 Dec–1 Jan)*. A major festival when many Stockholmers go out on the town. Traditional celebrations at Skansen include a reading of Tennyson's *Ring out wild bells...* on the stroke of midnight. Churches across the city ring their bells, and there is a spectacular fireworks display.

Christmas market at Stortorget in Gamla Stan, a traditional prelude to the festive season

JANUARY

Winter Games *(early Jan)*. This youth sports festival takes place at various venues around the city and features a selection of both indoor and outdoor sports.

FEBRUARY

Globen Gala *(early Feb)*. International athletics stars converge on the Globen arena for one of the world's best indoor competitions.
Antiques Fair *(mid-Feb)*. A highlight for antiques lovers, staged at Stockholm International Fairs, Älvsjö.

PUBLIC HOLIDAYS

New Year (1 Jan)
Epiphany (6 Jan)
Good Friday
Easter Monday
Ascension Day (6th Thu after Easter)
Labour Day (1 May)
Whit Monday (May/Jun)
Midsummer Eve (end Jun)
Christmas Day (25 Dec)
Boxing Day (26 Dec)

STOCKHOLM AT A GLANCE

The old conception of Stockholm as a small, rustic capital of a cold country far away to the north is no longer valid – the city has a rich cultural heritage and has become a dynamic Continental-style capital.

Stockholm is an unbelievably beautiful city, surrounded by clear water and unspoilt countryside which stretches right into the heart of the urban area. Stockholm's 750-year history has produced many beautiful buildings, as well as plenty of impressive cultural treasures which can be discovered in its fine museums.

To make your visit as rewarding as possible the following 10 pages give a quick guide to the best museums and palaces, the most distinguished architecture, and outstanding modern design. Activities along the city's quaysides and waterways are also described. Below is a selection of sights that should not be missed.

STOCKHOLM'S TOP TEN SIGHTS

Stadshuset
See pp114–15

Nordiska museet
See pp90–91

Skansen
See pp96–7

Drottningholm
See pp146–9

Historiska museet
See pp104–5

Moderna museet
See pp80–81

Stockholm's Archipelago
See pp150–51

Nationalmuseum
See pp82–3

Royal Palace and its Guard
See pp50–53

Vasamuseet
See pp92–4

◁ Gamla Stan, and its romantic streets like Österlånggatan, is one of Stockholm's leading attractions

Stockholm's Best: Museums

Stockholm has around 100 museums. Their remarkable collections cover every conceivable subject and interest. The "Top Ten" shown here are of particular note. Kungliga Slottet (the Royal Palace), for instance, is effectively four museums in one, while the most spectacular is the museum housing the *Vasa* warship, salvaged from the depths of Stockholm's harbour after 333 years and now an international attraction.

Hallwylska museet
Thanks to a methodical countess and her impeccable taste this lavishly decorated palace from the late 19th century has become a magnificent museum with a wideranging collection of objects displayed in an original setting.

VASASTADEN

Stockholms Medeltidsmuseum
Parts of the city wall from the 1530s can be seen in this underground Museum of Medieval Stockholm, which focuses on the capital's origins. The wall's reconstruction shows medieval building techniques.

CITY

SÖDERMALM

Nationalmuseum
The Nationalmuseum of Fine Arts, Sweden's largest art museum, has fine collections of 17th- and 18th-century Swedish paintings and handicrafts, 18th-century French and 17th-century Dutch art. Rubens's Bacchanal on Andros dates from the 1630s.

The Royal Palace
In addition to its own attractions, the Royal Palace houses four specialist museums: the Treasury, featuring the State Regalia; the Royal Armoury; Gustav III's Museum of Antiquities; and the Tre Kronor Museum.

0 metres	500
0 yards	500

Historiska museet
Behind the sculpted bronze gateways of the National Historical Museum is a wealth of material, including a section on Viking life. The Gold Room shows priceless prehistoric finds, such as the Timboholm Treasure (400–450 BC).

Moderna museet
Paradise *(1966) by Tinguely de Saint Phalle marks the way up to the Modern Museum with its superb collections of international and Swedish modern art.*

Sjöhistoriska museet
The stern of the royal flagship Amphion, *dating from the late 18th century, is one of the many treasures on display in the National Maritime Museum, designed by Ragnar Östberg.*

ÖSTERMALM

Nordiska museet
This colossal building from 1907 houses many different artifacts illustrating everyday Swedish life and customs, including this dancing pair from the 1780s.

SKEPPS-
HOLMEN

DJURGÅRDEN

Skansen
The world's first open-air museum, founded in 1891, shows the Sweden of bygone days with farms and manor houses, urban scenes and crafts people at work. Nordic fauna and flora are also on display.

Vasamuseet
A fatal capsizal in 1628 and a successful salvage operation 333 years later gave Stockholm its most popular museum. Over 75 per cent of the renovated warship Vasa *is original.*

Exploring Stockholm's Museums

Stockholm's wide range of museums gives the visitor a chance to experience exhibitions covering a multitude of different interests. Many are housed in magnificent historic palaces or institutions with notable collections and the resources to bring each subject to life. In addition, there are numerous specialist museums, including the homes of highly regarded artists. Various important private collections are open to the public. This guide lists more than 50 of the best museums Stockholm has to offer.

Karl XII's uniform, 1718, on show at Livrustkammaren

PALACE MUSEUMS

The period when Sweden was a great power (1611–1718) resulted in a number of beautiful buildings many of which are now museums. Foremost among these are the royal palaces in and around the city. **Kungliga Slottet** (Royal Palace, *pp50–53*) is a museum in itself. It also houses **Skattkammaren** (the Treasury) with Sweden's royal regalia, crowns and a large silver font for the baptism of royal children.

Also in the Royal Palace are **Gustav III's Antikmuseum**, containing the antique marble sculptures that Gustav III brought home from his Italian travels, and **Livrustkammaren** (Royal Armoury, *p48*) where visitors can see a variety of items used at the court through the centuries. **Museum Tre Kronor** reflects the history of the earlier castle.

Other royal museums include **Rosendals Slott** (*p98*) on Djurgården, a prefabricated building from the 1820s in Karl Johan (Empire) style. **Gustav III's Paviljong** (*pp122–3)* in Hagaparken has furnishings and decorations which are fine examples of the late 18th century Gustavian style. **Ulriksdals Slott** (*p125*) has some interesting interiors, including a living room for King Gustav VI Adolf and Queen Louise.

In a class of its own is **Drottningholms Slott** (*pp146–9*), a UNESCO heritage site, which includes a notable theatre museum.

HISTORICAL MUSEUMS

Several of Stockholm's museums focus on various historic aspects. **Historiska museet** (National Historical Museum, *pp104–5*) has treasures from prehistoric times in its magnificent Gold Room, as well as a wonderful section on the Vikings.

Nordiska museet (*pp90–91*) and the open-air **Skansen** (*pp96–7*) show Swedish customs and traditions alongside traditional wooden homes. **Stockholms Stadsmuseum** (City Museum, *p127*) tells the story of Stockholm and its citizens. It also has a reference library.

The city's earliest history is highlighted at **Stockholms Medeltidsmuseum** (Medieval Museum, *p59*). **Etnografiska museet** (National Museum of Ethnography, *p108*) features anthropological artifacts from all around the world.

The culture and history of Stockholm's Jewish population is the theme of **Judiska museet** (*p118*).

Medelhavsmuseet (Museum of Mediterranean and Near Eastern Antiquities, *p65*), with its marvellous 1905 stairwell, focuses on architecture and sculptures from the countries around the Mediterranean.

Östasiatiska museet (Museum of Far Eastern Antiquities, *p78*) contains large collections of arts and crafts from China, Japan, Korea and India.

ART MUSEUMS

The wide range of collections at the **Nationalmuseum** (National Museum of Fine Arts, *pp82–3*) cover European and Swedish paintings up to the early 20th century, as well as Swedish handicrafts and design. **Moderna museet** (*pp80–81*) on Skeppsholmen has an outstanding collection of contemporary Swedish and international art. **Arkitekturmuseet** (Museum of Architecture, *p78*), highlights Swedish building techniques over the last 1,000 years and provides an overview of the wider international picture.

Three magnificent art galleries are located in beautiful buildings on Djurgården. **Liljevalchs Konsthall** (*p95*) focuses on 20th-century Swedish and international art, while **Waldemarsudde** (*p99*) and **Thielska Galleriet** (*p99*) both specialize in Swedish and Nordic art from the late 19th to the early 20th century. **Scheffelerska Palatset** (the Haunted Palace, *p116*) shows Stockholm University's collection of classic Swedish paintings, from the 16th to the

Decorative Viking brooch, Historiska museet

19th century, as well as artistic Swedish glass.

Millesgården *(p150)* on Lidingö is where the sculptor Carl Milles lived and worked, and where he is now buried. Some of his best works are on show in a beautiful outdoor setting with a panoramic view of Stockholm.

MARINE MUSEUMS

A city located on water offers plenty of interest for anyone interested in ships and the sea.

One of the city's biggest attractions, **Vasamuseet** *(pp92–4)*, shows the magnificent and almost intact warship *Vasa*, which sank in Stockholm harbour after a maiden voyage of only 1,300 m (1,400 yd). In addition to the painstakingly restored hull, there are other exhibits which give an insight into life on board a 17th-century warship.

Close to *Vasa* are **Museifartygen** (Museum Ships, *p89*), including one of the last Swedish lightships, *Finngrundet* (1903), and the powerful ice-breaker *St Erik* (1915) featuring Europe's largest marine steam engine.

Sjöhistoriska museet (National Maritime Museum, *pp106–7*) features a fine collection of model ships as well as an interesting display of figure heads.

A short boat trip takes visitors to the **Fjäderholmarna** islands, where there are two boat museums devoted to traditional and recreational boating. There is also an angling museum and the Baltic aquarium, dramatically set into the side of a rock face *(p150)*.

MUSEUMS IN PRIVATE HOMES

One of the pearls among Stockholm's museums, **Hallwylska museet** *(p73)*, is an opulent private residence from the late 19th century, complete with original furnishings. The home of the dramatist and author August

Drawing room in the lavishly decorated Hallwylska house

Strindberg, which became **Strindbergsmuseet Blå Tornet** (Strindberg's Blue Tower Museum, *p69*), gives an insight into his life. A statue of Strindberg by Carl Eldh stands near **Carl Eldhs Ateljémuseum** (Studio Museum, *pp120–21*), the sculptor's former residence.

MUSEUMS FOR SPECIAL INTERESTS

Stockholm has many museums catering for special interests. **Kungliga Myntka-binettet** (Royal Coin Cabinet, *p48*) explains the history of money and shows coins and other methods of payment dating back 1,000 years.

Stage costume from *Les Ballets Suédois* (1920s), Dansmuseet

Junibacken *(p88)* is a charming museum, bringing to life the classic children's books by Astrid Lindgren.

Leksaksmuseet (Toy Museum, *p131*) is an attraction for all ages with its mechanical toys, models, dolls and dolls' houses.

A traditional wine shop and distillery can be seen at Vin- & Sprithistoriska museet (Wine and Spirits Museum, *p95*). Another human weakness, tobacco, is documented at Skansen's Tobaksmuseet (Museum of Matches and Tobacco).

Postmuseum (Postal Museum, *p55*) contains more than 4 million stamps from around the world.

Spårvägsmuseet (Transport Museum, *p130*) has some 40 original trams and a large collection of models. In the same area is the **Almgrens Sidenväveri & Museum** (Almgren's Silk-weaving Mill & Museum, *p127*).

The life of the 18th-century troubadour Carl Michael Bell-man *(p98)*, is portrayed at the **Bellmanmuseet** *(p132)* on Långholmen.

Dansmuseet (Dance Museum, *p65*) reflects all aspects of dance with a superb and varied inter-national collection.

Musik- & Teatermuseet (Museum of Music and Theatre, *p72*) has some 6,000 instruments and the country's biggest musical archive, which includes records covering 20,000 traditional ballads.

Stockholm's Best: Architecture

Sweden was spared the ravages of World War II, so Stockholm has preserved a rich variety of architectural treasures. Gamla Stan was the city's first built-up area. The surrounding districts known as Malmarna *(see p101)* remained mainly rural until an intensive period of building begun in the second half of the 19th century. From 1930 the city started to expand further and this period is reflected in a band of Functionalist-style buildings. Suburbs like Farsta and Vällingby were built after 1945. In the 1990s, new buildings began appearing in the inner city on former industrial sites.

Stadsbiblioteket
(Erik Gunnar Asplund, 1920–28). The City Library is Stockholm's most admired example of the 1920s Neo-Classicist style. The book hall has a fascinating cylindrical shape and many fine interior details. (See p117.)

Kungliga Dramatiska Teatern
(Fredrik Liljekvist, 1901–1908). The Royal Dramatic Theatre is one of Stockholm's few monumental buildings in Jugendstil. The façades are of white marble, and inside the staircase and foyer are embellished with lavish gold decorative work. (See p72.)

VASASTADEN

CITY

Nybrov

KUNGSHOLMEN

GAMLA STAN

Ström

SÖDERMALM

The Royal Palace
(Nicodemus Tessin the Younger 1690–1704; completed under Carl Hårleman). Work on the Royal Palace, based on plans by Tessin the Younger, started after the fire in 1697. The façade exhibits influences of Roman palaces; the magnificent interiors are of French and Swedish design. (See pp50–53.)

Wrangelska Palatset
(Nicodemus Tessin the Elder 1652–70). This is one of several majestic palaces built on Riddarholmen in the imposing style popular during the 17th century. Original details include the gateway and the courtyard arcade. (See p56.)

Tessinparken
(Arvid Stille, 1930 city plan by Sture Frölén). Functionalist style on a large scale was tested on the three-storey buildings on pillars at Tessinparken. (See p110.)

THE TESSIN TRIO

Nicodemus Tessin the Younger (1654–1728), who designed the Royal Palace *(see pp50–53)*, can be regarded as Sweden's leading architect because he influenced not only building design but also city planning, landscape gardening and handicrafts. His father, Nicodemus Tessin the Elder (1615–81), designed several country mansions, with Drottningholm Palace being his master work *(see pp146–9)*. The third-generation Tessin, Carl Gustaf (1695–1770), along with Carl Hårleman, introduced the Rococo style to Sweden.

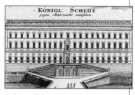

Etching of the Royal Palace, to which all three Tessins contributed

Nordiska museet
(Isak Gustaf Clason, 1889–1907). This museum was conceived as a national monument for Nordic culture. The impressive building in a Scandinavian version of Renaissance style is only one-fourth of its planned size. (See pp90–91.)

ÖSTERMALM

SKEPPS-HOLMEN

Moderna museet
(Rafael Moneo, 1995–8). The spacious Modern Museum was designed to be novel yet not to disturb the historically sensitive surroundings of the island of Skeppsholmen. (See pp80–81.)

DJURGÅRDEN

Söder Cottages
Wooden cottages for port workers started to spring up from the early 18th century. Quite a few remain in the Söder area, for example at Åsöberget and on Fjällgatan. (See p129.)

metres	500
yards	500

STOCKHOLM'S SURROUNDING AREAS

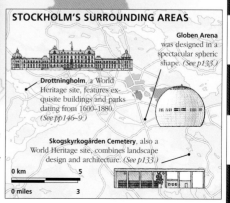

Globen Arena was designed in a spectacular spheric shape. *(See p133.)*

Drottningholm, a World Heritage site, features exquisite buildings and parks dating from 1600–1880. *(See pp146–9.)*

Skogskyrkogården Cemetery, also a World Heritage site, combines landscape design and architecture. *(See p133.)*

0 km	5
0 miles	3

Swedish Style

Swedish design first attracted international attention at the 1925 World Exhibition in Paris, when glassware in particular took the world by storm and the concept of "Swedish Grace" was launched. The nation's design tradition is characterized by its simplicity and functionality with an emphasis on natural materials. Swedish designers and architects are renowned for creating simple, attractive "human" objects for everyday use. The 1990s marked the beginning of a new golden age in which contemporary Swedish design once more won worldwide acclaim.

Stoneware, Hans Hedberg
Swedish stoneware from the 1940s, 1950s and 1960s attract. worldwide attention, and collec tors buy anything they can find

Armchair (1969), Bruno Mathsson
Bruno Mathsson, one of Sweden's most famous 20th-century furniture designers, is one of the creators of what came to be known as the "Swedish Modern" style. He designed the first version of the Pernilla armchair in 1942.

Pale wood and simplicity is the concept most closely associated with Swedish style.

Rag mats are an old Swedish weaving tradition taken up by Karin Larsson, whose skill as a textile designer is now widely recognized.

Bureau (1952), Josef Frank
Frank was born in Austria but worked in Sweden and was another disciple of the "Swedish Modern" style. He is best known for his printed textiles for Svenskt Tenn (see p186), but also designed furniture.

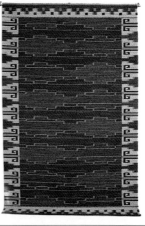

Carpet (1931), Märta Måås-Fjetterström
From 1919 Måås-Fjetterström wove her highly regarded carpets at her studio in southern Sweden. Her work was inspired by folklore and nature, and she created a design concept that was new but still deeply rooted in tradition.

Silver coffee pot (1953), Sigurd Persson

Persson had an unrivalled ability to handle metal. He made a big impact on the history of design with both his every-day industrial work and his exclusive artistic creations.

Flowers and plants along a windowsill and no curtains typify the Larssons' ideas on interior decoration.

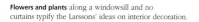

Chair (1981), Jonas Bohlin

The Concrete chair became the most remarkable piece of Swedish furniture design in the 1980s. A graduation project, it represented a completely new approach to furniture design.

Bookshelf (1989), John Kandell

Books are placed flat on the Pilaster bookshelf instead of stacking them in the usual way. The lines are simple and typically Scandinavian. The maker, Källemo, is one of Sweden's most unconventional furniture manufacturers.

Gustavian late 18th-century style elements have remained a strong feature in Swedish design through the centuries, and made a particular comeback in the 1990s.

CARL LARSSON'S SUNDBORN

The home created by the artist Carl Larsson (1853–1919) and his wife Karin, became an inspiration to the world when it featured in his watercolour series *A Home*. The mixture of old and new, pure colours, plants and windows without curtains was an expression of the "Beauty for All" movement.

Vase (1998), Ann Wåhlström

Wåhlström is one of the new young glass designers at Kosta Boda. Her vase, Cyklon, *is a good example of contemporary Swedish glass.*

WHERE TO SEE SWEDISH DESIGN

Asplund
Linnegatan 42.
Map 3 E3.
Contemporary Swedish and international design.
www.asplund.org

Design House Stockholm
Smålandsgatan 11.
Map 3 D4.
Exclusive and functional design with a Scandinavian touch. **www.**
designhousestockholm.com

R.O.O.M.
PUB, Plan 03, Hötorget.
Map 2 C4. www.room.se

Svenskt Tenn
Strandvägen 5. **Map** 3 E4.
Josef Frank, etc.
www.svenskttenn.se

Kosta Boda
Birger Jarlsgatan 15.
Map 3 D3.

Jacksons
Sibyllegatan 53. **Map** 3 E3.
www.jacksons.se

Stockholm, the City on the Water

The Swedish capital is often called "The Venice of the North", built as it is on 14 islands surrounded by the clear waters of Lake Mälaren and Saltsjön, an inlet from the Baltic Sea. For most visitors "the green city on the water" is a remarkable experience. Stockholm's quaysides and waterways offer a whole range of activities not normally associated with a capital city, which are made possible only because of the pollution-free environment. The waterside location is Stockholm's most beautiful feature.

Canoe Slalom on Strömmen
Spectacular canoe slalom competitions are held every year in the rushing water of the Strömmen channel below Gustav Adolfs Torg.

Sailing Race on Riddarfjärden
The waters of Stockholm are always busy with sailing boats. A ride along Riddarfjärden is particularly spectacular at night.

KUNGSHOLMEN

CITY

Riddarfjärden

GAMLA STAN

Strömmen

Långholmen

SÖDERMALM

Swimming in the Heart of the City
During the summer months, swimmers bathe in the clean, warm water (about 20°C/68°F) in the city centre. Långholmen (see p132) has sandy beaches and smooth rocks offering an ideal setting for a refreshing dip.

Fishing for a Living
For 400 years fishermen have cast their nets from boats near Kungliga Slottet (Royal Palace). Today only four boats remain. Of the 30 species found here, smelt is the most commonly caught fish.

Vintage Mahogany Boat
Lovingly renovated vintage motor boats with shining mahogany and brass fittings are often seen on the waterways of Stockholm, as well as the more exclusive Riva racing boats.

Exploring on Your Own
Kayaks, pedalos, rowing boats, motor boats, and sometimes sailing dinghies, can be hired near the Djurgården Bridge by visitors who want to explore the waters of Stockholm on their own.

| 0 metres | 500 |
| 0 yards | 500 |

ÖSTERMALM

Djurgårdsbrunnsviken

DJURGÅRDEN

Saltsjön

Fishing for Perch
The clean waters of the inner city are rich in edible fish. Anglers spin for sea trout, and here on Djurgårdsbrunn Canal bait-fishing for perch is popular, and fly-fishing in autumn.

KEY

---- Paved walking path

Open-air swimming

Cruise Ship Manoeuvres in Stockholm's Harbour
Cruise ships are an attractive sight when seen from the heights of Södermalm as they make their way through the narrow channel to their centrally located quay.

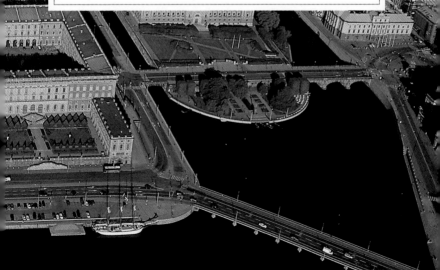

STOCKHOLM
AREA BY AREA

GAMLA STAN

Relics of Stockholm's early history as a town in the 13th century can still be found on Stadsholmen, Gamla Stan's (Old Town) largest island. The whole island is one huge area of historical heritage, with the many sights just a few metres apart.

The Royal Palace is the symbol of Sweden's era as a great power in the 17th and early 18th centuries *(see pp18–19)*, and its magnificent state rooms, apartments and artifacts are well matched to the Roman Baroque-style exterior. The historic buildings standing majestically

Anchor point on a palace façade

around Slottsbacken, underline Stockholm's role as a capital city.

This area has a special atmosphere with much to offer: from the bustling streets of souvenir shops, bookstores and antique shops to elegant palaces, churches and museums. Many medieval cellars are now restaurants and cafés, while the narrow streets recall a bygone era.

Bridges lead to Riddarholmen, with its 17th-century palaces and royal crypt, and to Helgeandsholmen for the newer splendours of Riksdagshuset (the Parliament building).

SIGHTS AT A GLANCE

Palaces and Museums
Kungliga
　Myntkabinettet ❸
Livrustkammaren ❷
Postmuseum ❿
The Royal Palace
　pp50–53 ❶
Stockholms
　Medeltidsmuseum ⓳

Public Buildings
Bondeska Palatset ⓱
Riddarhuset ⓰
Riksdagshuset ⓲
Stenbockska Palatset ⓯

Historic Buildings
Birger Jarls Torn ⓮
Tessinska Palatset ❹
Wrangelska Palatset ⓬

Streets and Squares
Evert Taubes Terrass ⓭
Mårten Trotzigs Gränd ❽
Stortorget ❻

Västerlånggatan ❾

Churches
Riddarholms-
　kyrkan ⓫
Storkyrkan ❺
Tyska Kyrkan ❼

KEY

▢ Street-by-Street map
　 See pp46–7

▭ Ferry landing point

🆃 Tunnelbana station

▭ Bus stop

0 metres　　　250
0 yards　　　250

◁ **Prästgatan in Gamla Stan with its yellow ochre plastering typical of the 18th century**

Street-by-Street: Slottsbacken

Slottsbacken is much more than just a steep hill linking Skeppsbron and the highest part of Gamla Stan (Old Town). It also provides the background for ceremonial processions and the daily changing-of-the-guard, and is the route for visiting heads of state and foreign ambassadors when they have an audience with the king at the Royal Palace. Alongside Slottsbacken the palace displays its most attractive façade, with the entrance to the Treasury (Skattkammaren), State Room (Rikssalen) and Palace Church (Slottskyrkan). Nicodemus Tessin the Younger's ambition to make Stockholm a leading European city in monumental terms was realized in 1799 with the addition of the Obelisk.

The Olaus Petri statue by Storkyrkan stands in front of a tablet telling the history of the cathedral since 1264.

Outer Courtyard

Axel Oxenstiernas Palats (1653) is, for Stockholm, an unusual example of the style known as Roman Mannerism. For 30 years, Axel Oxenstierna (1583–1654) himself was a dominant figure in Swedish power politics.

TRÅNGSUND

The Obelisk by Louis Jean Desprez was erected in 1799 to thank the citizens for their support of Gustav III's Russian war in 1788–90.

Stock Exchange *(see p54)*

STOR-TORGET

★ **Storkyrkan**
An impressive cathedral with a late Gothic interior, it is full of treasures from many different eras ⑤

STAR SIGHTS

★ Storkyrkan

★ Livrustkammaren

★ The Royal Palace

Stortorget
This square is the heart of the "city between the bridges", with a well dating from 1778. It was the scene of the Stockholm Bloodbath in 1520 ⑥

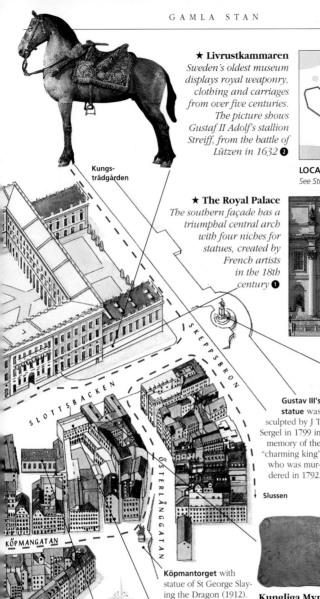

★ **Livrustkammaren**
Sweden's oldest museum displays royal weaponry, clothing and carriages from over five centuries. The picture shows Gustaf II Adolf's stallion Streiff, from the battle of Lützen in 1632 ❷

LOCATOR MAP
See Street Finder map 4

★ **The Royal Palace**
The southern façade has a triumphal central arch with four niches for statues, created by French artists in the 18th century ❶

Kungs-
trädgården

**Gustav III's
statue** was
sculpted by J T
Sergel in 1799 in
memory of the
"charming king"
who was mur-
dered in 1792.

Slussen

Köpmantorget with
statue of St George Slay-
ing the Dragon (1912).

Kungliga Myntkabinettet
In a 16th-century setting, the Royal Coin Cabinet has the world's largest stamped coin, dating from 1644 ❸

Finska Kyrkan, Slottsbacken's oldest building,
dates from the 1640s. It
was originally a royal ball-
games court for the palace,
but since 1725 it has been
the religious centre for the
Finnish community.

Tessinska Palatset
Built by and for Nicodemus Tessin the Younger, architect of the Royal Palace, in 1694–7, this palace has been the residence of the Governor of Stockholm County since 1968 ❹

SKEPPSBRON
SLOTTSBACKEN
ÖSTERLÅNGGATAN
KÖPMANGATAN

0 metres		100
0 yards		100

KEY

‑ ‑ ‑   Suggested route

The Royal Palace ❶

See pp50–53.

Livrust-kammaren ❷

Slottsbacken 3. **Map** 4 C2.
Tel 08-402 30 30. Ⓣ *Gamla Stan.*
🚌 *2, 43, 55, 76.* ☐ *Jun–Aug:*
10am–5pm daily; Sep–May: 11am–
5pm Tue–Sun (Thu also 5–8pm).
🎫 *Eng: Jul–Aug.* 📷 🔊 🚫 ♿ 🏠
www.livrustkammaren.se

Sweden's oldest museum,
Livrustkammaren (the Royal
Armoury) was founded in
1628 and is full of *objets d'art*
and everyday items used by
the Royal Family over the
past five centuries. The oldest
exhibit is Gustav Vasa's
crested helmet dating from
1548. The museum also
houses a variety of royal
items which illustrate
events in Swedish
history. Among
them are Gustav II
Adolf's stuffed
stallion, Streiff,
which he rode at
the Battle of Lützen
in 1632; Gustaf
III's costume from
the notorious
masked ball at
which he was murdered in
1792; and Karl XII's blue
uniform with the still muddy
boots he had on when he
died at the siege of
Frerikshald in Norway in 1718.

Coronation ceremonies are
illustrated by costumes such
as those worn by King Adolf
Fredrik and Queen Lovisa
Ulrika in 1751. The King's
attire alone was adorned with
some 2 kg (4 lb) of silver. The
coronation carriage, originally

**Sweden's first coin,
struck in about AD 995**

built in the 17th century, was
modernized for this event. Its
renovation in the 1970s took
eight years and cost 700,000
kronor. The cellar vault, once
used for firewood, is skilfully
lit, providing an imaginative
setting for the exhibits.

Kungliga Myntkabinettet ❸

Slottsbacken 6. **Map** 4 C3.
Tel 08-519 553 04. Ⓣ *Gamla Stan.*
🚌 *2, 43, 55, 59, 76.* ☐ *10am–4pm*
daily. 📷 *by arrangement.* 🔊 ♿ 🍴
☐ 🏠 **www.**myntkabinettet.se

The Royal Coin Cabinet is a
museum highlighting the
history of money from the
10th century to the present
day – from the little cowrie
shell via the drachma and
denarius to the cash card of
the 21st century. The
museum also gives an
insight into the art
of medal design
over the past 600
years and shows
both traditional
portrait medals and
more modern
examples like
those that have
been awarded to
Nobel laureates.
Visitors can also see the first
Swedish coin, struck in the
late 10th century by King Olof
Skötkonung. Other rarities
include Queen Kristina's coin
from 1644, weighing 19.7 kg
(43 lb) and reckoned to be
the world's heaviest coin.
From the island of Yap in
Micronesia the museum has
acquired the world's largest
means of payment, a so-
called "rai-stone" which greets
visitors in the foyer.

The many
sections in the
museum include
"The World's
Money", "State
Finance" and
"Saving in a Piggy
Bank and Bank".
"Summa
Summarum" is a
section designed
for children and
illustrates the use
of money in play
and real life.

**The elegant Baroque garden in
Tessinska Palatset's courtyard**

Tessinska Palatset ❹

Slottsbacken 4. **Map** 2 C3.
Ⓣ *Gamla Stan.* 🚌 *2, 43, 55, 59, 76.*
⭕ *to the public.*

The Tessin Palace at Slottsbacken is considered by
many to be the most beautiful
private residence north of
Paris. It is the best-preserved
palace from Sweden's era as a
great power in the 17th
century and was designed by
and for Tessin the Younger
(1654–1728), the nation's
most renowned architect.

Completed in 1697, the
building is located on a
narrow site which widens out
towards a courtyard with a
delightful Baroque garden.
The relatively discreet façade
with its beautiful porch was
inspired by the exterior
design of Roman palaces.
The decor and garden were
influenced by Tessin's time in
Paris and Versailles.

Tessin, who became a count
and State Councillor, spent
large sums on the building's
ornamentation. Sculptures and
paintings were provided by
the same French masters
whose work had graced the
Royal Palace. Later, however,
his son, Carl Gustaf, had to sell
the palace for financial reasons.

The building was acquired
by the City of Stockholm as a
residence for its Governor in
1773. In 1968 it became the
residence of the Governor of
the County of Stockholm.

**The coronation carriage of King Adolf Fredrik
and Queen Lovisa Ulrika in Livrustkammaren**

Storkyrkan 🕔

Trångsund 1. **Map** 4 B3. **Tel** 08-723
30 16. 🚇 Gamla Stan. 🚌 2, 43, 55,
59, 76. ⬜ May–Aug: 9am–6pm Mon–
Fri (to 4pm Sat & Sun); Sep–Apr: 9am–
4pm daily. 🕍 11am Sat & Sun. 📷
Eng: Jul–Aug: 1pm (tour of the tower
2pm). ♿ 📷 (during services). 🚪

Stockholm's 700-year-old
cathedral is of great national
religious importance. It was
from here that the Swedish
reformer Olaus Petri
(1493–1552) spread his
Lutheran message around the
kingdom. It is also used for
royal ceremonies.

Originally, a small village
church was built on this site
in the 13th century, probably
by the city's founder Birger
Jarl. It was replaced in 1306
by a much bigger basilica, St
Nicholas, which was altered
over the centuries.

The Gothic character of the
interior, acquired in the 15th
century, was revealed in 1908
when, during restoration
work, plaster was removed
from the pillars, exposing the
characteristic red tiling. The
late Baroque period provided
the so-called "royal chairs"
and the pulpit, while the
façade was adapted to bring it
into keeping with the rest of
the area around the Royal
Palace. The 66-m (216-ft) high

Storkyrkan's façade in Italian Baroque style, seen from Slottsbacken

tower, added in 1743, has 4
bells, the largest of which
weighs about 6 tonnes.

The cathedral houses some
priceless artistic treasures,
including St George and the
Dragon, regarded as one of
the finest late Gothic works of
art in Northern
Europe. The sculp-
ture, situated to
the left of the altar,
was carved from
oak and elk horn
by Lübeck sculp-
tor Berndt Notke.
Unveiled in 1489,
it commemorates
Sten Sture the
Elder's victory
over the Danes in
1471 (see p15).

The Last Judgment
(1696) is a massive
Baroque painting
by David Klöcker
von Ehrenstrahl.
The 3.7-m (12-ft)
high bronze can-
delabra before the
altar, likely to be
German, has
adorned the
cathedral for some
600 years. One of

the cathedral's most prized
treasures is the silver altar,
which gave the interior a
completely new appearance
in the 1650s. It was a
gift from the
diplomat Johan
Adler Salvius.

The pews
nearest to the
chancel, the
"royal chairs",
were designed
by Nicodemus
Tessin the
Younger in
1684 to be
used by royalty
on special
occasions. In
1705, the pulpit
was installed
above the grave of Olaus Petri.

On 20 April 1535, a light
phenomenon was observed
over Stockholm – six rings
with sparkling solar halos. The
Parhelion Painting, recalling
the event (see p14), hangs in
Storkyrkan and is thought to
be the oldest portrayal of the
capital. It shows the modest
skyline dominated by the
cathedral, at that time still the
basilica of St Nicholas.

**Storkyrkan's
silver altar
(detail)**

**The sculpture St George and the Dragon by
Bernt Notke (1489) in Storkyrkan**

The Royal Palace (Kungliga Slottet) ❶

Royal Sceptre

Defensive installations or castles have stood on the island of Stadsholmen ever since the 11th century. The Tre Kronor (Three Crowns) fortress was completed in the mid-13th century, but during the following century it became a royal residence. The Vasa kings turned the fortress into a Renaissance palace which burned to the ground in 1697. In its place the architect Nicodemus Tessin the Younger created a new palace in Roman style with an Italianate exterior and a French interior toned down by Swedish influences. The palace's 608 rooms were decorated by Europe's foremost artists and craftsmen. King Adolf Fredrik was the first king to move into the palace, in 1754. It is no longer the king's private residence, but remains one of the city's leading sights.

★ Changing of the Guard
Stockholm's most popular tourist event is the daily changing of the guard at midday in the Outer Courtyard.

Entrance to the State Apartments

The Western Staircase
Tessin was especially proud of the two staircases, made from Swedish marble and porphyry. On the western staircase stands a bust of the gifted architect.

★ The Hall of State
This opulent hall has an atmosphere of ceremonial splendour and forms an ideal setting for Queen Kristina's silver throne, probably the palace's most famous treasure.

The Guest Apartments

Entrance to Treasury and Royal Chapel

A ROYAL WORKPLACE

The king and queen have their offices at the palace, where they hold audiences with visiting dignitaries, and official ceremonies. They travel around the country attending special events, official openings and anniversaries, and they make regular State visits abroad. The king is well known for his interest in the environment while the queen is heavily involved with her work for children, especially the disabled.

King Carl XVI Gustav and Queen Silvia

The Royal Chapel
This delightful little church has a rich interior decorated by many different artists. The pulpit is the work of J P Bouchardon.

STAR FEATURES

★ Changing the Guard

★ The Hall of State

★ Karl XI's Gallery

Gustav III's State Bedchamber
Sergel's bust of Gustav III (1779) stands in the room where the king died after being shot at the Opera House. The decor by J E Rehn dates from the 1770s.

VISITORS' CHECKLIST

Gamla Stan. **Map** 4 B2.
Tel 08-402 61 30. 🚇 Gamla Stan, Kungsträdgården. 🚌 2, 43, 55, 71, 76. **The Royal Apartments, The Treasury, Gustav III's Museum of Antiquities, Tre Kronor Museum** ⬜ 15 May– 25 Sep: 10am–5pm daily; 26 Sep–14 May: noon–3pm Tue–Sun. 🚫 during official functions of the Court. 🎫 tours in English at 1 & 2pm. 📷 ⌀ ♿ 🛗 **The Royal Chapel** ⬜ Jun–Aug: noon–3pm Wed & Fri. ✝ Mass 11am Sun (year round). ⌀ ♿
www.kungahuset.se

The Bernadotte Apartments are situated on the floor below Karl XI's Gallery.

Tre Kronor Museum entrance from Lejonbacken.

★ Karl XI's Gallery
One of the most magnificent rooms in the palace, this fine example of Swedish Late Baroque is used for banquets hosted by the king and queen. In the cabinet is this priceless salt-cellar dating from 1627–8.

Carl Hårleman played an important role in the design of the palace. His bust adorns this niche.

Logården is the terrace between the palace's east wings.

Livrustkammaren *(see p48)*

Gustav III's Museum of Antiquities
The museum's collection includes antique statues brought home by Gustav III from his journey to Rome.

Exploring the Royal Palace

The public areas of the Royal Palace allow you to walk through grand rooms of sumptuous furnishings and priceless works of art and craftsmanship. The Hall of State and the Royal Chapel are both characterized by their magnificent lavish decor and Gustav III's Museum of Antiquities contains ancient marble sculptures from the king's journey to Italy. The palace also houses the Treasury with the State regalia; the new Tre Kronor Museum, which depicts the palace before the 1697 fire; and the Livrustkammaren *(see p48)*.

The Pillar Hall in the Bernadotte Apartments with original decor

Karl XI's Gallery, the finest example of the Late Baroque period in Sweden

THE STATE APARTMENTS

The royal family has lived at Drottningholm Palace *(see pp146–49)* since 1982, but official functions still take place in the State Apartments, including banquets hosted by the king during visits by foreign heads of state. Other official dinners are staged here, as well as the festivities held every year to honour the Nobel laureates.

These meals are served in Karl XI's Gallery, the finest example of Swedish Late Baroque, modelled on the Hall of Mirrors at Versailles. Each window is matched with a niche on the inner wall where some of the palace's priceless works of arts and crafts are exhibited. Most remarkable is the salt-cellar made from ivory and gilded silver designed by the Flemish painter Rubens (1577–1640). The room known as "The

King Karl XIV Johan's egg cup

White Sea" serves as a drawing room. Gustav III's State Bedchamber, where the king died after being shot at the Opera House in 1792 *(see pp22–3)*, is the height of Gustavian elegance. Along with Queen Sofia Magdalena's State Bedchamber, it was designed by the architect Jean Eric Rehn. The lintels on the doors to the Don Quixote Room, named after the theme of its tapestries, were made by François Boucher and are among the palace's most treasured pieces.

THE GUEST APARTMENTS

An imposing part of the palace, these apartments are where visiting heads of state stay. The beautiful rooms include the Meleager Salon, where official gifts and decorations are exchanged, and a large bedroom with a sculpted and gilded bed. Other impressive rooms are the Inner Salon, whose decor was inspired by the excavations in Pompeii, and the Margareta Room, named after the present king's grandmother, which displays some pictures painted by her.

The apartments contain remarkable works of craftsmanship by such 18th-century masters as Georg Haupt, Ephraim Ståhle and Jean Baptiste Masreliez.

THE BERNADOTTE APARTMENTS

This magnificent suite has earned its name from the gallery displaying portraits of the Bernadotte dynasty. The apartments have some notable ceiling paintings and mid-18th-century chandeliers, and are used for many a ceremonial occasion. The elegant Pillar Hall is the venue for investitures, and the East Octagonal Cabinet with probably the palace's best Rococo decor, is where the king receives foreign ambassadors. Along with the western cabinet, its interior has remained just as it was planned by Carl Hårleman more than 250 years ago.

Oscar II's very masculine Writing Room, dating from the 1870s, also still looks much as it did in his day. However, it is clear the palace was kept up to date with technical advances. Electricity was installed in 1883, and the telephone only one year later.

THE HALL OF STATE

Rococo and Classicism were brought together in perfect harmony by the architects Nicodemus Tessin the Younger and Carl Hårleman when they designed the two-storey Hall of State. It provides a worthy framework for Queen Kristina's silver throne, a gift for the coronation in 1650 and one of the most valuable treasures in the palace. The throne was given to the Queen by Magnus Gabriel de la Gardie and was made in Augsburg by the goldsmith Abraham Drentwett. The canopy was added 100 years later for the coronation of King Adolf Fredrik and was designed by Jean Eric Rehn.

The decor of the Hall of State is lavish. The throne is flanked by colossal sculptures of Karl XIV Johan and Gustav II Adolf, while those on the cornice symbolize Peace, Strength, Religion and Justice.

Until 1975 the Hall of State was the scene of the ceremonial opening of the Swedish Parliament (Riksdagen) which included a march past of the royal bodyguard in full regalia. It is now used more for other official occasions and, like the Royal Chapel, is a venue for summer concerts (see pp176–77).

The Hall of State, the most important ceremonial room in the palace

THE ROYAL CHAPEL

It took 50 years to build the Royal Palace, and a lot of effort went into the French Rococo interior decoration of the Royal Chapel. The work was carried out largely by Carl Hårleman under the supervision of Nicodemus Tessin the Younger. As with the Hall of State, the co-operation between the two produced a magnificent result, enhanced by the contributions of several foreign artists. The chapel was completed when the palace reopened in 1754.

A number of remarkable artifacts have been added over the centuries. The most recent was a group of six 17th-century-style bronze crowns, as well as two crystal crowns.

It also has some rare relics of the original Tre Kronor

fortress: new benches that had been ordered by Tessin. They had been rescued during the palace fire in 1697 and preserved but not put in the chapel until the 19th century. The benches were made by Georg Haupt, grandfather of the Georg Haupt who was to create some of the palace's most prized furnishings (see p82).

Erik XIV's crown, made by Cornelis ver Weiden in Stockholm in 1561

GUSTAV III'S MUSEUM OF ANTIQUITIES

Opened in 1794 in memory of the murdered king, the Museum of Antiquities initially housed more than 200 exhibits, mainly acquired during Gustav's Italian journey in 1783–4 and then supplemented with more purchases later.

In 1866 the museum's collection was moved to the city's National Museum (see pp82–3). During the 1950s the main gallery was renovated, followed by the smaller galleries 30 years later, which enabled the collection to be returned to its original setting.

The most prized exhibits are in the main gallery, the best known being the sculpture of Endymion, the eternally sleeping young shepherd and lover of the Moon Goddess Selene. The 18th-century sculptor Johan Tobias Sergel is represented by The Priestess, ranked as the collection's second most important piece. She is flanked by two large candelabras.

THE TREASURY

At the bottom of 56 well-worn steps, below the Hall of State on the south side of the palace, is the entrance to the Treasury (Skattkammaren) where the State regalia, the most potent symbols of the monarchy, are kept.

On the rare occasions that King Erik XIV's crown, sceptre, orb and the keys of the kingdom are taken out of their showcase, they are placed beside the uncrowned

King Carl XVI Gustaf. The 1-m (3-ft) high silver baptismal font, which took the French silversmith Jean François Cousinet 11 years to make, is 200 years old and is still used for royal baptisms. Hanging in the Treasury is the only undamaged tapestry among six dating from the 1560s, salvaged from the 1697 fire.

TRE KRONOR MUSEUM

In the oldest parts of the ruined Tre Kronor fortress, preserved under the north side of the royal palace, is the Tre Kronor (Three Crowns) Museum. About half of a massive 12th-century defensive wall and brick vaults from the 16th and 17th centuries provide a unique setting for the museum which illustrates the palace's history of almost 1,000 years.

Two models of the Tre Kronor fortress show changes made to the fortress during the second half of the 17th century and how it looked by the time of the fire. Among items rescued from the ashes are a schnapps glass, amber pots and bowls made from mountain crystal.

A glass bowl in the Tre Kronor Museum, saved from the 1697 fire

The imposing Stock Exchange on the north side of Stortorget

Stortorget ⑥

Map 4 B3. 🚇 Gamla Stan.
🚌 2, 3, 43, 53, 55, 76.
Nobelmuseet Tel 08-23 25 06.
⭘ mid-May–mid-Sep: 10am–5pm
daily, 10am–8pm Tue; mid-Sep–mid-
May: 11am–5pm Wed–Sun, 11am–
8pm Tue. 🎫 ♿ 🎦 🚻 🏠 🛒
www.nobelmuseum.se

It was not until 1778, when
the Stock Exchange (Börsen)
was completed, that
Stortorget, the square in the
heart of the Old Town,
acquired a more uniform
appearance. Its northern side
had previously been taken up
by several buildings that
served as a town hall. Since
the early Middle Ages the
square had been a natural
meeting point with a well and
marketplace, lined with
wooden stalls on market days.
  A pillory belonging to the
jail, which was once sited on
nearby Kåkbrinken, used to
stand on the square. It is now
in the Town Hall on
Kungsholmen (see p112).

The medieval layout is clear
on Stortorget's west side, where
the red Schantzska Huset (No.
20) and the narrow Seyfridtska
Huset were built in around
1650. The Schantzska Huset
remains unchanged and has a
lovely limestone porch adorned
with figures of recumbent
Roman warriors. The artist
Johan Wendelstam was
responsible for most of the
notable porches in the Old
Town. The 17th-century gable
on the Grilska Huset (No. 3)
is also worth closer study.
  The decision to construct
the Stock Exchange was taken
in 1667 but many wars delay-
ed the start of the building by
100 years. The architect was
the talented Erik Palmstedt
(1741–1803), who also created
the decorative cover for the old
well. However, 200 years of
trading on the floor of the
Stock Exchange came to an
end in 1990. Opened in 2001
to mark the centenary of the
Nobel Prize (see p68), the
Nobelmuseet explores the
work and ideas of more than

700 creative minds by means
of short films and original
artifacts. On the upper floor,
the Swedish Academy holds
its ceremonial gatherings, a
tradition maintained since
Gustav III gave his inauguration speech in 1786.

Tyska Kyrkan ⑦

Svartmangatan 16. **Map** 4 B3.
Tel 08-411 11 88. 🚇 Gamla Stan.
🚌 2, 3, 43, 53, 55, 76. ⭘ 9:30–
11:30am & 1–3pm Tue–Fri, 9am–
noon Wed. 🏠 11am Sun, German.
🎫 by appt in Swedish & German.
♿ **www**.svenskakyrkan.se

The German church is an
impressive reminder of the
almost total influence that
Germany had over Stockholm
during the 18th century. The
Hanseatic League trading
organization was in control of
the Baltic and its ports, which
explains why the basic layout
of Gamla Stan resembled that
of Germany. Germany's political
influence was only broken
after the Stockholm Bloodbath
and Gustav Vasa's accession
to the throne in 1523 (see p16),
but its cultural and mercantile
influence remained strong as
German merchants and
craftsmen settled in the city.
  The church's parish
assembly, which today has
some 2,000 members, was
founded in 1571. The present
twin-nave church was built in
1638–42, as an extension of
a smaller church which the
parish had used since 1576.
  In German Late Renaissance
and Baroque style, the interior
has a royal gallery, added in
1672 for German members of

THE STOCKHOLM BLOODBATH

**Detail of a painting of
the Bloodbath (1524)**

Stortorget is intimately linked with
the Stockholm Bloodbath of
November 1520. The Danish King
Kristian II besieged the Swedish
Regent, Sten Sture the Younger,
until he capitulated and the Swedes
chose Kristian as their king. He
promised an amnesty and ordered
a three-day feast at Tre Kronor
Fortress. Near the end of the
festivities, the revellers were suddenly shut in and arrested for
heresy. The next day more than 80
noblemen and Stockholm citizens
were beheaded in the square.

The royal gallery in the 17th-
century Tyska Kyrkan

the royal household. The pulpit (1660) in ebony and alabaster is unique in Sweden and the altar, from the 1640s, is covered with beautiful paintings surrounded by sculptures of the apostles and evangelists.

The sculptures on the south porch by Jobst Hennen date from 1643 and show Jesus, Moses and three figures portraying Faith, Hope and Love.

Mårten Trotzigs Gränd, the narrowest street in the city

Mårten Trotzigs Gränd ❽

Map 4 C4. Ⓣ *Gamla Stan.* 🚌 *2, 3, 43, 53, 55, 59, 76.*

At only 90 cm (3 ft) wide, Mårten Trotzigs Gränd is the city's narrowest street, and climbing up the 36 steps gives a good idea of how different parts of the Old Town vary so much in height and how tightly packed together the houses are.

Mårten Trotzigs Gränd is named after a German merchant called Traubzich, who owned two houses here at the end of the 16th century. After being fenced off at both ends for 100 years, the street was reopened in 1945.

Västerlånggatan ❾

Map 4 B3. Ⓣ *Gamla Stan.* 🚌 *2, 3, 43, 53, 55, 59, 76.*

Once a main road outside the city proper, built along parts of the original town wall, Västerlånggatan now runs through the heart of the Old

Town, and is usually thronging with people – tourists and locals – shopping or strolling. Starting at Mynttorget in the north, where the Chancery Office (Kanslihuset) and Lejonbacken are, the lively and atmospheric street finishes at Järntorget in the south, where the export of iron was once controlled. Alongside is Bancohuset, which served as the headquarters of the State Bank from 1680 to 1906.

The building at No. 7 has been used by the Swedish Parliament since the mid-1990s. Its late 19th-century façade has a distinctive southern European influence.

No. 27 was built by and for Erik Palmstedt, who also designed the Stock Exchange and the well at Stortorget. No. 29 is a really venerable building, dating from the early 15th century. The original pointed Gothic arches were revealed during restoration in the 1940s.

No. 33 is a good example of how new materials and techniques in the late 19th century made it possible to fit large shop windows into old houses. The cast-iron columns which can be seen in many other places also date from this period.

No. 68, Von der Lindeska House, has a majestic 17th-century façade and a beautiful porch with sculptures of Neptune and Mercury.

Postmuseum ❿

Lilla Nygatan 6. **Map** 4 B3. **Tel** 08-781 17 55. Ⓣ *Gamla Stan.* 🚌 *3, 53.* 🕐 *11am–4pm Tue–Sun, Sep–Apr also Wed 4pm–7pm.* 🎫 *by arrangement.* ♿ 🛗 📷 📽 🛍 **www**.postmuseum.posten.se

An attraction in itself, the Postmuseum building takes up a whole area bought by the Swedish Post Office in 1720. About 100 years later

Västerlånggatan, Gamla Stan's most popular shopping street

the majestic-looking Post Office was built, incorporating parts of the 17th-century buildings already there. Stockholm's only Post Office until 1869, it was turned into the Postal Museum in 1906.

Letters have been sent in Sweden since 1636, and the museum's permanent exhibits include a portrayal of early "peasant postmen" fighting the angry Åland Sea in their boat *Simpan*. Also on display is the first post bus which ran in northern Sweden in the early 1920s and a stagecoach used in eastern Sweden.

Mauritian stamp in the Postmuseum

The collection includes Sweden's first stamp-printing press and no less than four million stamps among which are the first Swedish stamps, produced in 1855. Also on display is the "Penny Black", the world's first stamp dating from 1840, and some stamps issued by Mauritius in 1847.

The museum library holds a large collection of literature on philately and postal history. There is also a charming workshop, *The Little Post Office*, where children can discover what it was like to work in a 1920s post office.

Riddarholms-kyrkan ⓫

Birger Jarls Torg. **Map** 4 A3.
Tel 08-402 61 30. Ⓣ Gamla Stan.
🚌 3, 53. ◯ 15 May–14 Sep:
10am–4pm daily. 🎫 Eng: 2pm &
4pm. 🖼 Ø ⅃ 🖼

This church on the island of
Riddarholmen is best
known as a place for royal
burials. Its interior is full of
ornate sarcophagi and worn
gravestones, and in front of
the altar are the tombs of the
medieval kings Karl Knutsson
and Magnus Ladulås.

Built on the site of the late
13th-century Greyfriars abbey,
founded by Magnus Ladulås,
the majestic brick church was
gradually enlarged over the
centuries. After a serious fire
in 1835, the church acquired
its present lattice-work,
cast-iron tower.

The church is surrounded
by ornate burial vaults which
date back as far as the 16th
century. The coffins rest on a
lower level with space for a
memorial above. The most
recent was built in 1858–60
for the Bernadotte dynasty.

The vaults contain the
remains of all the Swedish
monarchs from Gustav II
Adolf in the 17th century to
the present day with two
exceptions: Queen Kristina
was buried at St Peter's in
Rome in 1689 and Gustav VI
Adolf, who died in 1973,
was interred at Haga (see
pp122–3). The most magni-
ficent sarcophagus is that
of the 19th-century king,
Karl XIV Johan, which
had to be towed
here by sledge from
his porphyry work-

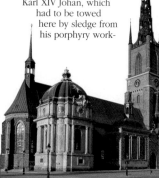

**Riddarholmskyrkan with the external
burial vault by Tessin and Hårleman**

shops in the Älvdalen region
in northern Sweden.

Particularly moving are the
graves of royal children who
met an early death, including
the many small tin coffins that
surround the last resting place
of Gustav II Adolf and his
queen, Maria Eleonora.

Wrangelska Palatset ⓬

Birger Jarls Torg 16. **Map** 4 A3.
Ⓣ Gamla Stan. 🚌 3, 53. ◯ to
the public.

Only two parts of the
fortification work which
Gustav Vasa undertook
around 1530 still remain –
Birger Jarl's Tower and the
southernmost tower of what
became the Wrangel Palace.
Built as a residence for the
nobleman Lars Sparre in
1629, it was extensively
rebuilt only a few decades
later. The owner by then
was Carl Gustaf Wrangel,
a field marshal during the
Thirty Years War, who
chose Nicodemus Tessin
the Elder as his
architect. The result was
Stockholm's largest
palace in private hands.

In 1693 Wrangel lost
many valuable posses-
sions in a major fire, and
four years later his
palace became a royal
residence when the
Royal Family moved to
Riddarholmen after the
Tre Kronor fortress (see
pp50–53) was ravaged
by another fire. The
palace then became

Wrangelska Palatset, a royal residence after the Tre Kronor fire of 1697

known as the King's House,
and it was here in 1697 that
the 15-year-old Karl XII took
the oath of office after the
death of his father. Three
years later the young king left
his palace to go to war; he
would never return to Stockholm. Gustav III was born
here, ten years before the
Royal Family moved back to
the new Royal Palace in 1754.

The Court of Appeal now
uses the whole building,
where in 1792 the assassin of
Gustav III was manacled in
the dungeons during his trial.

The court also rents the
Rosenhane Palace (Birger
Jarls Torg 10) and the
Hessenstein House (Birger
Jarls Torg 2), which was built
in 1630 by Bengt Bengtsson
Oxenstierna. It was named
after Fredrik Wilhelm von
Hessenstein, the son of
Fredrik I and his lover Hedvig
Taube. Later it was occupied
by Carl Gustav Tessin, son of
the Royal Palace architect and
a leading personality in the
world of culture.

**The city founder Birger Jarl's statue
on the square that bears his name**

Evert Taubes Terrass ⑬

Norra Riddarholmshamnen. **Map 4** A3. Ⓣ *Gamla Stan.* ▨ *3, 53.*

A statue of Evert Taube (1890–1976), the much-loved troubadour and ballad writer, stands on the terrace below Wrangelska Palatset looking out over the waters of Riddarfjärden. In an ideal position, given the poet's close links to the sea, the bronze sculpture was created by Willy Gordon in 1990. Close by, Christer Berg's *Solbåten* (the Sun Boat), an elegant sculpture in granite, was unveiled in 1966. Inspired by the shape of a shell, from some angles it looks like a sail.

Evert Taube (1890–1976)

Birger Jarls Torn ⑭

Norra Riddarholmshamnen. **Map 4** A3 Ⓣ *Gamla Stan.* ▨ *3, 53.* ⬤ *to the public.*

When the St Klara convent on Norrmalm was pulled down in 1527 following the Reformation, Gustav Vasa used some of its stonework to build a defensive installation on Riddarholmen. The northernmost of the two towers came to be known as Birger Jarls Torn in the 19th century when some thought it had been erected 600 years earlier. The tower has been linked with one of the legends that surround the founding of Stockholm by Birger Jarl. The story goes that the inhabitants of the town of Sigtuna floated a log on Lake Mälaren after a fire in 1187. It drifted on to the shore where the tower now stands, and it was this log – or "stock" in Swedish – that gave the capital its name. A famous picture in Storkyrkan *(see p14)*, dating from 1535, shows the waves breaking over the rocks beneath the tower.

The 16th-century Birger Jarls Torn

Stenbockska Palatset ⑮

Birger Jarls Torg 4. **Map** 4 A3. Ⓣ *Gamla Stan.* ▨ *3, 53.* ⬤ *to the public.*

Both externally and internally the Stenbock Palace is the best-preserved building on Riddarholmen. Built in the 1640s by the State Councillor

Stenbockska Palatset, the best-preserved nobleman's residence on Riddarholmen

Fredrik Stenbock and his wife Katarina de la Gardie, the family's coat of arms can be seen above the porch. The palace underwent major extension work in 1863 when it was taken over by the State Archives. Then in 1969–71 it was restored as the headquarters of the Supreme Court.

Many leading Swedish and foreign architects and artists have all played their part in enhancing the palace's outstanding appearance. The roof beams and flooring are from the Stenbock period, and the staircase was designed by Nicodemus Tessin the Elder.

Several beautiful ceilings are the work of the master of stucco, Carlo Carove from Italy (d. 1697), and there is a cabinet created by Rococo architect Carl Hårleman.

TIMELINE: RIDDARHOLMEN

1250s The island, then called Kidskär, is a cattle-grazing area outside the settlement	**1527** Following the Reformation, the monks are evicted from the island	**Late 17th century** The prosperity of the nobility starts to diminish. Palaces are replaced by government offices	**1697–1754** The royal family takes over Wrangelska Palatset after Tre Kronor fortress is destroyed by fire		**1865–66** The Parliament building and Hebbe House are rebuilt for new two-chamber Parliament

1200	**1300**	**1400**	**1500**	**1600**	**1700**	**1800**	**1900**

1270–85 The Greyfriars' abbey is founded. Kidskär is renamed Gråmunke-holmen. The abbey church is used for royal burials	**1625–35** Land is donated to noblemen and distinguished officers. The name is changed to Riddarholmen		**1830s** Fleming House used for Parliament by priests and burghers	**1905** Parliament moves to new building on Helgeands-holmen

Wrangelska Palatset

Riddarhuset in lavish Dutch Baroque style, built in the 17th century

Riddarhuset 🔟

Riddarhustorget 10. **Map** 4 A3.
Tel 08-723 39 90. Ⓣ Gamla Stan.
🚌 3, 53 🕐 11:30am–12:30pm
Mon–Fri. 🗺 📷 by arrangement.
www.riddarhuset.se

Often regarded as one of
Stockholm's most beautiful
buildings, Riddarhuset (House
of Nobility) stands on
Riddarhustorget, which as late
as the mid-19th century was
still the city's centre.

Built in 1641–7 on the
initiative of the State
Chancellor, it was designed
by the architects Simon and
Jean de la Vallée, Heinrich
Wilhelm and Justus
Vingboons. The nobility,
whose privileges were
granted in 1280, then
had a base for meet-
ings and events.

The building is a
supreme example
of Dutch Baroque
design and colouring.
Over the entrance on
the northern façade is
the nobility's motto *Arte et
Marte* (Art and War) with
Minerva, Goddess of Art and
Science, and Mars, God of
War, on either side.

The sculptures on the
vaulted roof symbolize the
knightly virtues. On the south
side is *Nobilitas* (Nobility) holding a small Minerva and spear.
She is flanked by *Studium*
(Diligence) and *Valor*
(Bravery). Facing the north is
the male equivalent, *Honor*,
flanked by *Prudentia* (Prud-
ence) and *Fortitudo* (Strength).

The interior is equally
impressive. The lower hall is
dominated by a magnificent
double staircase which leads

**The motto at
Riddarhuset**

up to the Knights' Room. This
has a masterly ceiling painting
by David Klöcker Ehrenstrahl
(1628–98) and Riddarhuset's
foremost treasure, a sculpted
ebony chair that dates from
1623. The walls are covered
by some 2,320 coats of arms.

Bondeska
Palatset 🔢

Riddarhustorget 8. **Map** 4 B3.
Ⓣ Gamla Stan. 🚌 3, 53.
🚫 to the public.

The seat of the Supreme
Court since 1949, the Bonde
Palace was created in 1662–73
by popular architect
Nicodemus Tessin the
Elder in the style of a
French town house.
The year previously,
the State Treasurer
Gustav Bonde had
bought the site
opposite Riddarhuset
to build a palace with
the idea of renting out
most of it.

Since then the Bonde
Palace has had several owners and
was damaged by fires in 1710

**Bondeska Palatset, now the seat of
the Supreme Court**

and 1753. In 1730 the building became the property of
the city and served as the City
Hall until 1915. After that,
there was little interest taken
in the palace until renovation
planned by the architect Ivar
Tengbom was begun in the
late 1940s. It had even been
suggested that the building
should be destroyed, but
public opinion ensured that it
remained intact.

Riksdagshuset 🔢

Riksgatan 3 A. **Map** 4 B2.
Tel 08-786 40 00. Ⓣ Gamla Stan.
🚌 3, 43, 53, 62. 🕐 tours & meetings
in the Chamber. 📷 ring for details
on tours of the building & art works.
♿ 🚻 **www**.riksdagen.se

The Parliament Building
(Riksdagshuset) and State
Bank (Riksbank) on Helge-
andsholmen were inaugurated
in 1905 and 1906 respectively.
Since 1983, when Parliament
returned after 12 years at
Sergels Torg, the two buildings have been combined
and enlarged. Parliament
also occupies two premises
in Gamla Stan, as well as an
information office at
Västerlånggatan 1. All the
buildings are connected by
underground passages and together amount to 130,000 sq m
(1,400,000 sq ft), with a staff
force of about 600, plus 250 in
the political parties' offices.

Parliamentary debates can
be watched from the public
gallery, which holds up to 500
visitors. There are guided tours
of the buildings every day
during the summer and only
at weekends in winter. Visitors
should use the public entrance
at Riksgatan 3A.

From the gallery level is a
striking view from as far as
Gustav Adolfs Torg to Riddarholmen. The main chamber
has benches of Swedish birch
and wall panelling in Finnish
birch, carved in Norway. A
large tapestry, *Memory of a
Landscape* (1983), by Elisabeth
Hasselberg-Olsson, covers
54 sq m (581 sq ft) of wall,
weighs 100 kg (220 lb) and
took 3,500 hours to make.

The old two-chamber
Parliament's beautifully

renovated rooms are now used for meetings of the majority party. The former Upper House has three paintings by Otte Sköld (1894–1958), and in the other chamber there are works by Axel Törneman and Georg Pauli, who realized Törneman's sketches after his death. Between the chambers is a 45-m (148-ft) long hall with an elegant display of coats of arms, paintings and chandeliers. The Finance Committee meets in the old oak-panelled library surrounded by old prints and Jugendstil lamps.

Facing the old entrance at Norrbro, the magnificent stairwell still retains its colouring from 1905. Other impressive survivors from opulent days include eight columns, a floor, steps and balusters all in various types of marble. The

The chamber where the 349 Members of Parliament meet

present entrance was the State Bank's main hall until 1976. It has magnificent columns, too, made from polished granite, and some outstanding paintings from the Parliamentary collection of 3,000 works.

The new Parliament building, with the older building behind

PARLIAMENTARY WANDERINGS

Sweden's first Parliament was opened in the 1860s on Riddarholmen in the combined properties of Fleming House and Hebbe House. From 1835–65, commoners – priests, burghers and farmers – met in Fleming House, which became known as the "House of Commons", while the noblemen sat in nearby Riddarhuset. Situated behind Riddarholmskyrkan at Birger Jarls Torg 5, Fleming House was constructed on the site of the Greyfriars abbey after the monks were forced to flee due to the Reformation in the 17th century *(see p57)*,

"Mother Svea" above the old Parliament building

and remains of the huge abbey can still be seen in the cellar.

A new base for Parliament, adapted for the needs of a two-chamber legislature, was inaugurated on Helgeandsholmen in 1905. When a single chamber was established in 1971, a lack of space meant that Parliament had to move to the newly built Kulturhuset *(see p67)* on Sergels Torg. It returned to Helgeandsholmen in 1983 into an extended and reconstructed Parliament building.

Stockholms Medeltidsmuseum

⑲

Strömparterren, Norrbro.
Map 4 B2. **Tel** 08-508 317 90.
🅃 *Kungsträdgården.* 🚌 *43, 62.*
◷ *11am–7pm Tue–Fri, 11am–5pm
Sat & Sun.* 🄯 🄵 🄶 🄾 🅆 **www.**
medeltidsmuseet.stockholm.se

This fascinating museum of medieval Stockholm is built around the capital's archaeological remains, mainly parts of the city wall that date from the 1530s. They were found during intensive archaeological research in 1978–80, which unearthed a number of remarkable finds from Stockholm's medieval history.

Situated, for the most part, below ground level, the museum also includes artifacts from other parts of the city. Among them is the 22-m (72-ft) long Riddarholm ship which was discovered off Riddarholmen in 1930 and dates from the 1520s.

The museum provides a good picture of Stockholm's early days. From the entrance, a 350-year-old tunnel leads into a reconstructed medieval world. There is a pillory in the square and the gallows hill with the tools of the executioner's grisly trade. The old harbour has been rebuilt. Boathouses, complete with salt barrels, seal skins and dried fish, as well as authentic nautical smells, tell the story of fishing and overseas trade. The spruce wreath hanging outside the wine cellar demonstrates that supplies of wine and beer have arrived from the Continent. The large house is built from 6,000 original bricks. The well-tended herb garden includes lavender, roses, tansy and sage. Herbs were important in the Middle Ages for their medicinal qualities as well as their use in food.

The museum runs regular themed exhibitions with a medieval emphasis and holds a programme of lectures and educational activities for children. The shop here sells books on the Middle Ages, plus postcards and jewellery.

CITY

The area known as City today was where, in the mid-18th century, the first stone-built houses and palaces outside Gamla Stan started to appear for the burghers and nobility. After World War II, the run-down buildings around Hötorget were demolished to form what is now Sergels Torg; many homes were replaced by rather dreary office blocks.

In recent years the area has been livening up after dark and become the true heart and commercial centre of Stockholm. A hub for public transport and banking, City is the place for the best department stores and shopping malls, exclusive boutiques and nightspots. The centre also has some beautiful parks and pleasant squares serving as popular meeting places. The unique landscape surrounding Stockholm permeates even City – here and there appear unexpected glimpses of the water with its bustling boat life and a string of anglers along the embankments.

Street light near Kungliga Operan

SIGHTS AT A GLANCE

Museums
Armémuseum ㉔
Dansmuseet ❹
Hallwylska museet ㉘
Medelhavsmuseet ❺
Musik- & Teatermuseet ㉕
Strindbergsmuseet Blå Tornet ⑰

Squares
Hötorget ⑫
Kungsträdgården ❶
Sergels Torg ⑪
Stureplan ⑳

Public Buildings
Arvfurstens Palats ❻
Centralbadet ⑮
Hovstallet ㉖
Konstakademien ❽
Kulturhuset and Stockholms Stadsteater ⑩
Kungliga Biblioteket ⑲
Kungstornen ⑭
Rosenbad ❼

Theatres and Musical Stages
Dansens Hus ⑯
Konserthuset ⑬
Kungliga Dramatiska Teatern ㉗
Kungliga Operan ❸

Churches
Adolf Fredriks Kyrka ⑱
Hedvig Eleonora Kyrka ㉓

Jacobs Kyrka ❷
Klara Kyrka ❾

Markets & Malls
Sturegallerian and Sturebadet ㉑
Östermalmshallen ㉒

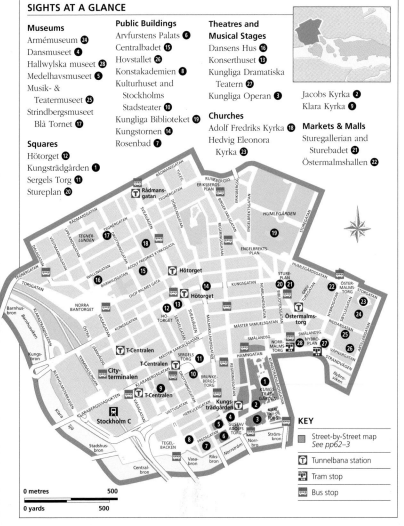

KEY

Street-by-Street map
See pp62–3

🇹 Tunnelbana station

Tram stop

Bus stop

0 metres   500
0 yards   500

◁ **Sagerska Palatset, official residence of the Prime Minister, between Rosenbad (left) and Arvfurstens Palats**

Street-by-Street: Around Kungsträdgården

With a history going back to the 15th century, the King's Garden (Kungsträdgården) has long been the city's most popular meeting place and recreational centre. Both visitors and Stockholmers gather here for summer concerts and festivals, or in the winter months to make the most of the ice skating rink. Close by is Sweden House where the tourist office is based, and around the park is a wealth of shops, boutiques, churches, museums and restaurants. A short walk takes you to Gustav Adolfs Torg, flanked by the Royal Opera House and other stately buildings, including the Swedish Foreign Office.

★ Medelhavsmuseet
This museum near Gustav Adolfs Torg has vast collections from prehistoric cultures around the Mediterranean **⑤**

Dansmuseet
Anything connected with dance such as costumes, stage set sketches and posters for the famous Les Ballets Suédois, can be seen here **④**

Gustav II Adolf's equestrian statue, designed by L'Archevêques, was unveiled in 1796.

FREDSGATAN

REGERINGSGATAN

Sagerska Palatset

STRÖMGATAN

GUSTAV ADOLFS TORG

STRÖMGATAN

NORRRBRO

NORRSTRÖM

SOPHIA·ALBERTINA ÆDIFICAVIT·

Arvfurstens Palats
The Swedish Foreign Office is based in this palace, built for Gustav III's sister Sofia Albertina in 1794 **⑥**

Opera-källaren (see p160)

★ Kungliga Operan
Built in 1898 with a magnificently ornate auditorium, the Royal Opera House replaced an earlier one from the time of Gustav III **③**

KEY

― ― ― Suggested route

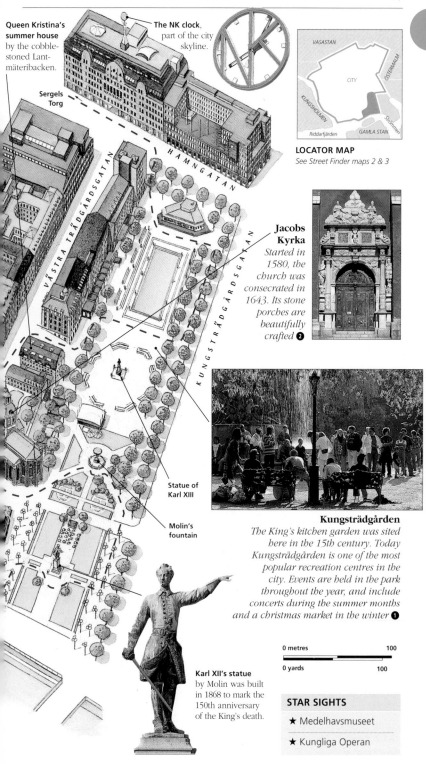

Queen Kristina's summer house by the cobble-stoned Lant-mäteribacken.

The NK clock, part of the city skyline.

Sergels Torg

HAMNGATAN

VÄSTRA TRÄDGÅRDSGATAN

KUNGSTRÄDGÅRDSGATAN

LOCATOR MAP
See Street Finder maps 2 & 3

VASASTAN

CITY

ÖSTERMALM

KUNGSHOLMEN

Skeppsholmen

Riddarfjärden   GAMLA STAN

Jacobs Kyrka
Started in 1580, the church was consecrated in 1643. Its stone porches are beautifully crafted ❷

Statue of Karl XIII

Molin's fountain

Kungsträdgården
The King's kitchen garden was sited here in the 15th century. Today Kungsträdgården is one of the most popular recreation centres in the city. Events are held in the park throughout the year, and include concerts during the summer months and a christmas market in the winter ❶

Karl XII's statue
by Molin was built in 1868 to mark the 150th anniversary of the King's death.

0 metres   100
0 yards   100

STAR SIGHTS

★ Medelhavsmuseet

★ Kungliga Operan

Kungsträdgården ●

Map 4 B1. Ⓣ *Kungsträdgården.*
🚌 *2, 47, 55, 59, 62, 65, 76.*

Once the royal kitchen garden in the 15th century, the "King's Garden" today is a popular meeting place for Stockholmers where there is something going on for everyone all year round. The park, Stockholm's oldest, is in the heart of the city and is encircled by avenues.
At the Strömgatan end of the park is a square: Karl XII's Torg with Johan Peter Molin's statue of the warrior king, unveiled in 1868, in the centre. The statue was commissioned to mark the 150th anniversary of the king's death. In Kungsträdgården itself there is a statue of Karl XIII (1809–18) by Erik Göthe. Also here is Molin's famous fountain, made from gypsum in 1866 and cast in bronze seven years later. The fountain is inhabited by mythological characters.

Molin's fountain

During Erik XIV's reign in the 16th century, the kitchen garden was transformed into a formal Renaissance garden and Queen Kristina had a stone summer house built in it. The 17th-century house still stands at Västra Trädgårdsgatan 2 next to the cobblestoned Lantmäteribacken.

Each year during the summer months nearly 150 events are staged in Kungsträdgården. The covered, outdoor stage here is the setting for various open-air concerts; Parkteatern, an outdoor theatre group, also puts on shows including musical productions, children's theatre, flamenco and other dance performances. Many of the events are free and enjoyed by thousands of Stockholmers who arrive with their picnics and blankets. The park also hosts numerous exhibitions, food festivals, dancing and live street theatre. Local radio stations also hold big festivals featuring a variety of local and international artists. In August, when the annual Gospel Choir Festival takes place, audiences are invited to sing along, whatever their musical abilities. At the garden's centre is a large cirular plaza and during the winter months this is transformed into a skating rink that attracts children and grownups alike. There is also a Christmas market held in the park every weekend throughout December.

Kungsträdgården has several outdoor cafés, art galleries, including the Galleri Doktor Glas, and restaurants at the two ends of the garden.

Jacobs Kyrka ●

Västra Trädgårdsgatan 2.
Map 4 B1. **Tel** 08-723 30 38. Ⓣ
Kungsträdgården. 🚌 *2, 55, 59, 62, 65, 76.* ◯ *noon–4pm Tue & Wed, noon–6pm Thu & Fri, 2–6pm Sat & Sun.* ✝ *(in English) Sun.* **Concerts** *5pm Fri.* 🎵 *by arrangement.* ♿

Even in medieval times there was a small chapel where Kungsträdgården now lies. Dedicated to St Jacob, the patron saint of wayfarers, the chapel and another modest-sized church in the area were destroyed by King Gustav Vasa in the 16th century. Johan III wanted to provide two new churches in Norra Malmen, as the area was then called, and work to build the churches of St Jacob and St Klara *(see p66)* started in 1580. St Jacob's was consecrated first, in 1643. It has been restored several times since then, in some cases rather clumsily. However, several valuable items have been preserved, including a baptismal font from 1634 and some church silver, as well as porches by stonemasons Henrik Blom and Hans Hebel.

The organ's façade was created by the architect Carl Hårleman and the large painting on the west wall of the southern nave is by Fredrik Westin, Sweden's most distinguished historical painter in the early 19th century.

Altar in Jacobs Kyrka, partly dating from the 17th century

Kungliga Operan ●

Gustav Adolfs Torg. **Map** 4 B1.
Tel 08-791 43 00.
Ⓣ *Kungsträdgården.* 🚌 *43, 62, 65.*
Ticket Office ◯ *noon–6pm Mon–Fri, noon–3pm Sat.* 🎵 *by arrangement.* ♿ 📶 ✝ **www**.operan.se

Opera has been performed in Sweden since 18 January 1773, when a performance took place at Bollhuset at Slottsbacken. Kungliga Operan (The Royal Opera House) on Gustav Adolfs Torg was inaugurated on 30 September 1782, but by the late 19th century it had become a fire hazard. The architect Axel Anderberg was commissioned to design a new opera house, which was

View of Kungsträdgården, towards Hamngatan

The 28-m (92-ft) long gold foyer at Kungliga Operan

transferred to the State in 1898 from a consortium founded by the financier K A Wallenberg.

The colouring of the building in late Renaissance style is in keeping with the Royal Palace and Parliament building, and some details of the architecture are common to all three. The beautiful staircase with ceiling paintings by Axel Jungstedt was inspired by the Paris Opera. The same artist's portrait of Oscar II hangs in the 28-m (92-ft) long gold foyer, where Carl Larsson was responsible for the decorative paintings. The wings at either side of the stage have been kept, as has the width of the proscenium arch (11.4 m/37 ft). Also saved was J T Sergel's group of angels, holding the national coat of arms, above the stage. An angel in Vicke Andrén's ceiling painting is holding a sketch of the Opera House.

Gold ceiling in Kungliga Operan

Dansmuseet ❹

Gustav Adolfs Torg 22–24.
Map 4 B1. **Tel** 08-441 76 50. Ⓣ
Centralen, Kungsträdgården. 🚌 2, 3,
43, 53, 59, 62, 65. 🕒 11am–4pm
Tue–Fri, noon–4pm Sat & Sun. 🎟 ♿
🖥 🛍 www.dansmuseet.se

In 1999 the Dance Museum moved into new premises on Gustav Adolfs Torg, in the former bank building opposite the Norrbro bridge. The

museum was originally founded in Paris in 1953 by the Swedish aristocrat Rolf de Maré (1888–1964). He was a noted art collector who founded the world-renowned Les Ballets Suédois.

The museum reflects all aspects of dance – costumes and masks, scenery sketches, art and posters, books and documents – and includes an archive on popular dance. Apart from the exhibition hall, there is also a data bank in the form of the Rolf de Maré Study Centre, with video facilities, a library and archives. The museum shop has Sweden's largest collection of dance DVDs for sale.

Medelhavs-museet ❺

Fredsgatan 2. **Map** 4 B1.
Tel 08-519 550 50. Ⓣ Kungsträdgården. 🚌 3, 52, 53, 62, 65.
🕒 noon–8pm Tue–Wed, 11am–4pm
Thu–Fri, noon–5pm Sat & Sun. 🎟 ♿
🖥 🛍 www.medelhavsmuseet.se

Gods and people from prehistoric cultures around the Mediterranean rub shoulders in Medelhavsmuseet (Museum of Mediterranean and Near East Antiquities). Its many treasures include a large group of terracotta figures discovered by archaeologists on Cyprus in the 1930s. Models made of unusual

materials like cork show how houses were once constructed, and the museum also has a fascinating gold room. The Islamic collections are complemented by temporary exhibitions.

The museum is housed in a former bank, originally built in the 17th century for Gustav Horn, a general in the Thirty Years War. The stairwell, dating from 1905, and the peristyles and colonnade around the upper part of the hall are worth a visit in themselves.

Arvfurstens Palats ❻

Gustav Adolfs Torg 1. **Map** 4 B1.
Ⓣ Kungsträdgården. 🚌 43, 62, 65.
⬤ to the public.

Opposite the Royal Opera House, on the other side of Gustav Adolfs Torg, stands Arvfurstens Palats (Prince's Palace), built for Gustav III's sister Sofia Albertina and inaugurated in 1794. She commissioned the architect Erik Palmstedt to carry out the work. He was a pupil of Carl Fredrik Adelcrantz, designer of the original opera house.

The palace and its decor are shining examples of the Gustavian style, thanks to the contributions of artists and craftsmen like Louis Masreliez and Georg Haupt and their pupils Gustaf Adolf Ditzinger, Johan Tobias Sergel and Gottlieb Iwersson. In 1906 the building was taken over by the Swedish Foreign Office.

Nearby is the elegant Sagerska Palatset (1894) in French Renaissance style, which is used by the Prime Minister as an official residence.

Arvfurstens Palats (1794), now the Swedish Foreign Office

had a vision of this area as an extension of his work.

Traces of the older buildings can still be seen. The interior of the small meeting room was designed by Carl Fredrik Adelcrantz around 1780 and two tiled stoves from the same period have been preserved, along with the main porch facing Jakobsgatan. The four allegorical female figures which were once at the entrance have been recast in cement and placed on the roof.

Rosenbad, home of the Government and City Council committees

Rosenbad **7**

Rosenbad 4. **Map** 4 A2.
Ⓣ *Kungsträdgården.* 🚌 *3, 53, 62, 65.*
🏛 *to the public.*

Since 1981, the Rosenbad complex – a collection of palatial buildings overlooking the Strömmen channel – has housed the Swedish Government and the Prime Minister's private office in three internally linked sites.

Three of the late 19th century's most notable architects were commissioned to design these buildings. The Venetian-style palace along Strömgatan was the last one to be added, in 1904. Designed by Ferdinand Boberg (1860–1916), it used to house private apartments, a bank and a popular restaurant, traces of which survive in the ornamentation of the open loggia facing the water.

Gustav Wickman (1858–1916) designed the pink sandstone house on the corner of Fredsgatan and Drottninggatan in exuberant, almost baroque, Jugendstil. The Skåne Bank moved into this building in 1900.

The Florentine-style house on Fredsgatan facing Rödbodtorget is 3 years older. It was designed by Aron Johansson (1860–1936), architect of the old Parliament building on Helgeandsholmen.

Rosenbad got its name from a former 17th-century bathhouse which offered bathers ` a choice of a lily bath, a chamomile bath or a rose bath – *rosenbad* in Swedish.

Konstakademien **8**

Fredsgatan 12. **Map** 4 A2.
Tel 08-23 29 45. Ⓣ *T-centralen.*
🚌 *3, 53, 62, 65.* ◯ *11am–5pm Tue–Fri, noon–4pm Sat & Sun.* ♿ *entrance Jakobsgatan 27C.* ▢

The art collections of Konstakademien (Royal Academy of the Arts) reflect more than 250 years of paintings and sculptures, mostly by past and present members. Today the Royal Academy has around 120 members.

Between Fredsgatan and Jakobsgatan, the imposing corner house was designed by Tessin the Elder in the early 1670s. The Royal Academy moved in while under the patronage of Gustav III in the late 18th century. It has been rebuilt several times, the latest in 1897 by the architect Erik Lallerstedt. Its present look ties in with the Royal Opera House *(see p62)* and the Royal Palace *(see pp50–53)*, whose architect Tessin the Younger

The Fredsgatan entrance of Konstakademien

Interior of Klara Kyrka with decor by Olle Hjortzberg

Klara Kyrka **9**

Klarabergsgatan 37. **Map** 2 C4.
Tel 08-411 73 24. Ⓣ *T-centralen*
🚌 *47, 52, 59, 65.* ◯ *10am–5pm daily.* ✝ *5pm Sat, 11am, 2pm (Swahili) Sun.* ♿ ▢

The convent of St Klara stood on the site of the present church and cemetery until 1527, when it was pulled down on the orders of Gustav Vasa. Later, his son Johan III commissioned a new church, completed in 1590.

The church was ravaged by fire in 1751 and its reconstruction was planned by the period's two outstanding architects, first Carl Hårleman and later C F Adelcrantz. The pulpit was made in 1753 to Hårleman's design, and J T Sergel *(see p83)* created the angelic figures in the northern gallery. A pair of identical angels adorn the exquisite chancel, based on the sculptor's gypsum originals.

In the 1880s, the 116-m (380-ft) tower was added and for many years could be seen from all over the city. The 20th-century church artist, Olle Hjortzberg, created the vault paintings, dating from 1904.

Edvin Öhrström's glass obelisk in Sergels Torg, with Kulturhuset behind to the left

Kulturhuset and Stockholms Stadsteater ⓾

Sergels Torg 7, Kulturhuset. **Map** 2 C4. **Kulturhuset** *Tel* 08-508 315 08. **Stockholms Stadsteater** *Tel* 08-506 202 00. 🔵 T-centralen. 🚌 47, 52, 56, 59, 69. ⬚ hours vary – check website. 🚻 some areas. ♿ 🍴 🛍 🔲 www.kulturhuset. stockholm.se; www.stadsteatern. stockholm.se

Opened in 1974, Kulturhuset is at the heart of Stockholm's cultural life. A creation of the architect Peter Celsing, the cultural centre is typical of its era and blends well with surrounding Sergels Torg. The building has a façade of glass all along the southern side of the square and is a symbol of Swedish Modernism.

Kulturhuset offers something for everybody: three galleries hold regularly changing exhibitions suitable for all tastes. Visitors can watch documentaries, short films and live broadcast concerts in the "Klara Cinema". Clubs, concerts and events are available in the "Sergels Torg 3" venue; there is also an open rooftop stage used during the summer months. The "Ecoteque" is a space dedicated to environmental issues where regular forums take place. There is also a coffee shop here and changing exhibitions. "Lava" is a meeting place for young people where dance, handi-craft and various other workshops are held.

There are five libraries in the centre. "Kidszone" caters for small children with storytelling and workshops; "TioTretton" is for children aged 10 to 13; "Serieteket" is Sweden's only library for fans of strip cartoons; the "Plattan Library" is stocked with international newspapers and magazines and also has a bank of computers for public use; the "Music and Film" section has a large archive of international music that visitors can listen to.

The centre has a variety of cafés and eateries as well as several shops selling items of contemporary Swedish design.

Kulturhuset also houses Stockholms Stadsteater (City Theatre). The theatre presents a varied programme of music and other events in its main auditorium. Here, some 1,400 performances take place every year for audi-ences totalling about 225,000.

Sergels Torg ⓫

Map 2 C4. 🔵 T-centralen. 🚌 47, 52, 59, 65, 69.

As part of the city centre's transformation, around 1930 there was a strong lobby in favour of extending Sveavägen through to Gustav Adolfs Torg. But in 1945 it was decided to end the road at the junction with Klarabergs-gatan and Hamngatan to form a new square, Sveaplan. In 1957 a two-level square was proposed – a lower level for pedestrians and an upper level for traffic. The plan was finalized in 1960 and the name changed to Sergels Torg.

In 1972 the sculptor Edvin Öhrström's glass obelisk, *Crystal Vertical Accent in Glass and Steel* was erected in the centre and now shimmers at night due to improved lighting.

CITY'S TRANSFORMATION

During the 20th century Stockholm's population grew from 250,000 to more than 1.6 million. By the 1920s it was obvi-

The first steps towards a new Hötorg City, 1958

ous that the old heart of the city did not meet the future needs of business, public administration and the growth in traffic. In 1951 a controversial 30-year pro-gramme to transform the lower Norrmalm city centre was launched. Slums on 335 of the 600 sites were pulled down and 78 new houses were built. Two-thirds of the area's buildings were added during this period.

Fresh produce on sale at Hötorget, a marketplace since the 17th century

Hötorget ⑫

Map 2 C4. Ⓣ *Hötorget.* ▣ *1, 52, 56.* ▤ *10am–6pm Mon–Thu, 10am–6:30pm Fri, 10am–4pm Sat.*

Tradition is still going strong on Hötorget (Hay Market). Formerly belonging to St Klara convent, in the 1640s the square evolved into an important place for trading in animal fodder, milk, vegetables and meat. Today it is still a lively market for fresh produce.

The buildings around the square are relatively new. The glass-fronted cinema complex opened in 1995, while the PUB department store was added in 1916 and Konserthuset in 1926. On nearby Sergelgatan, where the five high-rises of Hötorgs City were constructed in 1952–6, there is a reminder of the old city centre.

A tablet marks where the renowned sculptor Johan Tobias Sergel (1740–1814) had his studio. A later sculptor, Carl Milles *(see p150)*, created the well-noted fountain, *Orpheus*, that stands in front of Konserthuset.

Konserthuset ⑬

Hötorget 8. **Map** 2 C4. **Tel** 08-786 02 00. Ⓣ *Hötorget.* ▣ *1, 3, 52, 56.* **Ticket Office** ◯ *11am–6pm Mon–Fri, 11am–3pm Sat, and 2 hours before a concert.* ▣ ▤ ▣ ▣ www.konserthuset.se

A Nordic version of a Greek temple, Konserthuset (the Concert Hall) is a masterpiece of the architect Ivar Tengbom (1878–1968) and is an outstanding example of the 1920s' Neo-Classical style. Tengbom's tradition has been carried on by his son Anders (b. 1911), who was in charge of its renovation in 1970–71, and his grandson Svante

(b. 1942), who had a similar task in 1993–6.

Constructed in 1923–6, the main hall at the outset matched Ivar Tengbom's original concept. However, acoustical problems led to major reconstruction work and modernization. Its internal decor is rather frugal, but the Grünewald Hall, by the artist Isaac Grünewald (1889–1946), is more lavish in the style of an Italian Renaissance palace. The four marble statues in the main foyer are by Carl Milles, creator of the *Orpheus* sculpture group outside. Other artists who have contributed to the decor are Einar Forseth, Simon Gate, Edward Hald and Carl Malmsten.

The Concert Hall has been the home of the Swedish Royal Philharmonic Orchestra since it opened. The orchestra gives some 70 concerts every year and international star soloists perform here regularly. It is also the venue for the Nobel Prize presentations.

Kungstornen ⑭

Kungsgatan 30 and 33. **Map** 3 D4. Ⓣ *Hötorget.* ▣ *1, 43, 56.* ⬤ *to the public.*

In 1915 the young architect Sven Wallander submitted a sketch showing how Stockholm could be given a modern, USA-inspired main street. His plans were accepted during the 1920s, when a

The *Orpheus* sculpture group by Carl Milles at Konserthuset

THE NOBEL PRIZES

Alfred Nobel (1833–96) was an outstanding chemist and inventor, and the prestigious Nobel Prizes – consisting of a monetary award and a medal – have been presented every year since 1901 on 10 December, the date of his death. The ceremony takes place in Konserthuset, where prizes are presented for physics, chemistry, physiology or medicine, and literature. Since 1969 the Bank of Sweden has also given a prize for economic sciences in Nobel's memory. The Nobel Peace Prize is presented in Oslo's City Hall on the same day. In 1901 each prize was worth 150,000 kr, while in 2010 it had increased to 10 million kr.

The Nobel Medal, awarded annually

new road was excavated through the Brunkeberg hill linking Hötorget with Sture-plan. A bridge was built over what is now Kungsgatan, and a few years later the twin Kungstornen (King's Towers) were added.

Designed in Neo-Classical style by Wallander, the northern tower was originally owned by the sugar company Sockerbolaget. The southern tower was designed by Ivar Callmander and owned by L M Ericsson. Apart from a period when restaurants occupied the top of each one, the towers have been used only as offices. Both 16 floors high, the northern tower, covering an area of 7,000 sq m (75,320 sq ft), is referred to as the "male", with his more graceful, slightly larger twin, as the "female". At the entrance of the northern tower are some beautiful granite sculptures created by Eric Grate.

The "male" and "female" Kungstornen on Kungsgatan

Centralbadet ⓐ

Drottninggatan 88. **Map** 4 C4. **Tel** 08-545 213 13. Hötorget. 52. 11am–7pm daily. Sun in Jul. www.centralbadet.se

Designed by the architect Wilhelm Klemming in Jugendstil, Centralbadet swimming and fitness centre was completed in 1904. Since then, it has been rebuilt and extended but the façade remains the same, while the Jugendstil influence continues into the main pool and restaurant.

A protected cultural heritage building, the classic swimming

Centralbadet's characteristic Jugenstil façade

centre has a 23-m (25-yd) long pool, bubble and treatment pools, three saunas and skincare and massage departments.

The garden, situated between Drottninggatan and Centralbadet, was originally designed by the prolific 18th-century architect Carl Hårleman. A few of the trees growing there today are thought to date from his era. The garden is a delightful oasis set round an ornamental pool and fountain, and there is also a sculpture showing a Triton riding a dolphin, created by Greta Klemming in the 1920s.

Dansens Hus ⓑ

Barnhusgatan 12–14. **Map** 2 C3. **Tel** 08-508 990 90. T-centralen. 1, 47, 53. **Ticket Office** noon–6pm Mon–Sat. www.dansenshus.se

The "House of Dance" has been Stockholm's main permanent stage for modern dance since 1991 when it took over this site from the City Theatre which moved to Kulturhuset in 1990 (see p67). Dansens Hus has 2 auditoriums: 1 for audiences of more than 800, and Blå Lådan (the Blue Box) for experimental performances seating 150.

The theatre does not have a resident ensemble but during the season it presents a dozen national and international guest performances, usually staying for 3 to 5 days. Exhibitions are staged in the foyer,

designed by Sven Markelius (1889–1972). Seminars and lectures are also held here and it is the base for the Dance Production Service (DPS), a choreographers' organization.

Strindbergsmuseet Blå Tornet ⓒ

Drottninggatan 85. **Map** 2 C3. **Tel** 08-411 53 54. Rådmansgatan. 52, 69. noon–4pm Tue–Sun (Jul & Aug: 10am–4pm Tue–Sun). when booked in advance. www.strindbergsmuseet.se

The world-famous dramatist August Strindberg (1849–1912) had 24 different addresses in Stockholm over the years. He moved to the last of these in 1908, and gave it the name Blå Tornet (The Blue Tower). By then he had gained international recognition.

The house, now the Strindbergsmuseet, was built with central heating, toilet and lift, but lacked a kitchen. Instead he relied on Falkner's Pension, in the same building, for food and other services. On his last few birthdays the great man would stand on his balcony and watch his admirers stage a torchlight procession in his honour.

Opened in 1973, the museum includes reconstructions of the author's home with his bedroom, dining room and study, as well as 3,000 books and archives for photographs, press cuttings and posters. In the adjoining premises, a permanent exhibition portrays Strindberg as author, theatrical director, artist and photographer. Temporary exhibitions and other activities are often held here.

Strindberg's desk and writing materials in his study

Adolf Fredriks Kyrka ⑱

Holländargatan 16. **Map** 2 C3.
Tel 08-20 70 76. 🔵 Hötorget.
📷 52. ⭕ 1–7pm Mon, 10am–4pm
Tue–Sun. ⏰ 7pm Mon, 12:15pm
Wed & Thu, 11am Sun. 📷
by appointment. ♿📷📷

King Adolf Frederik laid the
foundation stone of this
church in 1768 on the site of
an earlier chapel dedicated to
St Olof. Designed by Carl
Fredrik Adelcrantz, in Neo-
Classical style with traces of
Rococo, the church has been
built in the shape of a Greek
cross and has a central dome.

The interior has undergone
a number of changes, but
both the altar and pulpit have
remained intact. The
sculptor Johan Tobias
Sergel created the
altarpiece, which is
probably his most
important religious
work. The memorial
to French philosopher
Descartes *(see p17)*
is also Sergel's
work. The
paintings on
the dome were
added in 1899–
1900 by Julius
Kronberg.
More recent
items of
value include
altar silver-

Memorial to Descartes

ware by Sigurd Persson.

The cemetery is the resting
place of the assassinated
Prime Minister Olof Palme,
as well as the politician
Hjalmar Branting, a key
figure of the Social Democratic
movement. J T Sergel is also
buried here.

The "Devil's Bible" from the early 13th century,
stored at Kungliga Biblioteket

Kungliga Biblioteket ⑲

Humlegården. **Map** 3 D3.
Tel 08-463 40 00. 🔵 Östermalmstorg. 📷 1, 2, 55, 56, 91, 96.
⭕ 9am–8pm Mon–Thu, 9am–7pm
Fri, 10am–5pm Sat; 1 Jun–31 Aug:
9am–6pm Mon–Thu, 9am–5pm Fri,
11am–3pm Sat. 📷 by appointment.
♿📷 www.kb.se

This is Sweden's national
library and an autonomous
Government department in
its own right. Ever since 1661,
when there were only nine
printing presses in Sweden,
copies of every piece of
printed matter have had to
be lodged with Kungliga
Biblioteket (Royal Library).
Since 1993 this requirement
has also applied to electronic
documents. As there are now
some 3,000 printers and publishers in Sweden the volume
of material is expanding
rapidly. The collection now
covers about 4 million books
and magazines, more than 14
million ephemera, 500,000
posters, 300,000 maps,
750,000 portraits and 500,000
pictures. The Department
of Audiovisual Material
(previously the Swedish
National Archive of Recorded
Sound and Moving Images) is
also here and holds a total of

8 million hours
of material that
includes TV and
radio programmes,
movies, videos,
Swedish music
and multimedia
recordings. The
library has made all
its material available
to the public.

The imposing
original building, inaugurated
in 1878, had to be expanded
in the 1920s, and again in the
1990s. This major extension
provided an auditorium and,
most importantly, two
underground book storage
areas covering an area in total
of 18,000 sq m (193,680 sq ft).

The library is in a beautiful
setting in Humlegården,
created by King Johan III in
the 16th century to grow hops
for the royal household. Since
the 18th century, the park has
been a favourite recreation
area for Stockholmers.

Stureplan ⑳

Map 3 D4. 🔵 Östermalmstorg.
📷 1, 2, 55, 56, 91.

A new town plan for Stockholm towards the end of the
19th century recommended
that the Stureplan area should
become the capital's new
centre. The proposal was
accepted and the area around
Svampen (The Mushroom)

Stureplan and *Svampen*, one of the
city's most popular meeting places

THE MURDERED PRIME MINISTER

Olof Palme (1927–86)

On 28 February 1986 the Swedish Prime
Minister Olof Palme was killed in a
Stockholm street on his way home from
a cinema without a bodyguard. The
murder happened at the corner of
Sveavägen and Tunnelgatan, whose
western section was renamed Olof
Palmes Gata. A memorial tablet has
been placed there. The murder
provoked strong reactions but to this
day remains unsolved. His grave is in
the nearby Adolf Fredrik cemetery.

rain shelter became a popular meeting place, as more and more shops and restaurants opened. However, a new street layout after the introduction of right-hand driving in Sweden in 1967 brought its halcyon days to a close.

But now Stureplan has staged a phoenix-like comeback out of the ashes of a major fire at the Sturebadet swimming pool in 1985. Plans to revamp the area were made: the pool was modernized and the Sturegallerian shopping mall was built, revitalizing the whole eastern part of the city. Once again Stureplan became one of the capital's most popular meeting places.

Sturegallerian and Sturebadet ㉑

Sturegallerian 36. **Map** 3 D4. ⊤ *Östermalmstorg.* 🚌 *1, 2, 55, 56, 91.* **Shopping mall** ◯ *10am–7pm Mon– Fri, 10am–6pm Sat, noon–5pm Sun.* **Pool Tel** *08-545 015 00.* ◯ *6:30am–10pm Mon–Fri, 9am–7pm Sat & Sun; other times by appointment & members only.* 💻 🍴

The original Sturebadet swimming pool, opened in 1885, was sited within the present-day StureCompagniet complex. Rebuilt on its present site in 1902, it was ahead of its time – even in the 1930s it was offering exercise facilities.

After a disastrous fire in 1985 some 600 million kr was invested, partly on reconstructing the pool according to its original design and partly on developing Sturegallerian, a world-class shopping mall. The architects managed to link the late 19th-century exterior with interiors of modern design using marble, granite, steel, copper, cedar and mahogany.

Indoor streets and squares with some 50 retail outlets have been created, including restaurants, cafés and various services. Today's swimming pool is now the most traditional part of the complex. It has a spa offering luxurious treatments and also has a gym on site.

Painstakingly restored Jugendstil decor at Sturebadet

Östermalms hallen ㉒

Humlegårdsgatan 1–3. **Map** 3 E4. ⊤ *Östermalmstorg.* 🚌 *56, 62.* ◯ *9:30am–6pm Mon–Wed, 9:30am– 7pm Thu & Fri, 9:30am–4pm Sat, 9:30am–2pm Sat in Summer.* ♿ 🍴

The temple of gastronomy, this market hall on Östermalmstorg is as far removed from a fast-food outlet as you could imagine. Nowhere else in the city is there such a range of high quality delicacies under one roof. But it was certainly an example of fast building. Taking only eight months to erect, the hall was opened by King Oscar II in 1888. It is regarded as a fine example of the city's late 19th-century architectural heritage. Construction of a brick building around a cast-iron shell was a novelty in Sweden, and the architects Gustaf Clason and Kasper Sahlin won acclaim for their design, inspired by the arcades of Mediterranean markets. In the early days there were 153 stalls, and after undergoing extensive restoration, there are now 13 larger specialist shops, selling local delicacies, and some popular lunch spots.

Hedvig Eleonora Kyrka ㉓

Storgatan 2. **Map** 3 E4. **Tel** *08-545 675 70.* ⊤ *Östermalmstorg.* 🚌 *62.* ◯ *11am–6pm daily.* ✝ *12:15pm Tue & Thu, 7pm Wed, 11am Sun.* 📷 *by appt.* ♿ 🚪

Founded in 1669 to give the Swedish Navy its own place for religious services, the church was not officially opened until 1737. The first plans were drawn up by Jean de la Vallée, but the work was completed with Göran Josuae Adelcrantz as architect. The dome was added in 1866–8. The main bell was cast in Helsingør, Denmark, in 1639 and hung in Kronborg Castle before being seized as a war trophy by General Carl Gustaf Wrangel *(see p56)*.

The church has many valuable artifacts. The altarpiece *Jesus on the Cross* was painted in 1738 by Engelhard Schröder. The designer of the majestic pulpit in Neo-Classical style was Jean Eric Rehn, who saw his work unveiled on Christmas Day in 1784.

The new organ was built in the mid-1970s, but Carl Fredrik Adelcrantz's 1762 organ façade is still in its original state. Included in the silverware is a Baroque chalice from 1650 and a christening bowl dated 1685. The 1678 font is now housed in the baptismal chapel, which was added at the time of the church's restoration in 1944.

Östermalmshallen, a culinary temple inspired by markets in southern Europe

Armémuseum, with the dome of Hedvig Eleonora Kyrka in the background

Armémuseum ❷❹

Riddargatan 13. **Map** 3 E4.
Tel 08-519 56 300. 🚇 Östermalmstorg. 🚌 47, 62, 69. ◯ 11am–8pm
Tue, 11am–5pm Wed–Sun. 🎫 📷
📷 ♿ 🛗 🎬 🛒
www.armemuseum.se

The old armoury on
Artillerigården has been the
home of the Armémuseum
(Royal Army Museum) since
1879. During the 1990s the
250-year-old building and its
exhibits underwent extensive
renovation. It is now one of
the capital's best-planned and
most interesting museums.

It puts Sweden's history in a
1,000-year perspective, present-
ing exciting information in a
more comprehensive way.
The march of history is
illustrated by life-size settings,
and visitors can see many
unique objects from the
collection of 80,000 exhibits.

Processions for royal visits
in the city start from the
museum, and during the
summer guardsmen march
from here to the Royal Palace
at 11:45am every day for the
changing of the guard.

Musik- &
Teatermuseet ❷❺

Riddargatan/Sibyllegatan. **Map** 3 E4.
Tel 08-519 554 90. 🚇 Kungsträdgården, Östermalmstorg. 🚌 2, 47,
52, 62, 69, 76. ◯ noon–5pm
Tue–Sun. 🎫 📷 ♿ 🛗 🛒
www.musikmuseet.se

The Museum of Music and
Theatre is housed in the
former royal bakery. The
site is the capital's oldest
preserved industrial building,
right in the city centre. Bread
was baked here for military
personnel in Stockholm

from 1640 right up to 1958.
The museum is laid out over
three floors and offers various
interactive exhibits that help
explore the world of music,
theatre and puppetry. Visitors
can try their hand at playing
a harp or an electric guitar,
and see stage sets, complete
with trap doors and wind
machines. Puppets from the
Marionetteatern in Stockholm
are on display, and there are
some superb marionettes
from China, Burma and Mali.
The museum shop sells a range
of small musical instruments.

Hovstallet ❷❻

Väpnargatan 1. **Map** 3 E4. **Tel** 08-
402 60 00. 🚇 Kungsträdgården,
Östermalmstorg. 🚌 2, 47, 55, 62, 69,
71, 76. ◯ for guided tours. 📷 public
hols. 🎫 15 Jan–29 May: 2pm Sat &
Sun; 27 Jun–12 Aug: 1pm Mon–Fri;
20 Aug–11 Dec: 2pm Sat & Sun.
📷 🛗 www.royalcourt.se

Formerly on Helgeands-
holmen, Hovstallet (the Royal
Mews) moved here in 1893
when the new Parliament
building was being constructed.
Alongside the Museum of
Music, it occupies a site next
to the Royal Dramatic Theatre.

The Mews arranges the
transport for the Royal Family

**Coach and four, with riders on the
left-hand horses, at Hovstallet**

and the Royal Household. It
maintains about 40 carriages,
a dozen cars and carriage
horses, and a few horses used
for riding. The royal horses
are Swedish half-breeds.

There are many treasures
among the carriages, such as
the State coach with glass
panelling known as a
"Berliner" made in Sweden at
the Adolf Freyschuss carriage
works. It was first seen at
Oscar II's silver jubilee in
1897 and is still used on
ceremonial occasions.

Incoming foreign ambassa-
dors travel to the Royal Palace
for their formal audience with
the monarch in Karl XV's
coupé. Open carriages from
the mid-19th century drawn
by two horses are normally
used for processions.

Kungliga Drama-
tiska Teatern ❷❼

Nybroplan. **Map** 3 E4. **Tel** 08-667 06
80. 🚇 Kungsträdgården, Östermalmstorg. 🚌 47, 62, 69, 76. **Ticket
Office** ◯ noon–7pm Tue–Sat,
noon–4pm Sun. 🎫 📷 ♿ 🛗
www.dramaten.se

When plans were drawn up
in the early 20th century to
build the present Kungliga
Dramatiska Teatern (Royal
Dramatic Theatre) at Nybroplan, the State refused to give
financial aid, so it was funded
by lotteries instead. The results
exceeded all expectations,
giving the architect Fredrik
Lilljekvist generous resources
which he used to the full.

The theatre, known as
Dramaten, was opened in
1908 after 6 years in
construction, and its decor
was remarkable for the era.

The Jugendstil façade
inspired by Viennese

architecture is in costly white marble. Christian Ericsson provided the powerful relief frieze, Carl Milles the centre section and John Börjesson the bronze statues *Poetry* and *Drama*. These are complemented in the foyer by *Tragedy* and *Comedy* by Börjesson and Theodor Lundberg respectively.

The lavish design continues inside, both in the choice of materials and in the contributions by leading Swedish artists. The ceiling in the foyer is by Carl Larsson, while the upper lobby's back wall was painted by Oscar Björk, and the auditorium's ceiling and stage lintel by Julius Kronberg. Gustav Cederström provided the central painting in the marble foyer, which also has some fantastic sculptures and busts.

Georg Pauli gave his name to a café where visitors can see his paintings and enjoy a meal without necessarily attending a performance.

The 805-seat auditorium and revolving stage with a diameter of 15 m (49 ft) have a classic beauty. When Gustav III founded the Royal Dramatic Theatre in 1788 it performed in a building on Slottsbacken. The probable colour scheme there – blue, white and gold – was chosen for the new national stage but was changed to the traditional "theatre red" in the 1930s. The auditorium was returned to its original colouring during renovation in 1988.

About 100 actors give some 1,200 performances every year on the theatre's 5 stages to large audiences of over 300,000.

Courtyard of Hallwylska museet, seen through the gateway arch

Hallwylska museet ㉘

Hamngatan 4. **Map** 3 D4. *Tel* 08-402 30 99. 🚇 *Östermalmstorg*. 🚌 *2, 47, 55, 62, 69, 76*. 🕐 *Jan–Jun & Sep–Dec: noon–4pm Tue–Thu & Sun (until 7pm Wed); July & Aug: 10am–4pm Tue–Sun.* 🎫 🚫 📷 **www**.hallwylskamuseet.se

The impressive façade of Hamngatan 4 is nothing in comparison with what is concealed by the heavy gates. The Hallwyl house was built from 1892–7 as a residence for the immeasurably rich Count and Countess Walther and Wilhelmina von Hallwyl. They decided quite early that the house should eventually become a museum. When the Countess died in 1930 the State was left a fantastic gift: an

The Steinway grand piano in Hallwylska museet

unbelievably lavish private house whose chatelaine had amassed a priceless collection of *objets d'art* over many decades. Eight years later the doors opened on a new museum with 67,000 catalogued items.

Wilhelmina left nothing to chance. The architect Isac Gustav Clason (1856–1930) had no worries about cost and nor did Julius Kronberg, who was a decorative painter and artistic adviser. Everything had to be perfect down to the smallest detail. A typical example is the billiards room which has gilt-leather wallpaper and walnut panelling, with billiard balls sculpted into the marble fireplace.

The paintings in the gallery, mostly 16th- and 17th-century Flemish, were bought over a period of only 2 years. Adjoining the gallery, the family skittles alley has become a showcase for top-class glazed earthenware. Visitors can also see a rich variety of household objects, which could well form a separate exhibition.

Various styles were chosen for the different rooms. The main salon in late Baroque style is built around four grandiose Gobelin tapestries and is finished in 24-carat gold leaf, clearly influenced by Hårleman's work at the Royal Palace (*see pp50–53*). It is difficult to believe that this was once a room in a private residence.

The most remarkable artifact is a Steinway grand piano, dating from 1896, adapted to fit into its majestic setting with a "casing" of hardwood and inlaid wood. In 1990 it was flown to New York in two sections, weighing a total of 900 kg (1,980 lb), for a renovation lasting several months. Visitors strolling through the salon can listen to a recording of music played on this magnificent piano.

Kungliga Dramatiska Teatern's Jugendstil façade in white marble

BLASIEHOLMEN & SKEPPSHOLMEN

Opposite the Royal Palace on the eastern side of the Strömmen channel lies Blasieholmen, a natural springboard to the islands of Skeppsholmen and Kastellholmen.

Several elegant palaces were built at Blasieholmen during Sweden's era as a great power in the 17th and early 18th centuries. But the area's present appearance was acquired in the period between the mid-19th century, when buildings like Nationalmuseum were erected, until just before World War I. In the early 1900s, stately residences such as Bååtska Palatset became overshadowed by prestigious hotels, lavish banks and

Porthole in wooden boat

entertainment venues. Blasieholmen is also the place for auction houses, art galleries, antique shops and second-hand bookshops. And the quayside is the departure point for sightseeing and archipelago boats.

Skeppsholmen is reached by a wrought-iron bridge with old wooden boats moored next to it. In the middle of the 17th century the island became the base for the Swedish Navy and many of its old buildings were designed as barracks and stores. Today they house some of the city's major museums and cultural institutions, juxtaposed with the avant-garde construction of the Moderna museet.

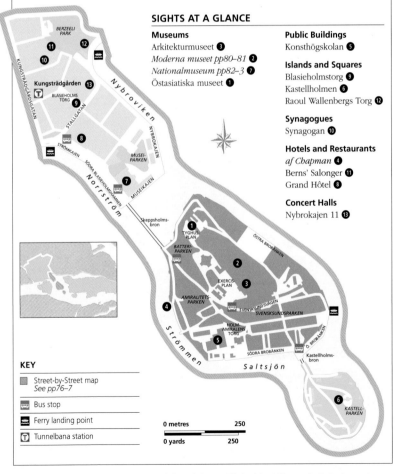

SIGHTS AT A GLANCE

Museums
Arkitekturmuseet ❸
Moderna museet pp80–81 ❷
Nationalmuseum pp82–3 ❼
Östasiatiska museet ❶

Public Buildings
Konsthögskolan ❺

Islands and Squares
Blasieholmstorg ❾
Kastellholmen ❻
Raoul Wallenbergs Torg ⑫

Synagogues
Synagogan ❿

Hotels and Restaurants
af Chapman ❹
Berns' Salonger ⑪
Grand Hôtel ❽

Concert Halls
Nybrokajen 11 ⑬

KEY

⬛ Street-by-Street map
See pp76–7

🚍 Bus stop

⚓ Ferry landing point

🅃 Tunnelbana station

0 metres ———— 250
0 yards ———— 250

◁ **Skeppsholmsbron linking Blasieholmen and Skeppsholmen, with the ship *af Chapman* in the background**

Street-by-Street: Skeppsholmen

Skeppsholmen has long since lost its importance as a naval base and has been transformed into a centre for culture. Many of the naval buildings have been restored and traditional wooden boats are moored here, but pride of place now goes to the exciting new Moderna museet.

The island is ideal for a full-day visit, with its location between the waters of Strömmen and Nybroviken acting as a breathing space in the centre of Stockholm. The attractive buildings, the richly wooded English-style park and the view towards Skeppsbron and Strandvägen also make Skeppsholmen an ideal place for those who would just prefer to have a quiet stroll.

Teater Galeasen is Stockholm's avant-garde theatre for new Swedish and international drama.

Skepps-holmsbron

Blasie-holmen

★ Östasiatiska museet
This belt plaquette in Ordos style from the 1st or 2nd century BC is included in a remarkable collection of arts and crafts from China, Japan, Korea and India, covering the period from the Stone Age to the 19th century ❶

Skeppsholmen Church (1824–42) in well-preserved Empire style.

Salute battery

Admiralty House

SVENSKSUNDSVÄGEN

Paradise (1963), a sculpture group by Jean Tinguelys and Niki de Saint Phalles for Montreal's World Exposition, has stood outside the site of the Moderna museet since 1972.

ÖSTRA BROBÄNKEN

Youth Hostel

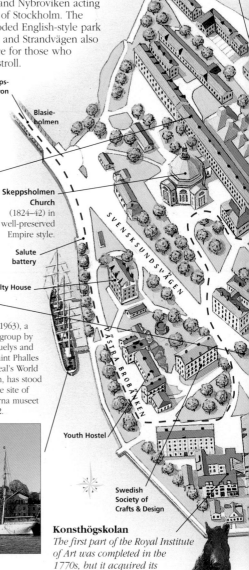

Swedish Society of Crafts & Design

Konsthögskolan
The first part of the Royal Institute of Art was completed in the 1770s, but it acquired its present appearance in the mid-1990s. This cast-iron boar stands at the entrance ❺

af Chapman
Built in 1888, the full-rigged former freighter and school ship has served as a popular youth hostel since 1949. Skeppsholmen Church (left) and the Admiralty House (1647–50, rebuilt 1844–6) are in the background ❹

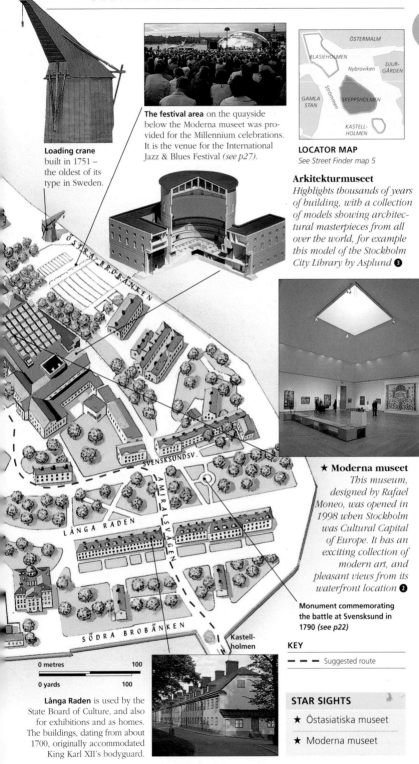

Loading crane
built in 1751 –
the oldest of its
type in Sweden.

The festival area on the quayside
below the Moderna museet was provided for the Millennium celebrations.
It is the venue for the International
Jazz & Blues Festival *(see p27)*.

LOCATOR MAP
See Street Finder map 5

Arkitekturmuseet
*Highlights thousands of years
of building, with a collection
of models showing architectural masterpieces from all
over the world, for example
this model of the Stockholm
City Library by Asplund* ❸

★ **Moderna museet**
*This museum,
designed by Rafael
Moneo, was opened in
1998 when Stockholm
was Cultural Capital
of Europe. It has an
exciting collection of
modern art, and
pleasant views from its
waterfront location* ❷

**Monument commemorating
the battle at Svensksund in
1790** *(see p22)*

KEY

– – – Suggested route

0 metres   100
0 yards   100

Långa Raden is used by the
State Board of Culture, and also
for exhibitions and as homes.
The buildings, dating from about
1700, originally accommodated
King Karl XII's bodyguard.

STAR SIGHTS

★ Östasiatiska museet

★ Moderna museet

Arkitekturmuseet, housed in the Neo-Classical former naval drill hall

Östasiatiska museet **❶**

Tyghusplan. **Map** 5 D2. **Tel** 08-519 557 50. Ⓣ Kungsträdgården. 🚌 65. ⛴ Djurgårdsfärja. 🕐 11am–8pm Tue, 11am–5pm Wed–Sun. 🎫 ♿ 🅿️ 🛗 🏪 www.ostasiatiska.se

It is not unusual for Western capitals to have a museum devoted to art and archaeology from China, Japan, Korea and India. But it is not every museum of Far Eastern antiquities that, like Östasiatiska museet, can claim one of the world's foremost collections of Chinese art outside Asia.

On a visit to the Yellow River valley in China in the early 1920s, the Swedish geologist Johan Gunnar Andersson discovered hitherto unknown dwellings and graves containing objects dating from the New Stone Age.

He was allowed by the Chinese to take a rich selection of finds back to Sweden, and these formed the basis for the museum, founded in 1926. A key figure in its development was the then Crown Prince, later to become King Gustaf VI Adolf, who was both interested in and knowledge-able about archaeology. He eventually bequeathed to the museum his own large collection of ancient Chinese arts and crafts.

The museum has been on Skeppsholmen since 1963, when it was moved into a restored house, which had been built in 1699–1700 as a depot for Karl XII's bodyguard.

Moderna museet **❷**

See pp80–81.

Arkitektur- museet **❸**

Exercisplan. **Map** 5 E3. **Tel** 08-587 270 00. Ⓣ Kungsträd-gården. 🚌 65. ⛴ Djurgårdsfärja. 🕐 10am–8pm Tue, 10am–6pm Wed–Sun. 🎫 by arrangement (for a fee). 🏪 ♿ 🛗 🍴 🖥️ 🅿️ 🛗 www.arkitekturmuseet.se

The Swedish Museum of Architecture shares an entrance hall and restaurant with the Moderna museet. It has also taken over its earlier home, the one-time naval drill hall.

In the permanent exhibition, over a hundred models guide visitors through a thousand years of building. These cover categories from the oldest and simplest of wooden houses to the highly varied building techniques and architectural styles of the present day.

It is fascinating to switch from an almost 2,000-year-old longhouse to a Konsum supermarket, in between encountering examples of architecture in Gothenburg dating from the 17th century to the 1930s and the Årsta bridge situated to the south of Stockholm.

Models of historic architec-tural works worldwide, from 2000 BC up to the present day, are also on show.

The museum offers an ambitious programme – albeit only in Swedish – alongside the permanent and temporary exhibitions, including lectures, study days, walks around the city, guided tours, school visits and family events on Sunday afternoons.

Detail of an earthenware tomb figurine in the Östasiatiska museet

THE SKEPPSHOLMEN CANNONS

A salute battery of four 57-mm rapid-fire cannons is sited on Skeppsholmen and are still in use. Salutes are fired to mark national and royal special occasions at noon on weekdays and 1pm at weekends: 28 January – the King's name day; 30 April – the King's birthday; 6 June – Sweden's National Day; 14 July – Crown Princess Victoria's birthday; 8 August – the Queen's name day; 23 December – the Queen's birthday.

The salute battery on Skeppsholmen

af Chapman ❹

Västra Brobänken. **Map** 5 D3.
Tel *08-463 22 66.* ⊤ *Kungsträd-gården.* 🚌 *65.* 🚢 *Djurgårdsfärja.*
🏨 *See **Where to stay** p154.*

The sailing ship *af Chapman* is one of Sweden's most attractive and unusual youth hostels and has 136 beds. The hostel also includes the 152-bed building facing the ship's gangway.

Visitors staying in more conventional accommodation can still go on board and enjoy *af Chapman*'s special atmosphere. The three-masted ship was built in 1888 at the English port of Whitehaven and used as a freight vessel. She came to Sweden in 1915 and saw service as a school ship until 1934. The City of Stockholm bought the ship after World War II and she has been berthed here since 1949. She is named after Fredrik Henrik af Chapman, a master shipbuilder who was born in Gothenburg in 1721.

Konsthögskolan ❺

Flaggmansvägen 1. **Map** 5 E3.
Tel *08-614 40 00.* ⊤ *Kungsträd-gården.* 🚌 *65.* 🚢 *Djurgårdsfärja.*
◯ *to the public for special events.*
♿ 🏨 *open 9:30am–4pm Mon–Fri.*

A stroll around Skeppsholmen provides an opportunity to have a closer look at the beautifully restored 18th-century naval barracks, which houses Konsthögskolan (the Royal Institute of Art). At the entrance there are two statues depicting a lion and a boar. "In like a lion and out like a pig" is an old saying among the lecturers and the 200 or so students at this institute, rich in tradition.

The institute started out in 1735 as an academy for painting and sculpture for the decorators working on Tessin's new Royal Palace. Gustaf III granted it a royal charter in 1773. Before it moved here in 1995, it was located on Fredsgatan as part of Konstakademien *(see p66)*, although since 1978 it had been run independently with departments for painting,

sculpture, graphics, digital media and video, as well as offering courses for architects.

The institute is not normally open to the public, apart from on Skeppsholms dagen and an "open house" in September. Then visitors can enjoy the beautiful interiors, especially the vaulted 18th-century cellars.

The medieval-style castle on Kastellholmen, built in 1846–8

Kastellholmen ❻

Map 5 F4. ⊤ *Kungsträdgården.*
🚌 *65.* 🚢 *Djurgårdsfärja.*

Right in the middle of Stockholm, Kastellholmen is a typical archipelago island with granite rocks and steep cliffs. From Skeppsholmen it is reached by a bridge built in 1880. Every morning since 1640 a sailor has hoisted the three-tailed Swedish war flag at the castle. Whenever a visiting naval vessel arrives, the battery's four cannons

fire a welcoming salute from the castle terrace.

The charming brick pavilion by the bridge was built in 1882 for the Royal Skating Club, which used the water between the two islands when it froze.

Nationalmuseum ❼

See pp82–3.

Grand Hôtel ❽

Södra Blasieholmshamnen 8. **Map** 4 C1. ***Tel*** *08-679 35 00.* ⊤ *Kungsträd-gården.* 🚌 *55, 59, 62, 65, 76. See* **Where to stay** *p154 and* **Where to eat** *p160.*

Oscar II's head chef, Régis Cadier, founded the Grand Hôtel, Sweden's leading five-star hotel, in 1874. And since 1901, the hotel has accommodated the Nobel Prize winners every year.

Traditional Swedish delicacies are served in an abundant *smörgåsbord* in the elegant Grands Veranda, while Franska Matsalen is a stylish gourmet restaurant. The Cadier Bar is named after the hotel's founder.

The hotel has 19 banqueting and meeting suites, the best known of which is the *Vinterträdgården* (Winter Garden) with a ceiling height of 20 m (66 ft) and space for more than 700 people. The *Spegelsalen* (Hall of Mirrors) is a copy of the one at Versailles and was where the Nobel Prize banquet was held until 1929, when the event became too big and was moved to the City Hall *(see p114)*.

Grand Hôtel on Blasieholmen, Sweden's first five-star hotel

Moderna museet ❸

The Museum of Modern Art is an airy, contemporary building, designed by the Catalan architect Rafael Moneo, in 1998. The museum has a top-class collection of international and Swedish modern art, including photography and film. Built partly underground, the museum includes a cinema and auditorium as well as the Pontus Hultén Study Gallery that provides a unique opportunity to view the former director's collection. A wide choice of books on art, photography, film and architecture can be found in the bookshop and the Restaurant MM Mat has attractive views over the water.

★ **Iván by the Armchair**
(1915) *Isaac Grünewald painted this portrait of his son after studying under Henri Matisse in Paris.*

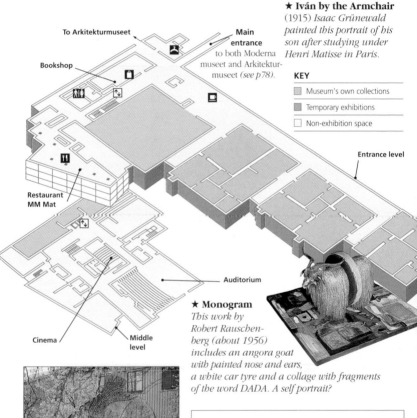

KEY

	Museum's own collections
	Temporary exhibitions
	Non-exhibition space

To Arkitekturmuseet

Main entrance to both Moderna museet and Arkitekturmuseet *(see p78).*

Bookshop

Entrance level

Restaurant MM Mat

Auditorium

Cinema

Middle level

★ **Monogram**
This work by Robert Rauschenberg (about 1956) includes an angora goat with painted nose and ears, a white car tyre and a collage with fragments of the word DADA. A self portrait?

Breakfast Outdoors (1962)
This sculpture group by Picasso, executed in sandblasted concrete by Carl Nesjar, stands in the museum garden near the entrance.

RAFAEL MONEO

Rafael Moneo (b. 1937) is one of the leading contemporary architects. As a young architect Moneo took part in the project to build the Sydney Opera House. His flair for adapting building design to sensitive surroundings was recognized in 1989 when he was chosen out of 211 entries as the winner of the competition to design the Moderna museet.

Moderna museet's northern façade

VISITORS' CHECKLIST

Exercisplan. **Map** 5 E3.
Tel 08-519 552 00.
🚇 Kungsträdgården. 🚌 65.
⛴ Djurgårdsfärja. ⏰
10am–6pm Wed–Sun,
10am–8pm Tue. ⬤ 24–25, 31
Dec, 1 Jan, Easter Mon, Whit
Mon, midsummer eve. 🎫 Eng:
summer. 📷 ⌀ ♿ 🎦 🛍 ⌂
🖥 www.modernamuseet.se

GALLERY GUIDE

*The large room on the entrance
level is used for temporary
exhibitions. Three rooms on
the same level have alternating
collections from three eras:
1900–45, 1946–70, and
1971–present. The middle
level has an auditorium,
cinema and the Pontus
Hultén Study Gallery. The
lowest level has an entrance.*

★ **The Child's Brain** (1914)
*The surrealist Giorgio de
Chirico gave his work the
title* The Ghost *but Louis
Aragon renamed it in a
pamphlet about the artist's
1927 retrospective exhibition.*

STAR EXHIBITS

★ Iván by the Armchair
  by Grünewald

★ Monogram
  by Rauschenberg

★ The Child's Brain
  by de Chirico

Blasieholmstorg ❾

Map 4 C1. 🚇 Kungsträdgården.
🚌 2, 55, 59, 62, 65, 76.

Two of the city's oldest
palaces are located in this
square, flanked by two bronze
horses. The palace at No. 8
was built in the mid-17th
century by Field Marshal
Gustaf Horn. It was rebuilt
100 years later, when it
acquired the character of an
18th-century French palace.
Foreign ambassadors and
ministers started to lodge here
when they visited
the capital, so it
became known
as the Ministers'
Palace. Later it
became a base for
overseas admin-
istration and soon
earned its present
name of Utrikes-
ministerhotellet
(Foreign Ministry
Hotel). Parts of the
building are now used as
offices by the Musical Academy
and the Swedish Institute.
 Bååtska Palatset stands
nearby at No. 6. Its restored
exterior dates from 1669 and
was designed by Tessin the
Elder. In 1876–7 it was partly
rebuilt by F W Scholander for
the Freemasons, who still
have their lodge here.
 Another interesting complex
of buildings can be found on
the square at No. 10. The
façade, which faces on to
Nybrokajen, along the water's
edge, is an attractive example
of the Neo-Renaissance style
of the 1870s and 1880s.

**Bronze horse on
Blasieholmstorg**

Synagogan ❿

Wahrendorffsgatan 3.
Map 4 C1. **Tel** 08-587 858 00.
🚇 Kungsträdgården. 🚌 7, 55, 59,
62, 65, 76. 🕐 8am Mon, Thu, Fri;
5:30pm Sat; Hebrew, partly Swedish.
🎫 Summer and on request. ♿
www.jfst.se

It took most of the 1860s
to build the Conservative
Jewish community's syna-
gogue on what was once the
seabed. When it was inaugurated in 1870, the synagogue
was standing on 1,300 piles,

**Monument to the victims of the
Holocaust during World War II**

which had been driven down
to a depth of 15 m (50 ft). It
is built in what the architect,
F W Scholander, called
"ancient Eastern style".
 Alongside this synagogue,
which can be
visited on guided
tours during the
summer, is the
congregation's
assembly room and
library. Outside is a
monument erected
in 1998 to the mem-
ory of 8,000 victims
of the Holocaust whose
relations had been rescued
and taken to Sweden during
World War II.
 There is also an Orthodox
synagogue in the city centre,
reached through the Jewish
Centre (Judiska Centret) on
Nybrogatan at No. 19.

Berns' Salonger ⓫

Berzeli Park, Nackströmgatan 8.
Map 3 D4. **Tel** 08-566 322 00. 🚇
Kungsträdgården, Östermalmstorg.
🚌 2, 55, 59, 62, 65, 76. ♿
www.berns.se **Where to eat** p160.

This has been one of Stockholm's most legendary
restaurants and entertainment
venues since 1863. Both
salons, with their stately
galleries, magnificent crystal
chandeliers and elegant
mirrors, have been restored
to their original splendour
by the British designer
Terence Conran to mark
the new millennium.
 The new-look Berns' is one
of Stockholm's biggest
restaurants with seating for
400 diners. The gallery level,
with its beautifully decorated
dining rooms, was made
famous by August Strindberg's
novel *The Red Room* (1879).

Nationalmuseum ❼

The Nationalmuseum is a landmark on the southern side of Blasieholmen. The location by the Strömmen channel inspired the 19th-century German architect August Stüler to design a building in the Venetian and Florentine Renaissance styles.

Completed in 1866, the museum houses Sweden's largest art collection, with some 16,000 classic paintings and sculptures. Drawings and graphics from the 15th century up to the early 20th century bring the total up to 500,000. The applied art and design section has 30,000 works spanning five centuries, including a 500-year-old tapestry, and Scandinavia's largest collection of porcelain. Renovations are due to begin in 2013, which will affect the location of exhibits; check the museum's website for details.

The Love Lesson (1716–17)
Antoine Watteau's speciality was the so-called fêtes galantes, depicting young couples in playful mood.

★ The Conspiracy of the Batavians under Claudius Civilis (1661–62)
Originally intended for Amsterdam, Rembrandt depicts the Batavians' conspiracy against the Romans, symbolizing the Dutch liberation campaign against Spain.

Level 2

Chest of Drawers (1780)
This impressive piece of furniture was created by Georg Haupt, who was one of the foremost Swedish cabinet-makers of the 18th century.

Atrium through levels 1 and 2

David and Bathsheba (1490)
This tapestry from Brussels is created in the decorative medieval style, with pomegranates, faces and hands forming an exquisite work.

Gravure gallery

Entrance

STAR PAINTINGS

★ The Conspiracy of the Batavians by Rembrandt

★ The Lady with the Veil by Roslin

Entry for wheelchairs

★ **The Lady with the Veil**
*Alexander Roslin's elegant
portrait (1769) is often
considered a symbol for
18th-century Sweden.*

VISITORS' CHECKLIST

Södra Blasieholmshamnen.
Map 5 D2. *Tel* 08-519 543 00.
🚇 Kungsträdgården. 🚌 65; or
2, 55, 59, 62, 76 to Karl XII:s
Torg. ◯ 11am–8pm Tue & Thu
(Jun–Aug: to 5pm Thu),
11am–5pm Wed, Fri & Sun.
● 1 Jan, 25 Jun, 24, 25 &
31 Dec. 🗣 English: tours twice a
week during summer. & 🛗 ⑪
🖥 www.nationalmuseet.se

The Upper Staircase
*At the back is Carl Larsson's
monumental mural* The Entry of
King Gustav Vasa of Sweden in
Stockholm 1523. *On the
opposite wall is his*
Midwinter Sacrifice.

**Amor and
Psyche** (1787)
*Johan Tobias Sergel
was the foremost
sculptor of the Gusta-
vian era. Inspired by
Greek mythology, this
piece shows a scene
from the story of
Amor and Psyche.*

Level 1

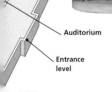

Auditorium

Entrance
level

KEY

- 🟦 Painting and sculpture
- ⬜ Applied art and design
- ⬜ Temporary exhibitions
- ⬜ Non-exhibition space
- ⬜ No admission

GALLERY GUIDE

*Level 2 is devoted to painting and
sculpture. The accent is on Swedish
18th- to early 20th-century art, but
the 17th-century Dutch and Flemish,
and 18th-century French schools are
also represented. Exhibits may
change. Level 1 shows mainly
Swedish applied art and design,
particularly furniture, porcelain,
silver and glass from the 15th century
up to modern Swedish design. To
the left of the main entrance is the
Gravure Gallery with temporary
exhibitions of graphics.*

Raoul Wallenbergs Torg ⑫

🚇 Östermalmstorg. 🚌 2, 55, 59,
62, 65, 76.

This square is dedicated
to Raoul Wallenberg (1912–
unknown), who during World
War II worked as a diplomat
at the Swedish Embassy in
Budapest. By using Swedish
"protective passports" he
helped a large number of
Hungarian Jews to escape
deportation to the Nazi
concentration camps.

In 1945, when Budapest
was liberated, he was impris-
oned by the Soviets and
according to Soviet sources
he died in Moscow's Lubianka
prison in 1947. His fate,
however, has never been
satisfactorily explained.

The small square adjoins
Berzelii Park and Nybroplan
and faces the Nybrokajen
waterfront. The definitive
design of the square has
been hotly debated because
it is set in a sensitive
architectural environment,
but great efforts have been
made to ensure that it
remains a worthy memorial
to Raoul Wallenberg.

Nybrokajen 11 ⑬

Nybrokajen 11. **Map** 4 C1.
Tel 08-401 16 00. 🚇 Kungsträdgården, Östermalmstorg. 🚌 47, 62,
69, 76. 🚢 Djurgårdsfärja. ◯ for
concerts (phone for details). &
www.nybrokajen11.rikskonserter.se

Constructed in the 1870s,
this building facing the waters
of Nybroviken once housed
the Musical Academy. Its concert hall, opened in 1878, was
the first in the country, and
was used for the first
presentations of the Nobel
Prize in 1901. Designed in
Neo-Renaissance style with
cast-iron pillars, the hall has a
royal box and galleries, and
can seat up to 600 people.

After extensive restoration,
it is now run by the state
musical organization
Rikskonserter, which has
provided a much-needed concert stage for chamber, choral,
jazz and folk music *(see p177)*.

DJURGÅRDEN

Museum tram

O nce a royal hunting ground, Djurgården is an island right in the centre of Stockholm covered by a natural park. It has very few buildings with only around 800 permanent residents and forms part of the Stockholm National City Park, the only one of its type in the world *(see p121)*.

From 1580 parts of Djurgården were a royal animal reserve where Johan III kept reindeer, red deer and elk. A century later the area was fenced off by Karl XI to be used for hunting. It developed into a popular recreational park during the 18th century, and in the time of troubador Carl Bellman *(see p98)* many inns appeared. The Gröna Lund funfair was established just a few decades before Artur Hazelius founded the fascinating outdoor museum of Skansen and Nordiska museet in around 1900. Today, there is a wealth of museums on Djurgården offering a mixture of nature, culture and entertainment. A royal connection survives in the beautiful Rosendal Palace which has magnificent Empire-style decor.

SIGHTS AT A GLANCE

Museums
Biologiska museet **7**
Junibacken **2**
Liljevalchs Konsthall **9**
Museifartygen **6**
Nordiska museet pp90–91 **3**
Skansen pp96–7 **12**
Thielska Galleriet **15**
Vasamuseet pp92–3 **5**
Vin- & Sprithistoriska museet **8**
Waldemarsudde **14**

Amusement Parks
Gröna Lund **10**

Historic Areas
Djurgårdsstaden & Beckholmen **11**
Rosendals Slott & Trädgårdar **13**

Memorials
Estoniaminnesvården **4**

Bridges
Djurgårds-
bron **1**

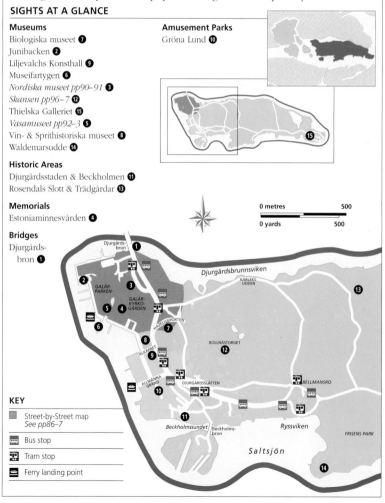

KEY

▨	Street-by-Street map *See pp86–7*
🚌	Bus stop
🚊	Tram stop
⛴	Ferry landing point

◁ Some of the 300-year-old oaks in Royal Djurgården, part of the National City Park

Street-by-Street: Around Lejonslätten

Lions were kept for animal-baiting up to 1792 on the
spot where Nordiska museet now stands, hence the name
of this area – Lejonslätten (The Lion Plain). Today visitors
can safely stroll along the waterfront, look at the boats, and
take in the panorama across to Nybroviken, Skeppsholmen
and the heights of Södermalm.

This area also offers several sights of cultural interest.
The majestic Nordiska museet, built in Neo-Renaissance
style, reflects Swedish cultural history over almost 500 years.
In Vasamuseet lies the beautifully restored 17th-century
warship and two more vintage ships are moored outside.
Nearby, Junibacken brings Pippi Longstocking and other
favourite children's book characters imaginatively to life.

Junibacken
*A fun place for children,
dedicated to the author
Astrid Lindgren. It also
features characters from
stories by other authors* ❷

★ Vasamuseet
The royal warship Vasa *was salvaged
after 300 years in the depths of Stockholm's harbour. It is now housed in
Stockholm's most popular museum* ❺

Museifartygen
*Alongside Vasamuseet are
two faithful vessels: the ice-
breaker Sankt Erik
and the lightship*
Finngrundet ❻

| 0 metres | 100 |
| 0 yards | 100 |

STAR SIGHTS

★ Vasamuseet

★ Nordiska museet

Estoniaminnesvården
*Near the Galär cemetery, a nat-
ional memorial has been erected
to the 852 people who lost their
lives in the* Estonia *ferry disaster
on the night of 27–28 September
1994. The ferry sank on its way
from Tallinn to Stockholm* ❹

Djurgårdsbron
There has been a bridge to Djurgården since 1661. The current bridge was built in 1896 to mark the Stockholm Exhibition the following year ❶

LOCATOR MAP
See Street Finder maps 5, 6 & 7

Blå Porten is a copy of one of the many blue-painted gateways once set in a 20-km (12-mile) fence around the former royal hunting reserve.

Strand-vägen

Villa Lusthusporten was built in the Italian style during the 1880s.

DJURGÅRDSBRUNNSVIKEN

Kaptens-udden

Lejon-slätten

DJURGÅRDSVÄGEN

Djur-gårds-brunns-bron

★ **Nordiska museet**
Artur Hazelius, creat-or of Skansen, also founded Nordiska museet, which portrays Swedish cultural history from the 1520s to the present day ❸

ROSENDALSVÄGEN

DJURGÅRDSVÄGEN

Vin- & Sprithistoriska museet

Galärkyrkogården (cemetery)

Biologiska museet
Swedish fauna is shown in realistic natural settings in this charming old museum ❼

Karl XV's equestrian statue by Charles Friberg was erected in 1909. The king (1826–72) was a great patron of the arts.

KEY

– – – Suggested route

One of the beautifully decorated pillars supporting Djurgårdsbron

Djurgårdsbron ❶

Map 3 F4. 44, 69, 76. 7. Djurgårdsfärja.

The Djurgården bridge came into use a few days before the major Art and Industrial Exhibition opened in Stockholm in May 1897. Made at the Bergsund plant in Södermalm, the bridge is richly ornamented with cast-iron railings in the form of stylized water plants. At that time Sweden was in union with Norway, and King Oscar II's monogram and motto "The sister nations' wellbeing" can be seen on the central span. The capital's patron saint, St Erik, is depicted on the pillar supports among sea gods and water lilies.

Wrought-iron lamps and sculptures portraying mythological gods, created by Rolf Adlersparre, adorn the four granite pillars at either end. On the Strandvägen side, the pillars show Heimdal, the watchman, and Frigga, the wife of Oden. On the opposite side is Thor, with his hammer, and Freja, goddess of love and fertility.

The gate of Blå Porten, just to the left on the Djurgården side, recalls the time when the island was a royal hunting ground during the 17th century, and the surrounding fence was punctuated by blue-painted wooden gateways. This gate, decorated with Oscar I's monogram, was made from cast iron in 1849.

Junibacken ❷

Galärvarvsvägen. **Map** 5 F1. **Tel** 08-587 230 00. 44, 69. 7. Djurgårdsfärja. Jan–May: 10am–5pm Tue–Sun; Jun: 10am–5pm daily; Jul–Aug: 9am–6pm daily; Sep–Dec: 10am–5pm daily. **www**.junibacken.se

You can find them all here – Pippi Longstocking, Mardie, Karlsson on the Roof, Emil, Nils Karlsson Pyssling, Ronja the robber's daughter, the Lionheart Brothers and many more characters from Astrid Lindgren's children's books. In accordance with the popular novelist's wishes, visitors can also meet the creations of other Swedish children's authors. When she heard about Staffan Götesam's project for a children's cultural centre she was adamant it should not be just an Astrid Lindgren museum.

Nevertheless Junibacken is still something of a tribute to the much-loved author. It was officially opened by the Royal Family in the summer of 1996 and has become one of the city's most popular tourist attractions. A mini-train takes

A colourful scene from one of Astrid Lindgren's stories seen from the mini-train

visitors from a mock-up of the station at Vimmerby (the author's home town) to meet some of her characters, finishing with a visit to Pippi's home in Villekulla Cottage, where children can play in the different rooms. There is also a well-stocked children's bookshop and a restaurant.

Nordiska museet ❸

See pp90–91.

Estoniaminnes-vården ❹

Galärkyrkogården. **Map** 5 F2. 44. Djurgårdsfärja.

On the night of 27–28 September 1994 the ferry MS *Estonia* sank in the Baltic on its journey from Tallinn to Stockholm with the loss of 852 lives. They came from many countries including Sweden, Estonia, Latvia, Russia, Finland, Norway, Denmark, Germany, Lithuania, Morocco, the Netherlands, France, the United Kingdom, Canada, Belarus, Ukraine and Nigeria. Their names and their fate will never be forgotten.

So reads the inscription on the national memorial to the victims of the *Estonia* disaster adjoining the cemetery of Galärkyrkogården. It was designed by the Polish artist Miroslaw Balka (b. 1958), who created it together

---

ASTRID LINDGREN AND PIPPI LONGSTOCKING

Astrid Lindgren wrote around 100 children's books, which have been translated into 74 languages, making her one of the world's most-read children's authors. Publishers turned down her first book about Pippi Longstocking, but she went on to win a children's book competition two years later with it, in 1945. Her headstrong and tough character Pippi soon won the hearts of children worldwide.

Following her death in 2002, the Swedish government created the world's largest prize for children's literature in her name.

Astrid Lindgren

Museifartygen: the lightship *Finngrundet* and ice-breaker *Sankt Erik* outside Vasamuseet

with the two landscape architects Anders Jönsson and Thomas Andersson.

Unveiled on 28 September 1997, the memorial is made of blasted granite and forms a roofless, triangular room with 11-m (36-ft) long sides and a height of 2.5 m (just over 8 ft). The exact position of where the ferry sank is given on a metal ring around a tree in the triangle. With relatives' consent, the names of most of the dead have been carved in the walls.

Vasamuseet ❺

See pp92–4.

Museifartygen ❻

Galärvarvet. **Map** 5 F2.
Tel *08-519 549 00.* 🚌 *44.* 🚋 *7*
🚢 *Djurgårdsfärja.* ⭘ *10 Jun–20 Aug: noon–5pm daily; also during various public holidays, ring for details.* 📷 📶 🚻
www.sjohistoriska.se

The two vintage ships moored alongside Vasamuseet are both fine examples of the ships built to handle various tasks in Swedish waters during the early 20th century. The lightship *Finngrundet,* built in 1903, used to be anchored during the ice-free season on the Finngrund banks in the southern Gulf of Bothnia. In the 1960s lightships started to be replaced by permanent automatic lighthouses, so *Finngrundet* was withdrawn from service and became a museum ship. At 31 m

(102 ft) long and 6.85 m (22 ft 6 in) wide, with a draught of 3.1 m (10 ft 3 in), she was designed for a crew of eight. The light had a range of 11 nautical miles.

Built in 1915, *Sankt Erik* was Sweden's first seagoing ice-breaker. This classic Baltic model slides up over the ice and crushes it. She also has a system that enables the ship to be rocked sideways to loosen the ice and widen the channel. One of the two three-cylinder engines is Sweden's largest working marine steam engine. The ice-breaker is 60 m (197 ft) long and 17 m (56 ft) wide and needs a crew of 30.

Biologiska museet ❼

Lejonslätten. **Map** 6 A3. ***Tel*** *08-442 82 15.* 🚌 *44.* 🚋 *7.* ⭘ *Apr–Sep: 11am–4pm daily; Oct–Mar: noon–3pm Tue–Fri, 10am–3pm Sat & Sun.* 📷 *by arrangement.* 📶 🚻
www.biologiskamuseet.com

The national romantic influences of the late 19th century inspired the architect Agi Lindegren when he was commissioned to design Biologiska museet (Museum of Biology) in the 1890s. He based his plans on the simple lines of the medieval Norwegian stave churches.

The man behind the museum was the zoologist, hunter and conservationist Gustaf Kolthoff (1845–1913). In 1892, he persuaded

the industrialist C F Liljevalch – who later financed the nearby art gallery – to form a company whose aim was "to develop and maintain a biological museum to include all the Scandinavian mammals and birds as stuffed specimens in natural surroundings". The result was the world's first museum of its type. Within a few months of opening in autumn 1893, Gustaf Kolthoff had delivered a couple of thousand stuffed animals, as well as birds' nests, young and eggs. Many of the creatures are shown against a diorama background, with about 300 species of Scandinavian birds and land mammals in their respective biotypes. Kolthoff's friend, the artist Bruno Liljefors, painted the backgrounds.

Since 1970 the Museum of Biology has belonged to the Skansen Foundation. During the 1990s it underwent extensive renovation and was reopened on 13 November 1993 – exactly 100 years after its original inauguration.

Biologiska museet's wooden façade, inspired by Nordic medieval design

Nordiska museet ❸

Resembling an extravagant Renaissance castle, Nordiska museet portrays everyday life in Sweden from the 1520s to the present day. It was created by Artur Hazelius (1833–1901), who was also the founder of Skansen (*see pp96–7*). In 1872, he started to collect objects which would remind future generations of the old Nordic farming culture.

The present museum, designed by Isak Gustaf Clason, was opened in 1907. Today it has more than 1.5 million exhibits, with everything from luxury clothing and priceless jewellery to everyday items, furniture and children's toys, and replicas of period homes.

Dolls' Houses
The dolls' houses show typical homes from the 17th century to modern times. This example illustrates one from 1860.

Level 3

Corridor to staircase

Level 2 (Main Hall)

Ground floor

State Bedchamber from Ulvsunda Castle
At the end of the 17th century, the lord of the manor at Ulvsunda accommodated prominent guests in this prestigious bedchamber.

STAR FEATURES

★ Table Settings

★ Strindberg Collection

★ Main Hall

GALLERY GUIDE

The museum has four floors. From the entrance, stairs lead up to the temporary exhibitions in the Main Hall. On the ground level is the Reference Room. Floor 3 has the Strindberg Collection, Dolls' Houses, Table Settings, Traditions and the Fashion and Textile Galleries. On the fourth floor are sections on Folk Art, Interiors, Swedish Homes, Small Objects and the Sami People and Culture.

Obelisk with an inscription meaning: "The day may dawn when not even all our gold is enough to form a picture of a bygone era".

Main entrance

★ **Table Settings**
In the mid-17th century, table settings were a feast for the eyes. A swan is the centrepiece at this meal.

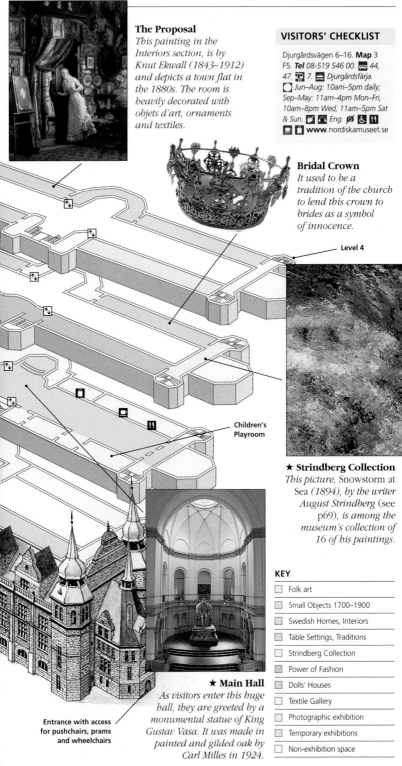

The Proposal
This painting in the Interiors section, is by Knut Ekwall (1843–1912) and depicts a town flat in the 1880s. The room is heavily decorated with objets d'art, ornaments and textiles.

VISITORS' CHECKLIST

Djurgårdsvägen 6–16. **Map** 3 F5. **Tel** 08-519 546 00. 44, 47. 7. Djurgårdsfärja. Jun–Aug: 10am–5pm daily; Sep–May: 11am–4pm Mon–Fri, 10am–8pm Wed, 11am–5pm Sat & Sun. Eng. www.nordiskamuseet.se

Bridal Crown
It used to be a tradition of the church to lend this crown to brides as a symbol of innocence.

Level 4

Children's Playroom

★ **Strindberg Collection**
This picture, Snowstorm at Sea (1894), by the writer August Strindberg (see p69), is among the museum's collection of 16 of his paintings.

KEY

- ☐ Folk art
- ☐ Small Objects 1700–1900
- ☐ Swedish Homes, Interiors
- ☐ Table Settings, Traditions
- ☐ Strindberg Collection
- ☐ Power of Fashion
- ☐ Dolls' Houses
- ☐ Textile Gallery
- ☐ Photographic exhibition
- ☐ Temporary exhibitions
- ☐ Non-exhibition space

Entrance with access for pushchairs, prams and wheelchairs

★ **Main Hall**
As visitors enter this huge hall, they are greeted by a monumental statue of King Gustav Vasa. It was made in painted and gilded oak by Carl Milles in 1924.

Vasamuseet ⑤

After a maiden voyage of just 1,300 m (4,265 ft) in calm
weather, the royal warship *Vasa* capsized in Stockholm's harbour on 10 August 1628. About 50 people
went down with what was supposed to be the pride of
the Navy, only 100 m (330 ft) off the southernmost point
of Djurgården. Guns were all that were salvaged from
the vessel in the 17th century and it was not until 1956
that a marine archaeologist's persistent search led to the
rediscovery of *Vasa*. After a complex salvage operation
followed by a 17-year conservation programme, the city's
most popular museum was opened in June 1990, less
than a nautical mile from the scene of the disaster.

Gun-port Lion
*More than 200 carved
ornaments and 500 sculp-
ted figures decorate* Vasa.

To the
restaurant

Museum
shop

★ Lion Figurehead
*King Gustav II Adolf, who com-
missioned Vasa, was known as
the Lion of the North. So a
springing lion was the obvious
choice for the figurehead.
It is 4 m (13 ft) long and
weighs 450 kg (990 lb).*

Information
desk

Entrance

Emperor Titus
*Carvings of 20
Roman emp-
erors stand on
parade on* Vasa

Bronze Cannon
*More than 50 of Vasa's
64 original cannons were
salvaged already in the
17th century. Three 11-kg
(24-lb) bronze cannons are
on display in the museum.*

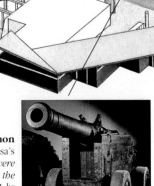

★ Stern
Vasa's stern was badly damaged but has been painstakingly restored to reveal the ship's magnificent ornamentation.

VISITORS' CHECKLIST

Galärvarvet. **Map** 5 F2.
Tel 08-519 548 00. 44, 69.
Djurgårdsfärja. 7.
10am–5pm daily (Wed until 8pm); 1 Jun–31 Aug: 8:30am–6pm daily. 1 Jan, 23–25 Dec, 31 Dec. English guided tours several times daily.
www.vasamuseet.se

The main mast was originally 52 m (170 ft) high.

The Gun Ports
Vasa *carried more heavy cannons on its two gundecks than earlier ships of the same size. This contributed to its capsizing.*

Reconstruction of the upper gun deck

A model of the *Vasa* to a scale of 1:10

Main film auditorium

Gun Deck
Visitors cannot board the ship, but there is a full-size copy of the upper gun deck with carved wooden dummies of sailors, which gives a good idea of conditions on board.

Upper Deck
The entrance to the cabins was towards the stern. This area was the grandest part of the ship, reserved for senior officers. Part of the original mainmast can be seen on the right.

STAR FEATURES

★ Lion Figurehead

★ Stern

Exploring the Vasamuseet

The Royal Warship *Vasa* has been restored to 95 per cent of its original appearance. The low salt content of the water saved the ship's timber – which came from more than 1,000 oaks – from attacks by ship worms. The hull was all present, but fitting the 13,500 loose pieces together was like doing a jigsaw puzzle without a picture, as there were no detailed designs to follow. The salvage operation produced more than 700 sculpted figures and carved ornaments, as well as many everyday items.

A sailor's simple belongings found on *Vasa*

Carved soldiers on Vasa's stern

THE SHIP

In 1628 *Vasa* was potentially one of the world's mightiest ships. It was able to carry 64 cannons and 300 soldiers (out of a total 450 men on board). *Vasa* was equipped for both traditional close combat and for artillery battles. From its high stern it would have been possible to fire down on smaller ships. The musketeers had shooting galleries for training, and on the upper deck were so-called "storm pieces", erected as protection against musketry fire.

All this may appear very impressive, but it is uncertain exactly what the ship's role would have been if it had survived. The main task of the Swedish navy at that time had been to transport weapons and soldiers as well as to protect shipping or block harbours. It seems doubtful that *Vasa* would have been suitable for these roles.

THE IMAGERY OF POWER

The Warship's many figures and elaborately carved ornaments formed an important part of that era's language of power and

were designed as a type of war propaganda. Many of the builders and carpenters who worked in the shipyard that built *Vasa* came from Holland, while most of the sculptors, whose work was typical of the late Renaissance and early Baroque eras, came from Germany. The German woodcarver Mårten Redtmer made most of the ship's larger sculptures. Created out of oak, pine and lime wood, the figures were inspired mainly by Greek mythology, as well as the Bible and 17th-century Swedish royal personalities.

LIFE ON BOARD

Vasa's destination on its maiden voyage, with about 150 people on board, was intended to be the Älvsnabben naval base in the southern Stockholm archipelago, where

300 soldiers were to embark. The ship was fully equipped, and the divers were able to recover many everyday items, including food and drink. But when the chief diver, Per Edvin Fälting, tasted the 333-year-old butter from a tub made of wood and tin, sores erupted around his mouth.

The museum has full-scale models of *Vasa* 's upper gun deck and the Admiral's cabin. The sailors and soldiers had to eat and sleep on deck among the cannons. No wonder that in the 17th century more died from illness than in battle.

In a fascinating exhibition of original artifacts, you can see the medical equipment that was used, an officer's backgammon game, some of the sailors' wooden spoons and plates and the officers' dinner service in pewter and earthenware. The divers also found about 4,000 coins, made mainly from copper, and a chest still neatly packed with hats, clothing and other personal belongings.

Replicas of some of these artifacts are on sale in the museum shop.

THE SALVAGE OPERATION

The marine archaeologist Anders Franzén had been looking for *Vasa* for many years. On 25 August 1956 his patience was rewarded when he brought up a piece of blackened oak on his plumb line. From the autumn of 1957, it took divers 2 years to clear tunnels under the hull for the lifting cables. The first lift with six cables was a success, after which *Vasa* was lifted in 16 stages into shallower water. Thousands of plugs were then inserted into holes left by rusted iron bolts. The final lift started on 24 April 1961, and on 4 May *Vasa* was finally towed into dry dock.

Vasa in dry dock after being salvaged in 1961

Vin- & Sprithistoriska museet ❽

Galärskjulen, Djurgården.
Map 6 A3. **Tel** 08-51 91 86 50.
🚇 Karlaplan. 🚋 Spårvagn City.
🕐 10am–6pm daily in summer;
10am–4pm daily in winter. 🎦 🔲 🔲
📷 www.vinosprithistoriska.se

The Swedish Museum of Wine and Spirits looks at the unique history of alcoholic beverages in Sweden. Spanning two floors, the museum is the only one of its kind in the country and boasts an impressive array of exhibits. The highlight of the museum is the Absolut Art Collection, which includes over 800 works by famous artists such as Andy Warhol, Keith Haring, Damien Hirst and Louise Bourgeois. The works were produced in conjunction with the advertising campaigns that helped make Absolut one of the best-known brands in the industry. It is the first time these works have been united under one roof.

Schnapps label, Vin- & Sprithistoriska museet

The museum is housed in Stockholm's historic Galärskjulen, or "galley sheds", which date from the 18th century. The sheds were modelled on a Venetian design and were built for the galleys of the Royal Navy, which were stored on land in these buildings. Thirty galley sheds once lined the shore but today only two remain, between Vasamuseet and the Vasa boat halls.

Liljevalchs Konsthall ❾

Djurgårdsvägen 60. **Map** 6 A3.
Tel 08-508 313 30. 🚋 44, 47. 🚌 7.
🚢 Djurgårdsfärja. 🕐 11am–8pm
Tue & Thu, 11am–5pm Wed & Fri–
Sun. 🎦 2:15pm Mon–Fri. 🎦 ♿
🔲 🔲 🔲 www.liljevalchs.com

Originally constructed thanks to a donation from the industrialist Carl Fredrik Liljevalch, this heritage building is regarded as one of northern Europe's most attractive art galleries. It was designed by the architect Carl G Bergsten and built in 1913–16 in a Neo-Classical style, which was typical of its era, particularly in Stockholm.

Liljevalch's portrait bust, sculpted in granite by Christian Eriksson, is set in the northern wall of this heritage building. On a high column outside the entrance is Carl Milles' sculpture *The Archer*.

The city of Stockholm owns and administers the gallery, which features Liljevalch's collections of Swedish, Nordic and international art over the 20th century, as well as handicrafts dating from the same period.

Every year four or five major exhibitions are staged, including the Spring Salon, which is always a major attraction for Stockholm art-lovers. The exhibitions are complemented by daily guided tours, lectures, debates and concerts.

Children and young people have a special section where they can create their own works of art from various different types of materials.

Liljevalchs Konsthall's spacious main exhibition hall

Gröna Lund funfair seen from Kastellholmen

Gröna Lund ❿

Lilla Allmänna gränd 9. **Map** 6 A4.
Tel 08-587 501 00. 🚋 44, 47. 🚌 7.
🚢 Djurgårdsfärja. 🕐 mid-Apr–mid-
Sep opening hours vary. 🎦 ♿ 🔢
🔲 www.gronalund.com

A tavern called Gröna Lund (Green Grove) existed on this site in the 18th century, and it was one of the haunts of the renowned troubadour Carl Michael Bellman*(see p98).* Jakob Schultheis used the tavern's name for the modest-sized funfair, which he opened here in 1883 with a two-level horse-drawn round-about as the main attraction. Today Gröna Lund is Sweden's oldest amusement park.

The 130-day season, starting the first week of May, is short but hectic. However, Gröna Lund draws about 1.2 million visitors each year. Its exciting attractions include a haunted house, a ghost train and an 80-m (262-ft) free-fall tower. There is also a wooden roller coaster.

The amusement park is well catered for with 13 restaurants and cafés. There are also three stages, a cabaret restaurant with space for 600 guests, and a theatre with 200 seats. The main stage has hosted world stars such as Bob Marley who, in 1980, played to a record audience of 32,000.

Gröna Lund's beautiful gardens include 30,000 pansies and 25,000 summer flowers.

Skansen ⑫

The world's first open-air museum, Skansen opened in 1891 to show an increasingly industrialized society how people once lived. About 150 houses and farm buildings were assembled from all over Sweden, portraying the life of both peasants and landed gentry, as well as Lapp *(Same)* culture. The Town Quarter has wooden urban dwellings and crafts like glass-blowing and printing. Nordic flora and fauna feature every-where, with bears, wolves and elks in natural habitat enclosures and more exotic creatures in the Aquarium. Many festivals are celebrated in Skansen *(see pp26–9).*

★ Älvros Farmstead
The living room in this 500-year-old wooden cottage from Härjedalen shows the tools for daily tasks.

A cable car runs from the Hazelius Gate entrance.

Tingsvallen/Bollnästorget is the venue for the Christmas market and Midsummer celebrations.

Swedenborg's Pavilion
Set in the rose garden is the pavilion which used to belong to the philo-sopher and scientist Emanuel Swedenborg (1688–1772).

Hazelius Gate

Skogaholm Manor
The main building in this Carlo-vingian manor estate (1680) comes from the Skogaholm ironworks village in central Sweden.

★ Town Quarter
Original Stockholm wooden town houses replicate a medium-size 19th-century town. Glass-blowers, bakers and other craftsmen demonstrate their traditional skills in restored workshops.

Solliden stage

Main entrance

Skansen Aquarium

Vastveit Storehouse
This storehouse from eastern Norway was built in the 14th century and is Skansen's oldest building.

VISITOR'S CHECKLIST

Djurgårdsslätten 49.
Map 6 B3.
Tel 08-442 80 00.
44. 7. Djurgårdsfärja.
10am–5pm daily (to 8pm in summer). Jun–Aug.
24 Dec.
Seglora Church 11am Sun.
www.skansen.se

★ **Bear Pit**
Skansen's brown bears are firm favourites, not least in April, when the new cubs emerge.

Wolves

Bredablick is a 30-m (98-ft) high viewing tower.

Seglora Church
This shingle-roofed wooden church was built in 1729–30 in western Sweden and has an interesting interior decor with a pulpit which is even older than the church itself. It is popular for weddings.

Skåne farmstead

0 metres 100
0 yards 100

Hornborga Cottage
A timber cottage with a straw and peat roof from western Sweden shows how poorer people lived in the 19th century.

STAR FEATURES

★ Älvros Farmstead

★ Town Quarter

★ Bear Pit

Djurgårdsstaden & Beckholmen ⓫

Map 6 A4. 🚌 *44.* 🚋 *7.*
🚢 *Djurgårdsfärja.*

Behind Gröna Lund amusement park lies Djurgårdsstaden, a tranquil oasis of wooden houses, providing flats for about 200 people. The area was originally developed from a town plan drawn up around the Admiralty churchyard in 1736, to house workmen at the nearby Johan Lampas shipyards.

When the Djurgården shipyard took over in 1768 the carpenters were given the opportunity to buy their homes. The company then erected the majestic two-storey stone building at Lilla Allmänna Gränd 15–17 with offices, employees' homes and a chapel. Other buildings on this street also date from the 18th century such as Apotekshuset, the shipyard manager's residence, and Mjölnargården, now belonging to the amusement park. Several two-storey wooden houses were built on the churchyard, which had fallen into disuse, in the 19th century.

At the junction of Östra Varvsgränd and Breda Gatan is the house of the ship's carpenter Sven Månsson. Enlarged in 1749, the building still looks much as it did then, with original tiled stoves and wood fires. It is now used by the Djurgården Local Culture Society.

Lying just to the south of Djurgårdsstaden is the island of Beckholmen which, during

The Karl Johan-style Rosendals Slott on Djurgården

the 17th century, was used as a warehouse for commercial goods. It was also used to store tar and pitch. The fire hazard meant that such dangerous items could not be stored any closer to the city centre.

In 1848 the Wholesalers' Society decided to build a shipping repair yard on the island and two docks were blasted out of the solid rock on the southern side. They were later widened to accommodate more wharves. In 1917 another large dock was opened, named after King Gustaf V and they were used by the Navy and the Finnboda shipbuilding firm. The fleet moved to the island of Muskö in 1969 and Finnboda remained until 1982. The docks and houses form an unusual industrial setting. The 18th-century tar inspector's residence, the dockmaster's 19th-century home, and workmen's cottages from the 1890s are well preserved.

Door lintel, Rosendals Slott's Gold Room

Skansen ⓬

See pp96–7.

Rosendals Slott & Trädgårdar ⓭

Rosendalsvägen. **Map** 6 C3. 🚋 *7.*
Palace Tel *08-402 61 30.* 🔓 *for guided tours Jun–Aug: Tue–Sun, Sep: Sat & Sun.* 📷 *every hour noon–3pm.*
🖼 ♿ **Gardens** 🔓 *all year.* 🏠 🚻 *summer.* **www**.royalcourt.se

What was considered elsewhere as Empire style was named Karl Johan style in Sweden after King Karl XIV Johan (1818–44). One of the best examples is Rosendal Palace, built as a summer retreat for the king.

Constructed in the 1820s and designed by Fredrik Blom, a prolific architect of the era, the palace was one of Sweden's first prefabricated homes. In 1913, it was opened to the public as a museum devoted to the life and times of Karl XIV Johan and represents a pioneering work of historic restoration.

The decor is magnificent, with Swedish-made furniture and lavish textiles in wonderful colours. The carpeting and curtains are worth a visit in themselves. The dining room

Well-preserved wooden homes in Djurgårdsstaden

AN IMMORTAL TROUBADOUR

Carl Michael Bellman (1740–95) was a much-loved troubadour. Gustav III gave him a job as secretary of a lottery, but he was best known around Stockholm's many taverns – particularly on Djurgården. His works about the drunken watchmaker Jean Fredman and his contemporaries (*Fredman's Epistles and Fredman's Songs*) have never lost their popularity and form part of Sweden's musical heritage. A bust of Bellman was unveiled on Djurgården in 1829 in the presence of Queen Desideria.

Bust of Bellman by J N Byström (1829)

is fitted out in heavily woven fabric to create the impression of being in a tent. Tiled stoves are everywhere, along with some grandiose artifacts and delightful details. In front of the palace is a large bowl made in porphyry from Karl XIV's own workshops at Älvdalen in central Sweden.

Close to the palace is Rosendals Trädgårdar, a biodynamic market garden managed by a foundation since 1984. Its aim is not just to use biodynamic cultivation methods but also to run courses, lectures and exhibitions. Plants are available to buy at the shop and there is a café.

Waldemarsudde ⓮

Prins Eugens Väg 6. **Map** 6 C4.
Tel 08-545 837 00. 🚌 47. 🚃 7.
⭕ 11am–8pm Tue–Thu, 11am–5pm Fri–Sun. 🚻 ♿ 🅿 🔔 🚻 📷
www.waldemarsudde.com

Prince Eugen's Waldemarsudde, which passed into State ownership after his death in 1947, is one of Sweden's most visited art museums. The prince was trained as a military officer but became a successful artist and was one of the leading landscape painters of his generation. He produced monumental paintings for Kungliga Operan, Kungliga Dramatiska Teatern and Rådhuset. Among his own works hanging in Waldemarsudde, his former home, are three of his most prized paintings: *Spring* (1891), *The Old Castle* (1893) and *The Cloud* (1896).

Based on works by his contemporaries, the collection represents early 20th-century Swedish art with names like Oscar Björck, Carl Fredrik Hill, Richard Bergh, Nils Kreuger, Eugène Jansson, Bruno Liljefors and Anders Zorn.

Prince Eugen was a generous patron to the next generation – for example, the group known as "The Young Ones" – so works by younger artists like Isaac Grünewald, Einar Jolin, Sigrid Hjertén and Leander Engström are also in the collection. Sculptors of the same era are well represented, particularly works by Per Hasselberg which can be seen in the gallery and the park.

Along with the architect Ferdinand Boberg, Prince Eugen drew up the sketches for the house, completed in 1905. The same architect was called in later to plan the gallery, which was finished in 1913. This now includes parts of the collection of some 2,000 works, as well as the Prince's own paintings.

The guest apartments remain largely unchanged to this day, and the two upper floors withthe Prince's studio at the top are used for temporary exhibitions.

Hornsgatan (1902) by Eugène Jansson, in Thielska Galleriet

Thielska Galleriet ⓯

Sjötullsbacken 6–8.
Map 7 F4. **Tel** 08-662 58 84.
🚌 69. ⭕ noon–4pm daily.
📷 by appt. ♿ 🅿
www.thielska-galleriet.se

When the magnificent apartments of the banker Ernest Thiel (1860–1947) on Strandvägenstarted to overflow with his excellent collection of contemporary paintings, he commissioned the well-known architect Ferdinand Boberg to design a dignified villa on Djurgården.

However, during World War I Thiel lost most of his fortune. In 1924, the State bought his collection, mostly covering Nordic art from the late 19th and early 20th centuries, and opened Thielska Galleriet in his villa 2 years later.

Thiel was regarded as something of a rebel in the banking world and he was particularly fond of works by painters in the Artists' Union, which had been formed in 1886 to counter the influence of the traditionalist Konstakademien *(see p66)*.

There are paintings by all the major Swedish artists who formed an artists' colony at Grèz-sur-Loing, south of Paris, such as Carl Larsson, Bruno Liljefors, Karl Nordström and August Strindberg. And there are paintings by Eugène Jansson, Anders Zorn and PrinceEugen, as well as wooden figures by Axel Petersson and sculptures by Christian Eriksson. Thiel also acquired works by foreign artists, not least his good friend Edvard Munch.

Prince Eugen's Waldemarsudde, seen from the water

MALMARNA & FURTHER AFIELD

As Stockholm started to grow, the heart of the city, Gamla Stan, became cramped and building spread out to the surrounding areas, known as "Malmarna" (the "ore hills"). Parts of these now make up present-day Stockholm.

Södermalm came into the ownership of the city in 1436. Much of Stockholm's old charm can still be found in the areas around Fjällgatan, Mosebacke and Mariaberget. To the north, the Norrmalm area expanded rapidly and became known as Stockholm's northern suburb in the 17th century. Much of Vasastan is a residential area, but in recent years it has become popular because of its wide choice of restaurants. The once-rural Östermalm

Window on Vikingagatan

was transformed in the late 19th century into an affluent residential area with grand, wide boulevards, contrasting with the 1930s Functionalist style of the adjoining Gärdet district. This is the location of some of Stockholm's most important museums, including Historiska museet with its impressive Gold Room, and Folkens Museum Etnografiska.

To the west is Kungsholmen, the centre for local government, with distinguished buildings like Stadshuset (the City Hall) and Rådhuset (the Law Court). Ekoparken (the National City Park), the first of its kind in the world, is a green area of ecological and cultural interest surrounding the city and reaching into its central districts.

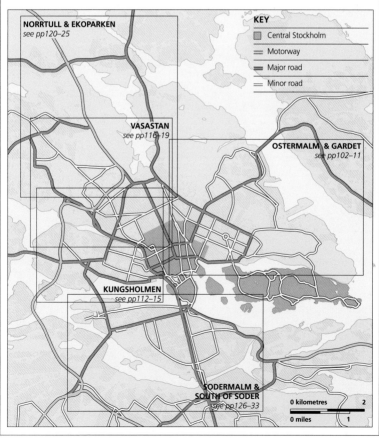

NORRTULL & EKOPARKEN
see pp120–25

KEY

▢ Central Stockholm

═ Motorway

▬ Major road

═ Minor road

VASASTAN
see pp116–19

OSTERMALM & GARDET
see pp102–11

KUNGSHOLMEN
see pp112–15

**SODERMALM &
SOUTH OF SODER**
see pp126–33

0 kilometres 2

0 miles 1

◁ **Stadshuset with Norr Mälarstrand on Kungsholmen and the Västerbron bridge in the background**

Östermalm & Gärdet

The four wide boulevards, Strandvägen, Karlavägen, Narvavägen and Valhallavägen, were created around 1870–80 as part of the development of Östermalm into one of the city's most affluent residential districts, adjoining the extensive green area of Ladugårdsgärde. Apart from embassies and the headquarters of Swedish Radio and TV, four leading museums are located in this green oasis, as well as Kaknästornet. The area between Östermalm and the former military exercise grounds was developed in the 1930s with housing in the clean lines of the Functionalist style typical of the period.

Housing at Karlaplan, built in the late 19th century

SIGHTS AT A GLANCE

Berwaldhallen ⑤
Diplomatstaden ⑥
Engelbrektskyrkan ⑱
Etnografiska museet ⑩
Filmhuset ⑬
Försvarshögskolan ⑮

Gärdet ⑨
Historiska museet (see pp104–5) ②
Kaknästornet ⑪
Karlavägen ③
Ladugårdsgärde ⑫
Sjöhistoriska museet ⑦

Stadion ⑯
Strandvägen ①
Sveriges Radio och TV ④
Tekniska Högskolan ⑰
Tekniska museet ⑧
Tessinparken ⑭

KEY

▨ Central Stockholm

▬ Major street

═ Other street

Ⓣ Tunnelbana station

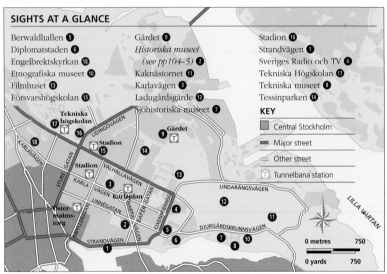

Strandvägen ①

Map 5 E1. 🚌 69, 76.
Ⓣ *Östermalmstorg, Karlaplan.* 🚊 7.

In the early 1900s Stockholm's 10 richest citizens lived in palatial new houses along Strandvägen. Seven of them were wholesale merchants. Up to 1897's major exhibition on Djurgården, the hilly and muddy former Ladugårdslands Strandgata had been moving

towards the goal of becoming "a street, the like of which will not be found anywhere else in Europe". It was a long process. Even after all the stately buildings had been completed the wooden quay erected in the 1860s was something of an eyesore. It was still used up to the 1940s by boats bringing fire wood from the archipelago islands.

All the same, Strandvägen and its three rows of lime

trees soon became the elegant boulevard envisaged and, then as now, it was a popular place for admiring the elegant façades, watching the boats and to see and be seen.

The financiers behind the housing projects of the early 1900s were wealthy and could call on the best architects, including I G Clason (1856–1930). Clason was influenced by Italian and French Renaissance styles for his work on No. 19–21 (Thaveniuska Huset) and No. 29–35 (Bünsowska Huset), where he designed gateways made of ship's timbers. No. 55 (Von Rosenska Palatset) was also created by him.

Strandvägen with stately houses and boats along the quayside

Historiska museet ②

See pp104–5.

Karlavägen 3

Map 3 E3. Ⓣ *Karlaplan, Stadion.* 🚌 *1, 42, 44.*

Until 1885 Karlavägen was known as Esplanaden, a 42-m (138-ft) wide avenue planted with lime trees and flower beds. Towards the end of the 19th century several impressive houses were built there, many in Neo-Renaissance style. The street has retained its character as a grand boulevard despite a lot of building and the arrival of shops and offices.

A major development was undertaken in the 1960s when the central section of the road was gradually converted into an open-air sculpture gallery. At the crossroads with Engelbrektsgatan is *The City* by Lars Erik Husberg; at Villagatan a female figure by the French sculptor Paul Cornet; at Floragatan Gunnar Nilsson's *Mimi*, which can also be seen at other places in the city; at Sturegatan *Living Iron* by Willy Gordon, a gift from the LKAB mining company, whose head office at No. 45 acquired a façade relief by Eric Grate in 1970. Also situated at this crossroads is *Scatola* by the Italian sculptor Arnoldo Pomodoro.

At Nybroplan is *Man – Horse – Carriage* by Asmund Arle; at Sibyllegatan *Woman with Hand Mirror* by Ebba Ahlmark-Hughes; in front of Östra Real a bust of the author August Blanche (1811–68) by Aron Sandberg; the secondary school building designed by Ragnar Östberg with sculptures by Carl Eldh; at Grevgatan *Incoming Sea* by Håkan Bonds; at Karlaplan a marble sculpture by Gert Marcus; at Tysta Gatan *Jeanette* by Curt Thorsjö; and at Banérgatan Urn by Hedy Jolly-Dahlström. Finally at No. 100 is the long Garrison administration building with a sculpture group at the entrance, a work in glazed stoneware by Gustav Kraitz.

The fountain and round pond at Karlaplan were added in 1929. *The Aviator* is by Carl Milles and was unveiled 2 years later.

Swedish Television's main building at Gärdet, next to Swedish Radio's headquarters

Radio- och TV-husen 4

Oxenstiernsgatan 20 & 34. **Map** 6 A1. Ⓣ *Karlaplan.* 🚌 *4, 56, 76.* **SR Tel** 08-784 50 00. 📷 *by appt.* ♿ **www**.sr.se **SVT Tel** 08-784 00 00. 📷 *by appt.* ♿ **www**.svt.se

The headquarters of Swedish Radio (SR) and Swedish Television (SVT) take up a 12 ha (30 acres) site alongside Ladugårdsgärde. The area's long history as a military training depot is reflected by several old buildings once used for stores. Now it is the site not just of the modern radio and TV buildings designed by the architects Erik Ahnborg and Sune Lindström but also of three old buildings with military connections: the gunpowder cellar from 1717, the old stone coach-house from 1750, and the Karl Johan storehouses from 1820. Both architects also designed Berwaldhallen *(see p106)*, the concert hall, which is linked to SR and SVT by a tunnel.

Swedish Radio started its transmissions from Malmskillnadsgatan on 1 January 1925. It moved to No. 8 Kungsgatan in 1928 and into its new premises in 1961.

SVT started transmissions from the Svea Artillery Regiment's old premises on 24 October 1954. In 1969 it moved into the new TV building in the former barracks area, where an office block was added 4 years later. Additions in 1983–7 included abuilding for news broadcasts. SVT now covers an area of 51,600 sq m (555,220 sq ft) with eight studios, three of which are used for news programmes.

Fountain on Karlaplan at the end of the tree-lined Karlavägen

---

BOATS ALONG STRANDVÄGEN

Until the 1940s sailing vessels used to carry firewood from Roslagen on the Baltic coast to the quayside at Strandvägen. This trade had lost its importance by the 1950s, and boating enthusiasts started buying up these old vessels. Some were

Old wood-carrying boats along the Strandvägen quay

renovated and sailed to the Caribbean, others became illegal drinking or gambling clubs on Strandvägen. New harbour regulations led to the formation of two associations to administer the boats. About 40 have survived and are owned by people who want to preserve a piece of cultural heritage. By every boat there is a sign describing its history.

Historiska museet ❷

Sweden's Historiska museet (National Historical Museum) was opened in 1943. It was designed by Bengt Romare and Georg Sherman. Bror Marklund (1907–77) was responsible for the decoration around the entrance and the richly detailed bronze gateways depicting events in early Swedish history. The museum originally made its name with its exhibits from the Viking era, as well as its outstanding collections from the early Middle Ages. Contemporary church textiles are also on show. Many of Historiska museet's gold treasures have been gathered together to form one of Stockholm's most remarkable sights, Guldrummet (the Gold Room).

Upper floor

Bronze Age Find
This Bronze Age artifact, thought to be a percussion instrument, was discovered in a bog in southern Sweden in 1847.

Courtyard

★ The Alunda Elk
This 21-cm (8-inch) stone axe, discovered in 1920 at Alunda in central Sweden, resembles an elk's head. It is a ceremonial axe, probably made in Finland or Karelia in around 2000 BC.

Ground floor

Rosen-gården

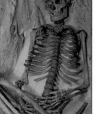

The Bäckaskog Woman
The 155-cm (5-ft) long Bäcka-skog woman lived around 5000 BC. She died at the age of 40–50 and was buried sitting in a cramped pit.

The Viking Era
This eventful era is reflected in a department, whose exhibits include a Viking sword with artistic embellish-ments, and or naments in the shape of Nordic animals.

STAR EXHIBITS

★ The Alunda Elk

★ Maria from Viklau

★ The Gold Room

The Skog Tapestry
This once hung in the wooden church at Skog in northern Sweden. It is one of the museum's oldest textile treasures.

Baroque Hall

History of Sweden

Stairs descending to the Gold Room

Main entrance

★ **Maria from Viklau**
This Madonna figure without child is the best-preserved example from Sweden's early medieval period. The colourful wooden sculpture is richly gilded.

VISITOR'S CHECKLIST

Narvavägen 13–17. **Map** 3 F4.
Tel 08-51 95 56 00. 📧 44, 56.
🚇 Karlaplan. ⬜ May–Sep:
10am–5pm daily; Oct–Apr:
11am–5pm Tue–Sun, 11am–8pm
Thu. ⬤ 24, 25 & 31 Dec. 📷 ♿
🚫 The Gold Room. 🖥 📷
www.historiska.se

GALLERY GUIDE
The exhibitions are divided chronologically on two floors with the prehistoric section on the ground floor and the Middle Ages on the upper floor, where there is also a Baroque Hall. In the basement, reached by a staircase from the entrance hall, is the Gold Room with priceless exhibits from prehistoric times to the medieval period.

KEY

🟦	Prehistoric Era
⬜	Middle Ages and Baroque
⬜	Temporary exhibitions
⬜	Non-exhibition space

★ **THE GOLD ROOM**
Since the early 1990s the museum's many priceless gold artifacts have been on show in Guldrummet (the Gold Room), a 700-sq m (7,500-sq ft) underground vault built with 250 tons of reinforced concrete to ensure security. The room is in two circular sections. The inner section houses the main collection, with 50 kg (110 lb) of gold treasures and 250 kg (550 lb) of silver from the Bronze Age to the Middle Ages.

The Elisabeth Reliquary was originally a drinking goblet which was mounted with gold and precious stones in the 11th century. In about 1230 a silver cover was added to enclose the skull of St Elisabeth. In 1631 it was seized as a trophy for Sweden during the Thirty Years War.

The Gold Collars were found between 1827 and 1864; the three-ringed collar in a stone quarry in eastern Sweden, the five-ringed in a ditch on the island of Öland, and the seven-ringed hanging on a spike in a barn.

The underground Gold Room in Historiska museet

Berwaldhallen, concert hall of the Swedish Radio Symphony Orchestra

Berwaldhallen ❺

Dag Hammarskiölds väg 3.
Map 6 A2. **Tel** 08-784 18 00.
🚇 Karlaplan. 🚌 56, 69, 76.
🕐 noon–6pm Mon–Fri. 📵 📷 🔲 🍴
www.berwaldhallen.se

On 30 November 1979 the
Swedish Radio Symphony
Orchestra and the Radio
Chorus acquired their own
concert hall, Berwaldhallen.
Since then the hall has
become a national showcase
for Swedish music. It is
named after Franz Berwald
(1796–1868), one of Sweden's
greatest composers. The
architects Erik Ahnborg and
Sune Lindström won an
award for their "wonderful
and sensitively designed
concert hall". Hans Viksten,
Hertha Hillfon and other
artists undertook the
decoration of the foyer.
Nature has made its own
contribution in the form of
untouched areas of rock,
which were blasted out to
accommodate two-thirds of
the six-sided building.
    The Swedish Radio Sym-
phony Orchestra and Radio
Chorus give between 70 and
80 performances every season
in the hall, which has established it as an internationally
renowned concert stage,
attracting audiences of 150,000
a year. Visiting ensembles
from all over the world also
perform here. In late August
the hall hosts the annual
Baltic Sea Festival in which
Swedish orchestras perform
well-known classical pieces.

Diplomatstaden ❻

Map 6 A2. 🚇 Karlaplan. 🚌 56,
69, 76.

The elegant villas which gave
the area of Diplomatstaden
its name stretch along
Nobelgatan and the eastern
part of Strandvägen (from
No. 74). The first house for a
foreign diplomat was built in
the 1910s, when the British
ambassador moved into
Nobelgatan 7. Nearby is
Engelska Kyrkan (the English
Church), which was built in
the city centre in the 1860s
but was moved to the
diplomatic quarter in 1913.
In the 1980s the church was
finally completed with the
addition of an octagonal
parish hall. Villa Bonnier at
No. 13 was designed by
Ragnar Östberg and was a gift
to the State by a prominent
publishing family. It is now
used by the Government for
official functions.
    The embassies of Hungary,
Turkey, South Korea, Norway,
Germany, the UK and USA are
all located in or near the area.
Nobelparken, the park
adjoining the embassies, is
named after the scientist
Alfred Nobel (1833–96). In the
early 20th century plans for a
Nobel Palace in the park were
drawn up by the architect
Ferdinand Boberg, but the
project never came to fruition.
On the north side of
Strandvägen is the Törner
Villa, a heritage wooden
house built in 1880. The villa
is named after a firemaster at
Nobel's gunpowder factory.

Sjöhistoriska museet ❼

Djurgårdsbrunnsvägen 24.
Map 6 C2. **Tel** 08-519 549 00.
🚌 69. 🕐 10am–5pm daily. 📷 📹
♿ 🔲 🍴 www.sjohistoriska.se

The National Maritime
Museum's architectural
design and location on
Djurgårdsbrunnsviken are
worthy of a country with a
long coastline and numerous
archipelagos and lakes.
Sjöhistoriska museet focuses
on shipping, shipbuilding and
naval defence, and there are
fascinating exhibits, both
permanent and temporary,
on these themes.
    There are some 100,000
exhibits, including more than
1,500 model ships. The oldest
ship was built in the 17th
century and the oldest Swedish
vessel is a reproduction of
the so-called "Cathedral ship"
from the early 1600s. The
collections include every
conceivable type of ship –
from small coasters and
Viking longboats to oil
tankers, coal vessels, dinghies,
full-riggers and submarines.

Majestic buildings in the diplomatic quarter at Djurgårdsbrunnsviken

A series of models on a scale of 1:200 show the development of ships in Scandinavia from the Iron Age to the present day.

There are also full-scale settings, which give a good idea of life on board the ships. Among them are the beautiful original cabin and elegant stern from the royal schooner *Amphion*. The ship was built at the Djurgården shipyard and designed by the leading shipbuilder F H Chapman. It was Gustav III's flagship in the 1788–90 war with Russia. Contrasting with this is the cramped and damp-preserved forecastle from the schooner *Hoppet*, where four crew members ate, slept and spent their time off watch.

The galley *Lodbrok*, one of many maritime models at Sjöhistoriska museet

The museum has some notable examples of ship decoration from the late 17th century. They include part of the national coat of arms recovered by divers in the 1920s from the stern of the *Riksäpplet*, which sank at Dalarö in 1676. When *Carolus XI*, an 82-cannon ship, was launched from the shipyard in Stockholm in 1678 the stern had a large relief portrayal of Karl XI on horseback. The relief was possibly removed some years later when the ship was renamed *Sverige*, but it was saved and is now in the museum. There are many fine figureheads in the collection, including one depicting Amphion, the son of Zeus, playing his lyre, which once adorned the schooner of the same name.

Linked to the museum is the Swedish Marine Archaeology Archive, which contains a mass of information, including a complete listing of shipwrecks with 10,000 entries from 1720 to the

Figurehead, about 1850

present day. The ship-design archive has documents covering most eras of maritime history and is used extensively by researchers. The photographic collection has 300,000 pictures, while the library covers all aspects of seafaring and war at sea. There is a special children's section with a workshop which is open on Saturdays, Sundays and during school holidays. During the summer a dinghy-sailing school is arranged for children aged 8–14.

The attractive museum building was one of the architect Ragnar Östberg's last works and was opened in 1938. On the gable facing Djurgårdsbrunnsviken is *The Sailor*, a monument to the victims of naval war by Nils Sjögren.

Tekniska museet ⑧

Museivägen 7. **Map** 6 C2.
Tel 08-450 56 00. 🚌 69. 🕐 10am–5pm Mon–Tue, Thu–Fri, 11am–8pm Wed, 11am–5pm Sat & Sun. 🅿 by appointment. 📷 ♿ 🎁 🚻 ☕
www.tekniskamuseet.se

Anyone planning to visit the Museum of Science and Technology should allow plenty of time. Throughout the 20th century it accumulated a wealth of exhibits connected with Sweden's technical and industrial history. It has 12,000 sq m (129,000 sq ft) of well-stocked exhibition space plus a library with 50,000 volumes and a large collection of technical magazines. It is also the home of Sweden's first Science Centre, Teknorama, with many "hands on" experiments aimed particularly at children and young people.

The machinery hall is the largest exhibition area with many powered machines from different eras. Among them is the country's oldest preserved steam engine, built in 1832 and once used in a coal mine in southern Sweden. The classic T-Ford is there, too, as well as early Swedish cars from Volvo, Scania and Saab.

The museum also has sections on the history of telecommunications and the computer, electric power, book-printing and the Swedish forestry industry. The mining and processing of iron and steel is also highlighted.

Ericsson telephone made in 1903 for Czar Nicholas II

Gärdet **9**

Rindögatan. Ⓣ *Gärdet*.
www.housingprototypes.org

Gärdet, one of the largest
residential neighbourhoods in
Stockholm, was built as the
result of a design competition
in the late 1920s, at a time
when the Swedish Modern
movement was in full swing.
The competition was won by
the architect Arvid Stille and
this area exhibits the graceful
form of Functionalism for
which Sweden became known
at the time, and which
continues to exert a strong
influence to this day. One
characteristic of Swedish
architecture from that period
was the emphasis it placed on
decoration whilst still adhering
to the basic principles of
Functionalist ideology.

The individual buildings in
Gärdet were designed and
built between 1935 and 1939
by a variety of architects,
including Sture Fröhlén, Albin
Stark, Ernst Grönwall, Wolter
Gahn, Björn Hedvall and
Swen Wallander, all within
Stille's overall plan.

Etnografiska museet **10**

Djurgårdsbrunnsvägen 34. **Map** 6 C2.
Tel 08-519 550 00. 🚌 69. ⏰ 10am–
5pm Mon–Tue & Thu–Fri, 10am–8pm
Wed, 11am–5pm Sat & Sun. 🅿 📷
♿ 🏪 🛒 🏛 www.etnografiska.se

The National Museum of
Ethnography is a showcase
for the collections brought
home to Sweden by travellers
and scientists from the 18th
century to the present day.
The imaginative displays are
intended to offer visitors not
only a better understanding of
the unknown or unfamiliar
from around the world,
but also of the cultural
connections between
such far-off places
and Sweden
through explaining
how and why the
objects came into
the museum's
collection.

The explorer Sven
Hedin (1865–1952),
who was the last
Swede to be ennobled (in
1902), contributed many
exhibits, including Buddha
figures and Chinese costumes,
as well as Mongolian temple
tents donated by leaders of
the Kalmuck people in western
China to King Gustav V.

A Japanese tea house, built
by 15 Japanese craftsmen to a
design by Professor Masao
Nakamura, was opened in
1990. It is a work of art in
itself, offering a space for
reflection and meditation
within a traditional setting.
During the summer months
visitors can take part in tea
ceremonies, while at other
times the house can be
viewed from outside.

Another section of interest
is dedicated to the native
peoples of North America.
Here there are masks, textiles
and ceramics from various
tribes, as well as totem poles
from western Canada.

Closer to home, the
museum also reflects upon
the multicultural influences

Religious mask from British Columbia

on Sweden brought about by
the large-scale immigration
into the country in the late
20th century.

Alongside the permanent
displays, the museum puts on
a changing series of
temporary exhibitions
highlighting different
aspects of the
collection. Every
year since 1936 it
has published the
international
magazine *Ethnos*.
There is also a good
reference library.
Visitors can
sample foods from
around the world in the
museum's bar-restaurant
"Babajan". Here you can try
one of 20 kinds of tea or
choose from an impressive
list of international beers. The
food is mainly African, Asian
and Middle Eastern.

Kaknästornet **11**

Ladugårdsgärdet. **Map** 7 D1.
Tel 08-667 21 05. 🚌 69.
⏰ Jun–Aug: 9am–10pm daily;
Sep–May: 10am–9pm daily. 🅿 by
appointment. 🏛 📷 ♿ 🏪 🛒 🏪

Anchored by 72 steel poles,
each one driven 8 m (26 ft)
into the rock, the 34-storey
Kaknästornet soars to a height
of 155 m (508 ft). The tower,
designed by the architects
Bengt Lindroos and Hans
Borgström, was opened in
1967. It was erected as a
centre for the country's
television and radio broad-
casting and also contains
technical equipment to
conduct conferences by

The Japanese tea house in the gardens of the Etnografiska museet

Kaknästornet with the buildings of Sjöhistoriska museet, Tekniska museet and Etnografiska museet in the foreground

satellite between European cities. Five dishes to the left of the tower – the largest of which has a diameter of 13 m (43 ft) – relay signals to and from satellites. The main hall containing the transmitters and receivers has been blasted out of the rock below the dishes.

The observation points on levels 30 and 31 provide a spectacular view of the city, and the restaurant on the 28th floor has panoramic windows. It is reached by two lifts, travelling at 18 km/h (11 mph). The restaurant also runs a busy tourist information office at the entrance level, selling souvenirs, maps and the Stockholm Card (see p190). Decorative features include a wall relief by Walter Bengtsson, which was inspired by the tower's daunting technology.

Ladugårdsgärde ⓬

Map 6 C1. 🚌 1, 69, 76.

As early as the 15th century there was a royal farm on the site where the Nobel Park now stands. After 250 years it had outlived its usefulness and for a few centuries it was used as a training area for the Stockholm garrison. Between Kungliga Borgen (Royal Fortress) and Hakberget are the remains of Karl XI's fort from 1672, which was largely rebuilt in time for the World Equestrian Championships, held here in 1990. During the 20th century what became

known simply as Gärdet lost its military role. In the early 1900s the area was used for May Day processions, and car races were staged here around 1920.

The fortress of Kungliga Borgen is a relic of the military training era, and it was from here that Karl XIV Johan used to watch his troops manoeuvring. He rode from here to Rosendal Palace on Djurgården (see p98) via a pontoon bridge near the present-day National Maritime Museum. The fortress was badly damaged by fire in October 1977, but it has since been rebuilt to its original appearance. A restaurant is open during the summer.

Something is always going on in Gärdet. It is the starting point for major fun runs and the venue for kite-flying festivals, and is used by the city's balloonists. It is also a favourite place to exercise horses and dogs.

Filmhuset ⓭

Borgvägen 1–5. **Map** 6 B1.
Tel 08-665 11 00. 🚇 Karlaplan.
🚌 56, 72, 76. ⬜ 8am–6pm
Mon–Thu, 8am–5pm Fri. **Film club, library & archives** ring for details.
♿ 🍴 🎬 www.sfi.se

The production of quality Swedish films is supported by the Swedish Film Institute. The institute also acts as guardian of the country's cinematic heritage and promotes Swedish films both at home and abroad. From 1971, all its activities were brought under one roof in Filmhuset, a Modernist structure by P Celsing.

The institute's archives include more than 18,000 films. Also there is a comprehensive library and a film database, accessible on the Internet. The institute publishes the *Film Annual*, and organizes the Film Gala at which the Gold Beetle prizes are presented. The film club shows Swedish and international films daily in their original languages.

Filmhuset, home of the Film Institute and Dramatic Institute

INGMAR BERGMAN

The playwright and producer Ingmar Bergman was born at Östermalm in 1918. His long series of masterly films made

Ingmar Bergman (1918–2007)

him world-famous, but he started his career in the theatre. From 1963–6 he was Director of Dramatiska Teatern, where he remained a guest producer. He created more than 100 theatrical productions. His most acclaimed are *Smiles of the Summer Night* (1955), *The Seventh Seal* (1957) and his final film *Fanny and Alexander* (1982), which won him four Oscars. He will also be remembered for his problematic private life, which his films often depicted.

Tessinparken, surrounded by Functionalist-style housing dating from the late 1930s

Tessinparken & Nedre Gärdet ⑭

Map 3 F2. Ⓣ *Karlaplan, Gärdet.* 🚌 *1, 4, 72.*

Three generations of the Tessin family of architects (*see p37*) have given their name to this park opened at Lower Gärdet in 1931. Tessinparken runs from north to south and is attractively designed with lawns, play areas, paths and ponds. The adjoining houses, built between 1932–7, have their own gardens and blend in such a way that they give the impression of being part of the park itself.

The earliest houses, nearest to Valhallavägen, still show signs of 1920s Classicism, although Gärdet's real hallmark is Functionalism (*see p37*). The lower white houses along Askrikegatan are Functionalist in style and noticeably different from other buildings in Gärdet. They mark the northern boundary of the park. Some 60 different architects were involved in designing the Gärdet development, including Sture Frölén.

A granite statue of a woman with a suitcase, *Housewife's Holiday*, stands in the part of Tessin Park adjoining Valhallavägen. It was made by Olof Thorwald Ohlsson in the 1970s. At the other end of the park is a colourful concrete statue, *The Egg*, by Egon Möller-Nielsen.

Functionalist façade at Tessinparken

Försvarshögskolan ⑮

Valhallavägen 117. **Map** 3 E2. 🚌 *4, 62, 72.* Ⓣ *Stadion.* 🌑 *to the public.*

Two decorative cannons, an aircraft propeller and an 18th-century anchor guard the entrance to Försvarshögskolan (the Military Academy). The building has been sympathetically renovated and appears to be lower than it really is because the adjoining Valhallavägen was built at a higher level.

It was originally the base for the Svea Artillery Regiment and is one of many notable military buildings designed by the architect Ernst Jacobsson. After Nybrogatan was blasted out through the Tyskbagarbergen hill, the regimental building provided a backdrop to the newly extended street.

The regiment moved out in 1949 to make way first for Swedish Radio and later for the Military Academy, in whose present gym Swedish

The restored façade of Försvarshögskolan (Military Academy) on Valhallavägen

TV started. A plaque reads: "From this building the first regular television programme was transmitted on 24 October 1954."

Stadion ⑯

Lidingövägen 1–3. **Map** 3 E2. *Tel* 08-508 283 51. Ⓣ *Stadion.* 🚌 *4, 55, 72, 73.* 🌑 *15 Apr–15 Oct.* 📷 *during events.* ♿ 🍴 💻

A new main arena was built for the 1912 Olympic Games in Stockholm. The architect of Stadion, Torben Grut (1871–1945), followed the National Romantic influences of the day. His design was based on his own interpretation of the commission to build a stadium "using modern construction methods adapted from traditional medieval brick-building techniques". It is no coincidence that the arena, which is the world's oldest Olympic stadium still in use, is often known as the "Stadium Fortress".

In addition to the 1912 Olympics, the stadium has also been the venue for ice hockey and bandy (a type of hockey) championships, the European Athletics Championships in 1958, and the World Equestrian Championships in 1990. The stadium is renowned for athletics events, and stages an international athletics gala every summer.

Stadion is listed as a heritage building and its twin towers are a familiar landmark. The complex is richly decorated. The clock tower has two figures by Carl Fagerberg, *Ask and Embla*, the counterparts of Adam and Eve in Nordic mythology. There are also busts of Victor Balck, the man behind the 1912 Olympics; P H Ling, the father of Swedish gymnastics; and Edwin Wide, the "flying teacher", who was a leading opponent of the Finnish master-athlete Paavo Nurmi in long-distance races during the 1920s.

Bruno Liljefors's statue *Play* outside Stadion

Four notable sculptures were added in the 1930s. The painter and gymnast Bruno Liljefors created *Play* at the main entrance, Carl Eldh made *The Runners*, and Carl Fagerberg provided *Relay Runners* and *The Shot-Putter*.

Tekniska Högskolan ⑰

Valhallavägen 79. **Map** 3 D1.
Ⓣ *Tekniska högskolan.* 🚌 4, 72, 73.

The renowned higher education establishment, Tekniska Högskolan, accounts for one-third of Sweden's technical research and engineering education at university level. It has 15,000 students, 1,000 active research students and a staff of 2,500. It was founded in 1827, and since 1917 its campus has been housed in heritage buildings on Valhallavägen, as well as in the suburbs of Haninge and Kista, and outside Stockholm in Södertälje, Gävle and Visby.

The main building on Valhallavägen was designed by Erik Lallerstedt and its opening in October 1917 was a milestone in Sweden's technological development.

The architect commissioned several contemporary artists to decorate the austere technical environment, so it has become something of an artistic treasure trove. The sculptors and painters whose works adorn the buildings included Einar Forseth, Olle Hjertzberg, Georg Pauli, Ivar Johnsson, Axel Törneman, Hilding Linnqvist and Carl Milles. Milles was also responsible for the fountain sculpture, *The Industrial Monument*, which rests on a marble base in the courtyard facing Valhallavägen.

Early in the 20th century the main building underwent a painstaking renovation. The surrounding park was also restored to its original state.

Engelbrektskyrkan & Lärkstaden ⑱

Östermalmsgatan 20. **Map** 3 D2.
Ⓣ *Tekniska högskolan.* 🚌 1, 42.
Engelbrektskyrkan Tel 08-406 98 00. ⭕ *11am–3pm Tue–Sun.* 🚻 *11am Sun, 11:30am Thu.* ♿ 🅿

One of Sweden's leading Jugendstil architects, Lars Israel Wahlman, designed the Engelbrekt Church as a result of winning an architectural competition in 1906. The church was opened on 25 January 1914 in the presence of King Gustaf V.

Engelbrektskyrkan gives the appearance of thrusting out from the rocks, and it dominates the surrounding area with its slender brick tower. In the chancel, the monumental paintings are by Olle Hjortzberg (1872–1959). The sculptor Tore Strindberg (1882–1968) was commissioned for the stucco reliefs both in the chancel and above the main entrance. Filip Månsson executed the frescoes in the west portico and elsewhere. The nave is the highest in Scandinavia, and the arches inside the church are supported by eight granite pillars.

Engelbrektskyrkan is located in Lärkstaden, a quarter which was developed around 1910 and is characterized by dark red façades and tiled roofs that blend in well with the church. The area has winding streets and natural differences in level – inspired partly by Austrian patterns.

Engelbrektskyrkan, dominating the surrounding area of Lärkstaden

---

ARENA FOR RECORDS

No other athletics arena can compete with Stockholm's Stadion when it comes to world records. The 1912 Olympics gave the statistics a flying start with 11 world records. The gold medallist Ted Meredith's time of 1 min 51.9 sec in the 800-m event can be compared with Wilson Kipketer's 1997 time of 1 min 41.73 sec over the same distance; the last world record set at Stadion. It has recorded a total of 83 world records. London is second with 68 and Los Angeles is third with 66 records. The top Swedish runner of the 1940s, Gunder Hägg, set seven world records and the Finn, Paavo Nurmi, had six.

Running track at Stadion, 1912

Kungsholmen

Once best known for its handicrafts and small industries, Kungsholmen changed in the late 19th century with the emergence of new apartment blocks and institutional buildings. By the early 1900s the area had a different status, exemplified by Ragnar Östberg's Stadshuset (city hall) – Stockholm's most notable architectural project of the 20th century – and Carl Westman's majestic Rådhuset (law court). These were followed by the elegant waterfront houses along Norr Mälarstrand. The area has a high concentration of government buildings, but it also offers many venues for entertainment and nightlife.

Stately buildings on Norr Mälarstrand line the Riddarfjärden waterfront

SIGHTS AT A GLANCE

Marieberg **6**
Norr Mälarstrand **3**
Rådhuset **2**
Rålambshovsparken **4**
Stadshuset (see pp114–15) **1**
Västerbron **5**

KEY

■ Central Stockholm
━ Motorway
━ Major road
━ Minor road
Ⓣ Tunnelbana station

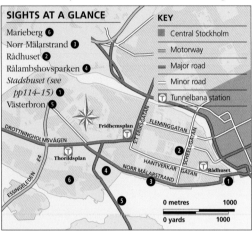

0 metres 1000
0 yards 1000

Stadshuset **1**

See pp114–15.

Rådhuset **2**

Scheelegatan 7. **Map** 2 A5.
Ⓣ *Rådhuset.* 🚌 *40, 52.*

In the early 20th century, the intention was to build a combined city hall and law court, but the plans changed when two separate architectural competitions were launched. The winning entry for Rådhuset (the law court), was a design by Carl Westman (1866–1936), who became a leading exponent of the National Romantic School along with Ragnar Östberg (1866–1945), architect of Stadshuset. Building began in 1911, and

Rådhuset was opened in December 1915. In his design, Westman drew inspiration from the Vasa Renaissance of the 16th century and was probably influenced by Vadstena Castle in southern Sweden. Rådhuset, with its prominent tower, is one of the best examples of the National Romantic style, but its solid scale also shows Jugendstil influences.

The sculptors Christian Eriksson and the brothers Aron and Gustaf Sandberg were responsible for the decoration, which also includes paintings by Olle Hjortzberg and Filip Månsson. Beside the staircase on the fifth floor is a copy of *Kopparmatte*, the pillory which once stood on Stortorget in Gamla Stan. The original pillory is at Stockholms Stadsmuseum *(see p127).*

Rådhuset, exterior detail

Norr Mälarstrand **3**

Map 1 C3. Ⓣ *Rådhuset, Fridhemsplan.* 🚌 *40, 52.*

When industries like textiles and dyeing left Norr Mälarstrand in the early 20th century, work began on exploiting Kungsholmen's attractive location along the bay of Riddarfjärden. Gradually an exclusive residential area emerged. During World War II a sculpture park was developed along the waterfront, where the excursion boats and vintage coasters are moored today. Willow, poplar, alder and birch trees thrive along the shoreline. A pavilion with a summer café stands on pillars above the water. It was designed by Erik Glemme, assistant to the city's master gardener Holger Blom (born 1906).

The architect of Stadshuset, Ragnar Östberg, designed Norr Mälarstrand 76. Cyrillus Johansson, Sven Wallander and J Norberg were the architects of Nos. 26, 28 and 30, where the figures on the gables above the steps were created by the metal craftsman Ragnar Myrsmeden. There is much to see in the small side streets, including the façades of No. 5 Jacob Westins Gata (architect Harald Wadsjö) and No. 9 Skillinggränd. The original service-flat building at No. 6 John Erikssongatan was designed by Sven Markelius, who was influenced by the ministerial couple Gunnar and Alva Myrdal. It is the first residential building in the Functionalist style typical of the 1930s to be listed as a heritage site.

Rålambshovs-parken ❹

Map 1 B3. Ⓣ *Fridhemsplan.*
🚌 *1, 4, 40, 56, 57, 62, 74.* 🏊

Rålambshovparken was created in 1935, when the Västerbron bridge was built. It adjoins other green areas, including Smedsudden and Marieberg and Fredhäll parks. These open spaces attract joggers and sun-bathers. In summer it is possible to swim from the beach at Smedsudden or the cliffs at Fredhäll.

When the city celebrated its 700th anniversary in 1953 an amphitheatre was opened in Rålambshovsparken, and a paddling pool and playgrounds were added. The park has been enhanced with Elli Hemberg's sculpture *The Butterfly*, Eric Grate's *Monument to an Axeman*, *Judgement* by Egon Möller-Nielsen and Lars Erik Falk's *Colour Tower*.

Rålambshovsparken on the north side of Västerbron bridge

Västerbron ❺

Map 1 B4. 🚌 *4, 40, 74.*

As Stockholm expanded and car use increased in the 1920s, it became necessary to build an additional bridge between the northern and southern shores of Lake Mälaren. German experts dominated the architectural competition launched in 1930, but their plans were implemented by Swedish architects and engineers and the bridge was completed in 1935.

The attractive design blends well with the landscape. The bridge is built in two spans of 168 m (551 ft) and 204 m (669 ft) with a vertical clearance of 26 m (85 ft). It is used by an average of 12,000 vehicles daily. A walk to the centre of Västerbron is rewarded with a magnificent view of central Stockholm.

Marieberg ❻

Map 1 A3. Ⓣ *Thorildsplan.*
🚌 *1, 49, 56, 62.* **Riksarkivet**
Tel *010 476 71 00.*

The area at the northern end of the Västerbron bridge, Marieberg, was once known for its porcelain factory and military installations. But since the early 1960s it has become the city's main newspaper district and the home of three of the four Stockholm dailies.

The architect Paul Hedqvist's 98.6-m (323-ft) high building for *Dagens Nyheter* and *Expressen* is one of the city's landmarks. The neon sign which tops the building at Gjörwellsgatan 30 was designed by P O Ultvedt, who also created the relief at the entrance. Works of art include Lennart Rodhe's walls made from glazed stoneware, *Day and Night*, and Arne Jones' sculpture *Nova*. Some older works of art were brought from the papers' original building in the central Klara district, including Stig

The Orb by Elli Hemberg (1970) in front of Riksarkivet

Blomberg's copper sculpture, *Freedom our Watchword*, made in 1951.

The offices of *Svenska Dagbladet* are not as richly decorated as their neighbours', but they are no less interesting architecturally. The building was inspired by Pirelli's high-rise offices in Milan and designed by Tengbom Architects in 1960–2.

The third interesting building in Marieberg is Riksarkivet, the state archive. It was built in 1968 by architects Åke Ahlström and Kjell Åström. Riksarkivet is one of Sweden's oldest public bodies, dating from the Middle Ages. At the entrance is Elli Hemberg's iron sculpture, *The Orb*. The main hall, which has 56 seats for researchers and 18 individual study rooms, is dominated by Lennart Rodhe's tapestry, *Symbol in the Archive*, created by the Friends of Handicrafts. In an adjoining room the public has access to archive documents, microfilm and microfiche.

Among the archives is one of the world's largest books – the accounts for the province of Östergötland dating from 1813. It has 12,390 pages, weighs 42 kg (92 lb) and is 1.13 m (3.7 ft) wide.

Guided tours of Riksarkivet can be arranged.

Västerbron bridge, opened in 1935, linking Kungsholmen with Södermalm across Lake Mälaren

Stadshuset ❸

Probably Sweden's biggest architectural project of the 20th century, the City Hall was completed in 1923 and has become a symbol of Stockholm. It was designed by Ragnar Östberg (1866–1945), the leading architect of the Swedish National Romantic style, and displays influences of both the Nordic Gothic and Northern Italian schools. Several leading Swedish artists contributed to the rich interior design. The building contains the Council Chamber and 250 offices for administrative staff. The annual Nobel Prize festivities take place in the Blue Hall and the Golden Hall.

Engel-brekt

★ **The Golden Hall**
The Byzantine-inspired wall mosaics by Einar Forseth (1892–1988) have 19 million fragments of gold leaf. The theme of the northern wall is Queen of Lake Mälaren.

Norra Trapptornet, crowned by a sun.

★ **The Blue Hall**
The banqueting room is made from hand-shaped dark bricks. The name comes from the original plan to use polished blue-painted bricks.

★ **The Prince's Gallery**
A fresco, The City on the Water, *in the Prince's Gallery, was painted by Prince Eugen (see p99), who donated it to the City Hall.*

Three Crowns
Sweden's heraldic symbol, Tre Kronor, dating from the 14th century, tops the 106-m (348-ft) tower.

Courtyard

VISITORS' CHECKLIST

Hantverkargatan 1. **Map** 2 B5.
Tel 08-508 290 58. T Rådhuset. 3, 62. for guided tours. 10–11 Apr; 9, 10, 24, 26, 31 Dec; and during special events. Swedish & English. Jun–Aug: 10am, 11am, noon, 2pm and 3pm daily; Sep–May: 10am & noon daily. Tornmuseet May–Sep: 10am–4pm daily. www. stockholm.se/stadshuset

The Council Chamber
Stockholm's 101 councillors meet in this magnificent chamber, which contains furnishings designed by Carl Malmsten.

Engelbrekt the Freedom Fighter by Christian Eriksson (1858–1935).

Marriage room

The Dance
The steps leading to Riddarfjärden are flanked by two statues by Carl Eldh (see p121). Dansen is the figure of a woman, Sången (The Song) is that of a man.

STAR FEATURES

★ The Golden Hall

★ The Blue Hall

★ The Prince's Gallery

Vasastan

Building started in Vasastan, the most northerly part of Norrmalm, in the 18th century. Today it is both a residential area, with houses built around 1900 for manual workers and craftsmen, and a lively part of the city with a wide choice of bars and restaurants. The area also includes some of Stockholm's most agreeable green open spaces, including Vasaparken and Vanadislunden. Stadsbiblioteket, the city library *(see p117)*, is one of Stockholm's most distinctive buildings, and there are several architecturally outstanding churches.

The old observatory (1748–53) at the top of the Observatory hill

SIGHTS AT A GLANCE

Gustav Vasa Kyrka ❺
Handelshögskolan ❸
Judiska museet ❻
Karlbergs Slott ❾
Observatoriemuseet ❷
Röda Bergen ❿
Rörstrandsgatan ❽
Schefflelerska Palatset ❶
Stadsbiblioteket ❹
Vanadislunden ⓫
Vasaparken ❼

KEY

- ▢ Central Stockholm
- ━ Motorway
- ▬ Major road
- ━ Minor road
- Ⓣ Tunnelbana station

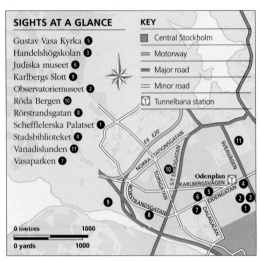

0 metres   1000
0 yards   1000

Schefflelerska Palatset ❶

Drottninggatan 116. **Map** 2 B3. *Tel* 08-16 47 07. Ⓣ *Rådmansgatan.* ▭ *52.* ◯ *only during prearranged tours.* 🗹 *groups only, by appt.* ⬟ *limited access.* 🚫

Until about 1900 the most northerly section of Drottninggatan formed the main road into the city from the north. Here is Schefflelerska Palatset (the "haunted palace"), built in the grand style popular during Sweden's time as a great power, thus dating it to around 1700. It has been suggested that it was designed by Tessin the Elder, but it is more likely that it was by his stepson, Abraham Winantz, who was ennobled in 1693

Orrefors bowl by Simon Gate, 1925

for his services as an architect. On show in the palace is Stockholm University's collection of 370 paintings from the 16th to the 19th century, and the Hellner collection of 700 pieces made at the Orrefors glassworks. Pehr Hilleström's painting *With the Fortune Teller* is included in the collection, but the emphasis is on foreign works such as *The Assault*, attributed to Pieter Bruegel the Elder (1567), and *Danae Banquet* and *Cleopatra's Banquet* by Tiepolo. The property was acquired in 1925 by the College of Higher Education, later Stockholm University, which handed it over to the State in 1960. Legend has it that the house has a ghost.

Observatoriemuseet ❷

Drottninggatan 120. **Map** 2 B2. *Tel* 08-545 483 90. Ⓣ *Odenplan/ Rådmansgatan.* ▭ *2, 4, 40, 42, 65, 72.* ◯ *hours vary – check website.* 🗹 *guided tours in English by appointment.* 🎨 ⬟ 🏠 www.observatoriet.kva.se

A number of institutions connected with science and education can be found on and around the hill of Brunkeberg. The oldest is the former observatory designed by Carl Hårleman for the Royal Scientific Academy and opened in 1753. In 1931 its astronomical research was moved to Saltsjöbaden in the Stockholm archipelago. The building has since become Observatoriemuseet (the Observatory Museum), where visitors can see the observation room, the two median rooms, the weather room and the instrument workshop. In good weather one can view the stars. There is a splendid view of Stockholm from the museum's dome.

The grove, which surrounds the old observatory, began to take shape in the 18th century. It is an idyllic enclosed area, which was first opened to the public in the 20th century. On top of Brunkeberg is Sigrid Fridman's statue *The Centaur*. A park stretches down to Sveavägen, where a large pond is fed by water from a stream running down the hillside. The statue *Dancing Youth* is by Ivar Johnsson. At the southern entrance of the park is Nils Möllerberg's sculpture *Youth*.

Handels-högskolan ❸

Sveavägen 65. **Map** 2 C2. **Tel** 08-736 90 00. Ⓣ Rådmansgatan. 🚌 59.

When the architect Ivar Tengbom (1878–1968) designed Handelshögskolan, Stockholm's School of Economics, in the early 1920s he was inspired mainly by the Renaissance and Neo-Classical styles. Tengbom himself took charge of the construction and the building was officially opened in 1926 in the presence of King Gustav V. The façade has stone reliefs and a gilded Mercury – the god of commerce – all by Ansgar Almquist, who also contributed a stucco relief with a lion gate based on the one in ancient Mycenae in Greece.

The school was founded in 1909 and was previously based in premises at Brunkebergstorg before moving to the newly built Handelshögskolan.

Entrance of Handelshögskolan, the School of Economics

The Stadsbiblioteket, Stockholm's main library

Stadsbiblioteket ❹

Sveavägen 73. **Map** 2 B2. **Tel** 08-508 311 00. Ⓣ Rådmansgatan. 🚌 4, 42, 46, 52, 53, 72. ◱ mid-Jun–mid-Aug: 9am–7pm Mon–Fri, noon–4pm Sat; mid-Aug–mid-Jun: 9am–9pm Mon–Thu, 9am–7pm Fri, noon–4pm Sat & Sun. ♿ ▢

Gunnar Asplund's master work, Stadsbiblioteket (City Library), is one of the capital's most architecturally important buildings (*see p36*). Asplund, the champion of the Functionalist style prevalent in the 1930s, designed a library, which was dominated by Classic ideals. It was opened in 1928.

Internally, the furnishings and many of the lightfittings were designed by Asplund himself. In the entrance hall are Ivar Johnsson's stucco reliefs with themes from Homer's *Iliad*. The sparkling mural painting in the children's section, *John Blund*, is by Nils Dardel, and the depiction of the stars in the heavens by Ulf Munthe. The door lintels, fine door handles and drinking fountains are by Nils Sjögren. Hilding Linnquist was responsible for the giant-sized tapestry, and also for four mural paintings using ancient fresco techniques.

The library lends more than a million books every year.

Gustav Vasa Kyrka ❺

Odenplan. **Map** 2 B2. **Tel** 08-508 886 00. Ⓣ Odenplan. 🚌 4, 40, 42, 46, 53, 69, 72. ◱ 11am–6pm Mon–Thu, 10am–3pm Fri, 11am–3pm Sat & Sun; Jun–Aug: 11am–6pm daily. ✝ noon Mon & Fri, 8:30am Wed, 6pm Thu, 11am Sun, in Swedish. ♿

Sweden's largest Baroque sculpture forms the altar in Gustav Vasa Kyrka, which was opened in 1906. The piece, by the court sculptor Burchardt Precht (1651–1738), was made for Uppsala Cathedral, from where it was removed in the late 19th century. It was bought by the Gustav Vasa parish congregation, whose church immediately gained a notable attraction.

The architect Agi Lindegren designed the central part of the church in Italian Neo-Baroque style with a 60-m (197-ft) high dome. Lindegren himself designed the marble pulpit and the font was created by Sigrid Blomberg. he baptismal chapel there is a 15th-century painting by an unknown Dutch artist. The paintings on the dome are by Vicke Andrén, who also portrayed the four evangelists in the transepts. The organ was built with the help of the composer Olle Olsson, the church organist for 50 years.

GUNNAR ASPLUND

Gunnar Asplund (1885–1940) was the dominant figure among Swedish and internationally renowned architects between the two world wars. His first major commission was the chapel at the Skogskyrkogården Cemetery, designed

Stockholm Exhibition, by Gunnar Asplund, 1930

in National Romantic style. His last work was Heliga Korsets Kapell, the cemetery's crematorium (1935–40). Regarded as a masterpiece in the Functionalist style, it has earned a place on the UNESCO World Heritage list (*see p133*). Asplund also designed Stadsbiblioteket (City Library, 1920–28). He pioneered the Functionalist style as chief architect for the Stockholm Exhibition in 1930.

An eight-stemmed *chanuki* (candlestick) in the collection of Judiska museet

Judiska museet ⑥

Hälsingegatan 2. **Map** 2 A2. *Tel 08-31 01 43.* Ⓣ *Odenplan.* 🚌 *4, 47, 72.* ⚪ *noon–4pm Mon–Fri & Sun.* 📷 *in English by appointment.* 📧 ♿ 🏠 🖥 www.judiska-museet.a.se

In 1774 Aaron Isaac became the first Jewish immigrant to settle in Stockholm and practise his religion. Half of Sweden's Jewish population of around 18,000 live in the Stockholm area. Judiska museet depicts the history of the Swedish Jews from Isaac's time up to the present day. It focuses on Judaism as a religion, its integration into Swedish society and, naturally, the Holocaust. A comprehensive collection of pictures and other items provide an insight into Jewish life in Sweden with its important traditions and customs. The beautiful *Torah* (the five books of Moses), the bridal canopy, and the collection of eight-stemmed *chanukiot* (candlesticks) are just some of the museum's remarkable spiritual artifacts.

Vasaparken ⑦

Map 2 A3. Ⓣ *S:t Eriksplan.* 🚌 *3, 4, 47, 72.*

Vasaparken dates from the early 20th century. It was typical of parks of its time with its emphasis on sport exemplified by the inclusion of a spacious grass sports field. During World War I the field was used for growing potatoes. A playground area was added in 1911.

It is a leafy and pleasant park. With few exceptions the trees were planted when the

park was opened, but a lime tree in the shape of a candelabra is believed to be more than 200 years old.

During a major facelift in the 1940s, the appearance of the section along Torsgatan was changed. Three terraced gardens were added with granite and concrete walls and reliefs. Gottfrid Larsson's bronze statue *The Workman* has stood in this part of the park since 1917. On the opposite side of the park is *Romeo and Juliet*, a small granite sculpture by Olof Th Ohlsson.

Vasaparken, a green lung in the built-up area of Vasastan

Rörstrandsgatan ⑧

Map 1 C1. Ⓣ *S:t Eriksplan.* 🚌 *3, 4, 42, 57, 72.*

This street takes its name from the no longer existing Rörstrand palace, built in the early 1630s. In the summer of 1726 the manufacture of Delft-style porcelain started in the building. Two hundred years later the now-famous

Rörstrand porcelain factory was moved to the Gothenburg area and then to its current home at Lidköping in south-west Sweden.

Rörstrandsgatan was the site of one of the city's first Chinese restaurants and today the many outdoor cafés give the street a colourful atmosphere during summer. The area around Rörstrandsgatan and Odengatan has several nice shops, bars and restaurants.

Karlbergs Slott ⑨

Map 1 B1. *Tel 08-514 390 00.* 🚌 *42, 72 to the station of Karlberg, then 15 min walk.* 📷 *groups only, by appointment.*

Admiral Karl Karlsson Gyllenhielm started to build Karlbergs Slott in the 1630s, during the Thirty Years War. From 1670 the palace was extended and rebuilt by Magnus Gabriel de la Gardie, with Jean de la Vallée as his architect. When Karlberg became royal property in 1688, it was one of Sweden's most majestic palaces. It was where the "hero King" Karl XII (1682–1718) grew up, and it was here that he lay in state after his death at the Battle of Fredrikshald (*see p19*).

In 1792 the architect C C Gjörwell converted the property into the Royal War Academy, which later became the Karlberg Military School, and since 1999 it has been one of the country's military academies.

Cadet balls at Karlberg are unforgettable experiences, not

Rörstrandsgatan, a popular area for restaurants and pubs

Karlbergs Slott, a palace dating from the 1630s – now one of Sweden's military academies

least because of the magnificent setting. The interior decorations include Carl Carove's magnificent stuccowork, which can be seen in the grand hall. The palace church has been renovated, but the 17th-century lamps are original. De la Gardie's "rarities room" is now the sacristy but once housed his collection of valuables.

Röda Bergen ❿

Map 2 A2. Ⓣ S:t Eriksplan.
🚌 3, 42, 47, 57, 69.

Turning off from Sveavägen into Vanadisvägen one soon reaches Matteus Kyrka, which dates from 1902–3. This church was designed by Erik Lallerstedt, who 20 years later undertook its renovation. The figure of St Matthew at the entrance, as well as the reredos figures, are the work of Ivar Johnsson. The mural paintings are by the artist Olle Hjortzberg.

The Röda Bergen ("Red Mountains") district starts at Vanadisplan with a sculpture made from reinforced plastic, *Transformation*, by Chris Gibson (1984). The area is a typical 1920s garden city where, as in Lärkstaden *(see p111)*, the architects abandoned the normal rigid road layout and allowed the

street plan to follow the terrain. After the rose gardens of Rödabergsbrinken, flanked by the parkland oases of Hedemora and Sätertäppan, comes Rödabergsgatan, an avenue of horse chestnut trees typical of the area. A Modernist sculpture in steel has sneaked in here – Björn Selder's *1 1/2 Spheres* (1979). In the background is a playground with Bo Englund's sculpture *Genesis* (1984).

Vanadislunden ⓫

Map 2 B1. 🚌 2, 40, 52. **Vanadisbadet** *Tel* 08-30 12 11. 🕐 mid-May–Sep: 10am–8pm daily. 🅿 ♿ 🍴 💷

Many places in Vasastan are named Vanadis, which derives from Norse mythology. It was not until the late 19th century that the area around the northern end of Sveavägen started to be developed. In the 1880s a park was laid out on the nearby hillside in which

the cultivated areas were created from a landfill site. A chapel, Stefanskapellet, at the southern end of the park, was opened in 1904. It was designed by Carl Möller, who was the architect responsible for Johannes Kyrka. During renovation in 1925–6 the chapel acquired its painted altar by Einar Forseth depicting the Passion.

It took almost a half-century to complete Vanadislunden The Vanadisbadet outdoor swimming pool was opened in 1938. Above the pool the sculpture *Girl in the Evening Sun* by Anders Jönsson looks out over Vasastaden. This is the highest part of Vanadislunden, and the streets around here have attractive black and white paving stones.

At one time there were numerous suburban mansions in the area. One of them, Cederdals Malmgård, can still be seen towards the northern end of the park.

Houses in Röda Bergen with their typical façades in warm colours

Norrtull & Ekoparken

Large parts of Ekoparken, the world's first National City Park, are spread around the Brunnsviken inlet, only a few kilometres north of the city centre. The English-style park, Hagaparken, with its many 18th-century buildings, extolled by the poet Carl Bellman *(see p98)*, is located in this oasis. To the north lies the majestic Baroque Ulriksdals Slott. In stark contrast, to the south visitors come abruptly to the inner city's built-up area at the old Norrtull gateway. The area has several museums, including Naturhistoriska Riksmuseet, Sweden's largest.

The Wenner-Gren Center's main building, Pylonen

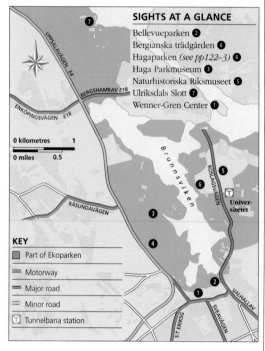

SIGHTS AT A GLANCE

Bellevueparken ❷
Bergianska trädgården ❻
Hagaparken *(see pp122–3)* ❹
Haga Parkmuseum ❸
Naturhistoriska Riksmuseet ❺
Ulriksdals Slott ❼
Wenner-Gren Center ❶

KEY

▨ Part of Ekoparken

═ Motorway

═ Major road

─ Minor road

Ⓣ Tunnelbana station

0 kilometres   1
0 miles   0.5

Wenner-Gren Center ❶

Sveavägen 166. **Map** 2 B1. 🚌 *2, 40, 52, 69.*

The industrialist Axel Wenner-Gren (1881–1961) had an almost religious faith in the potential of science. "Let us use science to solve mankind's problems" is an expression attributed to him. During the 1920s he launched products like vacuum cleaners and refrigerators through his company, Electrolux, which he founded in 1919. His name is preserved in three foundations and in the Wenner-Gren Center, whose 24-storey headquarters, Pylonen, stands like an exclamation mark at the northern end of Sveavägen.

It was opened in 1962, but Wenner-Gren lived only long enough to see the topping-out ceremony in 1961. In the semi-circular Helicon are 155 apartments for the use, at subsidized rents, of foreign scientists undertaking long-term research in Sweden.

The Wenner-Gren Foundation was set up to encourage scientific exchanges between Sweden and other countries. About 250 scientists take part in these every year, and international symposiums are arranged.

Bellevueparken ❷

South of Brunnsviken lake, Ekoparken 11346. 🚌 *2, 40, 53.*
Carl Eldhs Ateljémuseum
Lögbodavägen 10, Bellevueparken.
***Tel** 08-612 65 60.* ◯ *Apr: noon–4pm Sun; May: noon–4pm Sat & Sun; Jun–Aug: noon–4pm Tue–Sun; Sep: noon–4pm Sat & Sun; Oct: noon–4pm Sun (times listed are from April 2013 when the museum reopens).* ◪ *1:30pm in English.*
🖼 🔊 🚫 📷 🖥 ♨

Bellevue Park is part of the Ekoparken, Stockholm's National City Park. Built by architect Fredrik Magnus Piper, who also planned Haga Park, Bellevue offers winding paths, groves, tree-lined avenues and open green areas. The park also boasts 200-year-old lime trees and rare medicinal plants. The name "Bellevue", French for "beautiful view", was given to the park by Baron Carl Sparre who purchased a villa here on Bellevue Hill in 1782. The villa was built in 1757 by court painter John Pasch and today is used as a conference centre.

On Bellevue Hill is the Lögbodavägen viewpoint. The site is not easy to locate but those who do find it are richly rewarded. The point looks out over the Brunnsviken inlet and is close to the monument *The Young Strindberg in the Archipelago* by Carl Eldh (1873–1954).

The sculptor's studio, now preserved as the Carl Eldh's Ateljémuseum, is only a few metres from Lögbodavägen. The sheltering environment and panoramic view of Brunnsviken and Haga were important factors in Eldh's decision to locate his studio here. The sculptor was able to benefit from the northern light, and the garden belonging to the studio made it possible for Eldh to work in the open air. Today, the area exudes calm and it is easy to see why the artist chose to settle here.

In his time Carl Eldh was one of Sweden's most prolific sculptors. Like his colleague Carl Milles, he lived in Paris for several years and was influenced by Rodin's Impressionist style. Later his works were characterized by a more robust Realism. Eldh's sculptures can be seen at 30 public sites in Stockholm. The plaster casts of these works are on show in the studio. Examples include the *Branting Monument* at Norra Bantorget, the statue of Strindberg in Tegnérparken,

Carl Eldh's Ateljémuseum containing plaster cast originals of his works

and *The Runners* at Stadion (*see pp110–11*). Also here are drawings, tools and other personal belongings of the artist. The unusual wooden building which housed the artist's studio was built in 1919 and was designed by the City Hall's architect, Ragnar Östberg.

Haga Parkmuseum ❸

Mellersta Koppartältet, Hagaparken. *Tel* 08-27 42 52. Ⓣ *Odenplan then bus.* 🚌 *515.* 🕐 *Oct–May: 10am–3pm Thu–Sun, May–Sep: 11am–5pm Tue–Sun.* 📷 **www**.hagaparkmuseum.se

This museum is housed in the largest of the three copper-clad "tents" situated in the northwest corner of Hagaparken. It is dedicated to the history of the park and includes exhibits on the plans for its original design, its unusual collection of buildings, and the people associated with them, from the time of Gustav III to the present.

Originally built in 1787–90 as an open stable yard, the building housing the museum was completely destroyed by fire in 1953. The tent-like façade was restored to its former glory in the 1960s, including the painted copper cladding, but it was not until the 1970s that the stables behind were rebuild as a covered structure, in keeping with the original design.

The museum has its own café, whilst the "tents" on either side contain their own restaurant and accomodation. The large rolling lawn in front of the museum is popular with locals for sunbathing and picnics in summer.

EKOPARKEN – THE NATIONAL CITY PARK

Ekoparken – the world's first National City Park – was established by the Swedish Parliament in 1995. This has enabled the capital to safeguard the ecology of its "green lung", a 27-sq km (10.5-sq miles) area for recreation and outdoor activities in an urban setting. In fact, the park covers an area that is as large as Stockholm's inner-city. Ekoparken includes central districts like Skeppsholmen and the southern part of Djurgården, and continues north-west to northern Djurgården, Hagaparken, Brunnsviken and Ulriksdal. Much of the park was a royal hunting ground as early as the 16th century, scattered with beautiful palaces and other sights. The archipelago is represented with the Fjäderholmarna islands in the south.

There are no gates around Ekoparken so you may find you have entered the park without realising it. Guided boat tours are available around Brunnsviken, with stops at some of the more important sights. For more information on Ekoparken and bookings inquiries, call 08-587 140 40.

Isbladskärret in Ekoparken with its rich bird-life, including breeding herons

Hagaparken ④

In the mid-18th century King Gustav III decided to create a royal park in the popular Haga area. The king's vision was realized by the fashionable architect Fredrik Magnus Piper (1746–1824) with the help of leading architects and decorators, and the result was an English-style park with some unusual buildings. A royal palace inspired by Versailles in France was also planned, but construction halted after the king's death and it remained unfinished. Today Hagaparken is part of Ekoparken *(see p121)*, the world's first national city park – an oasis of nature and culture in the city centre.

***Gustav III's Pavilion* painted in 1811 by A F Cederholm**

Fjärils- & Fågelhuset
Hundreds of exotic butterflies and birds fly freely around the greenhouses containing humid tropical rainforest with waterfalls and luxuriant growth at a temperature of 25°C (78°F).

Haga Park-museum

★ **Koppartälten**
These "Roman battle tents" designed by Louis Jean Desprez were completed in 1790. They were originally used as stables and accommodation, but now house a restaurant, café and the Haga Parkmuseum.

These ruins are all that remain of Gustav III's unfinished royal palace.

Stora Pelousen
The lawns stretching down from Koppartälten to Brunnsviken are popular with Stockholmers for sun-bathing and picnics in the summer, and skiing or sledging in the winter. At the rear is Gustav III's Paviljong.

Haga Slott
Built in 1802–4 for Gustav IV Adolf, the palace was the childhood home of the present monarch, Carl XVI Gustaf. It is now the residence of Crown Princess Victoria and Prince Daniel.

VISITORS' CHECKLIST

4 km (2.5 miles) N of Stockholm.
🚌 515. **Haga Parkmuseum**
Tel 08-27 42 52. ⬜15 May–30
Sep: 11am–5pm Tue–Sun; 1 Oct–
14 May: 10am–3pm Thu–Sun.
Gustav III's Paviljong *Tel* 402
61 30. 📷 hourly Jun–Aug: 11am–
3pm Tue–Sun. **Fjärils- & Fågelhuset** *Tel* 08-730 39 81. ⬜ Apr–
Sep: 10am–4pm Tue–Fri, 11am–
5.30pm Sat & Sun; Oct–Mar:
10am–3pm Tue–Fri, 11am–4pm
Sat & Sun. ⬤ 24, 25 & 31 Dec. ⬜
🚹 www.hagaparkmuseum.se

Ekotemplet
This building designed by Louis Jean Desprez in the 1790s was a royal summer dining room. The acoustics made it possible to eavesdrop on secret conversations.

Kinesiska Pagoden
With the 18th century's fascination for anything Chinese, this pagoda was a natural part of Piper's plans for the park.

Old Haga

Royal
Cemetery

★ Gustav III's Paviljong
Olof Tempelman designed this Gustavian masterpiece and Louis Masreliéz undertook the interior decoration. The magnificent hall of mirrors is particularly worth seeing.

Turkish
Pavilion

0 metres   200

0 yards   200

STAR SIGHTS

★ Koppartälten

★ Gustav III's
Paviljong

Polar bear in a natural setting at Naturhistoriska Riksmuseet

Naturhistoriska Riksmuseet **5**

5 km (3 miles) N of Stockholm.
Tel 08-519 540 00. 🛈 *Universitetet.*
🚌 *40, 540.* ⏰ *10am–8pm Tue–Wed & Fri, 10am–7pm Thu, 11am–7pm Sat & Sun.* 🎫 *by appointment.*
🖼️🚻🛗📷🍴 www.nrm.se

Completed in 1916, the vast Naturhistoriska Riksmuseet (Natural History Museum) was designed by Axel Anderberg and decorated by Carl Fagerberg. The museum is a venerable institution, founded in 1739 by Carl von Linné (1707–78) as part of Vetenskaps-akademien (the Academy of Science). It is one of the 10 largest museums of its kind in the world. Over the centuries, the number of exhibits has risen to about 17 million.

During the 1990s it was modernized with the aim of providing "experience-based knowledge". There are permanent collections, such as "Treasures from the Earth's Interior" and "Marvels of the Human Body", along with temporary exhibitions. In "1.45 Billion Years" visitors can get acquainted with the dinosaurs and the earliest

human beings. "Life and Water" presents both the smallest creatures and the giants of the sea, while penguins, sea lions and polar bears await visitors in "The Polar Regions".

During the 1980s the restaurant and museum courtyard were given an artistic facelift by Nils Stenqvist, Gunnar Larsson and Pål Svensson, and a major extension was added in the early 1990s. This also saw the opening of Cosmonova, which is both a planetarium and an IMAX cinema. The architects were Uhlin & Malm. The domeshaped cinema screen is 25 times the size of a normal screen. It is largely due to Cosmonova that the museum is now a major visitor attraction.

Mola Mola, Naturhistoriska Riksmuseet

The *Vega Monument* was erected in front of the museum in 1930 to mark the 50th anniversary of explorer Adolf Erik Nordenskiöld's first voyage through the North-East Passage in his ship *Vega*. Designed by Ivar Johnsson, it is an obelisk in dark granite topped with a copper ship.

Bergianska trädgården **6**

3 km (2 miles) N of Central Stockholm.
Tel 08-545 917 00. 🛈 *Universitetet.*
🚌 *40, 540.* **Edvard Anderson Conservatory** ⏰ *Feb–Oct: 11am–5pm daily; Nov–Jan: 11am–4pm Mon–Fri, 11am–5pm Sat & Sun.* **Victoriahouse** ⏰ *May–Sep: 11am–4pm Mon–Fri; 11am–5pm Sat & Sun.* 🖼️🚻🛗📷🖥️
www.bergianska.se

Bergianska trädgården features more than 7,000 types of plants in beautiful natural settings, and provides an attractive display throughout the year. The most important parts of the gardens are the herb area with its botannical planting scheme, the park with its flower borders, Victoriahouse and the conservatories of Edvard Anderson, and the fruit and berry beds. There is a kitchen garden in the shade of 100-year-old spruce hedges, and an area for spices and medicinal plants. There are also trees and shrubs from northern Europe, Asia and America, as well as flowerbeds with both Nordic and Mediterranean plants, and rhododendrons. The spring spectacle of seas of flowering bulbs is the result of 100 years of dedicated care. The Japanese pool was added in 1991 to mark the 200th anniversary of the Bergius foundation, which made these gardens possible.

The Victoriahouse (1900) houses tropical water plants, utility plants and epiphytes. The Edvard Anderson Conservatory (1995) has large sections for Mediterranean and tropical plants.

Edvard Anderson Conservatory in Bergianska trädgården featuring Mediterranean and tropical plants

Ulriksdals Slott with its magnificent 18th-century Baroque exterior, seen from the palace park

Ulriksdals Slott ❼

7 km (4.3 miles) N of Stockholm.
Tel 08-402 61 30. 🚌 503. **Palace**
◯ *Jun–Aug: noon–4pm Tue–Sun.
Guided tours only in this period at
noon, 1, 2 and 3pm.* **Orangery** ◯
*Jun–Aug: noon–4pm Tue–Sun for pre-
booked groups.* **Coronation carriage**
◯ *For pre-booked groups.* 🚫 📷
♿ 🅿 🚻 🖥 www.royalcourt.se

Ulriksdals Slott is situated
between the two main roads
in the northern outskirts of
Stockholm – the E4 and
Norrtäljevägen. The palace
sits on a headland in the bay
of Edsviken. Its attractive
buildings and lush and leafy
surroundings are well worth a
visit. At the entrance to the
grounds is one of Stockholm's
best-known restaurants,
Ulriksdals Wärdshus *(see p170)*.

The original palace was
built in the 1640s and designed by Hans Jakob Kristler in
German/Dutch Renaissance
style. The owner, Marshal of
the Realm Jakob de la Gardie,
named the palace Jakobsdal.
It was bought in 1669 by the
Dowager Queen Hedvig
Eleonora. When she had a
grandson, Ulrik, 15 years later
she donated the palace to
him as a christening gift, and
it was renamed Ulriksdal.

Around this time the architect Tessin the Elder *(see p37)*
suggested some rebuilding
work, but only a few of his
proposals saw the light of
day. However, the stucco
work by Carlo Carove in the
southern wing can still be
seen. In the 18th century the
palace acquired its Baroque

exterior. After being a popular
place for festivities in the time
of Gustav III (1746–92), it
began to lose its glamour and
at one time was used as a
home for war invalids.

Interest in the palace was
revived under Karl XV
(1826–72), and furnishings
and handicrafts many
hundreds of years old are on
show in his rooms. The living
room of Gustav VI Adolf
(1882–1973) in the rebuilt
Knights' Hall, contains furnishings by the great architect
and designer Carl Malmsten.
The suite was a gift from the
Swedish people in 1923 to the
then Crown Prince when he
married Louise Mountbatten.
A staircase was built at
the same time to designs,
which Tessin the Elder had
suggested 250 years earlier.

The park was laid out in
the mid-17th century. It has
300-year-old lime trees, as
well as one of Europe's most
northerly beechwoods. Carl
Milles's two sculptures of wild
boars stand by the pool in

front of the palace. A stream
is crossed by a footbridge,
which is supported by Per
Lundgren's *Moors Dragging
the Nets*. More art can be seen
in the orangery, designed by
Tessin the Elder in the 1660s
and rebuilt in 1705. It now
houses a sculpture museum.

The palace chapel, a popular
place for weddings, was designed by F W Scholander and
built in 1865 in Dutch Neo-
Renaissance style. It has some
notable medieval stained-
glass windows.

It was from Ulriksdal that
Queen Kristina's Coronation
procession departed in 1650.
Legend has it that by the time
the queen reached the city,
some of her retinue had still
not left Ulriksdal. In one of
the stables there is a replica
of Kristina's carriage. A riding
school, built in 1671, was
converted into a theatre by
Carl Hårleman and C F
Adelcrantz in the 1750s. Performances are staged in the
theatre, named Confidencen,
every summer *(see p176)*.

Sculpture on display in the 17th-century orangery at Ulriksdals Slott

Södermalm & South of Söder

The Södermalm area, generally known as "Söder", rises
steeply from the water and is something of a city in
itself with its own character, charm and dialect. The
slopes are lined with old wooden cottages with an unrivalled view of Stockholm. The dramatic topography has
provided some hilly parks, and allotments are scattered
among the built-up areas. The area has plenty of shops,
bars and restaurants and a lively nightlife, as well as the
latest in modern architecture. South of Söder is Globen,
a spectacular indoor arena, and Skogskyrkogården
Cemetery which is on the UNESCO World Heritage list.

The towers of Mariaberget on a
steep hillside close to Slussen

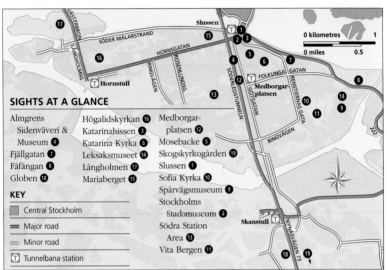

SIGHTS AT A GLANCE

Almgrens
    Sidenväveri &
    Museum ❹
Fjällgatan ❼
Fáfängan ❽
Globen ❶❽

Högalidskyrkan ❶❻
Katarinahissen ❸
Katarina Kyrka ❻
Leksaksmuseet ❶❹
Långholmen ❶❼
Mariaberget ❶❺

Medborgar-
    platsen ❶❷
Mosebacke ❺
Skogskyrkogården ❶❾
Slussen ❶
Sofia Kyrka ❶❶
Spårvägsmuseum ❾
Stockholms
    Stadsmuseum ❷
Södra Station
    Area ❶❸
Vita Bergen ❶❶

KEY

▨ Central Stockholm

━━ Major road

══ Minor road

Ⓣ Tunnelbana station

Slussen ❶

Map 4 C4. Ⓣ *Slussen.* 🚌 *2, 3, 43,
53, 55, 59 76.* ⛴ *Djurgårdsfärja.*

Steadily increasing traffic in
the early 1900s turned the
narrow road between Södermalm and Gamla Stan into a
bottleneck. All the boats sailing between Lake Mälaren and
the Baltic had to pass through
the locks here, and land
traffic was confined to a
narrow bridge. The congestion was eased in 1928, when
some of the boat traffic was
transferred to a new canal, but
the problem needed a more
radical solution. This took the
form of a clover-leaf system of
roundabouts devised by Tage
William-Olsson and Gösta
Lundborg. It was opened in
1935 and was so well
designed that it was able to
cope with the change to right-
hand driving in 1967.

At Slussplan, facing Södermalm and the lock that bears
his name, is a bronze statue
of Karl XIV on horseback by
Bengt Fogelberg, unveiled in
1854 by Oscar I on the 40th
anniversary of the union between Sweden and Norway
(1814–1905). Around the
same time, the locks were
rebuilt. New machinery
devised by the inventor Nils
Ericsson was installed. Today
the locks are used mostly by
pleasure boats, whose erratic
manoeuvres provide enter-
tainment for onlookers.

Although the construction
of Västerbron bridge and
Söderleden road have eased
the traffic burden, Slussen is
still a busy junction and is in
need of a thorough facelift.

The intricate traffic system at Slussen, opened in 1935

Stockholms Stadsmuseum ❷

Ryssgården. **Map** 4 B5.
Tel 08-508 316 00. ⓣ Slussen.
🚌 2, 3, 43, 53, 55, 76. ⏰ 11am–
5pm Tue–Sun, 11am–8pm Thu. 🗓
🚫 ♿ 🚻 🖥 www.stadsmuseum.
stockholm.se

Hemmed in between the traffic roundabouts of Slussen and the steep hill up to Mosebacke Torg is Stockholms Stadsmuseum (City Museum). It is housed in a late 17th-century building originally designed by Tessin the Elder as Södra Stadshuset (Southern City Hall). After a fire, it was completed by Tessin the Younger in 1685. It has been used for various purposes over the centuries, including law courts and dungeons, schools and city-hall cellars, theatres and churches. It became the city museum in the 1930s.

The museum documents the history of Stockholm. The city's main stages of development are described in a permanent exhibition, beginning at the first sign of settlement until the present day. There are also regular temporary exhibitions.

The library has a large archive of pictures and a documentary room where visitors can find out virtually anything they want to know about Stockholm. There are also children's activities, concerts and lectures.

**Stomatol neon-sign
Katarinahissen**

The museum's Stieg Larsson Millennium Tour visits the world of Larsson's best-selling Millennium books (the *Girl with the Dragon Tattoo* series), which are set in Södermalm. The tours are 2 hours long and start at Bellmansgatan 1, home of character Mikael Blomkvist. Tours in English take place on Saturdays at 11:30am.

Katarinahissen ❸

Stadsgården. **Map** 4 C5.
ⓣ Slussen. 🚌 2, 3, 43, 53, 55, 76.
⏰ 1 Sep–14 May: 10am–6pm Mon–
Sun, 15 May–31 Aug: 8am–10pm
daily. 🚫 ♿ 🚻 ♨

Katarinahissen is the oldest of Stockholm's "high-rise" attractions. The 38-m (125-ft) high lift was opened to the public in March 1883 and is still a prominent silhouette on the Söder skyline. The first Swedish neon sign was erected here in 1909 – a legendary advertisement for Stomatol toothpaste. Since the 1930s, the sign has been placed on a nearby rooftop.

The original lift was driven by steam, but it switched to electricity in 1915. In the 1930s it was replaced by a new lift when the Cooperative Association (KF) built its large office complex at Slussen. In its first year the lift was used by more than a million

**Almgrens Sidenväveri (*silk mill*), now a
museum with working 19th-century looms**

passengers, but its record year was 1945, when it carried 1.8 million people between Slussen and Mosebacke Torg.

The lift is still used every year by about 500,000 passengers who enjoy the great views from the top.

Almgrens Sidenväveri & Museum ❹

Repslagargatan 15 a.
Map 9 D2. **Tel** 08-642 56 16.
⏰ 10am–4pm Mon–Fri, 11am–
3pm Sat (25 Jun–6 Aug: 11am–3pm
Mon–Fri). 🎥 call for details. 🚫 🚻
www.kasiden.se

Karl August Almgren was the founder of Almgren's silk-weaving mill, now a museum, in 1833. While on a study tour to Lyon and Tours in France in 1825, Almgren learned about the punch-card system, which was one of the secrets of France's dominance of the silk business. Armed with this information, he returned to Sweden with designs for modern looms and opened his own mill. It soon became a leader in the market, which in the 1700s had seen the establishment of more than 30 silk-weaving mills in Stockholm.

The Almgren family continued the business until 1974, when the mill finally closed. Everything was left intact, and the mill took on a new role in 1991 as a living museum. In the weaving room there is a museum shop selling textiles. The area where the old steam-driven machinery stood is now used as a banqueting room with well-preserved 19th-century decorations.

Katarinahissen with Stockholms Stadsmuseum in the background

Mosebacke ❺

Map 9 D2. 🅣 *Slussen, then a short walk or take the lift at Katarinahissen.* 🚌 *59, then a short walk.* ❄

By taking the lift at Katarina-hissen *(see p127)* from Slussen, the district of Mosebacke with its distinctive atmosphere can be reached. The area got its name from a miller and landowner, Moses Israelsson, the son-in-law of Johan Hansson Hök who managed two mills on the hilltop plateau in the 17th century.

In the mid-19th century Mosebacke became increasingly attractive to Stockholmers as a centre for entertainment. A theatre was built in 1852. However, it was destroyed by fire soon after and replaced in 1859 by a new building, Södra Teatern, designed by Johan Fredrik Åbom. The gateway leading to Mosebacke Terrass and its spectacular panoramic views of the city was added at the same time.

Södra Teatern is a classic among Stockholm's stages. Around 1900 the auditorium was enhanced with a ceiling painting by Vicke Andrén. In the 1930s murals were added, some by Isaac Grünewald. Carl Eldh's bronze bust, *The Young Strindberg*, placed on the theatre's terrace in 1975, shows the author looking across the city from this very terrace, recalling the character of Arvid Falk in the beginning of Strindberg's novel *The Red Room* (1879).

Nils Sjögren's *The Sisters* stands behind railings on Mosebacke Torg. Attractive

Katarina Kyrka (1695) after its extensive restoration due to a devastating fire in 1990

steps lead up to Fiskargatan. At No. 12 is an experimental fireproof-gable design, *Morning Light*, an *al secco* painting on limestone plaster.

Katarina Kyrka ❻

Högbergsgatan 13. **Map** 9 D2. **Tel** 08-743 68 00. 🅣 *Medborgarplatsen, then 3 min walk.* 🚌 *2, 3, 53, 76.* ◻ *11am–5pm Mon–Fri, 10am–5pm Sat & Sun (Oct–Mar: Tue–Sun only).* 🎟 *by appointment.* ✝ *noon & 6pm Wed, 11am Sat, 11am Sun.* ♿ ⛪

The buildings on Katarina-berget date partly from the 18th century and surround a hilltop where various churches have been sited since the late 14th century. The earlier chapels were replaced in the 17th century by a more impressive and

appropriate building, Katarina Kyrka, designed by one of the era's greatest architects, Jean de la Vallée (1620–96). King Karl X Gustaf was also deeply involved in the project, and he insisted that the church should have a central nave with the altar and pulpit right in the middle. The church was founded in 1656, although it was not completed until 1695. In 1723 it was badly damaged by fire, but it was restored over the next couple of decades. Major restoration was also carried out in the 20th century, and a new copper roof was added in 1988. Two years later, on the night of 16 May 1990, there was another fire and, apart from the outer walls, the church and virtually all its fittings were destroyed.

The architectural practice of Ove Hidemark was commissioned to design a new church which, as far as possible, would be a faithful reconstruction of the original. It was not just the outer shell of the building that had to undergo detailed restoration. In order to make the best use of the surviving walls it was necessary to adopt 17th-century building techniques throughout the new building. Experts and craftsmen managed to join heavy timbering on to the central dome in the traditional way, and the collapsed central arch was rebuilt with specially made bricks in 17th-century style.

In 1995, the church was reconsecrated, more beautiful than ever in the view of many people, with the altar sited exactly where it was originally planned.

The reconstruction cost 270 million kronor, of which 145 million kronor was covered by insurance. Such was the popularity of the project that the rest was raised through public donations.

Mosebacke Torg with Södra Teatern in the background

Fjällgatan ⑦

Street light, Fjällgatan

Per Anders Fogelström (1917–98), probably Söder's best-known author, wrote: "Fjällgatan must be the city's most beautiful street. It's an old-fashioned narrow street which runs along the hilltop with well-maintained cobble-stones… and with street lights jutting out from the houses. Then the street opens up and gives a fantastic view of the city and the water…" This area offers an experience of the authentic Söder and its unique atmosphere.

The Heights of Söder
With its 300-year-old houses and terraced gardens, the Söder hilltop stands like a giant stage-set behind Stadsgården harbour.

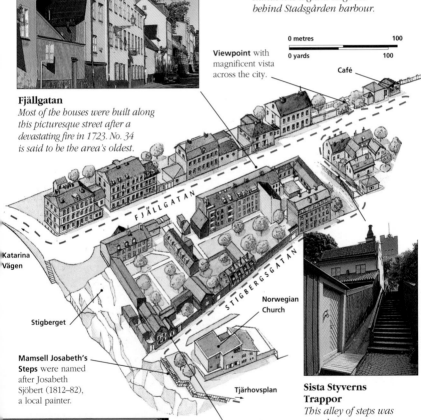

Fjällgatan
Most of the houses were built along this picturesque street after a devastating fire in 1723. No. 34 is said to be the area's oldest.

Viewpoint with magnificent vista across the city.

0 metres	100
0 yards	100

Café

Katarina Vägen

Stigberget

Mamsell Josabeth's Steps were named after Josabeth Sjöbert (1812–82), a local painter.

Norwegian Church

Tjärhovsplan

Söder Cottages
Typical well-preserved cottages can be found along Stigbergsgatan. One of them is No. 17, the house of the block-maker Olof Krok during the 1730s.

Sista Styverns Trappor
This alley of steps was once known as Mikaelsgränd after a 17th-century executioner. Later it was named after the inn on the harbour, Sista Styvern ("The Last Penny").

KEY

– – – Suggested route

Fåfängan ❽

Map 6 A5. 🚋 *53.* ▢ ☼

Fåfängan, at Södermalm's most easterly point, provides a grandstand view of the boats sailing in and out of Stockholm's harbour. In the 1650s, Field Marshal Erik Dahlberg made full use of its strategic location on a hilltop to build a defensive fortress. Some relics of this period can still be seen.

The hill and its park were given the name Fåfängan in the 1770s. The wholesale merchant Fredrik Lundin owned the area at that time, and he built a pavilion, which still stands on the hilltop in a square garden filled with flowerbeds. The word "Fåfängan" ("Vanity") originally denoted an area of land, which was not worth using. But in Stockholm it has a special meaning: "The pavilion on the hilltop with a marvellous view." It is a delightful place for a coffee break while exploring Söder.

Spårvägsmuseet ❾

Tegelviksgatan 22. **Map** 9 F3.
Tel 08-686 17 60. 🚋 53, 55, 66.
🕐 10am–5pm Mon–Fri, 11am–4pm Sat & Sun. 🎥 by appt. 📷 ♿ 🚻
💻 www.sparvagsmuseet.sl.se

The Tram Museum, Spårvägsmuseet, covers the development of the Stockholm public transport system, SL, from the horse-drawn buses of the 19th century to the high-tech underground trains of today. Visitors can try out old and new trams and buses for

Horse-drawn tram from the 1890s on display in Spårvägsmuseet

Sofia Kyrka and Vita Bergen park with its 18th-century cottages

comfort and can experience a driver's-eye view of the city traffic on film.

The museum has three permanent exhibitions covering 5,000 sq m (53,800 sq ft). One shows the history of public transport with the help of some 50 vehicles. Another section traces technical developments from different eras. The third section focuses on the artistically decorated underground stations (*see p202*). There is also a library and archive. On Saturdays and Sundays for most of the year visitors can take two free round trips on a vintage bus.

Sofia Kyrka ❿

Vitabergsparken. **Map** 9 F3. **Tel** 08-641 83 01. 🚋 3, 46, 76. 🕐 10am–4pm Mon–Fri, noon–4pm Sat & Sun. ✝ noon Wed, 6:30pm Thu, 11am Sun. 🎥 by appt. ♿ 🚻 **Concerts** 3pm Sat. www.svenskakyrkan.se

High up on Vita Bergen, surrounded by a leafy green park, is Sofia Kyrka, named after Oscar II's consort and built in 1902–06.

The 35-year-old architect Gustaf Hermansson, who had already designed several churches, including Oscars-kyrkan at Östermalm, created a monumental design with both National Romantic and Gothic influences and tall spires, the highest reaching 78 m (256 ft).

Three windows by Olle Hjortzberg are all that remain of the original decorations. The early 1950s saw the addition of the large altar fresco by Hilding Linnqvist with themes from the Old and New Testaments. The interior acquired its present appearance as part of a major renovation in the early 1980s when the layout of the church was radically altered.

Vita Bergen ⓫

Map 9 F3. 🚋 2, 3, 55, 66, 76.

Vita Bergen (White Mountains) is best known as a park, largely because of Swedish TV broadcasts from its open-air theatre. But it is more than just a park. Houses for workers at Söder's harbours and factories were built on and around the hilltop in the 18th century. They were simple homes, often with a small garden and surrounded by a fence. In 1736 the building of new wooden houses was forbidden because of the fire risk, but the slum districts were exempted. As a result, areas like Bergsprängargränd still have houses, which have retained their original character and give a good idea of life in bygone days.

Around 1900, when Sofia Kyrka was built, the area was turned into a leafy hillside park. This was complemented to the east by an area of allotment-garden cottages. Towards Malmgårdsvägen is the 300-year-old Werner Groen Malmgård (suburban mansion). The park has a bronze statue, *Elsa Borg*, by Astri Bergman Taube (1972), wife of the great troubadour Evert Taube (*see p57*).

Medborgar-platsen ⑫

Map 9 D3. ⓣ *Medborgarplatsen.* 🚌 *59, 66.*

Södermalm's natural centre is Medborgarplatsen. The square had been called Södra Bantorget for more than 100 years, but in 1939 it was renamed Medborgarplatsen (Citizen's Square) on completion of Medborgarhuset. The building, designed by Martin Westerberg in Functionalist and Neo-Classical styles, contains an auditorium, gym, swimming pool and library.

On the west side of the square is Söderhallarna, a complex of restaurants, delicatessens and a cinema. In 1984 the Göta Ark offices, designed by Claes Mellin and Willy Hermansson, were added on the north-west side.

Alongside the stairway to Södra Station is the Södertorn apartment block designed by the Danish architect Henning Larssen. At the entrance is *Nana's Fountain* by Niki de Saint-Phalle, who also created a large sculpture group at the Moderna museet *(see pp80–81)*. The western corner of Medborgarhuset features a 17th-century gateway. Closer to Götgatan is Gustaf Nordahl's *The Source of Life* (1983).

Göran Strååt's sculpture *Kasper* can be seen at the 17th-century Lillienhoffska Palatset. Stefan Thorén's sculpture *Dawn* in welded iron is a dominant feature on the square outside.

Södertorn tower and Ricardo Bofill's curved building near Södra Station

Södra Station Area ⑬

Map 8 C3. ⓣ *Medborgarplatsen or Mariatorget, then a short walk.* 🚌 *43, 55, 66.*

In the mid-19th century Fatburen lake existed to the west of Medborgarplatsen. It was filled in and in the 1860s a train station called Södra Station was opened nearby. In the 1980s the track site was transformed into a new residential area with about 3,000 apartments.

The district became a test-bed for the design concepts of the 1980s shaped by architects' efforts towards Stockholm's urban renewal. The most interesting developments were the work of the Spanish architect Ricardo Bofill. He designed the tower blocks near to the station building as well as the curved residential building – the area's most impressive Neo-Classical feature – which adjoins Fatbur Park.

The park has an open section close to Bofill's curved building with a wooded area further away. It is crossed by a path, which links Medborgarplatsen with

Medborgarplatsen, central Södermalm, with Lillienhoffska Palatset, once a poorhouse

Södermalmsallén and the rail-shuttle station. A 200-m (660-ft) long avenue with 16 sculptures cuts diagonally across the park with a fountain and pool in the middle. In the northern part of the park a flower garden has been named after the Swedish composer Johan Helmich Roman (1694–1758). The arches of Bofill's curved building shelter some interesting works of art.

Leksaksmuseet ⑭

Tegelviksgatan 22. **Map** 8 F3. **Tel** 08-641 61 00. ⓣ *Slussen.* 🚌 *2, 53, 55, 66.* ◯ *10am–5pm Mon–Fri, 11am–4pm Sat & Sun.* 📷 *by appt.* 🅿️ 🚻 www.leksaksmuseet.se

Toys, which have delighted children and adults alike over the past century, are on show at Leksaksmuseet (the Toy Museum). The museum was opened in 1980, and the main exhibition changes continuously as new toys are added to the collection.

One floor features musical instruments, including musical boxes, barrel organs and accordions. Another floor is devoted to mechanical toys, models and dioramas. A third section has dolls, dolls' houses, wooden toys, steam engines, and several working model railways. Private collections are also on show. There is a playroom and children's theatre.

Bastugatan, one of Mariaberget's well-preserved 18th-century streets

Mariaberget ⓰

Map 8 C2. Ⓣ *Mariatorget.*
🚌 *43, 55.*

A fire in 1759 destroyed the old buildings of Mariaberget. The area was rebuilt according to a 1736 law forbidding the construction of wooden houses in this part of Söder. The result of this purposeful 18th-century town planning remains intact. Mariaberget's stone buildings on the slopes down towards Riddarfjärden are among Stockholm's most distinctive, and the character of the steep winding streets and alleys has been well preserved.

Towards the end of the 20th century a conservation programme was implemented to safeguard the area's cultural heritage, including the view over Riddarfjärden. Near Bastugatan an attractive promenade, Monteliusvägen, has been built along the rock's edge. A new flight of steps leads down to the Söder Mälarstrand quayside.

The author Ivar Lo-Johansson (1901–90) lived in this area for more than half a century. A small park with a bust of the artist bears his name. The 18th-century poet C M Bellman (*see p98*) was born at Mariaberget, although he is more usually associated with Haga and Djurgården.

Mariaberget presents a pleasant contrast to the busy traffic artery of Hornsgatan. When the street was widened and levelled in 1901 a number of 18th-century buildings came into view. The area now features galleries and antique shops. On the opposite side of Hornsgatan is Maria Magdalena Kyrka on a site where there have been religious buildings since the 14th century. The predecessor of the present building was constructed in 1634. It burnt down in 1759 and was rebuilt 4 years later.

Högalidskyrkan ⓱

Högalids Kyrkväg. **Map** 1 C5.
Tel 08-616 88 00. Ⓣ *Hornstull.*
🚌 *4, 66, 74.* ⊙ *9am–noon &
1–3pm Mon, Tue, Thu, Fri, 1–3pm
Wed, 10am–4pm Sat & Sun.*
🕆 *noon Wed, 11am Sun.* ⬥ 🔲

The octagonal twin towers of Högalidskyrkan make the church easy to identify from many parts of the city. The impressive brick building in National Romantic style was completed in 1923. It was designed by Ivar Tengbom. He also put his mark on the interior decoration, which involved a number of leading artists and craftsmen.

Tengbom was enlisted to design the columbarium which was added in 1939. The most prolific artist was Gunnar Torhamn, who provided the Crucifix – the

The distinctive twin towers of Högalidskyrkan, built in 1923

largest in Scandinavia – as well as the frescoes in the baptismal chapel and the decoration of the pulpit and organ loft. Erik Jerke created the reredos in Byzantine style. In the cemetery chapel below the chancel, Einar Forseth designed an apse mosaic using the same techniques that he employed for Gyllene Salen (the Golden Room) in Stadshuset (*see p114*).

By no means everything in the church is new. The font is from the 16th century, and the seven-stemmed candlestick on the altar dates from the 18th century.

Exercise yard in the former royal prison on Långholmen

Långholmen ⓲

Map 1 B5. Ⓣ *Hornstull, then 3 min
walk.* 🚌 *66.* 🚢

Below the majestic Västerbron bridge (*see p113*) is the island of Långholmen, which is linked to Södermalm by two bridges. Långholmen is best known for the various prisons, which have been located here since 1724. During the 20th century the prison here was the largest in Sweden, housing 620 inmates. When it closed in 1975, the island became a popular recreational area.

The prison buildings were demolished in 1982, but the old royal jail dating from 1835 remains. The one-time cells now form part of a hotel, as well as a prison museum. There is also a youth hostel and an excellent restaurant, as well as a small museum to the poet C M Bellman with a café in the gardens which run down towards Riddarfjärden.

Långholmen's park has an open-air theatre, and offers excellent swimming both from the beaches and the rocks.

Globen ⓲

3 km (1.9 miles) S of Stockholm.
Ⓣ Globen. **Tel** 08-50 83 53 00.
◯ during events. 🎫 by appt. ♿
▣ 🖥 www.globen.se

In 1989 Stockholm acquired a new symbol in the shape of the indoor arena Globen. It is the world's largest spherical building and has given the southern part of the city a completely new silhouette.

Globen offers a wide programme, including 125 annual events. The ice hockey world championship in 1989 was the first major competition to be staged here. It has been followed by other world championships, including handball, boules, wrestling and indoor bandy (a type of hockey). Globen has also hosted European championships in gymnastics, athletics and volleyball and key equestrian events.

Concerts at Globen have featured international stars like Pavarotti, Sinatra and the Rolling Stones, as well as Bruce Springsteen, U2, Ozzy Osbourne, Bob Dylan and Depeche Mode.

Globen, designed by Berg Architects, has a circumference of 690 m (2,260 ft) and a height of 85 m (279 ft). The viewing screens each cover 13 sq m (140 sq ft). Globen City has sprung up around the arena with more than 150 shops, hotels and other services.

Chapel of the Holy Cross by Gunnar Asplund at Skogskyrkogården

Skogskyrko-gården ⓳

6 km (3.7 miles) S of Stockholm.
Tel 08-508 301 58. Ⓣ Skogskyrko-gården. 🚌 183 (weekends only). 🎫
Jul–Sep: 5pm Mon (in English). ♿ ▣

Nature and the splendid buildings have combined to provide a harmonious setting, which has placed Skogskyrko-gården Cemetery on the UNESCO World Heritage list. It is sited amid pinewoods, which provide a justly sombre framework for the chapels and crematorium.

Epitaph to Gunnar Asplund

The winners of a competition to design the cemetery in 1914 were Gunnar Asplund *(see p117)* and Sigurd Lewerentz, whose proposals were considered the most likely to safeguard the area's special character. Asplund's first significant work, Skogskapellet (Woodland Chapel), with its steep shingled roof, was opened at the same time as the cemetery in 1920. This was followed 5 years later by Uppståndelsekapellet (Resurrection Chapel), designed by Lewerentz.

In 1940 Asplund's last great work, Skogskrematoriet (Woodland Crematorium), was opened, along with its three chapels representing Faith, Hope and the Holy Cross. They are sited along Korsets Väg. John Lundqvist's *The Resurrection* stands in the pillared hall of Heliga Korsets Kapell – the largest of the three. Adjoining the chapel is Asplund's black granite cross.

A memorial park was added in 1961 to the north-west of the chapel. The Hill of Meditation lies to the west. The chapel has been decorated by artists like Carl Milles, Sven Erixson and Gunnar Torhamn.

Skogskyrkogården is the last resting place of both the unknown and the celebrated, among whom is Greta Garbo.

GRETA GARBO

The legendary Greta Garbo, one of the 20th century's outstanding film stars, was born in 1905 in a humble part of Södermalm. At the age of 17 she joined the theatre academy of Dramaten and made her film debut in *Peter the Tramp*. Her breakthrough came in 1924 in Mauritz Stiller's film of Selma Lagerlöf's book *The Atonement of Gösta Berling*. The following year she moved to Hollywood, where she soon became the reigning star. Garbo appeared in 24 films, including *Anna Karenina* (1935) and *Camille* (1936). She never married and lived a solitary life until her death in 1990. Her ashes were interred at the Skogskyrkogården Cemetery in 1999.

Garbo in *As You Desire Me* (1932)

The silhouette of Globen arena dominating the surrounding area

THREE GUIDED WALKS

Stockholm is a perfect city for walking. Not only is it flat, but it is also one of Europe's less crowded capital cities, making it ideal for stress-free strolling through the streets and thoroughfares. Many of Stockholm's pedestrian areas also have cycle paths running alongside them, so take care to observe the painted signs on the ground, indicating which side of the line you should walk. These guided walks have been devised to cover

The top of Kaknäs-tornet TV tower

some of the city's most appealing districts: discover residential Södermalm (also known as "Söder") south of the centre, with great views of the city centre; take in some of Stockholm's best parkland on Djurgården – the perfect destination for a picnic; and finally, explore the commercial heart of the Swedish capital, following a route which takes you past leading department stores and boutiques, as well as more sedate churches and monuments.

A view of Stockholm from Södermalm *(see p135)*

KEY

• • • Walk route

0 kilometres   1

0 miles   1

A 90-minute walk around the city centre *(pp138–9)*

Stadsbiblioteket (the city library) in central Stockholm *(see p139)*

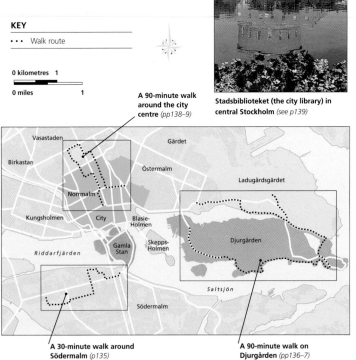

Vasastaden

Gärdet

Birkastan

Östermalm

Ladugårdsgärdet

Norrmalm

Kungsholmen   City   Blasie-Holmen

Skepps-Holmen

Ladugårdsgärdet

Djurgården

Riddarfjärden

Gamla Stan

Saltsjön

Södermalm

A 30-minute walk around Södermalm *(p135)*

A 90-minute walk on Djurgården *(pp136–7)*

A 30-Minute Walk around Södermalm

Winding through a charming mix of narrow residential streets and neighbourhood allotments with their red and white summer cottages, this walk also offers the best views of Stockholm from anywhere in the city. There is also the chance to browse in some of the more quirky stores or stop at a streetside café whilst exploring this largely undiscovered side of Stockholm.

Begin at Södermalms torg ①, the heart of one of Stockholm's main traffic interchanges, Slussen. Before leaving the square, glance up at the roofs of the surrounding buildings and you'll see

View of Riddarholmen from Blecktornsgränd ⑤

head north towards Söder's northern shore, then take a left into pretty, cobbled Bastugatan ④, full of 18th-century houses. Turn right into Blecktornsgränd ⑤ to see some of the finest views in the city, with open vistas out over Riddarholmen, Gamla Stan and the city centre. Follow the narrow path of Monteliusvägen ⑥ west, enjoying the sweeping views on your right; several of the

Boats serving as floating hotels lining Söder Mälarstrand ⑦

0 metres	500
0 yards	500

KEY

••• Walk route

🔆 Good viewing point

🚇 Tunnelbana station

Sweden's first ever neon sign for the now defunct Stomatol toothpaste. From Södermalms torg, head west along Hornsgatan ②. Söder has a plethora of good restaurants and unusual shops, and on the initial stretch of this long road you will also find many small, interesting art galleries. On the left as you make your way along Hornsgatan you'll soon pass the 17th century Maria Magdalena Kyrka ③ designed by the same architects as the Royal Palace.

Now leave the main road to walk along some of Söder's residential streets which are among Stockholm's most sought after addresses. Turn right into Bellmansgatan and

house-boats below on Söder Mälarstrand ⑦ now serve as floating hotels. At Timmermansgatan head south until you reach Wollmar Yxkullsgatan ⑧, considered by some to be the heart of Södermalm.

Now head right along Wollmar Yxkullsgatan until you reach Ringvägen. Cross this road and take the delightful Zinkens Väg ⑨ through an area of allotments and small summer cottages in the Zinkensdamm area ⑩. Owners often spend several days at a time here pottering in their gardens. After passing the Zinkensdamm youth hostel, head north up the steps of Pipmakartrappan back to Hornsgatan and the end of the walk ⑪.

TIPS FOR WALKERS

Starting point: The easiest way to get to the start of the walk is to take the T-bana to Slussen; Södermalms torg is just outside the main exit.

Length: 2.5 km (1.6 miles)

Duration: Half an hour

Stopping-off points: There are plenty of cafés and shops along Hornsgatan for a break or rest.

Ending the walk: At the end of the walk you can take the Zinkensdamm T-bana located on Hornsgatan (two stops west of Slussen).

A 90-Minute Walk on Djurgården

This delightful walk offers a chance to explore the former royal hunting grounds of Djurgården, an island which forms the northern side of Stockholm harbour. Heavily wooded and dotted with grand old houses, the island offers peace, tranquility and some of the city's most striking museums. There are also stunning views across Stockholm from the top of the Kaknäs TV tower.

Nordiska museet to Ryssviken

The walk starts at the palatial Nordiska museet ①, one of the city's best museums, which provides a good grounding in the history of everyday Swedish life. From the museum, follow Djurgårdsvägen south, looking out for the boat-shaped building behind the Nordiska museet. Here resides the former warship, *Vasa*, who sank in Stockholm harbour on her maiden voyage in 1628 (see pp92–4).

Continuing on, you will soon come to the eclectic Liljevalchs Konsthall art gallery ② (see p95) which hosts frequently-changing exhibitions of art and sculpture. Once at Almänna Gränd, you are entering the pleasure zone: there are often crowds of children here heading for the amusement park, Gröna Lund ③ (see p95), which features several

hair-raising rides including the "Free Fall", a vertical drop of around 100 m (330 ft). From here Djurgårdsvägen swings east on its way around Djurgården. Follow the road to the small inlet, Ryssviken ④, where you could end the walk if you wish and take the 47 bus back to the city.

The greenery of Djurgården as seen from the air

Ryssviken to Blockhusudden

From Ryssviken, take the path south to the promontory known as Waldemarsudde ⑤ (see p99) with its good views across the harbour and excellent art gallery

The Vasamuseet, home to the former warship, the *Vasa*

specialising in late 19th-century Nordic art. From here, it is a pleasant walk along the waterfront to another small promontory, Biskopsudden ⑥.

Heading east a short distance along Biskopsvägen, pick up another path along the shore which begins just south of the junction with Djurgårdsvägen ⑦. This path leads to the eastern end of Djurgården, Blockhusudden ⑧, which gives views of the hi-tech business centre, Nacka

---

TIPS FOR WALKERS

Starting point: Tram number 7 or bus 44 will bring you closest to the Nordiska museet.

Length: 8.5 km (5.3 miles)

Duration: One and a half to 2 hours

Stopping-off points: A great spot for lunch or a cup of coffee is the Blå Porten, Djurgårdsvägen 64, near the Liljevachs Konsthall art gallery. The café at the top of the Kaknästornet TV tower has the best views of Stockholm.

End point: You could end this walk early at Blockhusudden, which is conveniently the terminus for the 69 bus which runs all the way back into the centre of the city via Strandvägen and Sergels torg. From the end of the walk at Strandvägen buses 69 and 79 run back to the centre.

Strand, on the southern side of the harbour and the residential area, Jarlaberg, high on the cliffs above. The arcing sculpture of a boy atop a crescent of steel that you can see across the water, is *Gud på himmelsbågen*, by Stockholm sculptor Carl Milles *(see p150)*.

Blockhusudden is also home to Thielska Galleriet ⑨ *(see p99)*, a superb art gallery with a fine collection of 19th-century Scandinavian art. If you wish to end the walk at this point, there is a bus from here back to the city.

Carl Milles' sculpture, *Gud på himmelsbågen*

Blockhusudden to Berwaldhallen concert hall

On foot, continue northeast to Lilla Sjötullsbron bridge ⑩. The stretch of path before the bridge runs past a marshy pond, especially preserved for its birdlife. Once over the bridge, head west along the tranquil canal to meet upwith Djurgårds-brunnsvägen which leads towards the Kaknästornet TV tower ⑪ *(see p108)*. This is a long diversion from the main route, but worth it if you are feeling energetic. At 155 m (508 ft) high, the tower is one of the tallest buildings in Scandinavia and even boasts a café at around 120 m (390 ft) elevation.

From the tower, backtrack to the main walk and head west along the canal path past a clutch of museums on your right, including the Sjöhistoriska museet ⑫ *(see pp106–7)*, which reveals Sweden's maritime history. Further along the path, the imposing villas on the right are part of Diplomatstaden ("Diplomat's Town", *see p106*), home to several Embassies, including that of the United States of America ⑬. The spire rising from behind the waterfront houses belongs to Engelska Kyrkan ⑭, the English Church. To finish the walk, take the path around Nobel Parken and end at Strandvägen, with its elegant façades lining the waterfront ⑮.

DJURGÅRDEN

0 metres   500

0 yards   500

KEY

• • • Walk route

⚘ Good viewing point

🚌 Bus stop

🚋 Tram stop

Ⓣ Tunnelbana

Palatial waterfront houses along Strandvägen ⑮

A 90-Minute Walk around the City Centre

Mille's
Orpheus

This walk will take you right through the heart of Stockholm, giving you a chance to browse in the city's best shops or to enjoy a coffee and pastry in one of the many cafés you'll pass. It also provides a chance to see some of the imposing buildings that Stockholm has to offer, such as the magnificent Konserthuset or the architecturally interesting Stadsbiblioteket. The route also includes a park or two where you can take a break and escape the bustling streets.

Plaque in memory of Olof Palme ⑤

Sergels Torg to
Adolf Fredriks Kyrka

This walk begins at
Sergels Torg (see p67) ①,
a split-level square widely
regarded as the very centre
of the modern city. It is

Strindberg's study at Strindbergsmuseet Blå Tornet (The
Blue Tower) on Drottninggatan ⑦

marked by a tall glass obelisk
which is illuminated at night.
From this point, take
pedestrianised Sergelgatan
north to reach the city's main
market square, Hötorget (see
p68) ②, full of vegetables and
flowers for sale. It was in the
PUB department store here in

the square that film
legend Greta Garbo
sold hats in the millinery
department; there is a small
exhibition devoted to her by
the ground floor entrance.
   On the opposite side of
Hötorget is the grand
Konserthuset (see p68) ③,

home
to the
Swedish
Royal
Philarmonic.
In front of
Konserthuset
stands Carl
Mille's sculpture,
Orpheus. Across
Kungsgatan you will
see the Kungshallen
shopping mall ④,
which also contains
several cafés and restaurants.
From Kungsgatan turn left
into Sveavägen. At the
junction with Olof Palmes
Gata you will find a plaque
in the pavement that marks
the spot where the former

The colourful Hötorget market, outside Konserthuset ③

Swedish Prime Minister, Olof Palme, was gunned down in 1986 as he left a nearby cinema with his wife ⑤.

A short distance to the north, still on Sveavägen, Palme's grave can be visited in the churchyard at Adolf Fredriks Kyrka *(see p70)* ⑥.

Blå Tornet to Odenplan

Just after the church, turn left into Kammakargatan to reach the former home of writer August Strindberg, now a museum, Blå Tornet *(see p69)* ⑦, at the corner of Drottninggatan. Head uphill on Drottninggatan, past small quirky shops and various popular cafés ⑧.

Once past Kungstensgatan, Drottninggatan becomes Norrtullsgatan and continues north along the side of Observatorielunden ⑨, a leafy park which hides Stockholm's former observatory dating

The imposing Kungstornen (King's Towers) on Kungsgatan ⑮

from 1753. At the end of the road you'll reach another of Stockholm's main squares, Odenplan ⑩, a large open area of superb 19th-century architecture dominated by the Neo-Baroque Gustav Vasa Kyrka *(see p117)* ⑪. There is a T-bana station here if you want to cut the walk short.

Odenplan to Stureplan

From Odenplan, head east along Odengatan past some university buildings to reach the city library, Stadsbiblioteket *(see p117)* ⑫, designed by Gunnar Asplund and widely regarded as one of Stockholm's finest Functionalist buildings. Next take a right into Sveavägen and head south towards the prestigious Stockholm School of Economics ⑬, Handelshögskolan, where competition for places is extremely fierce.

From here turn left into Rehnsgatan and walk a short distance east before turning right into Döbelnsgatan which, leading south, eventually becomes Malmskillnadsgatan. Johannes Kyrka ⑭, a 19th-century Neo-Gothic church set in a small park, can be

seen on your left. The wooden steeple, which stands next to it was constructed much earlier in 1692.

Look out for a set of stone steps on the left which lead down onto Kungsgatan beside the Neo-Classical Kungstornen twin towers *(see pp68–9)* ⑮, which dominate this part of the city. Once on Kungsgatan, you will find a good selection of cafés and stylish shops, as well as several cinemas near the Kungstornen bridge.

The walk ends with a short stroll downhill to Stureplan, *(see pp70–71)* ⑯ an open square that is the centre of Stockholm's vibrant nightlife and a popular meeting place.

The impressive doorway of the Neo-Baroque Gustav Vasa Kyrka ⑪

TIPS FOR WALKERS

Starting point: Sergels Torg is easily accessible from Stockholm's main T-bana station, T-Centralen. When leaving the platform simply follow the signs for Sergels torg.
Length: 3.5 km (2.2 miles)
Duration: One and a half hours
Stopping-off points: For cafés, try the Kungshallen shopping mall at Hötorget or Kungsgatan and Stureplan. The Saluhallen indoor market in Hötorget is the best place in Stockholm for ethnic treats and delicious Middle Eastern snacks.

HUMLEGÅRDEN

BERGS-
-KEN GATAN
VEBERGS.

IVERSONSG.

AS BACKE

ENGELBREKTS-
PLAN
DAVID BAGARES GATA
HUMLEGÅRDSGATAN

BRUNNSGATAN

KUNGSGATAN ⑯
STURE-
PLAN

LÄSTMAKARGATAN
RGSG.

JAKOBSBERGSGATAN

MÄSTER SAMUELSGATAN
SMÅLANDSGATAN

HAMNGATAN
BERZELI
PARK
NYBRO-
PLAN

REGERINGS.

GREV TUREGATAN

NORRLANDSGATAN
BIBLIOTEKSGATAN

Östermalms-
torg

RIDDARGATAN

NYBROGATAN

0 metres   300

0 yards   300

KEY

• • • Walk route

✂ Good viewing point

Ⓣ Tunnelbana station

EXCURSIONS FROM STOCKHOLM

*S*tockholm's strategic location between the Baltic Sea and Lake Mälaren provides the backdrop for a range of excursions whichs offer an insight into Swedish life and history. To the east lies the beautiful archipelago with its 24,000 islands and skerries. To the west are the more sheltered beaches and islands of Mälaren with a cultural heritage stretching back to the time of the Vikings and before.

The wide stretches of water to the east and west of the capital are markedly different, in terms of both their natural environment and history. The Vikings and their ancestors headed west towards the present-day Lake Mälaren for defensive reasons before the gradual rising of the land transformed what was once a Baltic inlet into a freshwater lake.

A lighthouse in the archipelago

Sweden's first town, Birka, was founded on the island of Björkö in the 8th century, but archaeological finds indicate that the area was used for trading with other countries as long as 1,500 years ago. Evidence of these early residents can be found on Björkö to this day. Along with the royal palace of Drottningholm, on nearby Lovön, Birka is included on the UNESCO World Heritage list.

Around Lake Mälaren's sheltered shores are many other majestic palaces, elegant manor houses and several small towns like Mariefred, which has retained its old-time character.

To the east of the city, the rising of the land since the Ice Age has provided a fantastic and largely untouched archipelago with over 24,000 islands, rocks and skerries. The archipelago has often been the scene of enemy attacks from the sea, so it lacks the wealth of cultural treasures that characterize Mälaren. Instead, visitors are attracted by the natural scenery. The boat trip to the leafy Fjäderholmarna islands takes less than half an hour, but a full day should be allowed for an excursion to the outer archipelago with its smooth rocks and wide bays.

Archipelago boats ready for departure from Strömkajen, outside Stockholm's Nationalmuseum

◁ Gripsholms Slott, King Gustav Vasa's Renaissance fortress at Mariefred, founded around 1540

Excursions from Stockholm

Stockholm is surrounded by a remarkable natural landscape which provides an attractive setting for excursions. Idyllic towns, majestic castles and prehistoric settlements dot the shores of Mälaren to the west. On the eastern side are the islands of the archipelago with their traditional wooden houses, and cosy hotels and youth hostels. Annual sailing regattas attract yachting enthusiasts from all over the world. Everything is easily accessible by scheduled boat services, making the journey itself a memorable experience.

KEY

══	Motorway
▬	Major road
═══	Minor road
▭▭▭	Railway
───	Minor railway

Drottningholms Slott on Lovön in Lake Mälaren

GETTING THERE

All the excursion destinations on this map can be reached in summer by scheduled boat services from Stockholm's city centre. Those on Lake Mälaren are operated by Strömma Kanalbolaget or Gripsholms-Mariefreds Ångf. AB. Most of those in the archipelago are operated by Waxholmsbolaget *(see p204)*. Other destinations on the mainland can be reached by car or bus, and by train to Mariefred. See also the checklist for individual sights.

SIGHTS AT A GLANCE

Birka ❷	Millesgården ❺
Drottningholm pp146–9 ❶	Sandhamn ❿
Finnhamn ❾	Steninge Slott ❹
Fjäderholmarna ❻	Utö ⓫
Grinda ❽	Vaxholm ❼
Mariefred ❸	

EXCURSIONS BY STEAMBOAT

Traditional steamboats are a picturesque feature on the waters around Stockholm. Both in the archipelago and on Lake Mälaren visitors can still enjoy the quiet, calm atmosphere of a steamboat voyage. One of the real veterans, *SS Blidösund* (1911), is operated by voluntary organizations and serves mostly the northern archipelago. Some routes, for example Stockholm–Mariefred, are operated partly or completely by steamers. Most of the other passenger boats from the early 20th century have been fitted with oil-fired engines but still provide a nostalgic journey back in time.

SS Blidösund, one of the oldest in Stockholm's fleet of renovated steamboats still in regular service

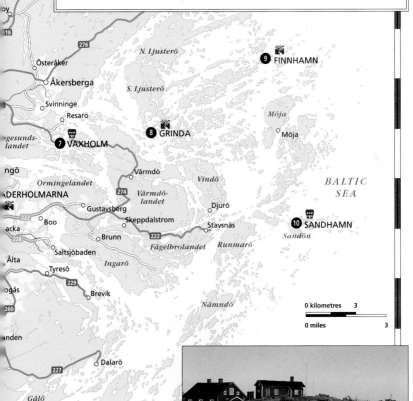

Huvudskär in Stockholm's outer archipelago

Drottningholm ❶

See pp146–9.

Birka ❷

30 km (19 miles) W of Stockholm.
🚢 *May–Sep from Stadshusbron.*
Birkamuseet *Tel 08-519 180 00.*
🔵 *May–Sep: 11am–4pm Mon–Fri,
11am–5pm Sat & Sun (Jul–mid-Aug:
11am–6:30pm daily).* 🎫 *of
exhibitions and excavations.* 🅿️ 🖥️
👤 www.raa.se/birka

The 16th-century Gripsholms Slott just outside Mariefred

The first town in Scandinavia was called Birka, on the island of Björkö in Lake Mälaren. It was founded in the 8th century by the king of Svea who then reigned over the central parts of present-day Sweden. His royal residence was on the nearby island of Adelsö. About 100 years later a contemporary writer gave the town this description: "In Birka there are many rich merchants and an abundance of all types of goods, money and valuable items." It was not a large town. There were only about 700 inhabitants, but they included craftsmen, whose work attracted merchants from distant countries.

Birka crucifix

The town was planned on simple lines. People lived in modest houses, which stood in rows overlooking the jetties where ships were moored. These vessels were used by the king's warriors, the Vikings, for their marauding expeditions. In 830 a monk named Ansgar came to Birka, bringing the Christian faith to Sweden. In the 10th century Birka was abandoned in favour of Sigtuna, 15 km (9 miles) to the north, which is now Sweden's oldest town.

Today Björkö is a flourishing island with gardens and juniper-covered slopes. But, most importantly, it is a popular excursion destination with a fascinating museum and continuing archaeological digs. During the early 1990s these excavations provided a lot of new information about Birka and the Vikings. Work has continued around the old fortifications, revealing much about the town's defences and the life of its inhabitants. The museum shows how Birka looked in its heyday, along with some of the archaeological finds. Visitors can also see freshly dug artifacts while excavations are in progress.

Mariefred ❸

65 km (40 miles) W of Stockholm.
🆔 *0159–231 60.* 🚢 *summer from
Stadshusbron.* 🚂 *from Central-
stationen to Läggesta, then bus.*
Gripsholms Slott 🔵 *15 May–15
Sep: 10am–4pm daily; 16 Sep–14
May: noon–3pm Sat & Sun.*
Grafikens Hus 🔵 *11am–5pm
Thu–Sun.* 🖼️ www.grafikenshus.se

Mariefred should ideally be approached from the water to get the best view of the magnificent Gripsholms Slott in all its splendour. The first fortress on this site was built in the 1380s by the Lord High Chancellor, Bo Jonsson Grip, who gave the castle its name. Work on the present building, initiated by King Gustav Vasa, started in 1537 but parts have been rebuilt or added – most notably during the time of Gustav III in the late 18th century. It was during this period that the National Portrait Gallery was established. It now contains more than 4,000 portraits and covers some 500 years of artistic endeavour, from the time of Gustav Vasa to the present day. It also has a collection of notable foreign portraits, which are shown in a separate section.

Gripsholms Slott's well-preserved interiors feature a wide collection of furniture, art and handicrafts. There are about 60 rooms. Highlights include Gustav III's late 18th-century theatre and the White Salon which is also from the same era.

The town of Mariefred, in the shadow of the castle, derives its name from a late

Iron Age burial ground at Birka on the island of Björkö in Lake Mälaren

15th-century monastery, Monasterium Pacis Mariae. It received its charter as a town in 1605, and an inn has stood on the site of the monastery since the early 17th century. The elegantly restored and rebuilt restaurant is an attraction in itself.

Visitors to Mariefred can stroll through the town and admire

Duke Karl's bedchamber, Gripsholms Slott

the 17th-century church and the 18th-century Rådhus (law courts' building), which also houses the local Tourist Information Office. There are a number of specialist shops, galleries and an excellent antiques shop.

The vintage railway attracts visitors of all ages. Those interested in art should head for Grafikens Hus (House of Graphics) on a hill leading up to the former royal farm, where stables and haylofts have been converted into an exhibition area.

The excursion can be made into a varied round trip. From Stockholm to Mariefred one can travel on Sweden's oldest steamboat service, dating from 1832. The steamboat *Mariefred*, which has operated on the route since 1903, travels at 6–7 knots and the journey takes about three and a half hours. Beautiful scenery and a lunch of classic "steamboat

beef" is on offer along the way. For the return journey, a vintage steam railway runs from Mariefred to Läggesta (a 40-minute journey) from where it is possible to catch an express train back to Stockholm (30 minutes).

Steninge Slott ➍

40 km (25 miles) N of Stockholm. **Tel** 08-592 595 00. 🚌 *summer from Stadshusbron to Rosersberg and connecting bus.* **Slottsgalleria** 🕐 *11am–6pm Mon–Fri, 10am–5pm Sat & Sun.* **Palace** 🕐 *11am–2pm Sat, 11am–3pm Sun; Jun–Aug: 11am–4pm daily.* 🎫 *call for tour information.* 🛒 💻 www.steningeslott.com

South-east of Sigtuna, Sweden's oldest town, and only 10 minutes from Arlanda Airport is Steninge Slott, one of the gems of Lake Mälaren. The palace ranks among the finest works of Tessin the

Younger *(see p37)* and was designed a decade before he started on Stockholm's Royal Palace. The roof is that of a traditional Swedish manor house of the time, but otherwise the design is influenced by Tessin's studies, mainly in Italy and France. The result is an Italianate palace in a rural Swedish setting, which Carl Gyllenstierna gave to his wife Anna Soop as a wedding gift in 1706. Since then Steninge has had several owners, the best known of whom was Count Axel von Fersen, reputed to have been the lover of the French Queen Marie Antoinette (1755–93). The park, planned by the landscape architect Johan Hårleman, has a monument of Count von Fersen.

In 1999 the estate was transformed into a cultural centre. The biggest attraction is the elegant Baroque palace. The staircase has similarities to its counterpart at the Royal Palace *(see p50)* and elsewhere there are details, which can also be seen in Tessinska Palatset *(see p48)*. The oval hall is a masterpiece of Swedish Baroque, decorated by the Italian stucco artist Giuseppe Marchi. It regained its original splendour as part of restoration work in the early 20th century, planned by the architect G Clason. At the same time Julius Kronberg contributed paintings on the door lintels and ceilings.

A 19th-century stone barn houses the Slottsgalleria with glassworks, pottery, candlemaking, shop and restaurant.

Steninge Palace, one of the most perfect examples of late 17th-century manor house design

Drottningholm ➊

With its palace, theatre, park and Chinese Pavilion,
the whole of Drottningholm has been included in
UNESCO's World Heritage list. The royal palace on
the island of Lovön emerged in its present form
towards the end of the 17th century, and was one of
the most lavish buildings of its era. Contemporary
Italian and French architecture inspired Tessin the
Elder (1615–81) in his design, which was also
intended to glorify royal power. The project was
completed by Tessin the Younger, while 18th-century
architects like Carl Hårleman and Jean Eric Rehn put
the finishing touches to the interiors. The Royal
Family uses part of the palace as its private residence.

Baroque Garden
The bronze statue of Hercules
*(1620s) by the Dutch Renais-
sance sculptor Adrian de Vries
adorns the parterre in the
palace's Baroque Gardens.*

**The Upper South
Bodyguard Room**
*This ante-room to the State
Room, used for ceremonial
occasions, was decorated with
stucco works by Giovanni and
Carlo Carove, and ceiling
paintings by Johan Sylvius.*

**Apartments of the
Royal Family**

STAR FEATURES

★ Queen Lovisa
Ulrika's Library

★ The Staircase

★ Queen Hedvig Eleo-
nora's State Bedroom

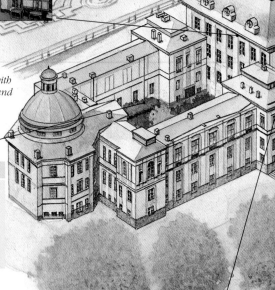

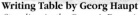

Writing Table by Georg Haupt
*Standing in the Queen's Room is this
masterpiece (1770) commissioned by
King Adolf Fredrik as a gift to Queen
Lovisa Ulrika. Textiles for the walls
and furnishings date from the 1970s.*

★ **Queen Lovisa Ulrika's Library**
The Queen commissioned Jean Eric Rehn (1717–93) to decorate this splendid library which emphasizes her influence on art and science in Sweden in the 18th-century.

VISITORS' CHECKLIST

10 km (6 miles) W of Stockholm.
🚇 Brommaplan, then bus 176,
177, 301, 323. 🚢 *May–Sep fr
Stadshusbron.* **Palace Tel** *08-
402 62 80.* 🕐 *Sep:* 11am–
3:30pm daily; Oct & Apr: 11am–
3:30pm Sat & Sun; Nov–Mar:
noon–3:30pm Sat & Sun.
🚫 *public hols.* 🗹 🗹 🚫 🗗
Chinese Pavilion 🕐 *May–Sep.*
🗹 🗹 🗹 **Theatre Museum**
Tel 759 04 06. 🕐 *May–Sep.*
🗹 🗹 **www**.royalcourt.se

The Palace Church
in the northern
cupola was com-
pleted by Hårleman
in the 1720s.

★ **Queen Hedvig Eleonora's State Bedroom**
Morning receptions ("levées") were held in this lavish Baroque room designed by Tessin the Elder. It took about 15 years for Sweden's foremost artists and craftsmen to decorate the room, which was completed in 1683.

Entrance

★ **The Staircase**
Trompe l'oeil paint-ings by Johan Sylvius adorn the walls, giving the impression that the already spacious interior stretches further into the palace.

Exploring Drottningholm

The Palace of Drottningholm is complemented by the Court Theatre (Slottsteatern), the world's oldest theatre still in active use, the Theatre Museum (Teatermuseum) and the elegant Chinese Pavilion (Kina Slott). The complex is situated on the shores of Lake Mälaren, surrounded by Baroque and Rococo gardens, and lush English-style parkland. In summer the theatre stages opera and ballet; and the church is used for High Mass and concerts.

Karl XI's gallery at Drottningholm, featuring the victory at Lund, 1667

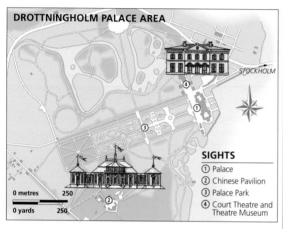

DROTTNINGHOLM PALACE AREA

STOCKHOLM

0 metres 250
0 yards 250

SIGHTS

① Palace
② Chinese Pavilion
③ Palace Park
④ Court Theatre and Theatre Museum

THE PALACE APARTMENTS

The first thing that meets the eye on entering the apartments is a Baroque corridor with a view that frames part of the gardens in all their splendour. The central part of the palace is dominated by the staircase, crowned by a lantern with ceiling paintings by Ehrenstrahl. There are examples of Baroque stucco work by Giovanni and Carlo Carove. Marble statues of the nine muses and their protector, Apollo, are placed at the corners of the balustrades.

Medallion showing life and death

The Green Salon is reached from the lower vestibule via the Lower Northern Bodyguard Room. This is the beginning of the main ceremonial suite, which continues with Karl X's Gallery where paintings illustrate his major military exploit, the crossing of the ice in the Store Bælt (Great Belt) by the Swedish army in 1658.

Queen Hedvig Eleonora (1636–1715) held audiences in the Ehrenstrahl Salon, named after the artist whose paintings dominate the walls. More prominent guests were received in the State Bedroom, which later in Queen Lovisa Ulrika's time was in fact used for sleeping. Her Meissen porcelain can be seen in the Blue Cabinet; the Library has her collection of more than 2,000 books. Behind the Upper Northern Guards Room with a ceiling by Johan Sylvius is a Gustavian drawing room, with a bureau by Johan Niklas Eckstein. In 1777, following Gustav III's assumption of power, the Blue Salon was decorated in the Neo-Classical style.

The Chinese Salon was used as a private bedroom by King Adolf Fredrik. It is directly above the Queen's State Bedroom and there is a hidden staircase linking the two floors. The "bureau"

opposite the tiled stove is also a sofa bed. The Oscar Room was refurbished by Oscar I (1799–1859) and is adorned by a tapestry dating from the 1630s. After the General's Room, Karl XI's Gallery commemorating the victory at Lund (1667), and the Golden Salon comes the Queen's Salon. Just as the adjoining State Room had portraits of all the European monarchs, the portraits in the Queen's Salon were of European queens. This floor finishes with the Upper South Bodyguard Room, an ante-room to the State Room and lavishly decorated by the Carove stucco artists and the ceiling painter Johan Sylvius.

THE CHINESE PAVILION

On her 33rd birthday in 1753 Queen Lovisa Ulrika was given a Chinese pavilion by her husband, King Adolf Fredrik. It had been manufactured in Stockholm and the previous night it was shipped to Drottningholm and assembled a few hundred metres from the palace. It had to be taken down after 10 years because rot had set in,

The Chinese Pavilion, an extravaganza in blue and gold

and was replaced by the Chinese Pavilion (Kina Slott) which is still one of the major attractions at Drottningholm. The polished-tile building was designed by D F Adelcrantz (1716–96).

At this time there was great European interest in all things Chinese. In 1733 the newly formed East India Company made its first journey to China. After Lovisa Ulrika's death in 1782 this interest waned, but it was rekindled in the 1840s. The Chinese Pavilion is a mixture of what was considered 250 years ago to be typical Chinese style along with artifacts from China and Japan. Efforts have been made to restore the interior to its original state with the help of a 1777 inventory.

Four smaller pavilions belong to the building. In the north-eastern pavilion the king had his lathe and a carpenter's bench. Alongside is the Confidencen pavilion, where meals were taken if he wished to be left undisturbed. The food was prepared in the basement, the floor opened and the dining table hauled up. The adjoining Turkish-style "watch tent" was built as a barracks for Gustav III's dragoons.

Tiled stove in a cabinet in the Chinese Pavilion

THE PALACE PARK

The palace's three gardens are each of a completely different character but still combine to provide a unified whole. The symmetrical formal garden started to take shape in 1640. The garden was designed to stimulate all senses with sights, sounds and smells. It starts by the palace terrace with its "embroidery" parterre and continues as far as the Hercules statue. The water parterre is situated on slightly higher ground and is broken up with waterfalls and topiaries. The sculptures, mainly carved by the Flemish

sculptor Adrian de Vries (1560–1626) were war trophies from Prague in 1648 and from Fredriksborg Castle in Denmark in 1659.

The avenues of chestnut trees were laid out when the Chinese Pavilion was completed, as well as the Rococo-inspired garden area – a cross between the formal main garden and the freer composition of the English park. The English park has natural paths and a stream with small islands, along with trees and bushes at "natural" irregular intervals. Gustav III is reputed to have been responsible for its design and also planned several buildings. Not all his plans were realized, but he added four statues which he had bought during his travels in Italy.

The first 300 of a total of 846 lime trees were planted in the avenues flanking the Baroque garden as early as 1684.

THE COURT THEATRE AND THEATRE MUSEUM

The designer of the Chinese Pavilion, Carl Fredrik Adelcrantz, was also responsible for the Drottningholm Court Theatre (Slottsteatern), which dates from 1766. The theatre was commissioned by Queen

The magnificent 18th-century stage in the Drottningholm Court Theatre

Lovisa Ulrika, but Adelcrantz did not have the same resources as the architects of the palace itself. This simple wooden building with a plaster façade is now the world's oldest theatre still preserved in its original condition. The interior and fittings are masterpieces of simple functionality. The pilasters, for example, are made from gypsum and the supports from papier maché. The scenery, with its wooden hand-driven machinery, is still in working order.

After Gustav III's death in 1792 the theatre fell into disuse until the 1920s, when the machinery ropes were replaced, electric lighting was installed, and the original wings were refurbished.

The scenery is adapted to 18th-century plays. It can be changed in just a few seconds with the help of up to 30 scene-shifters. The sound effects are simple but authentic: a wooden box filled with stones creates realistic thunder, a wooden cylinder covered in tent cloth produces a howling wind. Every summer there are about 30 performances, mainly opera and ballet from the 18th century. The theatre is open daily for visitors to the palace.

A Theatre Museum and shop are housed in Duke Carl's pavilion, built in the 1780s. The museum focuses on 18th-century theatre, with decoration sketches, paintings, scenery models and costumes. A *Commedia dell'arte* room contains paintings by Pehr Hilleström and sketches for Gustav III's dramatic productions by Louis Jean Desprez.

Court Theatre stage machinery: the world's oldest still in use

Millesgården, home of the sculptor Carl Milles in the early 20th century

Millesgården ❺

Herserudsvägen 30, Lidingö.
🚇 Ropsten, then bus 207 or train to Torsvik. **Tel** 08-446 75 90.
🕐 15 May–30 Sep: 11am–5pm daily; 1 Oct–14 May: noon–5pm Tue–Sun. 🎟 by appointment. ♿ ✍
🖥 📷 www.millesgarden.se

Carl Milles (1875–1955) was one of the 20th century's greatest Swedish sculptors and the best known internationally. From 1931 he lived for 20 years in the USA, where he became a prolific monumental sculptor with works like the *Meeting of the Waters* fountain in St Louis and the *Resurrection* fountain in the National Memorial Park outside Washington DC. In Stockholm visitors can see 15 of his public works, including the *Orpheus* fountain in front of Konserthuset *(see p68)*.

In 1906 Milles bought land on the island of Lidingö on which he built a house, completed in 1908. He lived here with his wife until 1931, and also after his return from the USA. In 1936 he and his wife donated the property to the Swedish people.

Millesgården covers 18,000 sq m (194,000 sq ft) in a series of terraces and includes Milles' studios with originals and replicas of his work. It has a magnificent garden – a work of art in itself – and a fine view over the water.

Fjäderholmarna ❻

6 km (4 miles) E of Stockholm.
🚢 53. ⛴ May–Sep from Nybrokajen and Slussen.

With the inclusion of the Fjäderholmarna islands in The National City Park *(see p121)* the city's "green lung" has acquired a small part of the archipelago. The main island, Stora Fjäderholmen, is only a 25-minute boat journey from Nybrokajen or Slussen.

The island already boasted an inn in the 17th century, conveniently sited for the archipelago islanders on their way to and from the city to sell their wares. The inn was closed during World War II when the area was taken over by the military and landing was forbidden.

Access to the public was restored in the mid-1980s and the main island now has an attractive harbour, three restaurants and an ice-cream parlour as well as a tour of the country's first whisky distillery, Mackmyra Distillery. There are also three museums, two of which are devoted to traditional and recreational boating and the

The Fjäderholmarna islands, a popular summer excursion just 25 minutes by boat from the city

third that explores the history of Vodka in Sweden and its growing popularity.

Various handicrafts are practised on the island, including metalwork, weaving, textile printing, wood-carving, pottery and glassmaking. There is also an art gallery and an outdoor theatre that, during the summer months, hosts popular theatre weeks for children.

The other three islands have a rich bird-life and one of them, Libertas, has Sweden's last remaining gas-powered lighthouse.

Vaxholm Fortress, strategically sited on the approach to Vaxholm

Vaxholm ❼

25 km (16 miles) NE of Stockholm.
🚌 670. ⛴ from Strömkajen and Nybrokajen. **Vaxholm Fortress** and **Vaxholm Fortress Museum** *Tel* 08-541 718 90. 🕐 Jun: noon–4pm daily; Jul–Aug: noon–5pm daily; first two weekends of Sep: 11am–5pm. ✍

The archipelago's main community, Vaxholm, has been a strategic point for shipping since the 19th century. It is easily reached by boat from Stockholm on a delightful one-hour journey through the inner archipelago.

Vaxholm has been inhabited since the 16th century. In 1548 Gustav Vasa ordered that the nearby island of Vaxholmen should be fortified. Some 300 years later a new fortress was built here, but it soon lost its military importance and was used as a civil prison. Today the imposing citadel houses an interesting military museum.

Two of Stockholm's best-known architects have left their mark on Vaxholm town. The 100-year-old law-courts' building was given its present appearance in 1925 by Cyrillus Johansson. On the headland nearest to the harbour is a rather stately hotel designed in 1899 by Erik Lallerstedt, and traces of its Jugendstil ornamentation can still be seen.

The wooden buildings around the square and along Hamngatan with their souvenir shops provide a pleasant stroll, and the harbour is always busy.

Grinda ❽

30 km (19 miles) E of Stockholm. ⓕ 08-542 494 91. 🚌 670 from Östra station to Vaxholm, then boat. ⛴ from Strömkajen and Nybrokajen. 🏠 (summer only). 🚻

Grinda is a leafy island, typical of the inner archipelago. It has some excellent beaches and rocks for swimming, as well as good fishing. Boats and bicycles can be hired, making it an ideal place to visit while exploring the archipelago. It takes about one and a half hours by boat from the city.

The architect Ernst Stenhammar, who designed the Grand Hôtel (see p79), built a large Jugendstil villa here, which is now a restaurant and pub and has guest rooms. There are chalets for rental, a campsite and a youth hostel in a former military barracks.

Finnhamn ❾

40 km (25 miles) NE of Stockholm. ⓕ 08-542 462 12. ⛴ from Strömkajen and Nybrokajen. 🏠 🚻

Finnish ships used to moor at Finnhamn on their way to and from Stockholm. This attractive group of islands lies two and a half hours by boat from the city at the point where the softer scenery of the inner archipelago gives way to the harsher landscape of the outer islands. As on Grinda, the main island has a wooden villa designed by Ernst Stenhammar (1912). Today it is the largest youth hostel in the archipelago. There is a restaurant, chalets for rental and a campsite. Smaller islands nearby are accessible by rowing boat.

Sandhamn, the yachting centre in Stockholm's outer archipelago

Sandhamn ❿

50 km (31 miles) E of Stockholm. ⓕ 08-57 03 45 67. 🚌 433, 434 from Slussen to Stavsnäs, then boat. ⛴ from Strömkajen and Nybrokajen. 🏠 🚻

Over the past 200 years Sandhamn, on Sandön, has been a meeting point for sailors, particularly yachting enthusiasts. The Royal Swedish Yacht Club has been based at Seglarrestaurangen (Sailors' Restaurant) for more than 100 years. Every year the world's yachting elite flock to Sandhamn to take part in the Round Gotland Race.

Once a pilot station, Sandhamn is a charming village with narrow alleys and houses adorned with decorative carvings. There are now about 100 permanent residents. The Customs House, built in 1752, is a listed heritage building.

Smooth rock formations at Utö in the southern archipelago

A customs inspector who worked here, Elias Sehlstedt (1808–74), made his name as a poet and artist.

Sandhamn has shops, handicraft centres, and a swimming pool. Guided tours can be arranged. Camping is not permitted, but hotel, bed-and-breakfast and chalet accommodation is available.

Utö ⓫

50 km (31 miles) SE of Stockholm. ⓕ 08-501 574 10. ⛴ in summer, from Strömkajen. 🏠 🚻
www.utoturistbyra.se

No other island in the archipelago has as rich a history as Utö, which was inhabited before the Viking era. In the 12th century the islanders started to mine iron ore, and this activity continued until 1879. Their story is told in the Mining Museum adjoining the hotel. Today's holiday homes along Lurgatan were built as miners' cottages in the 18th century. A windmill, built in 1791, provides an unrivalled view of the island.

Utö is one of the best seaside resorts in the Stockholm area, and is ideal for a weekend or full-day excursion. Its facilities include a variety of restaurants. The hotel's restaurant is sited in the old mine offices.

Hotel, youth hostel, camping, chalet and bed-and-breakfast accommodation are all available. Bicycles, rowing boats and canoes can be hired, and there are also regular fishing trips and archipelago safaris.

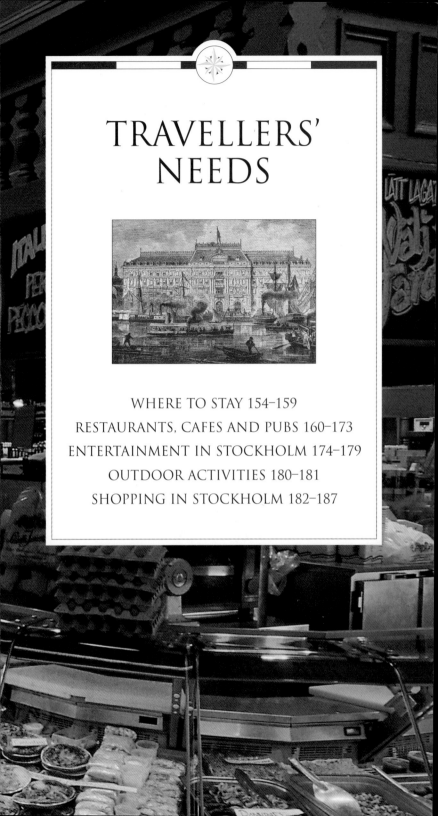

TRAVELLERS' NEEDS

WHERE TO STAY

Stockholm's hotel scene could be said to revolve around Blasieholmen, where the Grand Hôtel offers accommodation which is just as princely as the Royal Palace on the opposite side of Norrström. Only a short distance away is *af Chapman*, a ship which is probably one of the world's most beautiful youth hostels. Stockholm's hotels are not

Door-man

usually built in the same grandiose style as their counterparts in southern Europe, but they offer a high level of comfort and service and often have magnificent views or locations.

The listings on pages 156–59 cover about 40 hotels in Stockholm and the immediate area, from budget accommodation and youth hostels to luxury hotels, with the large medium-price chain hotels in between.

Exterior of the elegant Hotel Diplomat *(see p158)*

CHOOSING A HOTEL

When you stay at a beautifully located classic hotel, you pay for the quality. But although most of Stockholm's hotels fall into the rather expensive category, it also has perfectly acceptable budget accommodation, maybe with a shower and toilet along the corridor.

The cheapest accommodation is offered by the dozen or so youth hostels, most of which have high standards. Other value-for-money options include the many Bed & Breakfast establishments.

Stockholm has become one of the world's most important cities for conferences, so occupancy at the city's hotels is high – around 80 per cent between May and November but much lower in July. Visitors are strongly advised to book hotel accommodation well in advance.

You should also try to avoid the peak seasons for trade fairs, or events like the

Stockholm Marathon in June. The **Stockholm Information Service** (SIS) events calendar posted on the Internet (www.stockholmtown.com) is useful for finding out when the busiest periods are.

HOW TO BOOK

If you do not book a hotel through your travel agent, you can easily make your own reservation through the **Stockholm Visitors Board** either over the counter, by phone or by using the centre's website. This user-friendly site includes a simple booking form (in English), which you complete and send back by e-mail. The agency makes bookings for hotels in the whole of Greater Stockholm, including the archipelago and the Mälardalen area. Advance booking on the Internet and by telephone or fax is free of charge, but a small fee is charged for bookings over the counter.

Of course, reservations can also be made directly with the hotel by telephone or fax, and in most cases also on the

The lobby at the Victory Hotel in Gamla Stan *(see p156)*

Internet. Web addresses for the larger hotel chains' reservation centres are listed opposite.

HOTEL CHAINS

Several international and national hotel chains are represented in Stockholm. **Scandic Hotels**, with more than 100 hotels, is the leading Scandinavian chain and it puts emphasis on its environmentally friendly policies. It has eight hotels in the city and six outside, including two on the way to Arlanda Airport.

Radisson SAS, a chain partly owned by Scandinavian Airlines, has three large hotels in Stockholm and two at Arlanda Airport.

Choice Hotels Scandinavia has two hotels in Stockholm under the "Comfort" banner, indicating a high-standard room-and-breakfast hotel. It also has a hotel near Arlanda and three conference hotels in the "Quality" category.

The environmentally conscious Scandinavian chain **First Hotels** has three categories – First Hotel, First Express and First Resort. There are three First Hotels in the city centre and three First Express properties outside the city.

Rica City Hotels, a partner chain of Braathens and Supranational Hotels, has three centrally located hotels in Stockholm, two near Hötorget and one in Gamla Stan.

The Collector's Hotel is a group of three small and exclusive hotels located in the Old Town – Victory, Lord Nelson and Lady Hamilton – which all have artistic and maritime features.

◁ **Östermalmshallen houses an abundance of delicacies in a well-preserved 1880s setting**

Grand Hôtel's Bernadotte Suite *(see p157)*

PRICES AND PAYMENT

Prices in the hotel listing are for the cheapest double room, including breakfast, service and VAT. All hotels offer rooms at much reduced rates at weekends year-round and daily in the summer. For the cheaper hotels this involves a price reduction of 100–300 kr per night; for the medium-priced hotels about 500 kr; and for deluxe hotels up to 1,000 kr.

Nearly all hotels accept the main credit cards. The larger hotels will also change foreign currency, but the best and cheapest way of changing money is to use one of the bureaux de change *(see p194)*.

YOUTH HOSTELS

There are 13 youth hostels in Stockholm, the four largest of which are affiliated to the **Swedish Touring Club** (STF/IYHF). Apart from the city's flagship, *af Chapman*, three more floating hostels are moored right in the city centre: *Gustav af Klint* at the Stadsgården quay, and *MS Rygerfjord* and *Den röda båten Mälaren* at Söder Mälarstrand. The ships each

Cabin at the floating youth hostel *af Chapman (see p157)*

have about 100 beds, as well as fully licensed restaurants and superb views.

The standard of Stockholm's youth hostels is generally high, especially the four affiliated to STF. Some hostels are open only in the summer.

Prices are around 200 kr per night in a double room, with a discount of about 40 kr for STF members, but come down to about 100 kr in a larger room or dormitory. Prices usually exclude breakfast and bed linen hire.

The Stockholm Visitors Board can book youth hostel accommodation, but only over the counter and for a stay the same night. Beds can be booked directly with the hostel. A complete list of hostels is available from Hotellcentralen or on the Internet.

BED & BREAKFAST

Bed & breakfast accommodation is widely available in central Stockholm and the suburbs, as well as the archipelago. There is usually a choice between a single room, double room or a whole apartment. Breakfast is normally included in the price – apart from apartments, where self-catering is the rule – and bed linen and hand towels always are. B&B prices range from 300–500 kr per person per night. A double room costs 500–700 kr while an apartment, which often has to be rented for four or five days, costs from 600 kr per night.

B&B can be booked in advance through **Bed & Breakfast Service Stockholm** directly or via the Internet. A small booking fee is charged.

DIRECTORY

CENTRAL BOOKING

Stockholm Visitors Board
(Central booking agency for hotels and youth hostels)
Vasagatan 14,
111 20 Stockholm.
Map 2 C5.
Tel 08-508 285 08.
Fax 08-508 285 09.
www.stockholmtown.com

HOTEL CHAINS

Choice Hotels Scandinavia
Tel 08-442 70 40.
www.choicehotels.se

First Hotels
Tel 020-411 111.
www.firsthotels.com

Radisson SAS
Tel 020-238 238.
Fax see individual hotel.
www.radissonsas.com

Rica City Hotels
Tel 08-723 72 10.
Fax see individual hotel.
www.rica.se

Scandic Hotels
Tel 08-517 517 00.
Fax 08-517 517 11.
www.scandic-hotels.com

The Collector's Hotel
Tel 08-506 400 50.
Fax 08-506 401 71.
www.victory-hotel.se

YOUTH HOSTELS

Swedish Touring Club (STF)
Tel 08-463 21 00.
Fax 08-463 21 06.
www.svenskaturist foreningen.se

BED & BREAKFAST

Bed & Breakfast Service Stockholm
Sidenvägen 17,
178 37 Ekerö.
Tel 08-660 55 65.
Fax 08-663 38 22.
www.bedbreakfast.a.se

Choosing a Hotel

The hotels listed here have been selected on the basis of their price category, value for money, comfort and location. The listing starts with the central areas and continues with hotels outside the city centre. For map references, see the street finder maps on *pp206–15*. For restaurant listings, *see pp164–71*.

PRICE CATEGORIES
The following price ranges are for a standard double room and taxes per night during the high season. Breakfast is not included, unless specified.
ⓚ under 1,000 kr
ⓚⓚ 1,000–1,500 kr
ⓚⓚⓚ 1,500–2000 kr
ⓚⓚⓚⓚ 2000–2,500kr
ⓚⓚⓚⓚⓚ over 2,500 kr

GAMLA STAN

First Hotel Reisen
ⓚⓚ

Skeppsbron 12, 111 30 **Tel** *08-22 32 60* **Fax** *08-20 15 59* **Rooms** *144*　　　　**Map** *4 C3*

Housed in three 18th-century buildings and a historic steamship (for the conference facilities) anchored nearby in the harbour, the Reisen is a lively location. The hotel bar was voted one of the top three bars in Stockholm and famous DJs work the turntables here at weekends. **www.firsthotels.com/reisen**

Lady Hamilton Hotel
ⓚⓚⓚ

Storkyrkobrinken 5, 111 28 **Tel** *08-50 64 01 00* **Fax** *08-50 64 01 10* **Rooms** *34*　　　　**Map** *4 B3*

Named after Lord Nelson's mistress, exquisite folk art and maritime antiques adorn the rooms and corridors of this delightful 15th-century building. The Lady Hamilton is a superior family hotel located in the heart of Gamla Stan amongst shops, museums, and the hustle-bustle of historic Stockholm. **www.ladyhamiltonhotel.se**

Lord Nelson Hotel
ⓚⓚⓚ

Västerlånggatan 22, 111 29 **Tel** *08-50 64 01 20* **Fax** *08-50 64 01 30* **Rooms** *29*　　　　**Map** *4 B3*

Built in the 1600s and filled with nautical antiques, this is the narrowest hotel in Stockholm as well as being a fascinating museum. The main floor and lobby resemble the inside of a ship, with the rooms decorated along the same lines. Guests can relax on the roof terrace, which is a unique experience in Gamla Stan. **www.lordnelsonhotel.se**

Rica Hotel Gamla Stan
ⓚⓚⓚ

Lilla Nygatan 25, 111 28 **Tel** *08-723 72 50* **Fax** *08-723 72 59* **Rooms** *51*　　　　**Map** *4 B4*

Charming winding streets lead to the doorstep of this cosy establishment. Located close to the Royal Palace, portraits of Swedish royalty dating from the 1650s adorn the walls of every room. Here you will find all the modern amenities you could wish for, including conference facilities in the historic wine cellars. **www.rica.se**

Victory Hotel
ⓚⓚⓚ

Lilla Nygatan 5, 111 28 **Tel** *08-50 64 00 00* **Fax** *08-50 64 00 10* **Rooms** *45*　　　　**Map** *4 B3*

The flagship of the Collector's Hotel chain and housed in a beautifully maintained townhouse, this exclusive boutique hotel has business facilities in every room. One of Stockholm's finest hotels, the service is exceptional and the maritime design timeless. Includes the landmark Leijontornet Restaurant *(see p164)*. **www.victoryhotel.se**

CITY

Comfort Hotel Stockholm
ⓚⓚ

Kungsbron 1, 111 22 **Tel** *08-56 62 22 00* **Fax** *08-56 62 24 44* **Rooms** *163*　　　　**Map** *2 B4*

Modern business hotel located in the World Trade Center and close to the central train station. The rooms are small, clean and simply furnished. The Comfort does not have a restaurant, but does serve a buffet breakfast. Well-equipped for business travellers with a 24-hour front desk. **www.choicehotels/hotels/se030**

Berns' Hotel
ⓚⓚⓚ

Näckströmsgatan 8, 111 47 **Tel** *08-56 63 22 00* **Fax** *08-56 63 22 01* **Rooms** *82*　　　　**Map** *3 D4*

Located in the heart of bustling central Stockholm, this lively boutique hotel first opened in 1863. Fine dining is available in its restaurant or on the terrace, as well as world-class nightlife with five bars and a popular night club in the basement. A favourite venue for international singers and musicians. **www.berns.se**

Hotel Crystal Plaza
ⓚⓚⓚ

Birger Jarlsgatan 35, 11 45 **Tel** *08-406 88 00* **Fax** *08-24 15 11* **Rooms** *111*　　　　**Map** *3 D3*

Built in 1895 and situated close to Stureplan *(see p70)*, all the rooms at the Crystal Plaza are decorated in a variety of styles, including speciality rooms in the bell tower (one of which even includes a Finnish spa). The hotel offers the Plaza Studios for travellers looking for long-term stay options. **www.crystalplazahotel.se**

Key to Symbols *see back cover flap*

Rica Hotel Kungsgatan

Kungsgatan 47, 111 56 **Tel** *08-723 72 20* **Fax** *08-723 72 99* **Rooms** *260*

Map *2 C4*

Located on the upper stories of the PUB department store, the Kungsgatan is one of the largest hotels in Scandinavia and has views of Hötorget *(see p68)*, Stockholm's oldest marketplace. There is no restaurant but breakfast is served in the rooms, which are medium-sized and modern. An ideal location for travellers wishing to shop. **www.rica.se**

Sheraton Stockholm Hotel & Towers

Tegelbacken 6, 101 23 **Tel** *08-412 34 00* **Fax** *08-412 34 09* **Rooms** *465*

Map *4 A1*

A large international luxury hotel, the Stockholm is centrally located overlooking Gamla Stan and the train station. Its Threesixty Bar and Restaurant offers a dynamic dining experience with an international ambience. Rooms are of the typically high standard expected from this chain. **www.sheratonstockholm.com**

Radisson SAS Royal Viking Hotel

Vasagatan 1, 101 24 **Tel** *08-50 65 40 00* **Fax** *08-50 65 40 01* **Rooms** *459*

Map *2 C5*

One of Stockholm's best known hotels, the Royal Viking offers two bars, one in the ground floor atrium and the exciting Sky Bar on the top floor, as well as the excellent Stockholm Fisk Restaurant. This hotel maintains high standards suited to both business and leisure travellers. **www.radissonsas.com**

Scandic Hotel Sergel Plaza

Brunkebergstorg 9, 103 27 **Tel** *08-51 72 63 00* **Fax** *08-51 72 63 11* **Rooms** *403*

Map *4 A1*

This award-winning hotel, situated close to Central Station, offers the full range of services for both tourists and business travellers. Guests can relax in the large rooms or comfortable lobby and enjoy the excellent Scandinavian breakfast buffet. Car rental is available within the hotel. **www.scandic-hotels.se**

Hotel Riddargatan

Riddargatan 14, 114 35 **Tel** *08-55 57 30 00* **Fax** *08-55 57 30 11* **Rooms** *78*

Map *3 E4*

The Hotel Riddargatan is one of the best hotels in the city and has a good location in Stockholm's "golden triangle", just behind the Royal Dramatic Theatre. Close to restaurants, bars and nightlife, sometimes visiting world-famous jazz musicians stay and perform here. **www.profilhotels.se**

Scandic Anglais

Humlegårdsgatan 23, 102 44 **Tel** *08-51 73 40 00* **Fax** *08-51 73 40 11* **Rooms** *230*

Map *3 D3*

This modern hotel is situated in the heart of central Stockholm. Guests can relax in the hotel's spa or the more energetic can take advantage of the free gym and bike hire. The hotel boasts a restaurant and a terrace bar that offers magnificent views of the city. **www.scandic-hotels.com/anglais**

BLASIEHOLMEN & SKEPPSHOLMEN

af Chapman & Skeppsholmen (STF/IYHF)

Flaggmansvägen 8, 111 49 **Tel** *08-463 22 66* **Fax** *08-611 71 55* **Rooms** *293 beds*

Map *5 D3*

One of the most beautiful youth hostels anywhere in the world offering beds on board a classic ship *(see p79)* permanently moored across from the Royal Palace or in Hantverkshuset. The gangway to the ship is raised at 2am and a healthy breakfast is served in the morning. Book early – it fills up quickly. **www.stfchapman.com**

Radisson SAS Strand Hotel

Nybrokajen 9, 103 27 **Tel** *08-50 66 40 00* **Fax** *08-50 66 40 01* **Rooms** *152*

Map *5 D1*

Exceptional waterfront location, with views over Nybroviken from the piazza restaurant and piano bar, the Strand offers 24-hour room service and many other amenities for the business traveller. Discount entry for guests to the nearby Sturebadet spa is a bonus. Excellent buffet breakfast. **www.strand.stockholm.radissonsas.com**

Grand Hôtel Stockholm

Södra Blasiehomshamnen 8, 103 27 **Tel** *08-679 35 00* **Fax** *08-611 86 66* **Rooms** *368*

Map *4 C1*

Magnificently located just a stone's throw from the Nationalmuseum *(see pp82–3)* and Kungsträdgården *(see pp62–3)*, the Grand is one of the world's great hotels. In addition, the Cadier Bar *(see p178)* and the Mathias Dahlgren Restaurant are unrivalled in Stockholm. **www.grandhotel.se**

DJURGÅRDEN

Scandic Hotel Hasselbacken

Hazeliusbacken 20, 100 55 **Tel** *08-51 73 43 00* **Fax** *08-51 73 43 11* **Rooms** *112*

Map *5 D3*

A beautifully restored traditional hotel dating from 1765 and adjoining Skansen *(see pp96-7)*, the Hasselbacken is close to the city centre, but surrounded by woodland in a peaceful location. Medium-sized rooms are a mixture of Swedish design with wooden features. Excellent restaurant, terrace grill and summerhouse bar. **www.scandic-hotels.se**

ÖSTERMALM & GÄRDET

Clarion Collection Hotel Tapto

Jungfrugatan 57, 115 31 **Tel** *08-664 50 00* **Fax** *08-664 07 00* **Rooms** *117* **Map** *3 F2*

This is a comfortable, cosy hotel, located just a short walk away from the city centre. It offers a 24-hour front desk service and has a relaxation area with both men's and women's saunas. Rooms are elegantly decorated and all mod-cons are provided. An evening buffet is included in the price. **www.choicehotels.no**

Mornington Hotel

Nybrogatan 53, 102 44 **Tel** *08-50 73 30 00* **Fax** *08-50 73 30 39* **Rooms** *215* **Map** *3 E3*

British-themed hotel with tartan-clad staff and interior design inspired by the theatre world. The Mornington is located across from Stockholm's largest auction house and many antique shops. Guests can enjoy the health club with full gym and spa facilities. **www.mornington.se**

Villa Källhagen

Djurgårdsbrunnsvägen 10, 115 27 **Tel** *08-665 03 00* **Fax** *08-665 03 99* **Rooms** *36* **Map** *6 B2*

Elegant establishment with outstanding location on Djurgårdsbrunnsviken Bay. All rooms have a view of the Djurgårdsbrun canal. There are beautiful conference facilities in this historic hotel, which also has a top-class restaurant, summertime garden café, and its own bakery. A peaceful retreat. **www.kallhagen.se**

Esplanade, Hotel

Strandvägen 7A, 114 56 **Tel** *08-663 07 40* **Fax** *08-662 59 92* **Rooms** *34* **Map** *3 E4*

Frequented by representatives of nearby embassies and others who enjoy its traditional charm, the Esplanade is a cosy tourist hotel set in a majestic patrician house. It is located on fashionable Strandvägen, close to Stockholm's best boutique shopping, and has individually decorated rooms in Jugendstil style. **www.hotelesplanade.se**

Hotel Diplomat

Strandvägen 7C, 114 56 **Tel** *08-459 68 00* **Fax** *08-459 68 20* **Rooms** *130* **Map** *3 E4*

With a prestigious address on Strandvägen, this hotel offers every amenity and a renowned standard of service to its guests. In a well-preserved Jugendstil building that dates from 1911, the rooms have typical Swedish decor and elegant bathrooms. Weekend highlights include a "tea house" and the T/Bar's popular brunch. **www.diplomathotel.com**

KUNGSHOLMEN & VASASTAN

Vanadis Hotel

Sveavägen 142, 113 46 **Tel** *08-30 12 11* **Fax** *08-31 23 91* **Rooms** *67* **Map** *2 B2*

Efficient budget hotel located on the outskirts of Stockholm with easy access to motorways. Family friendly, it is connected to Stockholm's largest water park, a popular destination in summer – hotel guests can use the facilities for free. Note that not all rooms are en suite. **www.vanadishotel.com**

Elite Palace Hotel, Best Western

St Eriksgatan 115, 100 31 **Tel** *08-56 62 17 00* **Fax** *08-56 62 17 01* **Rooms** *216* **Map** *2 A1*

Large and comfortable hotel with triple and 4-bed rooms, particularly good for families. This establishment is close to Hagaparken *(see pp122–3)* and has easy access to motorways. The hotel's own pub, the Bishop's Arms, found at street level, serves beer and whisky. Great gym and sauna facilities also available. **www.elite.se**

August Strindberg Hotel

Tegnérgatan 38, 113 59 **Tel** *08-32 50 06* **Fax** *08-20 90 85* **Rooms** *27* **Map** *2 C3*

A small boutique hotel with its own courtyard, the August Strindberg lies in a quiet location on top of a ridge in Tegnérlunden Park, one of the highest points in Stockholm. The central train station, a number of theatres and surrounding shopping streets are within easy walking distance. **www.hotellstrindberg.se**

Hotel Tegnérlunden

Tegnérlunden 8, 113 59 **Tel** *08-54 54 55 50* **Fax** *08-54 54 55 51* **Rooms** *102* **Map** *2 B3*

Near to the August Strindberg museum on Drottninggatan *(see p69)*, the Tegnérlunden offers a family atmosphere and a quiet location. Breakfast buffet is served on the roof with spectacular views over the city centre. This hotel is superbly situated for exploring all parts of the city. **www.hoteltegnerlunden.se**

Nordic Sea Hotel

Vasaplan 4, 101 37 **Tel** *08-505 630 00* **Rooms** *367* **Map** *2 B4*

The staff at the Nordic Sea Hotel are attentive and happy to provide information on the best places to visit. All rooms are decorated individually in Scandinavian style. It is also home to the coolest of bars: Absolut Icebar Stockholm *(see p178)* with a permanent temperature of -5 degrees. **www.nordicseahotel.com**

Key to Price Guide *see p156* **Key to Symbols** *see back cover flap*

SÖDERMALM

Tre Små Rum Hotel ⊗

Högbergsgatan 81, 118 54 **Tel** *08-641 23 71* **Fax** *08-642 88 08* **Rooms** *7*   **Map** *8 C3*

This inexpensive but cosy modern hotel was started by a traveller hoping to offer an economical and friendly option with a central location. All the rooms are non-smoking, and none *en suite*. Healthy breakfasts are created to your individual order. Early booking is essential. Bicycles are available for hire. **www.tresmarum.se**

Ersta Konferens & Hotel 〼P⑪ ⊗⊗

Erstagatan 1K, 116 91 **Tel** *08-714 63 41* **Fax** *08-714 63 51* **Rooms** *22*   **Map** *9 F2*

Good value for money, this small hotel is located in a large, busy complex in a historic setting. It offers comfortable Scandinavian-style rooms, conference facilities, café, restaurant, bookshop, museum and a church. Professional and accommodating staff make this an excellent choice for conferences. **www.erstadiakoni.se**

The Red Boat Mälaren P⑪ ⊗⊗

Söder Mälarstrand 6, 117 20 **Tel** *08-644 43 85* **Fax** *08-641 37 33* **Rooms** *97 beds*   **Map** *1 C5*

Two converted boats moored where Lake Mälaren meets the Baltic Sea make up this hotel and youth hostel. The rooms and lobby are decorated to resemble a ship and have been well maintained. The Red Boat is within walking distance of all parts of downtown Stockholm. Breakfast is not included. **www.theredboat.com**

Columbus Hotel P⑪ ⊗⊗⊗

Tjärhovsgatan 11, 116 21 **Tel** *08-50 31 12 00* **Fax** *08-50 31 12 01* **Rooms** *40*   **Map** *9 E3*

This small, intimate hotel occupies a building that dates back to 1780. The location is quiet and peaceful, with the beautiful Katarina Church close by. One of the city's hidden treasures, the Columbus boasts a delightful courtyard where breakfast is served during the summer. **www.columbus.se**

Långholmen Hotel 〼P⑪ ⊗⊗⊗

Kronohäketet, Långholmen, 102 72 **Tel** *08-720 85 00* **Fax** *08-720 85 75* **Rooms** *102*   **Map** *1 B5*

A converted former prison, the Långholmen offers accommodation in modernised "cells" on a leafy island in the city centre. The restaurant is in the warden's residence, dating from the 1670s, and there is also a pub, a wine cellar, a prison museum, and even a private bathing beach. Youth hostel available from 19 June to 9 August. **www.langholmen.com**

Hilton Hotel Slussen 〼P⑪≋♨♠⊟ ⊗⊗⊗⊗

Guldgränd 8, 104 65 **Tel** *08-51 73 53 00* **Fax** *08-51 73 53 11* **Rooms** *289*   **Map** *9 D2*

Well-equipped modern international hotel with two restaurants, a bar and a wine cellar. High on a hill overlooking Gamla Stan and Riddarfjärden, the Slussen has magnificent views from the summertime terrace bar. Pets welcomed by prior arrangement. Excellent gym facilities. **www.hilton.com**

FURTHER AFIELD

Ariston Hotel Lidingö 〼P⑪〽 ⊗

Stockholmsvägen 70, 181 42, Lidingö **Tel** *08-54 48 13 00* **Fax** *08-54 48 13 33* **Rooms** *27*

Three sisters run this pleasant hotel in a quiet part of the residential island of Lidingö, about 15 minutes from the city centre. Close to several golf courses, it has its own tennis courts as well as a full indoor gym. The rooms are spacious and individually decorated. Pets allowed by arrangement. **www.aristonhotell.se**

Ibis Hotel Stockholm Hägersten 〼P⑪〽 ⊗

Västertorpsvägen 131, 129 44, Hägersten **Tel** *08-55 63 23 30* **Fax** *08-97 64 27* **Rooms** *190*

Located on the southern approach to Stockholm, near the world's largest IKEA. This hotel offers high standards at reasonable prices. Friendly, multi-lingual staff help make this hotel a popular choice for business and leisure travellers alike. Approximately 15 km (9 miles) from the city centre. **www.ibishotel.se**

First Hotel Royal Star 〼P⑪♣ ⊗⊗

Mässvägen 1, 125 30, Älvsjö **Tel** *08-99 02 20* **Fax** *08-99 39 09* **Rooms** *103*

Personable business and conference hotel, close to Stockholm International Fairs exhibition centre. This establishment is 10 minutes from the city centre by shuttle train. The large clean rooms have basic amenities. Connecting rooms are available for families and large groups. The restaurant serves traditional Scandinavian cuisine. **www.firsthotels.com**

Quality Hotel Globe 〼P⑪〽⊟ ⊗⊗⊗

Arenaslingan 7, 121 26 **Tel** *08-686 63 00* **Fax** *08-686 63 01* **Rooms** *287*

Well-equipped large hotel near the Globe Arena and a large shopping mall, with women-only rooms and facilities for conferences and special events. Breakfast is served in the Arena Restaurant, one of the hotel's two restaurants. There is also a lounge/bar area. A convenient eight minutes by subway to the city centre. **www.globehotel.se**

RESTAURANTS, CAFES AND PUBS

Stockholm has become one of Europe's liveliest and most varied cities for eating out. Swedish cuisine has won many international awards and several of the country's restaurants have been awarded Michelin stars. Many of the best restaurants are relatively small and informal as a number of top chefs have opened their own establishments. Various ethnic styles of cooking are often combined to create innovative and delicious dishes in what is called "cross-over" cuisine. Traditional Swedish dishes are frequently served at lunchtime and are excellent value for money. If you want to eat inexpensively in the evening there are plenty of fast-food outlets, pubs, Chinese restaurants, pizzerias and kebab houses. Hot-dog kiosks, providing filling snacks, can be found dotted all over the city.

Swedish hot dog

WHERE TO EAT

There is a wide choice of restaurants all over the capital, not just in the city centre or the busiest shopping streets. Restaurants and cafés can also be found in the larger department stores and shopping malls, as well as at most museums. Hot meals can be had on many of the archipelago ferries, and several of the boats offering sightseeing tours also include dinner (*see p204*).

The market halls at Östermalmstorg, Hötorget and Medborgarplatsen have some excellent restaurants and cafés but they are not open in the evening for dinner.

Sandwiches with a variety of fillings can be bought at cafés and cake shops, which often serve inexpensive hot dishes at lunchtime as well.

Outdoor cafés spring up in the summer on many streets and squares, and also in green areas like Djurgården and Hagaparken (*see p122*).

TYPES OF RESTAURANT

Fashionable restaurants usually attract a young clientele, and the most trendy places sometimes have a rather stark decor and extremely high noise levels. If you are looking for somewhere quieter which also has good service, it is often best to choose an established restaurant. There are many specialist restaurants serving cuisine from abroad, or "cross-over" cooking, which is a combination of styles.

Inn sign, Gamla Stan

Most restaurants charge roughly the same prices, regardless of quality. If you are looking for somewhere cheaper to eat, there are plenty of pizzerias, pubs, kebab houses, hamburger joints or cafés to choose from.

Those with a sweet tooth will be well-catered for in Stockholm's many modern cafés or traditional cake shops, which offer delicious Danish pastries, cinnamon buns, cakes and gateaux.

Stockholm has few bars (*see pp178–9*) as such and the best can be found at the most popular restaurants (*see pp164–71*).

Dress is usually informal, even at the more elegant restaurants, although shorts are not acceptable. Men are not normally required to wear a tie.

Smoking is banned in all public bars and restaurants.

OPENING TIMES

Most restaurants open for lunch at 11.30am and close at around 10pm. Dinner is served from 6pm or even earlier. A number of restaurants are closed on Sundays or Mondays as well as during the winter. Smaller restaurants may close for their annual holiday during July.

Prices for lunch are often extremely reasonable, even at the more elegant establishments, so lunchtime can be spent enjoying an inexpensive meal at a pleasant restaurant. *Dagens lunch* (Lunch of the Day) is generally not served after 2pm, even if the restaurant is open in the afternoon.

For those who like to eat late, a number of restaurants and pubs serve food right up to midnight or even later, particularly those which have

Magnificent interior of Café Opera, next to Operakällaren (*see p165*)

Outdoor café in Riddarhustorget in Gamla Stan

entertainment, music or a disco. Anyone still hungry during the night can find 24-hour hot-dog kiosks.

VEGETARIAN FOOD

Interest in vegetarian food is increasing in Sweden, and this is reflected by the fact that excellent vegetarian cuisine now is served at most Stockholm restaurants. There are also several completely vegetarian restaurants.

BOOKING A TABLE

Reservations should be made for evening meals, but many restaurants do not accept bookings for lunch. If you want to be sure of a table at midday, it is best to arrive at the restaurant before 11.30am or after 1pm, by which time most of the lunchtime clientele will have left.

CHILDREN

All children are welcome in restaurants without exception. They will usually be offered a special children's menu, or half portions from the normal menu. Highchairs are generally available.

PRICES

Prices of meals at Stockholm restaurants are very similar. At most places hot dishes cost from about 100 kr, or 200 kr at the more expensive restaurants. Lunch prices are around 70 kr, and that often includes bread, salad, a soft drink and coffee. However, the price of beer, wine and other alcoholic drinks can vary considerably. It generally follows that the more expensive the restaurant, the higher the price of the wine. The house wine is usually the cheapest, with a bottle normally costing from 250 kr. Beer is cheaper in pubs than in restaurants. Tap water is free of charge, and Stockholm's drinking water is of excellent quality.

Tips are always included in the price, but if you want to reward good service you can round up the bill. If the restaurant has a manned cloakroom, the normal price is 10 kr per person. A number of restaurants do not allow guests to take their outdoor clothing into the dining room. Credit cards are accepted in virtually every restaurant.

READING THE MENU

Dinner at a Stockholm restaurant usually includes a starter, hot main course and dessert. Most offer one or more fixed-price meals with a choice of two or three dishes at a lower price than the à la carte menu. It is perfectly acceptable to have just a starter or main course. At lunchtime most people order only one course. The meal is nearly always served on the plate, but the more elegant restaurants often have dessert or cheese trolleys. Many restaurants have menus in English. But if they don't, the serving staff are usually familiar with English and will be pleased to explain the menu. A number of menus have a section labelled *Husmanskost,* which features traditional dishes of Swedish "home-cooking".

Some restaurants serve a typical Swedish *smörgåsbord,* usually on Sundays. During December a *Julbord* is usually available. This is similar to the normal *smörgåsbord,* but with a lavish buffet selection of traditional seasonal dishes. You can eat as much as you like at a fixed price, but drinks are not included.

WHAT TO DRINK

Wine and beer are the normal accompaniments to a meal, as well as mineral water. The wine list often features wine from countries outside Europe, along with a house wine. Vintage wines are usually not available at medium-price restaurants.

Beer is graded into three classes, with class I the weakest. Many pubs and restaurants offer a wide selection, often with one or more on draught. A few smaller Swedish breweries make an excellent non-filtered beer.

Herring or "home-cooking" is usually washed down with beer, sometimes accompanied by one of the many varieties of schnapps as well.

Spirits and wines are more expensive in Swedish restaurants than in most other countries because of the high duty on alcohol and the State retail alcohol monopoly.

Café Tranan in Vasastan, one of Stockholm's many popular small restaurants *(see p169)*

The Flavours of Stockholm

Thanks to strict regulations, Sweden is one of most unpolluted countries in Europe and produces some of the purest food. Salmon can be caught in the heart of Stockholm, zander and herring are fished from the nearby coastal waters and the lakes and rivers are full of crayfish and other delicacies. Fish is a staple, but other gastronomic treats are also on offer. Wild game, such as grouse, reindeer and elk, is abundant in autumn and winter. The forests are full of berries and mushrooms, and the rich pastures produce superlative dairy produce, including several fine cheeses.

Fresh dill

Fresh anchovies on offer at Östermalmshallen food market

THE SMÖRGÅSBORD

The *smörgåsbord* made its first appearance on Swedish tables sometime in the 18th century, when it consisted of a spread of hot and cold hors d'oeuvres that would be served as a prelude to a grand lunch or dinner. All this was washed down with ice-cold "schnapps" (vodka). Gradually, however, it has grown into a full-scale meal. A traditional *smörgåsbord* will start with a selection of different herring appetizers, followed by a variety of cold dishes such as hard-boiled eggs, meat pies and salads. Then a number of hot dishes are served, including such offerings as meatballs, fried potatoes and Jansson's Temptation (a gratin of potatoes, onions, anchovies and cream). Finally an array of desserts will be placed on the table. Diners help themselves, changing their plates between courses.

Some Swedes will prepare a *smörgåsbord* as a good way of using left-overs. Inventive cooks often improvise a very simple version when unexpected guests arrive, using larder staples, such as eggs, slices of cheese and cooked meats, and tinned or pickled fish.

Selection of items typically found on a cold *smörgåsbord*

Beetroot & orange salad
Rye crispbread
Pickled herring
Cucumber salad
Egg with lumpfish roe
Cheese
Lingonberry tartlets
Pork liver på
Smoked ham

LOCAL DISHES AND SPECIALITIES

A typical Swedish breakfast often includes yoghurt or *filmjölk* (a type of soured milk yoghurt) with cereal. Many Swedes, however, prefer a more savoury start to the day and cheese, ham and even liver paté may be on offer. Bread spread with *kaviar* (a cod's roe paste) is also eaten at breakfast. For lunch, most people reach for something quick and simple to prepare. Salad, perhaps served with a seafood, ham or vegetable quiche, is common and pasta is popular too. As well as the main meals, a break for coffee and pastries, known as *fika*, is taken at any time of the day. This strong Swedish tradition is a sociable event as much as an occasion to eat. In the evening, families usually get together for the main meal of the day, dinner, a more elaborate, but still homely, affair.

Lingonberries

Gravad Lax, *a salmon fillet, marinated for two days in sugar, salt and dill, is served with a creamy mustard sauce.*

A colourful vegetable stall at Hötorget market

During the Christmas season, many Stockholm restaurants serve a special *smörgåsbord*, known as a *Julbord*, which will include dishes using nearly every part of the pig, such as various ham, trotters and a special brawn called *sylta*, made from the head.

RUSTIC FARE

The Swedes are very good at using cheap cuts to prepare delicious dishes and seasoning is usually kept simple with salt, pepper and fresh dill. Such homely fare, known as *husmanskost*, is central to the Swedish diet and regularly features on the menus of many Stockholm restaurants. One favourite is yellow pea soup, traditionally served on Thursdays, accompanied by sausages or lightly salted meat and

mustard. This is generally followed by pancakes with jam, washed down with hot *punsch*. Other popular dishes include *pytt i panna* (a hash of meat, onions and potatoes) and meatballs, served with lingonberry jam.

A selection of fine fish from Sweden's pristine coastal waters

SWEDEN'S DINING "REVOLUTION"

The turn of the 21st century has witnessed a renaissance of gourmet cooking in Sweden, with people now visiting Stockholm for its food as well as its culture. Traditional dishes, made with the finest – usually organic – ingredients are being given an original, modern twist. Instead of simple meatballs with lingonberries, chefs are increasingly offering delights such as *foie gras* with a spiced mixed berry and apple chutney and turning cheap staples, such as pig's offal, into magnificent, melt-in-the-mouth mousses.

WHAT TO DRINK

Beer Along with vodka, beer is the most popular drink to accompany a *smörgåsbord*. In the past, little was on offer other than insipid lagers, but a beer-making revival has made styles from dark porters to pale ales available, including some interesting fruit beers.

Vodka About 60 types of "schnapps", each flavoured with different herbs and spices, are made in Sweden.

Punsch This sweet arak spirit is often taken with coffee or served hot with pea soup.

Wine A huge variety of fine wines are imported, but are usually very expensive.

Jansson's Temptation *is a dish of layered potato, anchovy and onion with cream, baked until golden.*

Meatballs *made from beef or pork are drenched in a rich meaty sauce and served with lingonberries.*

Apple cake *is a delicious buttery dessert traditionally served piping hot with cold vanilla sauce.*

Choosing a Restaurant

This listing covers over 80 restaurants in all the price categories, which have been selected for good value, excellent food and/or their setting. The restaurants are listed area by area, starting with the inner city. For map references, see the maps on *pp206–15*. Note that alcohol, particularly wine, is expensive in Sweden.

PRICE CATEGORIES
The following price ranges are the average prices for a three-course meal for one, half a bottle of house wine and unavoidable charges such as service and cover.

Ⓚ under 400 kr
ⓄⓄ 400–550 kr
ⓄⓄⓄ 550–700 kr
ⓄⓄⓄⓄ over 700 kr

GAMLA STAN

Brasserie Pontus by the Sea   Ⓚ Ⓚ
Tullhus 2, Skeppsbron, 111 30 Stockholm **Tel** *08-20 20 95*   **Map** *9 D1*

Owned by one of Stockholm's star chefs, Pontus Frithiof, this restaurant offers a reasonably priced, accessible menu including a large seafood platter and the cold meat platter, both of which are worth trying. The food is excellent, as you would expect from this chef. In summer you can sit outside and watch the ships come into port. Closed Sundays.

Grill Ruby   Ⓚ Ⓚ
Österlånggatan 14, 111 31 Stockholm **Tel** *08-20 60 15*   **Map** *4 C3*

Wonderful grilled steaks at very reasonable prices as well as good classical Swedish dishes, such as *biff rydberg* (thin sliced tenderloin of beef) and *slottstek* (beef stew) with pressed cucumber, are on the menu here. Grill Ruby also offers a special brunch menu on Saturdays. Open daily from 5pm and from 1pm on Saturdays.

Fem Små Hus   Ⓚ Ⓚ Ⓚ
Nygränd 10, 111 30 Stockholm **Tel** *08-10 87 75*   **Map** *4 C3*

The restaurant has its premises in five adjoining houses (one of which dates back to 1651), furnished with European antiques and oil paintings to give the place an air of grandeur like a private castle. A favourite on the menu – for the last 30 years – is *Kalvfilé Anna Lindberg* (veal fillet), named after a proprietor who ran an illegal tavern here in 1694.

Källaren Movitz   Ⓚ Ⓚ Ⓚ
Tyska Brinken 34, 111 35 Stockholm **Tel** *08-20 99 79*   **Map** *4 B3*

Located in a 17th century vault, this restaurant serves predominantly Swedish cuisine and some French and Italian dishes. Try the veal medallions with fresh tomatoes, white wine and mozzarella. For dessert, the house ice cream with fresh berries is superb. There is a stylish pub upstairs for post-dinner drinks.

Den Gyldene Freden   Ⓚ Ⓚ Ⓚ Ⓚ
Österlånggatan 51, 103 17 Stockholm **Tel** *08-10 90 46*   **Map** *4 C4*

An artists' restaurant with a long tradition, serving excellent Swedish/French cuisine alongside Swedish "home cooking". The fish is well prepared with good sauces. The scallops with mushroom jelly are worth a try. It is quite a tourist trap, but the interior makes it worth a visit. Open evenings Monday to Friday and lunchtime on Saturdays.

Leijontornet   Ⓚ Ⓚ Ⓚ Ⓚ
Lilla Nygatan 5, 111 28 Stockholm **Tel** *08-50 64 00 80*   **Map** *4 B3*

Leijontornet's Head Chef Gustav Otterber's vision of a Nordic, ecological and innovative approach to cuisine has won this restaurant a Michelin star. Housed in a historic medieval cellar it holds 1,100 different wines and more than 10,000 bottles, some of which feature on the interesting wine list. If you can afford it this is a must-do experience.

CITY

Ett litet Hak   Ⓚ Ⓚ
Grevx Turegatan 15, 114 46 Stockholm **Tel** *08-660 13 09*   **Map** *3 E4*

Lively, pleasant local restaurant with trendy Continental cuisine and friendly staff. Ett litet Hak means "a tiny bit", which describes the approach precisely. You can enjoy chorizo or a slice of goat's cheese pie washed down with an ice-cold beer. This open-air restaurant offers great value. Open daily for lunch and dinner.

Bakfickan   Ⓚ Ⓚ Ⓚ
Operakalaren, Operahuset, Karl XIIs Torg, 111 86 Stockholm **Tel** *08-676 58 00*   **Map** *3 B4*

A real little gem for its many regular customers, including artists from the nearby opera house, Bakfikan is ideal if you are looking for a quick bite to eat. The bar menu consists of Swedish "home-cooked" specials, along with a selection of delicious open sandwiches. More complex meals are also available. Closed Sundays.

Key to Symbols *see back cover flap*

Bistro Jarl
Birger Jarlsgatan 7, 111 45 Stockholm **Tel** *08-611 76 30*
Map *3 D4*

This small luxurious restaurant serves Mediterranean, Swedish and Asian dishes and is a favourite spot for the hip crowd. The bistro's bar offers vintage champagne in a room filled with crystal chandeliers. One of the best dishes is a beautifully presented beef tartar. The deep-fried taleggio is also delicious. Closed Sundays.

Nalen
Regeringsgatan 74, 111 39 Stockholm **Tel** *08-50 52 92 01*
Map *3 D3*

Formerly the Grand National, this eatery now has the same name as the jazz club around the corner. The food is traditional Swedish using the best local ingredients such as reindeer, bleak roe and cloudberries. Since Mathias Nordin became the head chef, it can be difficult to get a table, so book ahead. Closed Sundays.

Restaurang Hälsingborg
Mäster Samuelsgatan 60, 111 21 Stockholm **Tel** *08-673 34 20*
Map *2 C4*

The theme at this popular restaurant is sea, land and forest. The menu changes daily and you can sample classic Swedish cuisine, such as braised elk tongue and meatballs. There is also a lunch menu available Monday to Friday. Closed Sundays.

Riche
Birger Jarlsgatan 4, 114 34 Stockholm **Tel** *08-54 50 35 60*
Map *2 C2*

Offering traditional Swedish fare along with foreign influences, customers can enjoy a variety of food from seared cod with truffle supremesauce and panchetta to calf's liver "Anglaise". The restaurant is set in a playful interior with cartoon characters decorating napkin-rings and menus. Closed Sundays.

Smakpå Restaurangen
Oxtorgsgatan 14, 111 57 Stockholm **Tel** *08-22 09 52*
Map *3 D4*

Owner and chef, Melker Andersson, serves small taster-style dishes in his stylish restaurant. You can choose 3, 5, or 7 dishes and the best of these are the desserts. The menu is dominated by strong flavours, from *wasabi* to Swedish anchovies. Choosing from the menu is a tick-box affair, where you mark a cross next to the dishes of your choice.

Sturehof
Stureplan 2, 114 46 Stockholm **Tel** *08-440 57 30*
Map *3 D4*

Sturehof consists of an oyster bar, an elegant restaurant and an outdoor café. Magnificent glass artworks separate the bar area from the dining room where fish and shellfish and the very best Swedish home cooking are on offer. Located in the very centre of town, Sturehof has a good reputation and is a great place for people-watching.

F12 restaurant
Fredsgatan 12, 111 52 Stockholm **Tel** *08-24 80 52*
Map *2 C5*

Star chefs Melker Andersson and Danyel Couet run this exclusive restaurant with world-class cooking combining the cuisines of many different countries. They have a wonderful *menu dégustation* including sweetbreads. The artichoke hearts and oyster *granité* are also well worth a try. Closed Sundays.

Operakällaren
Operahuset, Karl XII:s Torg, 111 86 Stockholm **Tel** *08-676 58 01*
Map *4 B1*

Awarded Restaurant of the Year by the prestigious White Guide, the chefs here are young and creative. The dining room, with its lavish 19th-century ceiling paintings and Jugendstil bar, are attractions in themselves. Café Opera has lower prices and an afternoon cake buffet, and when it is warm you can sit outside. Closed Sundays and Mondays.

Prinsen
Mäster Samuelsgatan 4, 111 44 Stockholm **Tel** *08-611 13 31*
Map *3 D4*

Fun but traditional restaurant with wood-panelled walls and attractive paintings, not to mention good food, which is mostly Swedish. A classic dish here is *Toast Pelle Jansson* (brioche with bleak roe). Prinsen is a popular meeting place for Stockholm's rich bohemians, artists and writers.

Vassa Eggen
Birger Jarlsgatan 29, 103 95 Stockholm **Tel** *08-21 61 69*
Map *3 D3*

The ceiling of this restaurant has a beautiful, coloured, domed glass cupola. Carefully chosen local ingredients are prepared with sophistication, and there are wonderful reduced sauces. The bouillabaisse and the oxtail tortellini with mascarpone in consommé are musts, and there is also a very good wine list. Closed Sundays.

BLASIEHOLMEN & SKEPPSHOLMEN

Atrium in the Nationalmuseum
Södra Blasieholmshamnen 4, Box 16017, 10321 Stockholm **Tel** *08-611 34 30*
Map *3 E5*

Situated in a unique space in the middle of the Nationalmuseum, chef Orjan Klein serves a selection of lovely salads and cold meats. However, it is always the dish of the day that is particularly tempting, such as *laxpudding*, sautéed baltic herring, or poached fish with a great lobster sauce. Open for lunch only. Closed Mondays.

Pauli in Dramaten Theatre

Nybroplan 2, 102 41 Stockholm **Tel** *08-665 61 43*

Map *3 E4*

A lovely, grand and old-fashioned restaurant on the third floor of this impressive theatre. Traditional *husmanskost* (wholesome home cooking) is served here, such as the delicious Swedish meatballs. George Pauli was a well known Swedish artist and the restaurant is decorated with portraits of famous actors painted by equally famous artists.

Pontus!

Brunnsgatan 1, 111 30 Stockholm **Tel** *08-545 27 30 00*

Map *3 D3*

With influences from London and New York, this is one of Stockholm's most modern restaurants. The downstairs dining room is decorated with Pontus!-designed wallpaper and eclectic, colourful tables and chairs; modern Swedish/fusion cuisine is on the menu. Upstairs is the bistro and bar with resident DJs. Closed Sundays.

Wedholms Fisk Restaurang

Nybrokajen 17, 111 48 Stockholm **Tel** *08-611 78 74*

Map *4 C1*

People travel a long way to eat the turbot here, served with a mustard hollandaise that has a nutty, buttery taste. Wedholms Fisk's secret is simplicity, and through this it has become the best fish restaurant in town. It is also very prettily located by the old boats on the strand. Closed Sundays.

DJURGÅRDEN

Rosendal's TrädgårdsKafe

Rosendalsterrassen 12, 115 21 Stockholm **Tel** *08-54 58 12 70*

Map *6 3C*

This is an oasis of delicious organic food located in a beautiful open garden. The renowned cakes and buns are all made in Rosendal's own bakery. Their wonderful bread, baked in a wood-fired stone oven, can be bought in the adjacent gift shop, which also stocks superb biodynamic vegetables grown in the garden. Guided tours are available.

Hasselbacken Restaurang

Hazeliusbacken 20, 100 55 Stockholm **Tel** *08-51 73 43 07*

Map *6 A3*

Well-prepared traditional Swedish food served in a finely restored 1850s setting. In summer there is an outdoor café, prettily situated next to Skansen on Djurgården. It has a tendency to be a little touristy, but you will really get a sense of old-time Sweden in this grand building. Open daily 4pm–10pm.

Wärdshuset Ulla Winblad

Rosendalsvägen 8, 115 21 Stockholm **Tel** *08-534 897 01*

Map *6 A3*

Beautifully located restaurant next to Skansen with an old-fashioned atmosphere and decorated as if out of a Carl Larsson painting. Serves well-prepared classic Swedish cuisine, as well as modern dishes, such as perchpike served with chanterelle sauce. The outdoor café is very popular in the summer.

ÖSTERMALM & GÄRDET

Dell'Attore

Skeppargatan 60, 114 59 Stockholm **Tel** *08-442 61 18*

Map *3 F2*

"Dell'Attore" means actors' restaurant – an apt name for this small, buzzing place decorated from floor to ceiling with photographs of famous actors. It boasts the most delicious pizzas in town for which people join lengthy queues to order. It is advisable to book in advance.

Kjellsons Restaurang

Birger Jarlsgatan 36, 114 29 Stockholm **Tel** *08-11 00 45*

Map *2 C2*

Opened as a family business in 1921, and run by the Kjellson family, it was formerly a bakery and café. Now the restaurant and bar is popular for a beer after work or dining out before enjoying the many attractions nearby. Serving local specialitites like meatballs and stew, it has a nostalgic atmosphere that makes people feel at home.

Spring

Karlavägen 110, 104 51 Stockholm **Tel** *08-783 15 00*

Map *3 E2*

With such a complex mix of influences, including Asian, North African and South American, each item comes with a detailed description on the menu. There are some good combinations to be found, such as Thai meatballs or corn chicken; all the food here is delicious. Open for lunch only.

Gerdas Fiskrestaurang

Östermalms Saluhall, 114 39 Stockholm **Tel** *08-55 34 04 40*

Map *3 E4*

A fun place to visit when looking for good seafood. Located in a lively area close to the Östermalm market (a place where all visiting foodies should go without fail), Gerdas is hugely popular and always busy. Their creamy fish soup is an absolute must. To avoid disappointment, book a table in advance. Closed Sundays.

Key to Price Guide *see p164* **Key to Symbols** *see back cover flap*

Brasserie Bobonne
Storgatan 12, 114 44 Stockholm **Tel** *08-660 03 18*

Map *3 F4*

A French brasserie serving classic dishes such as *moules marinière, boef bourguignon* and well matured French cheeses. The menu changes every Monday in order to provide variety and take advantage of the freshest ingredients. Helpful, knowledgeable staff. Open for dinner only. Closed Sundays.

Brasserie Godot
Grevturegatan 36, 114 36 Stockholm **Tel** *08-660 06 14*

Map *3 E3*

This is a trendy place that attracts lots of young people with its great cocktails and substantial food. The menu has a strong French flavour with such dishes as *moules marinière* and steak and chips. However, there are Swedish favourites too, including potato blini with bleak roe and sour cream. Closed Sundays.

Divino
Karlavägen 28, 114 31 Stockholm **Tel** *08-611 02 69*

Map *3 D3*

Arguably the best Italian in town, Divino's has a lovely interior and the food is quite superb The *antipasti* is original, and the small slices of lobster and monkfish with fennel and vanilla sauce are worth trying. All this is at a very reasonable price, and there is an extensive wine list. Closed on Sundays (and Mondays in July).

Eriks Bakficka
Fredrikshovsgatan 4, 115 23 Stockholm **Tel** *08-660 15 99*

Map *3 F4*

Named after Erik Lallerstedt, who also owns the renowned Gondolen *(see p170)*, Bakficka specialises in Swedish classics mixed with modern, innovative cuisine. Look out for the great desserts and (affordable) champagne by the glass. Open daily.

Grodan Grev Tur
Grev Turegatan 16, 114 46 Stockholm **Tel** *08-679 61 00*

Map *3 E2*

Whether you choose to enjoy your meal in the beautiful dining room or in the simpler but charming bar section, the outcome is the same: good food, with the likes of the club sandwich and fish soup as long-standing favourites. The same menu is available in both areas. For a fun atmosphere the bar is always busy in the evenings and on weekends.

Halv Grek Plus Turk
Jungfrugatan 33, 114 44 Stockholm **Tel** *08-665 94 22*

Map *3 E3*

The incongruous Greek-Turkish mix on offer here actually works really well. The menu is tapas-style with a wide selection of *meze* dishes. The decorfollows suit, though with an unexpected lean towards the Scandinavian. The bar is worth a visit just for the beautiful design alone. Closed on Sundays.

T/Bar Scandinavian Brasserie
Strandvägen 7C, 114 56 Stockholm **Tel** *08-459 68 00*

Map *3 E4*

Located in the Hotel Diplomat, this brasserie is a great place for breakfast, lunch, dinner or even afternoon tea. On offer is Swedish fare – try the fillet of venison with logonberry sauce and pickled mushrooms – and there are good views of the archipelago. The outdoor lounge is open during the summer for al fresco dining.

Undici
Grevturagatan 30, 114 36 Stockholm **Tel** *08-661 66 17*

Map *3 D3*

Near Stureplan and set in a modern, trendy environment, the Undici shows a strong Italian influence, mixed with traditional Swedish food from Norrland. Try the truffle and cauliflower cream with bleak roe and potato *cris*. Undici doubles as a nightclub later in the evening. Closed on Sundays and Mondays.

Teatergrillen
Nybrogatan 3, 114 34 Stockholm **Tel** *08-54 50 65*

Map *3 E3*

One of Stockholm's oldest restaurants, Teatergrillen serves a mix of French fine dining cuisine and classic Swedish dishes. The restaurant is known for its "Silvervagnen", a trolley that circles the tables serving guests the finest entrecôte. Another speciality is the beef Rydberg, cubes of stewed beef tenderloin with potatoes. Closed Sundays.

Villa Källhagen
Djurgårdsbrunnvagen 10, 115 27 Stockholm **Tel** *08-665 03 00*

Map *7 D3*

Stunningly located on Djurgårdsbrunnsviken Bay, this excellent restaurant serves classic Swedish cuisine with Continental influences. The seasonal gourmet menu uses the finest and freshest ingredients and the outdoor terrace offers wonderful views over the bay. In winter, enjoy a glass of wine by the fire from the well stocked wine cellar.

KUNGSHOLMEN

Restaurang Kungsholmen
Nor Mälarstrand, Kajplats 464, 112 20 Stockholm **Tel** *08-505 244 50*

Map *1 B3*

With a perfect location by the Mälaren river, this trendy, ambient lounge-cum-dining room has seven separate open kitchens: Raw, Nordic, Organic, Fast Food, Classic, Spice and Fruit Bar. It wouldn't be complete without a cocktail bar, and here celebrities mingle with the beautiful people sipping both classic and modern mixes. Seats 200 diners.

Spisa Hos Helena

Scheelegatan 18, 112 28 Stockholm **Tel** *08-654 49 26*

Map *2 A5*

Lit by hundreds of candles, the atmosphere here is cosy and welcoming and the food highly recommended. Do try the tuna steak and Helena's Bookmaker (fillet steak, horseradish, dijon mustard and tomatoes with chips), which has been on the menu since 1996 and is a real favourite. All the main courses are cheaper on Sundays. Open daily.

Göken

Pontonjärgatan 28, 112 37 Stockholm **Tel** *08-654 49 28*

Map *1 C3*

Excellent value for money, this restaurant offers everything from Swedish "home cooking" to French "bistro style" with an oriental touch, not to forget the delicious homemade bread. Owned by the inventive Lena Nygården, this restaurant combines a cosy atmosphere and friendly service with splendid views from the outdoor terrace.

La Famiglia

Alströmergatan 45, 112 47 Stockholm **Tel** *08-650 63 10*

Map *1 B2*

Particularly popular with children, La Famiglia serves classic Italian cuisine at budget prices in a friendly atmosphere. One dish to try is the excellent shellfish pasta. A good place to take the whole family, as the name suggests. Frank Sinatra even made a special visit here just to try the signature dish, sauteed calves' liver. Open daily.

Roppongi

Hantverkargatan 76, 112 38 Stockholm **Tel** *08-650 17 72*

Map *1 B3*

The superb quality of fish and the creative use of ingredients used at Roppongi ultimately makes this the best sushi restaurant in town. It is never quiet here so be prepared to get up close and personal with other sushi fans. A wide range of artistic dishes feature on the menu and are temptingly laid out for perusal. A take-away service is available.

Rosmarin

Hantverkargatan 14, 112 21 Stockholm **Tel** *08-653 87 63*

Map *2 A5*

A popular family-run restaurant, best known for its charcoal-grilled meat, which is always top quality, followed by its pork chops. The restaurant endorses the belief that rosemary is particularly good for the brain; the fragrant herb features in their delicious home-baked bread and fried, sliced potatoes.

Tabbouli

Norra Agnegatan 39, 112 29 Stockholm **Tel** *08-650 25 00*

Map *2 A4*

One of the many Lebanese restaurants that have sprung up in Stockholm, Tabbouli specialises in grilled meats and *meze*, and makes for a refreshing change if you are enjoying an extended stay in Stockholm. The food is good quality and the atmosphere lively Middle-Eastern.

Terreno Vinotek

Scheelegatan 12, 112 28 Stockholm **Tel** *08-653 19 88*

Map *2 A5*

An original concept lies behind this venture: a Swede buys an Italian vineyard and sells the wine by the glass along with delicious tapas-style food. You buy a charge card which you put into a slot, and then you order by pressing once for a 4cl taster glass and three times for a full glass. A lovely idea which works exceptionally well.

Mäster Anders

Pipersgatan 1, 112 24 Stockholm **Tel** *08-654 20 01*

Map *2 A5*

Specializing in grilled meats and fish, including a delicious chilli bearnaise that leaves a wonderful tingle in the mouth, Mäster Anders also does good traditional Swedish food. The 1913 interior consists of Bentwood chairs, parquet flooring and yellow tiled walls.

Stadshuskällaren

City Hall, Hantverkargatan 1, 112 21 Stockholm **Tel** *08-506 322 00*

Map *2 B5*

Located in a cellar next to the City Hall where the Nobel Prize ceremony takes place, this restaurant originally opened in 1923 and the decoris typical of that era. The omelettes are delicious if you just want a light snack. For private parties you can choose from any of the past Nobel dinner menus served on the Nobel dinner service.

Lux

Primusgatan 116, 112 62 Stockholm **Tel** *08-619 0190*

Originally the old canteen for Electrolux, but don't let these humble beginnings put you off. Today Lux sports a Michelin star and is among the top restuarants in Stockholm. The chefs experiment brilliantly with traditional ingredients combining, for example, perch with crab and caviar. Closed Mondays.

VASASTAN

Storstad

Odengatan 41, 113 52 Stockholm **Tel** *08-673 38 00*

Map *2 C2*

This is where people go if they want to be seen, and the bar is usually packed. Here you will find minimalist décor, comfortable seating and courteous staff serving excellent, if a little fanciful, food. Meat and fish are the famed specialities and the dress code is smart and elegant. Closed Mondays; bar menu Sundays.

Key to Price Guide *see p164* **Key to Symbols** *see back cover flap*

Clas på Hörnet

Surbrunnsgatan 20, 113 48 Stockholm **Tel** *08-16 51 36*　　**Map** *2 C2*

This rather decadent-looking building houses a lovely, old fashioned restaurant with extremely good Swedish food. Duck sausage is a speciality, as are the sauteed sweatbreads with leeks and cured ox tongue and the rosehip soup with vanilla ice cream. Head chef Ulf Kappen is a master and no-one can cook fish like he does. Closed Sundays.

Döden I Grytan

Norrtullsgatan 61, 113 45 Stockholm **Tel** *08-32 50 95*　　**Map** *2 B2*

Döden I Grytan literally translates as "death in the pot." However, don't let this strange name put you off – the Italian food here is outstanding, the portions generous and the dishes earthy, such as the polenta and spare ribs, or their succulent carpaccio. You can even take time out to relax on their comfortable sofas after a good meal.

Paus Bar & Kök

Rörstrandsgatan 18, 113 40 Stockholm **Tel** *08-34 44 05*　　**Map** *1 C1*

Local restaurant with sober decorand elegant, modern and advanced cuisine. This street is famous for its restaurants with every other door opening onto a different gastronomic world. The menu at Paus Bar & Kök is quite adventurous, with dishes such as duck liver on toast with figs and apple sauce. Open daily.

Stockholm Fisk

Vasagatan 1, 111 20 Stockholm **Tel** *08-506 541 00*　　**Map** *2 B4*

Just a hop and a jump from Central Station, this cosy yet luxurious brasserie specialises in fish and seafood, with dishes like fried herring with puréed potatoes and lingonberries on the menu. Also on offer are fun group activities such as wine-tasting or the popular Floyd evenings where three-course meals are prepared with the chef.

Stockholms Matvarufabrik

Idungatan 12, 113 45 Stockholm **Tel** *08-32 07 04*　　**Map** *2 B1*

As its name (Stockholm's Food Factory) indicates, this restaurant serves a wide range of classic dishes from a well-planned menu. Very friendly, it is considered one of Vasastan's favourite neighbourhood restaurants. They are well known for making the best omelettes in Stockholm, and the atmosphere is buzzing. Closed Sundays.

Tranan

Karlbergsvägen 14, 113 27 Stockholm **Tel** *08-527 281 00*　　**Map** *2 B2*

A bit off the beaten track, this popular and reliable French bistro-style restaurant serves international cuisine and top-class Swedish "home cooking". The menu is in Swedish only, but the waiters are happy to translate. A speciality is fillet of beef with sauteed potatoes and horseradish. There is a lively bar on the floor below.

Wasahof

Dalagatan 46, 113 24 Stockholm **Tel** *08-32 34 40*　　**Map** *2 B3*

Friendly brasserie-style restaurant, popular among theatre and opera goers. The speciality here is seafood, and they always have an excellent catch of the day. Swedish and French dishes also feature on the menu. The waiters are good at recommending wines from the well-stocked cellar. Adjoins a pleasant oyster bar. Closed Sundays.

Grill

Drottninggatan 89, 113 60 Stockholm **Tel** *08-31 45 30*　　**Map** *2 C3*

This is another of Melker Andersson and Danyel Couet's success stories – it is an enormous establishment with 200 covers. Most of the food is grilled and the speciality meats do not disappoint. There are lots of young people sipping lattes on the sofas and colourful cocktails at the bar, sometimes to live jazz music.

Rolf's kök

Tegnérgatan 41, 111 61 Stockholm **Tel** *08-10 16 96*　　**Map** *2 C3*

Rolf doesn't run this restaurant any more, but those who have taken over do a very good job. The food is imaginative – red wine-braised cheeks of ox with truffle – and the atmosphere and decorfun, with chairs hanging on the walls. If you choose the communal table you never know who you might meet.

NORRTULL & NORTH OF STOCKHOLM

Stallmästaregården

Norrtull, 113 47 Stockholm **Tel** *08-610 13 00*　　**Map** *2 A1*

A 17th-century inn set in an idyllic location on Brunnsviken Bay. It serves the epitome of Swedish cuisine, with dishes from the charcoal grill and rotisserie. Specialities include cold-smoked wild duck with truffle foam and fillet of char fish filled with chanterelles. There is also a pleasant outdoor café.

Ulriksdals Wärdshus

Ulriksdals Slottspark, 170 79 Solna **Tel** *08-85 08 15*

Magnificent location in a beautiful and historic inn. Wårdshus offers elegant top-class cuisine and the largest collection of wines is the world (according to the Guiness Book of Records). Famous for its outstanding *smörgåsbord*, especially at Christmas, for which people book their parties a year in advance.

SÖDERMALM

Crêperie Fyra Knop
Svartensgatan 4, 116 20 Stockholm **Tel** *08-640 77 27*

Map *9 D2*

For a change from local food, try this slice of Normandy in the middle of Stockholm. It is the only crêperie in the city, and has a lovely warm atmosphere, especially in winter. They also serve delicious *galettes*. It is a small popular restaurant so it is worth booking ahead to ensure a place. Good value. Open daily.

Chutney Vegetarian Restaurant
Katarina Bangata 19, 116 39 Stockholm **Tel** *08-640 30 10*

Map *9 D3*

A candle-lit dinner below the paintings of local artists or the buzz of the outdoor restaurant make Chutney a popular choice. However, it is famous firstly for its superb vegetarian food, particularly influenced by the Mediterranean, Mexico and Asia. Potato pancakes, vegetarian steaks and plantation stew feature and wash down well with some organic wine.

Hermans
Fjällgatan 23B, 116 28 Stockholm **Tel** *08-643 94 80*

Map *9 E2*

A vegetarian restaurant with a difference, Hermans uses only organic ingredients and ecologically friendly methods. With myriad spices and seasonings on their shelves, their extensive World cuisine buffet features dishes such as Tex Mex, Indian, Asian, Middle Eastern, Mediterranean and native Scandinavian. In summer they do a BBQ buffet, too.

Marie Laveau
Hornsgatan 66, 118 21 Stockholm **Tel** *08-668 85 00*

Map *8 B2*

A minimalist, stylish eatery, yet hidden beneath the clean-cut lines lies a big soul: with flavours of Cajun and Creole, it is the Louisiana and New Orleans menu that attracts the foodies here. The super-cool cocktail bar serves every drink imaginable to full-bellied customers under the midnight sky, and for those inclined there is a nightclub, too.

Zucchero
Borgmästargatan 7, 116 29 Stockholm **Tel** *08-644 22 87*

Map *9 E3*

Named after a famous café in Rome, Zucchero is fun and popular with young people, partly because the Italian cuisine served here is very good value. But the main appeal is the retro feel and dishes that are prepared with love. The decor is reminiscent of 1950s Italy and the film La Dolce *Vita*.

Folkoperan Bar & Kök
Hornsgatan 72, 118 21 Stockholm **Tel** *08-658 51 80*

Map *8 B2*

A favourite haunt of those going to the alternative opera house, the food here is good and the bar bustling with activity – worth a visit for the cosy atmosphere alone. There are three menus: the bar offers small starter-size dishes; the other two usually feature either meat or fish. Closed Sundays.

Hosteria Tre Santi
Blekingegatan 32, 118 56 Stockholm **Tel** *08-644 18 16*

Map *9 D4*

Run by Italians who will burst into song if you ask them nicely, Tre Santi is the closest you will get to Italy outside Italy. The interior is rustic, as is the style of food, such as *tortellacci* with artichokes and ricotta. They also do a mouthwatering bruschetta. You'll need to book a table to avoid disappointment. Closed Sundays.

Koh Phangan & Same Same But Different
Skånegatan 57, 116 37 Stockholm **Tel** *08-642 50 40*

Map *9 E3*

Even when it is snowing outside, inside the Oriental décor, bamboo and lanterns makes you feel that you are actually in Thailand –there are even realistic sound effects. The food is delicious with a wide selection of fantastic spicy dishes. Very good value. Book ahead as it is very popular. Closed Saturdays and Sundays.

Matkultur
Erstagatan 21, 116 36 Stockholm **Tel** *08-642 03 53*

Map *9 F3*

Run by much-travelled enthusiasts who serve food from all over the world. The excellent cuisine in this charming restaurant is exotic in style. The interior is Asian-inspired, as is the menu – some of their Indian specialities are just incredible. Matkultur means "food culture" and that is a true reflection of the ethos to be found here. Closed Sundays.

Pelikan
Blekingegatan 40, 116 62 Stockholm **Tel** *08-556 090 90*

Map *9 D4*

More than 100 years old, this is a Swedish restaurant through and through, with all the staples such as meatballs and *pytt i panna* (Swedish hash). The interior is very Swedish too, with painted ceilings and wood-panelled walls. Choose beer and schnapps, rather than wine, as they make for perfect accompaniments to the delicious herrings on the menu.

Erik's Gondolen
Stadsgården 6, top of Katarinahissen, 104 65 Stockholm **Tel** *08-641 70 90*

Map *9 D2*

Probably one of the best views of the city is to be had from this restaurant. To sample the excellent French food you first need to take a lift, called Katarinahissen *(see p127)*, to get to this elevated establishment. Next door is the Köket restaurant, which also serves superb food in a rustic setting but at significantly lower prices. Closed Sundays.

Key to Price Guide *see p164* **Key to Symbols** *see back cover flap*

Jimmy's Steakhouse 🔲 ⓌⓌⓌ
Tjärhovsplan 33, 116 28 Stockholm **Tel** *08-644 06 66* **Map** *9 E2*

Dining out Wild West style, this is Stockholm's first authentic grill house. Among the finger-licking delights are steaks (you can choose your own size), ribs, chops, burgers and chicken, cooked in front of your eyes at the large grill in the centre of the restaurant. The relaxing rustic interior with wooden furniture adds to its charm.

Lo Scudetto 🚹♿ ⓌⓌⓌ
Åsögatan 163, 116 32 Stockholm **Tel** *08-640 42 15* **Map** *9 E3*

The football pictures on the walls make Lo Scudetto popular among sports fans. Top-class Italian dishes, both traditional and innovative, are served with a smile. Try the grilled scallops with truffle risotto, followed by warm chocolate fondue with praline centre och Bellini sorbet – just delicious.

Rival 🚹♿🔲 ⓌⓌⓌ
Mariatorget 3, 118 91 Stockholm **Tel** *08-545 789 15* **Map** *8 C2*

Owned by Benny Andersson of the pop group ABBA, this restaurant is great fun and well worth a visit. The cooking is a mix of French and Swedish with dishes such as topside of elk marinated with juniper berries and Belgian Abbey Beer and served with porcini mushroom cream. Popular for Sunday brunch.

Sjögräs 🚹♿ ⓌⓌⓌ
Timmermansgatan 24, 118 55 Stockholm **Tel** *08-84 12 00* **Map** *8 C2*

This simple, lively restaurant is located in a pleasant residential neighbourhood by Mariatorget Park. The decor and furniture are contemporary and there is an open kitchen. The French-inspired menu is made up of generous portions of flavourful dishes with some local influences. Over 300 choices of rum.

Mistral 🚹♿ ⓌⓌⓌⓌ
Sockenvägen 529, 121 34 Enskededalen **Tel** *08-10 12 24*

This must be the smallest and one of the best restaurants in town. The menu intrigues with dishes like calves' brisket served with squid and bone marrow, and *rillettes* made with smoked eel and pig's cheek. Frederik Andersson and Bjorn Vasseur, both chefs and owners, have ensured that there is rarely a table free. Closed Sundays and Mondays.

FURTHER AFIELD

Sjöpaviljongen 🚹🔲 ⓌⓌ
Tranebergsstrand 4, 167 40 Bromma **Tel** *08-704 04 24*

With its own jetty, Sjöpaviljongen is particularly popular with businessmen at lunchtime who want to impress their clients. The view is tremendous, offering a panorama of all the islands around Stockholm. The food is, by comparison, slightly uninteresting, but the service is reliable and the view unbeatable. Open daily.

Båthuset 🚹🔲 ⓌⓌⓌ
Hamnen, 193 21 Sigtuna **Tel** *08-59 25 67 80*

A floating restaurant in Sigtuna's harbour. In the summer you can watch the boats go by whilst you sit at the bar, whilst in the winter there is an open fire and cosy kitchen inside. Their forte is seafood – cod with crayfish sauce is a speciality. Definitely worth a trip out of Stockholm for this. Closed Mondays, Tuesdays and Sundays.

Fjäderholmarnas Krog 🚹🔲 ⓌⓌⓌ
Stora Fjäderholmen, 100 05 Stockholm **Tel** *08-718 33 55*

Situated on an island in Stockholm's archipelago, this restaurant serves delightful Swedish titbits during the summer months. It is a great place for those who haven't been to the archipelago before to get a taste of Sweden's biggest asset. The food is equally fantastic. Boats from central Stockholm take about 25 minutes.

Restaurant J 🚹♿🔲 ⓌⓌⓌ
Värdshusvägen 14–16, 181 63 Lidingö **Tel** *08-601 34 00*

New England-style food, including clams, oysters and lobster, are the speciality of this American restaurant. The head chef is a master with fish such as turbot and arctic char. In summer, try the fresh salads; in the winter nothing is more warming than a bowl of his delicious soup. Great atmosphere for families.

Edsbacka Bistro 🚹♿🔲 ⓌⓌⓌⓌ
Sollentunavägen 223, 191 35 Solentuna **Tel** *08-631 00 34*

International-class cuisine at an inn dating from 1626, with a setting and service to match. The food is cooked with only the best Swedish ingredients, expertly prepared and beautifully presented by Christer Lingström, who has won a Michelin Star for his efforts. It is definitely worth the 20-minute trip out of Stockholm. Closed Sundays.

Oaxen Skärgårdskrog 🚹♿🔲 ⓌⓌⓌⓌ
Oaxen Skärgårdskrog, 153 93 Hölö **Tel** *08-55 15 31 05*

Awarded two Michelin stars, the food at this seasonal restaurant – experimental Swedish cuisine – is extraordinary and painstakingly prepared. The chef is Magnus Ek, and his partner, Agneta Green, works at front-of-house. If you want the best meal of your life, this is probably where you will find it in Sweden.

Cafés and Pubs

Swedes love their coffee. At work people take a coffee break at around 3pm, and if they are out and about, they are likely to pop into a café. The cake shops (indicated by the sign "Konditori") have a long tradition. They serve typical Swedish pastries, with everything from sweet small buns to tempting gateaux. The best cake shops have their own bakeries and sell a variety of pastries and sandwiches. Cafés were once cheaper and more popular than the elegant cake shops, but the differences have been evened out and there are now many Continental-style cafés serving espresso, cappuccino and caffe latte. Many cafés open for breakfast early in the morning, and they usually serve lunch as well. The old Swedish "beer cafés" have been replaced by the city's many pubs, which also serve simple dishes at reasonable prices.

CAFÉS AND CAKE SHOPS

Café culture is flourishing in Stockholm, and the style ranges from American or Italian to traditional Swedish and classic cake shops. The café is a good choice if you feel peckish between meals, need to rest your legs or simply want a meeting place. Apart from coffee, sandwiches and cakes, nearly all serve simple lunches – quiches and salad, for example – soft drinks and ice cream. Typical cafés serve Swedish-style strong coffee, along with sandwiches, buns and cakes. Don't miss the delicious *prinsesstårta* cream cake, by far the most popular one. Cafés usually close at around 6pm.

Many cafés have tables outside in the summer. If you feel like sitting under a fruit tree where you can enjoy the birdsong, **Rosendals Träd-gårdsKafé** on Djurgården is the place. The salad buffet is a feast for the eye and the palate, consisting of organically grown vegetables and home-baked bread. It is open only during the summer and in December. **Lasse i Parken** is another rustic idyll in the city with home-baked bread and delicious cheesecakes.

Sturekatten is a classic cake shop decorated in the style of an early 20th-century upper-class home with many small rooms and unrivalled pastries. **Vete-Katten** is one of Stockholm's most authentic cake shops. Its pastries are outstanding and chocaholics

won't be able to resist the home-made pralines. After a hectic day's shopping, head for the trendy **Hotel Diplomat T/Bar**, which serves English-style afternoon tea. Another oasis in the shopping district is **Gateau**, one floor up in Sturegallerian. The pastries are delicious, and the gentle piano music is particularly enjoyable and relaxing.

Rather more unusual is **Legym**, which serves nutritious yet tasty Middle Eastern vegetarian delicacies with biodynamic bread. Another one is **Café Julia**, where the selection of excellent fresh cheeses are home-made. It also serves excellent hot chocolate and provides a choice of eight different types of cheesecake, each as mouth-watering as the other.

Mellguist Caffé is a very popular place for hanging out close to Sankt Eriksplan. The moreish turkey and horse-radish cream panini is particularly addictive.

Wayne's Coffee is Södermalm's most popular meeting place with giant sandwiches and cakes, comfortable armchairs and an elegant clientele. **Coffee Cup** serves bagels with various fillings and many different types of coffee. At **Tabac** you can mingle with the locals as you enjoy a café au lait and home-baked brownies. Absolutely the finest espresso is served at **Tinta-rella di Luna**, an authentic Italian café which also has the city's best *panini*.

Coffee connoisseurs should not miss **Robert's Coffee**, where they roast their own beans. They also stock a range of exclusive beans which you can buy to take home.

PUBS

The old Swedish beer cafés have either closed down, transformed into a local restaurant (Tranan at Odenplan is a typical example – *see p169*) or are now pubs with an international flavour. Irish, Scottish or English pubs are all popular, but there are also influences from Belgium, the Czech Republic, Germany, Australia and the USA.

Stockholmers have a great interest in beer, so the pubs usually have a wide selection of brews and the staff are knowledgeable. Try some of the beers from three small, acclaimed, quality breweries: Tärnö, Stockholm's own brewery; Slottskällan in Uppsala; and Pilgrimstad from northern Sweden.

One of the busiest and most traditional pubs is the **Tudor Café**, opened in the 1960s, where English is the normal language and many of the regular customers are British. Scots and Americans head for the **Bagpiper's Inn**, where bagpipes are provided on the upper floor and Scottish beers are available. One floor down is the **Bald Eagle** where drinkers can enjoy rock music, and there is usually a queue for the billiards table. The adjoining pub, **Boomerang**, features music from Down Under, everyone is "mate", and the staff are Australian. The steakhouse serves kangaroo or ostrich steaks.

Anyone feeling homesick for Ireland only needs to go through the door of **Limerick** to enjoy some Guinness or Kilkenny. Irish music is performed there at weekends. **O'Leary's** has many expat regulars and also serves excellent food. **The Dubliner** is yet another Irish pub, with a large selection of malt whiskeys. Live music contributes to the atmosphere. On Södermalm, **Soldaten Svejk** specializes in

Czech draught beer and offers rustic country cooking.

Beer connoisseurs or whisky drinkers should head for **Akkurat**, which has about 400 different types of whisky and beer from all over the world, but particularly from Belgium. Mussels are always on the menu, but there is also a good choice of other hot dishes and delicious snacks. Beer and whisky tastings take place frequently, the staff are knowledgeable and service is quick. **Oliver Twist** is reckoned to be one of the city's best pubs for draught beer, imported from all over the world. The staff here are also dedicated and know-ledgeable. Business people head for **Man in the Moon** after work, and the atmos-phere is rather more refined than at most other pubs. A pleasant rural feel pervades the **Anchor Pub**, which specializes in unusual beers and has live music 3–4 nights a week.

Lundgrens is one of Sweden's best lagers and can be enjoyed on Kungsholmen, where it is brewed by the Tärnö brewery. It is served on draught at both **Mackinlay's** and **Kings Head**, two pleasant local pubs. **Tennstopet** was once a meeting place for journalists and some have remained loyal customers. It is pleasant but noisy, and there is a darts board. Swedish "home cooking" is available. The clientele is typically in the upper middle-age bracket.

Like their predecessors, the beer cafés, the pubs serve not just drinks but also snacks and value-for-money hot food from lunchtime till late in the evening. Many Stockholmers now regard going out to the pub as a pleasant and often less expensive alternative to their local restaurant.

Most pubs are open daily. Many open for lunch and usually close at 11pm, while a few remain open to midnight or 1am (see also pp178–9).

FAST FOOD

If you are looking for a quick snack, there are plenty of street kiosks selling hot dogs, hamburgers or kebabs. Several of them are open 24 hours. The Kungshallen complex at Hötorget has a lot of restaurants and fast-food outlets – particularly useful for groups who are undecided on the type of food they want to eat. There are also plenty of pizzerias of varying standards, as well as Chinese restaurants where you can eat well and inexpensively.

DIRECTORY

CAFÉS AND CAKE SHOPS

Café Julia
S:t Eriksgatan 15.
Map 1 B3.
Tel 08-651 45 15.

Coffee Cup
Sergelstorg 12.
Map 2 C4.
Tel 08-21 72 00.

Gateau
Sturegallerian.
Map 3 D4.
Tel 08-611 65 93.

Hotel Diplomat T/Bar
Strandvägen 7 C.
Map 3 E4.
Tel 08-459 68 02.

Lasse i Parken
Högalidsgatan 56.
Map 1 B5.
Tel 08-658 33 95.

Legym
Hornsgatan 80.
Map 8 B2.
Tel 08-669 35 35.

Mellguist Caffé
Rörstandsgatan 4.
Map 1 B1.
Tel 08-30 23 80.

Robert's Coffee
Kungsgatan 44.
Map 2 C4.
Tel 08-791 88 80.

Rosendals TrädgårdsKafé
Rosendalsterrassen 12.
Map 6 C3.
Tel 08-545 812 70.

Sturekatten
Riddargatan 4.
Map 3 D4.
Tel 08-611 16 12.

Tabac
Stora Nygatan 46.
Map 4 B4.
Tel 08-10 15 34.

Tintarella di Luna
Drottninggatan 102.
Map 2 C3.
Tel 08-10 79 55.

Wayne's Coffee
Götgatsbacken 31.
Map 9 D2.
Tel 08-644 45 90.
Kungsgatan 14.
Map 3 D4.
Tel 08-791 00 86.

Vete-Katten
Kungsgatan 55.
Map 2 C4.
Tel 08-20 84 05.

PUBS

Akkurat
Hornsgatan 18.
Map 8 C2.
Tel 08-644 00 15.

Anchor Pub
Sveavägen 90.
Map 2 C2.
Tel 08-15 20 00.

Bagpiper's Inn/Bald Eagle
Rörstandsgatan 21.
Map 1 C1.
Tel 08-31 18 55.

Boomerang
Rörstandsgatan 23.
Map 1 C1.
Tel 08-33 04 11.

Copperfields
Eriksgatan 36–38.
Map 2 A2.
Tel 08-654 80 00.

The Dubliner
Hollandargatan 1.
Map 2 C4.
Tel 08-679 77 07.

Limerick
Tegnérgatan 10.
Map 2 C3.
Tel 08-673 43 98.

Mackinlay's
Fleminggatan 85.
Map 1 C2.
Tel 08-650 83 20.

Man in the Moon
Tegnérgatan 2 C.
Map 2 C3.
Tel 08-458 95 00.

O'Leary's
Götgatan 11.
Map 4 B5.
Tel 08-644 69 01.

Oliver Twist
Repslagargatan 6.
Map 9 D2.
Tel 08-640 05 66.

Soldaten Svejk
Östgötagatan 35.
Map 9 D3.
Tel 08-641 33 66.

Tennstopet
Dalagatan 50.
Map 2 A2.
Tel 08-32 25 18.

Tudor Café
Grevgatan 31.
Map 3 F4.
Tel 08-660 27 12.

ENTERTAINMENT IN STOCKHOLM

Within the past couple of decades Stockholm has become an important city for entertainment. The capital, which was once said to have a "cold beauty", is now a vibrant, trend-setting metropolis full of theatres, bars and music venues. International stars increasingly put Stockholm on their touring schedule, not least because of the magnificent indoor arena, Globen. Another

Jazz musician

factor is Swedish pop music's great position on the world stage which has made it an important export item. A wide range of entertainment is on offer and the short distance between venues is another benefit. The Royal Opera House, for instance, is only a few minutes' walk from the intimate clubs of Gamla Stan. Stockholm also has a rich cultural life with concerts, drama and exhibitions.

Kungliga Operan (Royal Opera House), Gustav II Adolfs Torg *(see p64)*

ENTERTAINMENT LISTINGS

A reliable source of information about special events is the official guide *What's On Stockholm* which is available free of charge at most hotels, conference centres and tourist information offices. It is published 10 times a year in both English and Swedish. Daily newspapers also have detailed information on

forthcoming events in a special section or in weekend supplements (but only in Swedish).

The Internet has several good sites with up-to-date information on special events. **Stockholm Visitors Board**, SVB *(see p191)* has an official "tourist site" (www.stockholmtown.com), which is constantly updated with detailed information and includes some useful links. **www.alltom stockholm.se** gives a wealth of information about entertainment and events in Stockholm, including everything from museums and restaurants to concerts.

A third extremely useful and user-friendly site on entertainment in the capital is **www.ticnet.se**. Information on all three websites is partly in English.

Stampen, in Stora Nygatan, one of Stockholm's great jazz clubs *(see p179)*

BOOKING TICKETS

Tickets for events can usually be bought at the ticket office of the relevant theatre or sports arena. But to be sure of reserving a seat it is advisable to book in advance either with the help of your hotel or of the Stockholm Visitors Board's main office, located at Vasagatan 14, or the Hotellcentralen office in the Central Station. You can also use one of the city's ticket agencies, for example **Ticnet**, which can make bookings by telephone for theatres, concerts, sporting events and excursions. A booking fee of 10–45 kr is charged depending on the price of the ticket. Tickets for various events can be bought over the counter at the centrally located **Boxoffice**. Tickets booked direct can also be picked up here.

OUTDOOR CONCERTS AND FESTIVALS

Major outdoor events get under way in mid-May with the annual **Kungsträd-gården** programme. This includes a wide variety of music with regular lunchtime and evening concerts. In the second week of June the **Slottsgalorna** event takes place at Ulriksdals Slott with international stars and the country's top musicians. **Skansen** stages a wide range of music, especially in July, with jazz on Monday evenings. The **Stockholm Jazz Festival** is held on Skeppsholmen in mid-July,

A sea of people at the Royal Philharmonic Orchestra's outdoor concert

and attracts the big names in jazz and blues.

For classical music lovers, the **Royal Philharmonic Orchestra**'s outdoor concert at Sjöhistoriska (the National Maritime Museum) on the second Sunday in August is one of the summer's highlights. The concert is an annual tradition and attracts audiences of 25,000–30,000.

Other events worth attending include **A Taste of Stockholm** at Kungsträd-gården on the first weekend in June and the **Boules Festival** on the last weekend in May for those interested in the game.

NIGHT-TIME TRANSPORT

The Tunnelbana stops around 3:30am Sunday to Thursday nights, but on Friday and Saturday nights it runs until 4am. It is replaced by night

buses. Several night buses depart from Sergels Torg, and most bus stops have maps showing the night routes. Taxis are usually not difficult to find, even on a Saturday evening *(see p201)*.

STOCKHOLM FOR CHILDREN

Compared with many major cities, Stockholm is an extremely child-friendly place and ideal for family visits.

It is easy to take prams and pushchairs on to the new buses, and there is plenty of space for them inside *(see also p191)*.

Most of the museums have children's corners with special activities. Museums and other important sights often have a cafeteria or restaurant with special menus or smaller portions for children. Toilets with a baby-changing table are frequently available.

Many of the favourite places for children are on Djur-gården. **Junibacken** has an exciting journey through the fantastic world of the children's author Astrid Lindgren. The nearby **Vasamuseet** is also child-friendly. For decades the **Gröna Lund** funfair has been a mixture of traditional and exciting modern attractions, making it an ideal excursion for families with both teenagers and younger children.

Gröna Lund's roller-coaster

DIRECTORY

EVENTS LISTINGS

Stockholm Visitors Board
Vasagatan 14, 111 20
Stockholm. **Map** 2 C4.
Tel 08-508 28 508.
www.stockholmtown.com
Other good Internet sites:
www.alltomstockholm.se
www.ticket.se

TICKET BOOKINGS

Boxoffice
Norrmalmstorg. **Map** 3 D4.
Tel 08-10 88 00.
www.boxoffice.se

Ticnet
Tel 077-170 70 70.
www.ticnet.se

STOCKHOLM FOR CHILDREN

Fjäderholmarna *p150*
Gröna Lund *p95*
Junibacken *p88*
Kulturhuset *p67*
Skansen *pp96–7*
Stockholms
  Medeltidsmuseum *p59*
Naturhistoriska
  Riksmuseet/
  Cosmonova *p124*
Leksaksmuseet *p131*
Vasamuseet *pp92–3*

The open-air museum **Skansen**, with all its animals and exciting activities, can keep a family happily occupied for a whole day.

Special children's weeks are organized on **Fjäderholmarna**, a group of islands, which can be reached from the city centre in only 25 minutes. **Leksaksmuseet** (the Toy Museum) on Söder is a safe bet for children. At **Stockholms Medeltidsmuseum** children can experience what life was like in Stockholm in the Middle Ages. In the city centre **Kulturhuset** has a variety of children's activities with a cultural content.

Naturhistoriska Riksmuseet (Museum of Natural History) houses the Cosmonova planetarium and IMAX cinema, which is a big attraction for children.

Drama and Classical Music

Stockholm's year as Cultural Capital of Europe in 1998 was a well-deserved honour, as all the city's various areas of culture reflect a high degree of dedication and talent. This applies particularly to the world of music, which has seen many top-class international artists emerge from the capital's stages. As a result opera, ballet and classical music is well supported by Stockholmers who have a wide home-grown repertoire to enjoy, which is complemented by a number of guest artists from all over the world.

BALLET AND DANCE

Classical ballet of the highest quality is mainly staged at the over 100-year-old **Kungliga Operan** (see pp64–5). Every season three of the best-known ballets, for example *The Nutcracker*, *Swan Lake*, and *Romeo and Juliet*, are performed to packed houses. Thanks to the choreographer Birgit Cullberg, now deceased, Stockholm has also become a noted centre for modern dance. Many established dance companies make guest appearances at **Dansens Hus** (see p69) which has taken over the previous home of Stadsteatern. **Moderna Dansteatern** in the old torpedo factory on Skepps-holmen is another important stage for modern dance.

OPERA

Traditional productions in their original language are staged mainly at **Kungliga Operan**. Lunchtime operas or concerts are sometimes performed in the Gustav III opera café. During the summer, major operas are presented at **Drottning-holms Slottsteater** (see pp146–49). Dating from the 18th century, the theatre's stage settings and scene-shifting machinery are preserved in their original condition and are still in good working order. All the operas performed here are also from the 18th century, and over the years the theatre has revived several unknown works by Mozart, using instruments typical of that era. The theatre is open for guided tours.

Sweden's oldest Rococo theatre, **Confidencen**, is located near Ulriksdal (see p125). Between June and September weekly opera and ballet performances are held here. Another genre of classical opera is staged at **Folkoperan**, which performs the classics in Swedish and without elaborate scenery.

Regina-Stockholm Operamathus is a rebuilt cinema where audiences can dine in comfort while enjoying the opera.

THEATRES AND MUSICALS

Stockholm has a flourishing theatrical life, but perform-ances are usually in Swedish. **Kungliga Dramatiska Teatern**, often known simply as "Dramaten" (see pp72–3), is Sweden's national theatre and has five stages. Internat-ional and Swedish classics are regularly performed here, from Shakespeare to Strind-berg, as well as modern foreign and Swedish produc-tions. Ingmar Bergman was the theatre's director from 1963–6, and he has returned as an acclaimed guest director many times since then.

Södra Teatern (see p128) often presents modern pro-ductions despite having roots that go back to the 19th century. **Stockholms Stads-teater**, based in Kulturhuset (see p67), has a widely varied programme. A summer speci-ality is the popular series of **Parkteatern** productions in several of the city's parks with drama, dance and children's theatre. **Judiska Teatern** has a repertoire of new Jewish drama, as well as dance, poetry and film shows. **Teater Galeasen** is Stockholm's avant-garde stage for new Swedish and foreign drama.

Marionetteatern has puppet shows for both children and adults, along with a puppet museum on the same premises. **Pantomimteatern** is a theatre company which performs not only in Stock-holm but tours rural areas, too.

Light-hearted plays are often staged at **China-Teatern**, and its programmes include some highly popular musicals and some much-loved plays for children. High quality musicals are also performed at **Oscars-Teatern**, **Göta Lejon** and **Cirkus**.

CLASSICAL MUSIC

World-standard classical music is regularly performed at **Berwaldhallen** (see p106). The hall is dedicated to the great Swedish composer Franz Berwald (1796–1868) and is home to the Swedish Radio Symphony Orchestra which has thrived under musical directors like Sergiu Celibidache and Esa-Pekka Salonen. The Swedish Radio Chorus, which is regarded as one of the world's great *a cappella* ensembles, is based here, too. Concerts are also given in the hall by other symphony orchestras and smaller ensembles.

Konserthuset (see p68) is the home of the Royal Philharmonic Orchestra, an internationally acclaimed 100-piece orchestra whose season runs from August to May. Its programme includes a couple of chamber music series and a jazz series, as well as performances for families on Saturdays. An annual composition festival is held every November.

Nybrokajen 11 (see p83) was formerly the home of the Musical Academy. Apart from July and August, its large hall is now used almost daily for concerts. In addition to classical music, you can hear performances of jazz, choral music and folk music. **Music at the Palace** is an annual summer series at the Royal Palace (see pp50–53) with two concerts every week, usually classical music but sometimes other styles. The concerts are normally staged in the Hall of

State or the Royal Chapel. The majestic staircase of **Nationalmuseum** *(see pp82–3)* is the setting for summer concerts. **Riddarhusmusik** at Riddarhuset *(see p58)* is a series by the Stockholm Sinfonietta.

FOLK AND CHURCH MUSIC

Rural folk music still flourishes in the capital, and this tradition is particularly fostered at **Skansen** *(see pp96–7)*, where fiddlers and folk dance teams play a major role in the various festivals held there *(see pp26–7)*. Folk music is also on the programme at **Nybrokajen 11**.

Concerts are regularly given in the city's churches, for example visitors can relax and enjoy beautiful church music in the tranquil surroundings of **Jacobs Kyrka** in Kungsträdgården *(see p64)* every Saturday at 3pm. Afternoon concerts usually take place in **Storkyrkan** *(see p49)* on Saturday and Sunday during spring and autumn.

BOOKING TICKETS

Tickets for Stockholm's theatres and concert halls can be booked through **Ticnet**; directly at the relevant box office; or ordered by telephone *(see p175)*.

DIRECTORY

BALLET & DANCE

Dansens Hus
Barnhusgatan 12–14.
Map 2 C3.
Tel 08-508 990 00.
www.dansenshus.se
Tickets on sale: 2–6pm Mon–Fri, 2–7pm Sat, 11am–3pm Sun (during performances).

Kungliga Operan
Gustav Adolfs Torg.
Map 4 B1. *Tel* 08-24 82 40; 08-791 44 00 (tickets).
www.operan.se
Tickets on sale: noon–6pm Mon–Fri, noon–3pm Sat.

Moderna Dansteatern
Slupskjulsvägen 30, Skeppsholmen.
Map 5 E2.
Tel 08-611 14 56.
www.modernadans teatern.se
Tickets on sale: from Dansteatern/home page.

OPERA

Confidencen
Ulriksdals Slottsteater.
Tel 08-85 60 10.
www.solna.se

Drottningholms Slottsteater
Drottningholm Palace, Lovön. *Tel* 08-660 82 25.
www.dtm.se

Folkoperan
Hornsgatan 72. **Map** 8 B2
Tel 08-616 07 00; 08-616 07 50 (tickets).
www.folkoperan.se
Tickets on sale: noon–7pm Wed, noon–6pm Thu & Fri.

Kungliga Operan
Gustav Adolfs Torg.
Map 4 B1.
Tel 08-24 82 40; 08-791 44 00 (tickets).
www.operan.se
Tickets on sale: noon–6pm Mon–Fri, noon–3pm Sat.

Regina-Stockholm Operamathus
Drottninggatan 71 A.
Map 2 C3. *Tel* 08-411 63 20. www.regina-operamathus.com
Tickets on sale: noon–6pm Tue–Sat.

THEATRE

China-Teatern
Berzelii Park 9.
Map 3 D4.
Tel 08-566 323 50.
www.chinateatern.se
Tickets on sale: 11am–6pm Mon–Fri.

Cirkus
Djurgårdsslätten.
Map 6 A4. *Tel* 08-587 987 00. www.cirkus.se
Tickets on sale: 11am–5:30pm Mon–Wed, 11am–7:30pm Thu, 11am–9pm Fri, 1–7:30pm Sat.

Kungliga Dramatiska Teatern
Nybroplan.
Map 3 E4.
Tel 08-667 06 80.
www.dramaten.se
Tickets on sale: noon–5pm Tue–Sat, noon–3pm Sun.

Drottningholms Slottsteater
Drottningholm Palace, Lovön. *Tel* 08-660 82 25 / 556 931 00. www.dtm.se

Göta Lejon
Götgatan 55.
Map 9 D3. *Tel* 08-643 67 00. Tickets on sale: 11am–6pm Mon–Fri.

Judiska Teatern
Djurgårdsbrunnsvägen 59.
Map 7 E2.
Tel 08-660 02 71.
www.judiskateatern.se

Marionetteatern
Brunnsgatan 6. **Map** 3 D3.
Tel 08-506 201 00.

Oscars-Teatern
Kungsgatan. 63.
Map 2 B4.
Tel 08-20 50 00.
www.oscarsteatern.se

Pantomimteatern
S:t Eriksgatan 84.
Map 1 C1.
Tel 08-31 54 64. www.pantomimteatern.com

Parkteatern
Tel 08-506 201 00.

Stockholms Stadsteater
Sergels Torg. **Map** 2 C4.
Tel 08-506 201 00.
www.stadsteatern.stockholm.se
Tickets on sale: noon–7pm Tue–Fri, noon–6pm Sat, noon–4pm Sun.

Södra Teatern
Mosebacke Torg 1–3.
Map 9 D2.
Tel 08-531 994 90.
www.sodrateatern.com
Tickets on sale: noon–6pm Mon–Fri, noon–4pm Sat.

Teater Galeasen
Slupskjulsvägen 32, Skeppsholmen. **Map** 5 E2.
Tel 08-611 00 30.
www.galeasen.se

CLASSICAL MUSIC

Berwaldhallen
Dag Hammarshjolds Väg 3.
Map 6 A2.
Tel 08-784 50 00.
www.berwaldhallen.se

Konserthuset
Hötorget 8.
Map 2 C4.
Tel 08-506 677 88.
www.konserthuset.se

Music at the Palace
The Royal Palace, Slottsbacken.
Map 4 C2.
Tel 08-10 22 47.

Nationalmuseum
Södra Blasieholmshamnen.
Map 5 D2.
Tel 08-519 543 00.
www.nationalmuseum.se

Nybrokajen 11
Nybrokajen 11 **Map** 4 C1.
Tel 08-407 16 00.
www.nybrokajen11.rikskonserter.se

Riddarhusmusik
Riddarhuset, Riddarhustorget 10.
Map 4 A3.
Tel 08-723 39 90.
www.riddarhuset.se

CENTRAL TICKET AGENCY

Ticnet
Tel 077 170 70 70.
www.ticnet.se

Nightlife and Entertainment

In common with most capitals, Stockholm has a rich variety of nightlife and entertainment, with something for everyone. Pop music is one of the country's biggest exports so there is no shortage of groups following in the footsteps of ABBA. Top-class musical entertainment is provided on a large scale in Globen or on a smaller more intimate basis in the pubs, clubs and bars. The Swedish jazz scene thrives in several venues where live music is played nightly.

ROCK AND POP

Stockholm's **Globen** is the city's biggest stage for rock and pop music. It attracts all the biggest international artists as well as leading Swedish groups. **Cirkus** and **Södra Teatern** (see p176) are other favourite venues for rock and pop, and they stage both musical and theatrical productions in beautiful settings. **Münchenbryggeriet**, a former brewery, also provides a great venue. Hard rock enthusiasts are well-catered for at **Anchor Pub** three or four times a week.

Debaser is Sweden's biggest club scene for pop and rock. Based in three locations across the city, the club has attracted the likes of Bob Dylan, The Strokes, Bright Eye's and Sweden's very own, The Ark.

JAZZ MUSIC

A wide choice of jazz can be found in Stockholm. **Fasching Jazzklubb** has an international reputation for good music with performances virtually every day of the week. Another classic jazz spot is **Stampen** in Gamla Stan, which attracts a rather older clientele. **Nalen** holds frequent jazz events, and usually provides live music to dance to on Sundays. **Glenn Miller Café** has a cosy atmosphere, with jazz nightly from Monday to Saturday. During the summer the vintage steamboat **SS Blidösund** (see p143) operates special jazz cruises around the archipelago four times a week. The annual **Stockholm Jazz Festival** hosts up-and-coming artists as well as international stars. See www.stockholmjazz. com for more details.

MUSIC PUBS

Life in Stockholm's pubs and bars has changed in recent years as a number of establishments have introduced live music. Irish bands often play at **The Dubliner** (see p172), and live music is also performed at the **Engelen** and **Akkurat** pubs. Engelen has a variety of music while the accent is on rock at Akkurat.

Apart from these musical watering holes, there are plenty of traditional British and Irish pubs in the capital, generally with a wide choice of beer and whisky and snack meals (see pp172–3).

BARS

The best bars are usually found in the hotels and restaurants, but those in the latter are often noisier and smokier. The most fashionable tend to have a long queue, supervised by a doorman, waiting to enter. For a quieter atmosphere with comfortable armchairs, hotel bars are the best bet. The minimum age for buying alcohol is 18, and young customers must be prepared to show proof of age.

The **Cadier Bar** in the Grand Hôtel (see pp79 & 157) undoubtedly has the most elegant clientele because this is where the rich and famous stay. From the verandah there is a fine view of the Royal Palace and the archipelago boats and in the background gentle music is played on the white grand piano.

Operabaren is a sight in itself with well-preserved Jugendstil decor, marble tables and leather sofas. The regulars often include authors, artists and intellectuals.

Erik's Gondolen at the top of Katarinahissen (see p127) offers arguably the most beautiful view of Stockholm and is a perfect place for a drink at sunset. It has comfortable leather armchairs, skilled bartenders and a relaxing atmosphere. **Sky Bar**, high up in the Royal Viking Hotel, has a panoramic view of the city, seen at its best after dark when the lights come on. The **Sheraton Living Room** is a classic international bar where business people from all over the world relax to the accompaniment of piano music while skilled bartenders fix their favourite cocktails.

Absolut Icebar Stockholm, located in the Nordic Sea Hotel, is the world's first permanent ice bar. All of the interior fittings are made of pure ice. The bar can cater for up to 30 people at a time. **Sturehof Bar** is a sophisticated and modern nightspot, particularly popular with people from the advertising and media worlds and other local night owls.

NIGHTCLUBS AND CASINOS

Most of Stockholm's best nightclubs are located around Stureplan (see pp70–71). The traditional discotheque evenings are Friday and Saturday, and on other days of the week they are often hired by various clubs providing particular styles of music. The nightlife scene is changing all the time as new clubs come and go. **Café Opera**, Stockholm's most historic international-class nightclub, is located to the rear of Kungliga Operan (see pp64–5). It has a mixed clientele of both the young and trendy and a more soberly dressed older generation. **Sturecompagniet** is a large disco on several floors which also has a rock bar at street level. **Fasching Jazzklubb** has soul from the 1960s and 1970s on Saturdays. **Spy Bar** is the place to rub shoulders with Swedish celebrities and international artists on tour. However, it is often crowded and a membership card may be necessary. **Ambassaduer** is another "in" place with a fashion-conscious clientele. The younger generation enjoy dancing to a variety of music at **Mondo**. In the city centre is **Casino Cosmopol**, Stockholm's first casino.

CABARETS

Good food and top-class entertainment are on the menu at **Hamburger Börs**, which features cabaret shows performed by leading Swedish artists. **Wallmans Salonger** offers musical entertainment provided by the waiters and waitresses along with the food.

FILM

Films are not dubbed into Swedish, so non-Swedish speaking visitors can more often than not go to a cinema and enjoy a film that is in their own language. Films in languages other than English are usually screened at **Zita**, and **Sture** is also a good venue for cineasts. There are both classic cinemas like **Rigoletto**, showing quality international drama, and multi-screen complexes like **Filmstaden Sergel**, which screens most of the current Hollywood repertoire.

DIRECTORY

ROCK AND POP

Anchor Pub
Sveavägen 90. **Map** 2 C2.
Tel 08-15 20 00.
◯ *3pm–3am daily.*

Cirkus
Djurgårdsslätten.
Map 6 A4.
Tel 08-587 987 00.

Debaser
Medborgarplatsen 8.
Map 9 D3.
Karl Johans Torg 1.
Map 4 C4.
Johannesgränd 1.
Map 4 C3.
Tel 08-462 98 60.

Globen
Globentorget 2.
Tel 0771 310 000.
3km (1.9 miles) S of Stockholm.

Münchenbryggeriet
Torkel Knutssonsg 2.
Map 8 B1. *Tel 08-658 20 00; for tickets: 0771 707070.*

Södra Teatern
Mosebacke Torg 1–3.
Map 9 D2.
Tel 08-531 994 90.

JAZZ

Fasching Jazzklubb
Kungsgatan 63. **Map** 2 B4. *Tel 08-534 829 60.*
◯ *7pm–1am Mon–Thu, 7pm–4am Fri–Sat, 5pm–1am Sun.*

Glenn Miller Café
Brunnsgatan 21 A.
Map 3 D3. *Tel 08-10 03 22.* ◯ *11am–1am Mon–Thu, 11am–2am Fri, 5pm–2am Sat.*
♫ *from 8pm.*

Nalen
Regeringsgatan 74.
Map 3 D3.
Tel 08-505 292 00.

Stampen
Stora Nygatan 5.
Map 4 B3.
Tel 08-20 57 93.
◯ *8pm–1am Mon–Thu, 8pm–2am Fri & Sat.*

SS Blidösund
Skeppsbron 10. **Map** 4 C2. *Tel 08-24 30 90.*
◯ *May–mid-Sep: boat departing at 7pm Mon–Thu.*

MUSIC PUBS

Akkurat
Hornsgatan 18. **Map** 8 C2. *Tel 08-644 00 15.* ◯ *11am–1am Tue–Fri, 11am–midnight Mon, 3pm–1am Sat, 6pm–1am Sun.*

The Dubliner
Holländargatan 1. **Map** 2 C3. *Tel 08-679 77 07.*
◯ *3pm–1am Mon–Thu, 2pm–3am Fri, noon–3am Sat, 1–11pm Sun.*
♫ *from 10pm daily.*

Engelen
Kornhamnstorg 59 B.
Map 4 B4.
Tel 08-20 10 92.
◯ *5pm–3am Mon–Sun.*

BARS

Absolut Icebar Stockholm
Vasaplan 7. **Map** 2 B4.
Tel 08-505 630 00.

Cadier Bar
Grand Hôtel, Södra Blasieholmshamnen 8.
Map 4 C1.
Tel 08-679 35 00.

Erik's Gondolen
Stadsgården 6. **Map** 4 C5. *Tel 08-641 70 90.*

Operabaren
Kungsträdgården.
Map 4 B1.
Tel 08-676 58 00.

Sheraton Living Room
Tegelbacken 6.
Map 4 A1.
Tel 08-412 34 00.

Sky Bar
Vasagatan 1.
Map 2 B4.
Tel 08-506 540 00.

Sturehof Bar
Stureplan 2.
Map 3 D4.
Tel 08-440 57 30.

NIGHT CLUBS AND CASINOS

Ambassaduer
Kungsgatan 18.
Map 3 D4.
Tel 08-24 47 00.
◯ *9pm–5am Tue, 7pm–3am Thu, 10pm–4am Fri & Sat.*

Café Opera
Operahuset, Kungsträdgården. **Map** 4 B2.
Tel 08-676 58 07.
◯ *11pm–3am daily.*

Casino Cosmopol
Kungsgatan 65. **Map** 2 B4. *Tel 08-781 88 00.*
◯ *1pm–5am daily.*

Fasching Jazzklubb
Kungsgatan 63.
Map 2 B4.
Tel 08-534 829 60.
◯ *Soul club: midnight–4am Sat.*

Mondo
Medborgarplatsen 8.
Map 9 D3.
Tel 08-673 10 32.
◯ *3pm–midnight.*

Spy Bar
Birger Jarlsgatan 20.
Map 3 D3.
Tel 08-545 076 55.
◯ *11pm–5am Wed–Sat.*

Sturecompagniet
Sturegatan 4. **Map** 3 D3.
Tel 08-545 076 10.
◯ *10pm–3am Thu–Sat.*

CABARETS

Hamburger Börs
Jakobsgatan 6. **Map** 3 D5.
Tel 08-787 85 00.

Wallmans Salonger
Teatergatan 3. **Map** 3 E5.
Tel 08-505 560 00.

FILM

Filmstaden Sergel
Hötorget. **Map** 2 C4.
Tel 08-562 600 00.

Rigoletto
Kungsgatan 16. **Map** 2 B4. *Tel 08-562 600 00.*

Sture
Birger Jarlsgatan 41.
Map 3 D3.
Tel 08-22 99 10.

Zita
Birger Jarlsgatan 37.
Map 3 D3.
Tel 08-23 20 20.

OUTDOOR ACTIVITIES

Hot-air balloon over Stockholm

As a city built around water and where the countryside reaches into the centre, Stockholm is ideally positioned for all kinds of open-air pursuits. The great outdoors plays an important role in the Swedish lifestyle, and the capital offers a plethora of activities throughout the year – for the energetic and not so energetic – from walking, cycling and ice-skating to fishing, skiing and hot-air ballooning. In spring, summer and autumn around 80 golf courses are open to visitors, as well as well-planned jogging and cycle tracks. Outdoor swimming pools are popular on hot summer days, and in winter long-distance skating between the islands and cross-country and downhill skiing are the things to do.

In many cases, it is simple to make your own contacts, but the Stockholm Visitors Board (SVB) will be able to advise you *(see p191)*.

Hagaparken, an inviting area for exercise and recreation *(see pp122–3)*

JOGGING, WALKS AND CYCLING

It can be both practical and rewarding to take some exercise while exploring the capital. Everything in the city centre is within easy walking distance, including major sights, beautiful parks and modern shopping malls. A walk in Stockholm always takes you close to the water or some unusual sight. The organized walks in the city are usually conducted in Swedish but there are also tours of Gamla Stan with English-speaking guides. Contact Stockholm Information Service (SIS) for advice on a route.

Even if you want to head out of the city centre, there is no need to travel far. The No. 47 bus goes out to Djurgården, where you can have a walk or jog along the shores, through the avenues under the oak trees, or over green fields. Walking paths along the city's waterfronts *(see pp40–41)* provide both good routes and stunning views. There are many floodlit jogging tracks, and plenty of fun-run events to choose from *(see pp26–9)*.

Those who prefer to move at a gentler pace can head for **Skansen** open-air museum *(see pp96–7)* or the **Gröna Lund** amusement park *(see p95)*, both suitable for the whole family, providing a day out in the open air.

Djurgården has plenty of cycle paths and bicycles can be hired from **Cykel Moped-uthyrningen** or **Stockholm City Bikes** *(see p205)*, which has locations all over Stockholm. Roller-blades can also be hired near the bridge.

Cyclists planning to take a longer tour should visit SIS and ask to be put in touch with the Cykelfrämjandet cycling organization.

HORSE RIDING

Several riding schools near the city centre, such as **Stockholms Ridhus**, offer lessons. For those who prefer to discover Stockholm's surrounding areas, tours on Icelandic ponies are operated from quite a few stables.

Rundemars Gård hires out horses to experienced riders to explore the Tyresö nature reserve, southeast of the city, after an initial briefing.

WATER SPORTS

There are excellent opportunities for water sports. Canoes, rowing boats, pedalos and larger boats for longer tours, can be hired from **Tvillingarnas Båtuth-yrning** near Djurgårdsbron. A good area for canoeing is the canal near Djurgården *(see pp85–99)*, where **Djurgårdsbrons Sjöcafé** hires out canoes.

Fishing at Blasieholmskajen in the centre of the city

SWIMMING

During the summer there are plenty of outdoor swimming pools to choose from. They include **Eriksdalsbadet** in Södermalm, **Kampementsbadet** at Gärdet and **Smedsuddsbadet** at Rålambshov Park Beach. There are several good places for a swim along the Kungsholmen shores of Riddarfjärden. And on Långholmen there are both sandy beaches or rocks to swim from (see p132).

For a completely different bathing experience, try the Japanese **Yasuragi** at Hasseludden. For indoor pools, try Centralbadet (see p69) or Sturebadet (see p71).

GOLF

Golfers will find about 80 golf courses within easy reach of the city centre. The closest, such as **Djursholms Golfklubb**, are in delightful settings.

The courses are popular and advance bookings are recommended. Golf information is available on Stockholm's official website (www.stockholmtown.com).

OTHER ACTIVITIES

Brightly coloured hot-air balloons hovering over the city are a common sight in the evening. Several companies operate charter trips in balloons. You can book via SIS or directly with a company such as **Far & Flyg**.

Game fishing for salmon and trout is possible right in

Outdoor swimming in Stockholm

the city centre near the Royal Palace. Suitable tackle can be hired at **Fiskarnas Redskapshandel**. **Sportfiskarma Stockholm** can provide information on fishing in and around Stockholm.

Outdoor tennis courts are available at several places, including **Kungliga Lawn Tennishallen**, where the Stockholm Open ATP indoor tournament is held every November.

You can go scuba-diving around Stockholm too. Contact SIS for details of diving schools and equipment hire.

Ice-skaters are in their element once the open waters of the archipelago have frozen over. Meanwhile, the artificial rink at Kungsträdgården is open throughout the winter, and hires out skates.

The outdoor activities organization **Friluftsfrämjandet** provides information on skating and skiing in the area.

Visitors with disablities can find out more about the availability of outdoor pursuits by contacting **De Handikappades Riksförbund** (see p191).

DIRECTORY

HORSE RIDING

Rundemars Gård
Rundmars Gård, Tyresö.
Tel 08-770 23 29.
www.rundemarsgard.com

Stockholms Ridhus
Storängsvägen 29. **Map** 3 F1.
Tel 08-664 61 79.
www.stockholmsridhus.se

WATER SPORTS AND FISHING

Djurgårdsbrons Sjöcafé
Galävarvsvägen 2. *Tel 08-660 57 57.* www.sjocafe.se

Fiskarnas Redskapshandel
S:t Paulsgatan 2–4. **Map** 8 C2.
Tel 08-556 096 50.

Sportfiskarma Stockholm
Tel 08-704 44 80.

Tvillingarnas Båtuthyrning
Grönviksvägen 120.
Tel 08-588 155 80.

SWIMMING

Eriksdalsbadet
Hammarby Slussv. 8.
Map 9 D5. *Tel 08-508 402 58.*

Kampementsbadet
Sandhamnsgatan (Gärdet).
Tel 08-661 62 16.
◯ 25 May–25 Aug.

Yasuragi
Hasseludden Konferens & Yasuragi.
▨ 35-min journey from Slussen.
Tel 08-747 61 00. ◯ 8am–7pm Mon–Fri, 9am–5pm Sat, 10am–4pm Sun. www.yasuragi.se

GOLF

Djursholms Golfklubb
Hagbardsvägen, Djursholm.
Tel 08-544 964 50. www.dgk.se

OTHER ACTIVITIES

Far & Flyg
Gröndasvägen 38nb.
Tel 08-645 77 00.
www.farochflyg.se

Kungliga Lawn Tennishallen
Lidingövägen. *Tel 08-459 15 00.*
www.kungl.tennishallen.se

Friluftsfrämjandet
Tel 08-447 44 40.
www.frilufts.se

One of Stockholm's many golf courses

SHOPPING IN STOCKHOLM

Stockholm is worth visiting for the shopping alone. All the best shops in the central area are within easy walking distance and they stock virtually everything anyone could want. There are plenty of small boutiques for fashion and interiors, as well as antique shops, luxury international designer outlets and well-stocked department stores.

Shopping is good all over the city. Exclusive shops can be found in fashionable Östermalm. Gamla Stan is a good place for handicrafts and unusual knick-knacks. Södermalm and Vasastan have antique and second-hand shops. Cameras, mobile telephones, furs, children's clothing, toys and Swedish glass are cheaper in Sweden than in most other countries. No expedition is complete without a visit to one of the city's splendid market halls which sell Swedish delicacies like reindeer and elk meat, caviar and cloudberries.

Dala horse
(see p184)

OPENING TIMES

Most shops usually open at 10am and close at 6pm, although many in the city centre remain open until 7pm. Most shops are open until 2pm on Saturdays, and the major department stores stay open until 5pm. Large stores, shopping malls and a number of shops in central Stockholm are open on Sundays. Market halls are closed on Sundays and public holidays. Larger supermarkets are open daily until 8pm.

PAYMENT

All the main credit cards and travellers' cheques are accepted in most shops. If you pay by card you may be asked for proof of identity; many shops require a pin number. Goods can be exchanged if you produce the receipt. Purchases can usually be made on a sale-or-return basis, providing this is noted on the receipt.

VALUE ADDED TAX

Value added tax ("moms" in Swedish) is charged on all items except daily newspapers. The VAT rate is 25%, except on food, for which the rate is only 12%. VAT is always included in the total price.

TAX-FREE SHOPPING

Residents of countries outside the European Union are entitled to a refund of the VAT they have paid on their purchases. Tax-free shopping with Global Refund gives visitors a cash refund of 15–18 per cent on their departure from the EU. Look for the "Tax-free shopping" sign. Global Refund is at all departure points, including Arlanda Airport.

Biblioteksgatan, an attractive shopping street in Stockholm

SALES

Twice a year Stockholm's shops and department stores have sales with reduced prices on clothing, shoes and other fashion goods. Sales are indicated by the *rea* sign. The year's first sales start after Christmas and continue throughout January. The second sales period lasts from late June to the end of July.

SHOPPING CENTRES AND DEPARTMENT STORES

Stockholm's best-known superstore is **IKEA**, which has become a popular tourist attraction in its own right. It sells not just furniture but also everything else for the home, and all at attractive prices. The textiles section is particularly good, as well as the kitchenware and porcelain departments. IKEA's store is located outside the city but is

NK, Stockholm's most exclusive department store

Nordiska Kristall, a major outlet for Swedish glass in Stockholm

easy to reach by a free shuttle bus from Regeringsgatan 13 to Kungens Kurva, hourly on weekdays from 10am to 5pm.

Another well-known store is the fashion house **H&M** (Hennes & Mauritz), which has branches in many European cities and several outlets in Stockholm. H&M stocks the latest fashions at low prices. It has its own designers and makes clothing for women, men, teenagers and children. The shops also sell accessories, jewellery, underwear, perfume and cosmetics.

Nordiska Kompaniet (NK) on Hamngatan is Stockholm's leading department store, where many well-known names in fashion and cosmetics have their own shops. NK also stocks Swedish-designed products, jewellery, handicrafts and souvenirs as well as cameras, films, books and CDs.

PUB on Hötorget is another established department store with a wide selection of goods.

One of Arsenalsgatan's fine antique shops

The **Cervera** boutique chain has a good choice of table coverings and decorations, both classic and modern.

Most shopping items can be bought inexpensively at **Åhlens** department store in City, Vasastaden, Kungsholmen and Östermalm, as well as some suburbs.

There are several indoor shopping malls. **Gallerian** on Hamngatan is the largest and the prices are lower than in the elegant **Sturegallerian** near Stureplan with its many trendy boutiques. Also there are shopping centres in most suburbs where nearly all the retail chains are represented.

MARKETS

A traditional Christmas market is held at Skansen *(see p96)* every Sunday in December. Stortorget in Gamla Stan *(see p54)* also has a delightful market at Christmas.

Vegetables, fruit and flowers are sold from Monday to Friday at Hötorget *(see p68)*, Östermalmstorg *(see p71)* and Medborgarplatsen *(see p131)*. Street stalls along Drottninggatan and around Sergels Torg sell watches, clocks, toys and other knick-knacks.

Stockholm's flea market, **Skärholmens Loppmarknad**, offers a wide variety of clothes, practical objects and bric-a-brac for sale.

WINES AND SPIRITS

The only shops selling alcohol in Sweden are run by Systembolaget, the State monopoly chain. They are open Monday to Friday 10am–6pm (some open on

DIRECTORY

SHOPPING CENTRES & DEPARTMENT STORES

Cervera
Svavägen 24 . **Map** 2 C4.
Tel 08-10 45 30.
www.cervera.se

Fältöversten
Karlaplan 13.
Map 3 F3. *Tel 08-692 69 00.*
www.faltoverstencentrum.se

Gallerian
Hamngatan 37.
Map 3 D4. *Tel 08-696 32 78.*
www.gallerian.se

H&M
Hamngatan 22. **Map** 3 D4.
Tel 08-524 635 30.
Sergels Torg 12. **Map** 2 C4.
Tel 08-796 54 46.
www.hm.com

IKEA
Kungens Kurva, Skärholmen.
Tel 08-744 83 60.
Barkarby, Järfälla.
Tel 08-795 40 00. www.ikea.se

NK
Hamngatan 18–20. **Map** 3 D4.
Tel 08-762 80 00. www.nk.se

PUB
Hötorget. **Map** 3 C4.
Tel 08-789 19 30. www.pub.se

Sturegallerian
Grev Turegatan 9.
Map 3 D4. *Tel 08-453 52 00.*
www.sturegallerian.se

Åhléns
Klarabergsgatan 50. **Map** 2 C4.
Tel 08-676 60 00.
Fridhemsplan. **Map** 1 B2.
Tel 08-728 53 00.
Odenplan. **Map** 2 B2.
Tel 08-728 53 00.
www.ahlens.com

MARKETS

Skärholmens Loppmarknad
P-huset. Skärholmen.
Tel 08-710 00 60. ☐ *11am–6pm Mon–Fri, 10am–4pm Sat, 11am–4pm Sun.*

Saturdays 10am–3pm, but not on a public holiday weekend). The minimum age for buying alcohol at Systembolaget shops is 20 *(see also p191)*.

What to Buy in Stockholm

Elk candlestick

The Dala wooden horse must be the most typical Swedish souvenir. But it is facing strong competition from the elk, which has become a symbol for a country with vast tracts of unspoilt countryside. The Swedes love the great outdoors, so there are plenty of shops selling top-class sporting equipment. Swedish glass and crystal are renowned around the world. Orrefors and Kosta are just two of several glassworks producing both classic and modern glassware. Educational toys in natural materials are a Swedish speciality and so are clogs, which can be found in many shoe shops.

Hand-painted clogs

HANDICRAFTS & DESIGN

Modern Swedish design is a familiar concept in many households worldwide, even for simple everyday items (*see pp38–9*). Handicrafts have a long tradition in Sweden and contemporary designers often use wrought-iron work, weaving, pottery and woodcarving.

Dala Horse and Cockerel
Originally the brightly painted Dala horses and cockerels were toys carved from left-over fragments of wood. Later the horse became a national symbol and is sold in many variants.

Swedish Glass
Hand-blown sets of glassware are made in Sweden's glassworks, as well as artistic crystal creations and beautiful objects for everyday use.

Nobel glass carafe from Orrefors by Gunnar Cyrén

Traditional schnapps glasses

Tray with design by Josef Frank, Svenskt Tenn

Cheese slicer and knife by Michael Björnstierna

Designer Objects
The larger department stores often commission well-known designers for porcelain, glass, textiles and household items which make highly desirable gifts.

Mama, a humorous clothes hanger

Crux rug by Pia Wallén

Children's Toys
Colourful wooden children's toys from Brio are worldwide favourites. Educational picture books, games and puzzles are all excellent gifts for children.

OUTDOOR GEAR

Many Swedes enjoy outdoor pursuits like fishing, hunting, sailing, golf, camping and all types of winter sports, so there are many well-equipped sports shops around. Unique items include Lapp handicrafts beautifully made from reindeer horn or skin.

Hand Knits
Caps and gloves with attractive designs, known as lovikka, are made from a special wool which gives good protection in cold or wet conditions.

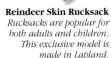

Drinking vessel in carved wood

Reindeer Skin Rucksack
Rucksacks are popular for both adults and children. This exclusive model is made in Lapland.

Spinning Reel and Lures
ABU-Garcia makes top-quality fishing tackle perfect for Sweden's long coastline, countless lakes and rivers with their rich and varied fishing.

Lapp Handicrafts
A hunting knife with a sheath of reindeer horn, or a kåsa, a drinking vessel carved in birch, are not only attractive but useful when out walking in the wild.

SWEDISH DELICACIES

Popular preserves are made from wild berries such as bitter lingonberries (for meatballs) or sweet cloudberries (served with whipped cream). Herring, crispbread and ginger biscuits can be bought in all groceries, and sweets are sold loose. Schnapps miniatures come in gift packs.

Lingonberry preserve   **Cloudberry jam**

Pickled Herring
Pickled herring should be enjoyed with new potatoes cooked with dill, chopped chives and crème fraîche. Versions flavoured with mustard, dill or other herbs or spices are also available.

Swedish schnapps gift-pack miniatures

"Raspberry boat" candy   **Salt liquorice**   **Crispbread**   **Box of ginger biscuits**

Where to Shop in Stockholm

Clothing from all the well-known international fashion houses can be found in Stockholm, and many have their own shops. If you want something rather different it is worth seeking out the creations of younger Swedish fashion designers. Swedish interior design is famous for its clean lines, functionalism and the use of pale wood, and Stockholm is a paradise for anyone interested in design. Handicrafts are of a high quality. Leisurewear and sports goods offer excellent value for money.

FASHION

Stockholm's top places for fashion are in the "golden triangle" bounded by Stureplan, Nybroplan and Norrmalmstorg. Clothing at more moderate prices can be bought around Sergels Torg.

If you are looking for Swedish designers, **NK** has a selection of clothing created by younger designers as well as mainstream local products. Classic men's clothing of high quality is designed by Oscar Jacobsson, while Stenström shirts are sold in department stores and the more elegant menswear boutiques. **Björn Borg** has his own shops selling men's and women's clothing and underwear, perfume and accessories. **Johan Lindeberg** produces unusual fashions for the daring man, while fashion-conscious young people shop at **Sneakersnstuff**. The designer **Filippa K** produces smart clothing for trendy women. **Anna Holtblad** has a good selection of stylish women's garments, while **Thalia** in Östermalm has a good range of exclusive party outfits.

DESIGN AND INTERIOR DECORATION

The city centre, Östermalm and Hornsgatan in Södermalm have a number of interior decoration shops selling the products of young designers and artists. To see the latest on offer, visit **DesignTorget**, where young designers display their work. **R.O.O.M** on Kungsholmen, **Asplund** in Östermalm and **Norrgavel** in City are just a few of the most up-to-date shops and they all have a good selection of products.

Svenskt Tenn is the city's oldest shop for interior decoration, with both modern and classic designs. **Nordiska Galleriet** has exclusive modern furniture and decoration items while **Georg Jensen** specializes in silver. **Kao-Lin, Nutida Svenskt Silver, Blås&Knåda** and **Galleri Metallum** stage exhibitions and sell Swedish-designed products. Modern printed textiles can be found at **Tio-Gruppen** in Södermalm. **Orrefors Kosta Boda** and **Nordiska Kristall** both have a wide choice of Swedish glassware, which can also be found at the various department stores.

ANTIQUES

A large number of antique shops can be found along Odengatan, Upplandsgatan and Roslagsgatan in Vasastan. Gamla Stan also has many shops offering collectables. Shops selling art, silver and porcelain of a more exclusive variety are on Arsenalsgatan on Blasieholmen, and also around Östermalmstorg. Södermalm has small shops selling bric-a-brac.

MUSIC AND MULTIMEDIA

Many Swedish pop bands now have an international reputation. Exciting new talents continue to find their way into the charts, and the latest products can often be bought in the record shops before they become available outside Sweden. Apart from pop and rock, Sweden has a long folk-music tradition, as well as many skilled jazz musicians and opera singers. **Pet Sounds** has a wide selection of CDs, as do the large department stores.

SPORT AND LEISURE

The Swedes devote a lot of time to outdoor sports and activities. **Naturkompaniet** and **Peak Performance** have an exclusive selection of sportswear and equipment. **Stadium** and **Alewalds** have a varied choice of sports clothing and equipment at attractive prices. Equipment and exclusive clothing for hunting or fishing can be bought at **Walter Borg**.

SOUVENIRS AND HANDICRAFTS

Glasses for schnapps, silver jewellery, hand-painted clogs, Lapp *(Same)* crafts, hand-knitted woollen gloves and caps, hand-made candles, traditional Christmas decorations and wrought-iron products can all be bought in the main department stores. Alternatively you can go to the Gamla Stan shops like **Carl Wennberg Sameslöjd** and **Handkraft Swea**. **Svensk Hemslöjd** and the various museum gift shops are also good places to shop. Visitors to Skansen *(see pp96–7)* can buy handicrafts made in its shops. **Nordic Souvenirs** sells Swedish handicrafts and quality souvenirs.

BOOKS

Photography books, cookery books, books on Swedish design and children's books make good souvenirs to take home. Apart from the **NK Bookshop** and at other department stores, **Hedengrens Bokhandel** has a large foreign-languages selection. The **Sweden Bookshop** has a good selection of books on Stockholm and Sweden in English.

TOYS AND BABY EQUIPMENT

It is worth buying high-quality baby prams and pushchairs produced by Emmaljunga and baby equipment by Babybjörn. **Babyland** and **Bonti** have a wide selection of these and other well-made products for children. Brio's wooden toys and other attractive toys are also favourite presents. **Bulleribock** and **BR Leksaker** offer a wide choice. Practical children's clothing can be found at **Polarn och Pyret** or at the larger department stores.

SWEDISH DELICACIES

The capital has three superb market halls: **Östermalmshallen, Hötorgshallen** and **Söderhallarna**. Delicacies on sale include salmon, bleak roe, smoked eel and smoked

reindeer meat, which are all delicious culinary souvenirs. The food sections of the major department stores sell tinned herrings, lingonberry or cloudberry jam, crispbread, gingerbread and sweets, which make good presents.

DIRECTORY

FASHIONS

Anna Holtblad
Grev Turegatan 13.
Map 3 E4.
Tel 08-545 022 20.

Björn Borg
Sergelg 12.
Map 2 C4.
Tel 08-21 70 40.

Filippa K
Grev Turegatan 18.
Map 3 E4.
Tel 08-545 882 56.

Johan Lindeberg
Grev Turegatan 9.
Map 3 D4.
Tel 08-678 61 65.

NK
Hamngatan 18–20.
Map 3 D4.
Tel 08-762 80 00.

Sneakersnstuff
Åsögatan 124.
Tel 08-743 03 22.

Thalia
Karlavägen 62.
Map 3 E3.
Tel 08-660 54 30.

DESIGN AND DECORATION

Asplund
Linnegatan 42. **Map** 3 E3.
Tel 08-662 52 84.

Blås&Knåda
Hornsgatan 26.
Map 4 B5.
Tel 08-642 77 67.

DesignTorget
Kulturhuset, Sergels
Torg 3. **Map** 2 C4.
Tel 08-21 91 50.
Götgatan 31.
Map 9 D2.
Tel 08-644 16 78.

Galleri Metallum
Hornsgatan 30.
Map 4 B5.
Tel 08-640 13 23.

Georg Jensen
Birger Jarlsgatan 13.
Map 3 D4.
Tel 08-545 040 80.

Kao-Lin
Hornsgatan 50.
Map 8 C2.
Tel 08-644 46 00.

Konsthant-verkarna
Södermalmstorg 4.
Map 9 D2, 4 B5.
Tel 08-611 03 70.

Nordiska Galleriet
Nybrogatan 11.
Map 3 E4.
Tel 08-442 83 60.

Nordiska Kristall
Kungsgatan 9.
Map 3 D4.
Tel 08-10 43 72.

Norrgavel
Birger Jarlsgatan 27.
Map 3 D3.
Tel 08-545 220 50.

Nutida Svenskt Silver
Arsenalsgatan 3.
Map 3 D4.
Tel 08-611 67 18.

Orrefors Kosta Boda
Birger Jarlsgatan 15.
Map 2 C2.
Tel 08-611 91 15.

R.O.O.M
PUB, Plan 03, Högtorget.
Map 3 C4.
Tel 08-692 50 00.

Svenskt Tenn
Strandvägen 5.
Map 3 E4.
Tel 08-670 16 00.

Tio-Gruppen
Götgatan 25.
Map 9 D2.
Tel 08-643 25 04.

MUSIC AND MULTIMEDIA

Pet Sounds
Skånegatan 53.
Map 9 E3.
Tel 08-702 97 98.

SPORT AND LEISURE

Alewalds
Kungsgatan 32.
Map 6 D3.
Tel 08-21 90 00.

Naturkompaniet
Sveavägen 62.
Map 2 C3.
Tel 08-24 30 02.
Kungsgatan 26.
Map 3 D4.
Tel 08-24 19 96.

Peak Performance
Biblioteksgatan 18.
Map 3 D4.
Tel 08-611 34 00.

Stadium
Sergelgatan 8.
Map 2 C4.
Tel 08-14 09 90.

Walter Borg
Kungsgatan 57.
Map 2 C4.
Tel 08-14 38 65.

SOUVENIRS AND HANDICRAFTS

Carl Wennberg Sameslöjd
Svartmangatan 11.
Map 4 B3.
Tel 08-20 17 21.

Handkraft Swea
Västerlånggatan 24.
Map 9 D1, 4 B3.
Tel 08-20 06 36.

Nordic Souvenirs
Hamngatan 27.
Map 3 D4.
Tel 08-24 24 70.

Svensk Hemslöjd
Sveavägen 44. **Map** 2 C3.
Tel 08-23 21 15.

BOOKS

Hedengrens Bokhandel
Stureplan 4. **Map** 3 D4.
Tel 08-611 51 28.

NK Bookshop
Hamngatan 18–20.
Map 3 D4.
Tel 08-762 83 39.

Sweden Bookshop
Slottsbacken 10.
Map 4 C2.
Tel 08-453 78 80.

TOYS AND BABY EQUIPMENT

Babyland
Karlbergsvägen 40. **Map** 2 A2. **Tel** 08-31 58 00.

Bonti
Norrtullsgatan 33.
Map 2 B2.
Tel 08-30 69 16.

BR Leksaker
Gallerian, Hamngatan 37.
Map 3 D4.
Tel 08-545 154 40.

Bulleribock
Sveavägen 104. **Map** 2 C2. **Tel** 08-673 61 21.

Polarn och Pyret
Gallerian, Hamngatan 35.
Map 3 D4.
Tel 08-411 22 47.

SWEDISH DELICACIES

Östermalmshallen
Östermalmstorg.
Map 3 E4.

Hötorgshallen
Hötorget. **Map** 2 C4.

Söderhallarna
Medborgarplatsen.
Map 9 D3.

SURVIVAL
GUIDE

PRACTICAL INFORMATION

Over the years, Stockholm has become one of the most popular tourist destinations in Scandinavia. Its bustling cruise ship terminals and its full event calendar bring thousands of tourists to the city each year, while many more come to experience the city's cultural and historical sites. It is easy to be a foreign visitor in the city, not least

Tourist office symbol

because most Swedes are happy to help tourists. The city's official tourism organization, the Stockholm Visitors Board, provides an excellent range of services. Stockholm is a small capital and is generally safe, but it still has its share of pickpockets. It is therefore wise to take care in the busy shopping areas and when travelling around the city at night.

VISAS AND PASSPORTS

Citizens of virtually all countries can enter Sweden without a visa. Since 2001, passports are not needed by visitors from European countries that have signed the Schengen agreement, as long as they are entering directly from a Schengen member country. However, to enter or depart from a Schengen country, visitors must carry a government-issued national ID card. Visitors arriving from outside the Schengen region must carry a valid passport.

Visitors are advised to check their visa and passport requirements with their local Swedish consulate or embassy prior to travelling.

TOURIST INFORMATION

Stockholm's official tourist information organization is the **Stockholm Visitors Board (SVB)**. The organization's website can answer most commonly asked questions and allows visitors to book hotel accommodation, check the calendar of special events and purchase tickets. It also provides web addresses for the most important sights. In addition SVB operates *Interactive Stockholm*, a service which offers the same information as the website but is available on dedicated public computers. These computers can be found at Central Station as well as in many of Stockholm's hotels.

Hotel staff are usually well informed and can answer most questions related to sightseeing in the city. A free monthly activity brochure, *What's On Stockholm*, gives information

Inside the Stockholm Visitors Board at Vasagatan 14

about events and can be found in most hotels, department stores and museums. Other good resources include the **Visit Stockholm** website and the **Museums in Stockholm** website, which provides an excellent overview of the city's museums and links to their respective websites.

The Stockholm Card, giving free admission to many museums

OPENING HOURS AND ADMISSION CHARGES

Most museums and other sights are open between 10 or 11am and 5 or 6pm all year, with extended opening hours during the summer. Some museums are closed on Mondays.

Entrance fees are generally between 50 and 100 kr, with discounts available for students, children and senior citizens. The Stockholm Card *(Stockholmskortet)* provides free admission to more than 80 museums and other attractions along with free travel on public transportation and a number of other discounts. The card can be purchased online at www.stockholmtown.com or at most major hotels in the city. Cards for adults cost 425 kr for 1 day, 550 kr for 2 days, 650 kr for 3 days and 895 kr for 5 days. There are significantly reduced rates for children.

Shops are generally open from 10am to 6pm during the week and from 10 or 11am to 4 or 5pm at weekends.

Tickets for theatres, concerts and sporting events can be bought at the venue box offices, at the SVB or through ticket agencies such as Boxoffice and Ticnet *(see p174)*.

◁ **The ice-covered waters of Riddarfjärden, transformed into walking grounds**

LANGUAGE AND ETIQUETTE

Visitors will find that English is widely spoken. This is especially true among hotel and restaurant staff, as well as most shop employees. The Swedes are usually friendly and glad to help foreign tourists. The use of first names is the norm and "Hej!" (pronounced "Hi!") is a familiar greeting.

Casual clothing is acceptable almost everywhere, including restaurants and most theatres. Tips are always included in restaurant prices, but it is usual to round up the bill by up to 10 per cent for good service.

The logo of *Systembolaget*, the State-owned liquor store

ALCOHOL AND SMOKING

Swedish policy towards alcohol is restrictive. Wines and spirits can be bought only in the shops run by the state monopoly *Systembolaget*. They are open Monday to Friday from 10am to 6pm, and on Saturdays from 10am to 1pm, although some shops have longer opening hours. The minimum age for buying liquor in these shops is 20 and you maybe required to show proof of age.

Most restaurants and pubs stop selling alcohol at 1am, but some city centre bars stay open until 5am. The minimum age for buying liquor in restaurants is 18, with some establishments setting higher age minimums.

The maximum permitted blood alcohol level is only 0.2 mg per mil, so drinking is effectively banned for drivers.

Bans on smoking are widespread in Sweden. Smoking is not permitted in public places, including all forms of public transport, bars and restaurants. Customers wishing to purchase tobacco must be over 18 and establishments will often ask for ID as proof of age.

TRAVELLERS WITH SPECIAL NEEDS

Under Swedish law, public areas have to be accessible to physically or visually disabled people and Stockholm is well ahead of many other cities in this respect. The Tunnelbana network is adapted for disabled passengers, and most buses "kneel" at bus stops to make it easier to board or disembark. Those travelling with pets on public transport even have allocated areas to separate them from allergy sufferers. Car drivers with a disability permit from their home country can park in designated areas.

Disabled visitors can obtain information in English before they travel from **De Handikappades Riksförbund**.

TRAVELLING WITH CHILDREN

Families with children will find it easy to travel around Stockholm. The under 20s travel at a reduced rate on all forms of public transport, while children under 7 do not need a ticket when travelling with a paying passenger. Children between the ages of 7–11 travel free with a paying passenger from Fridays at noon through to midnight on Sunday. In addition, at all times, one adult may accompany a baby or toddler in a pram on city buses free of charge.

Children are warmly welcome in Stockholm's many cafés and restaurants, and most museums and movie theatres offer reduced tickets for children *(see p175)*.

RESPONSIBLE TOURISM

Stockholm is known for its efforts to reduce pollution and improve the level of environmental awareness among its inhabitants. The city has established over 700 km (435 miles) of cycle lanes, while all inner city buses and trains run on renewable fuels. Greenhouse emissions have been lowered by 25 per cent since 1990 and Stockholm was presented with the

DIRECTORY

TOURIST INFORMATION

Arlanda Visitor Centre
Arrival Hall Terminal 5, Arlanda Airport, 190 45 Stockholm-Arlanda.
Tel 08-797 60 00.

Museums in Stockholm
www.stockholmmuseum.com

Stockholm Visitors Board
Vasagatan 14, 111 20 Stockholm.
Map 2 C5.
Tel 08-508 285 08.
www.stockholmtown.com

Visit Stockholm
www.visit-stockholm.com

TRAVELLERS WITH SPECIAL NEEDS

De Handikappades Riksförbund
Tel 08-685 80 00.
www.dhr.se

EMBASSIES AND CONSULATES

United Kingdom
Skarpögatan 6–8.
Map 6 B2.
Tel 08-671 30 00.
www.ukinsweden.fco.gov.uk

United States
Dag Hammarskjölds väg 31.
Map 6 B2.
Tel 08-783 53 00.
www.stockholm.usembassy.gov

European Commission's first European Green Capital Award in 2009.

Recycling containers for cans and plastics are found in public areas throughout the city and travel by public transport is highly encouraged. Over 30 Stockholm hotels are deemed eco-friendly and several restaurants offer purely organic menus. The Stockholm Visitors Board lists many such establishments. For those wishing to sample local produce, a farmers' market can be found at Hötorget 7 days a week, while others are open at Katarina Bangata on Södermalm and at Tessinparken in Gärdet from 10am to 3pm on Saturdays during the summer, as well as during the Christmas holidays.

Personal Security and Health

Police symbol

Stockholm is outstandingly safe compared with virtually any other major city. To a great extent the city has been spared violence and terrorism, and natural disasters like earthquakes and severe storms do not occur. However, as with any major city, caution is recommended in the centre of town, particularly at night.

Sweden has a well-developed network of emergency services as well as highly efficient hospital emergency clinics and rescue services.

Policeman   **Security guard**

POLICE

Police in Stockholm are usually extremely helpful and competent in English and visitors can feel free to address them with any questions or concerns.

Police patrolling on foot or in cars are a routine sight in the city centre, and mounted police are common at special events. There are police stations in every part of the city, and police are also available at the Central Station/T-Centralen. To report an incident that does not require immediate police assistance call the **non-emergency** telephone number.

In addition to the police, security guards are a familiar feature in many public places, such as shopping centres.

WHAT TO BE AWARE OF

Although Stockholm is basically safe, as with any major city, tourists can still run into trouble. The many popular events attract bag-snatchers and pickpockets, especially during the summer months. Always keep an eye on your bag and camera in crowded public areas.

When going out, it is a good idea to lock passports and travel documents in your room safe or in the hotel strongbox. It is equally important not to leave any valuables in your car; ideally, choose a hotel with its own parking facilities. There is no need to carry large amounts of cash when exploring the city. ATM machines are widely available and all of the main credit and debit cards are accepted in virtually all shops and restaurants. Note that many places now require you to enter your PIN number when using a debit or credit card.

Stockholm is easy to explore on foot or by Tunnelbana (underground railway). The Tunnelbana is safe at most times, but avoid empty carriages.

Care should also be taken when walking around the city at night. In addition, visitors should avoid using unauthorized taxis, particularly when arriving at Arlanda Airport.

It is illegal to buy sexual services in Sweden so it is the buyer, not the prostitute, who is prosecuted. As a result of this law, street prostitutes are a rare sight in the inner city.

IN AN EMERGENCY

The emergency telephone number for police, fire or ambulance is **112**. It can be dialed free of charge from all public and mobile telephones, but should be used only in emergencies. For minor illnesses or concerns, ring the **Healthcare Information Service** (*Sjukvårdsupplysningen*).

LOST AND STOLEN PROPERTY

Lost or stolen property should be reported to the nearest police station. The **Police Lost Property Office** (*Polisens Hittegodsexpedition*) is open Monday to Friday from 10am to 3pm (until 7pm on Thursdays). Telephone enquiries are accepted Monday and Tuesday from 1pm to 3pm and Friday from 10am to noon. The **Swedish State Railways** (*Statens Järnvägar*) has its own lost property office for items lost on SJ trains. For property lost on *Storstockholms Lokaltrafik* (SL) buses, Tunnelbana trains or local trains, check with the **SL Lost Property Office** (*Hittegodsavdelning*), which is open from 8am to 7pm Monday, 8am to 5pm Tuesday to Friday and 8am to 2pm Saturday.

Ambulance

Police car

Fire engine

Entrance to Karolinska Sjukhus, a hospital in Stockholm

HOSPITALS AND PHARMACIES

Several city hospitals have accident and emergency clinics, including **Karolinska Sjukhus**, **Astrid Lindgrens Barnsjukhus** (children), **Danderyds Sjukhus**, **S:t Görans Sjukhus** (privately owned) and **Södersjukhus**.

Patients should not report to individual emergency clinics without contacting the **Healthcare Information Service** beforehand. This service can provide advice in English and its staff are responsible for assigning patients to a suitable hospital or duty doctor. It is always advisable to make use of this service; those who do not and go directly to a hospital emergency clinic with minor ailments are likely to experience long waiting times.

For severe toothache or eye emergencies, patients can report to **S:t Eriks Sjukhus** between 7:45am and 8:30pm.

Pharmacies can dispense medicines for most minor ailments without a prescription, and staff can usually give good advice on suitable medication.

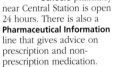

Pharmacy sign

Pharmacies across the city are normally open Monday to Friday from 8:30am to 4 or 6pm. Some are also open on Saturday. The **C W Scheele** pharmacy near Central Station is open 24 hours. There is also a **Pharmaceutical Information** line that gives advice on prescription and non-prescription medication.

Visitors to Sweden do not need special vaccinations.

MINOR HAZARDS

Mosquitoes can be a nuisance between June and late September, especially at dusk. This is particularly the case in parks, along waterways and, above all, in the archipelago. Pharmacies can supply mosquito repellent.

In the wooded areas around Stockholm and in the archipelago, ticks are a serious problem. As ticks in this region often carry borrelia or TBE, they should be removed from the skin with tweezers as quickly as possible. If redness develops around the bite, a doctor should be consulted.

The cobbled streets of Gamla Stan, the city's old quarter, can prove treacherous for tourists. Sturdy shoes are recommended when visiting this area, particularly in the winter.

TRAVEL AND HEALTH INSURANCE

Foreign visitors are advised to take out medical insurance before departure to cover medical care or hospital in-patient treatment. EU citizens are entitled to free medical care in Sweden on production of a European Health Insurance Card and a valid passport or other form of identification. As not all treatment is covered by the card, separate medical insurance is advisable.

DIRECTORY

POLICE

Non-emergency
Tel *114 14.*

IN AN EMERGENCY

Ambulance, Police, Fire Brigade
Tel *112.*

LOST AND STOLEN PROPERTY

Police Lost Property Office
Bergsgatan 54. **Map** 1 C3.
Tel *08-401 07 88.*

SL Lost Property Office
Klara Östra Kyrkogata 6.
Map 2 C5.
Tel *08-600 10 00.*

Swedish State Railways Lost Property Office
Central Station, Vasagatan.
Map 2 C4.
Tel *08-501 255 90.*

MEDICAL INFORMATION SERVICES

Healthcare Information Service
Tel *08-32 01 00 (24-hr).*

Pharmaceutical Information
Tel *0771 450 450*
(7am–9pm Mon–Fri,
8am–6pm Sat & Sun).

HOSPITALS AND PHARMACIES

Astrid Lindgrens Barnsjukhus
Karolinska Hospital. **Map** 2 A1. **Tel** *08-517 771 02.*

C W Scheele
Klarabergsgatan 64.
Map 2 C4.
Tel *07-714 504 50 (24-hr).*

Danderyds Sjukhus
Mörbygårdsvägen.
Tel *08-655 50 00 (24-hr).*

Karolinska Sjukhus
Karolinska Vägen.
Map 2 A1.
Tel *08-517 700 00 (24-hr).*

S:t Eriks Sjukhus
Polhemsgatan 50. **Map** 1 C2. **Tel** *08-672 31 00.*

S:t Görans Sjukhus
S:t Görans Plan 1. **Map** 1 A2. **Tel** *08-587 010 00.*

Södersjukhus
Sjukhusbacken 10. **Map** 8 B4. **Tel** *08-616 10 00.*

Banking and Local Currency

As Sweden remains outside the European Monetary Union (EMU), goods are priced only in Swedish kronor and not in euros. Visitors can change currency in banks, which provide an efficient service, but better rates can often be obtained at bureaux de change, which have longer opening hours and are strategically located in the city centre. Automatic cash machines can be found outside most banks and in shopping centres. Credit and debit cards are accepted nearly everywhere, and some of the larger stores accept the major foreign currencies. Traveller's cheques are no longer accepted in shops and can only be exchanged in banks and bureaux de change.

Bankomat ATM

BANKS AND BUREAUX DE CHANGE

There are plenty of banks in the city centre, all of which offer currency exchange services, and can help visitors who need to report lost or stolen bank or credit cards. The major banks – **Handels-banken**, **Nordea** and **SEB** – have numerous branches throughout Stockholm. Their opening times vary, but the normal hours are from 9:30am to 3pm. Some banks stay open until 6pm at least once a week. All banks are closed on weekends and on public holidays, as well as the day before a public holiday.

Various bureaux de change chains are represented in Stockholm, including **Forex** and **X-Change**. They generally provide a better exchange rate than the banks and they are easily accessible. In the city centre, there is always an office close at hand.

Currency and traveller's cheques can be changed at one of Forex's or X-Change's Arlanda Airport locations from 5:30am, and from 7am at the Forex or X-change offices at Stockholm Central Station. All of these outlets are open for more than 12 hours daily. At Central Station, Forex and X-Change are both located in the main entrance hall and on the underground train level. Other exchange offices can be found in the Nordiska Kompaniet and PUB department stores, and in the Gallerian shopping centre on Hamngatan (*see p183*).

Changing money in your hotel can be an expensive option so remember to check the exchange rates and commission charges before going ahead.

ATMS

Automatic cash machines (ATMs) are widely available, operate efficiently and are generally safe to use. Foreign visitors can use all the city's cash machines to make withdrawals provided that

DIRECTORY

BANKS

Handelsbanken
Kungsträdgårdsgatan 2.
Map 4 C1. **Tel** *08-701 10 00.*

Nordea
Hamngatan 12. **Map** 3 D4.
Tel *077-122 44 88.*

SEB
Sergels Torg 2. **Map** 2 C4.
Tel *077-136 53 65.*

BUREAUX DE CHANGE

Forex
Central Station. **Map** 2 C5.
Tel *08-411 67 34.*
Arlanda Airport, Terminal 2.
Tel *08-593 622 71.*
Arlanda Airport, Terminal 5.
Tel *08-593 622 20.*
Vasagatan 14. **Map** 2 C5.
Tel *08-10 49 90.*
www.forex.se

X-Change
Arlanda Airport, Terminal 5.
Tel *08-797 85 57.*
Kungsgatan 30. **Map** 3 D4.
Tel *08-506 107 00.*
www.x-change.se

CREDIT AND DEBIT CARDS

American Express
Tel *077-129 56 00 or*
077-129 54 29.

Diners Club
Tel *08-14 68 78.*

MasterCard
Tel *020-791 324 (emergency assistance for international visitors).*

Visa
Tel *020-795675.*

The head office of Handelsbanken at Kungsträdgårdsgatan

they have an internationally accepted credit or debit card with a PIN code. The majority of ATMs accept **Visa** and **MasterCard**. Please note that credit card companies often charge a high fee for such cash advances.

Machines usually have instructions in several languages, including English. The charge for withdrawing cash varies according to the type of card and additional fees may be charged by the cardholder's bank. As criminals are known to watch ATMs to gather PIN code information, make sure you shield the keypad with your hand or body when entering your PIN.

CREDIT AND DEBIT CARDS

All the well-known credit and debit cards, including Visa, MasterCard, **American Express** and **Diners Club**, are accepted not just by the larger hotels and restaurants but by nearly all shops and services. Customers paying by credit or debit card may be asked to produce proof of identity, and many stores require use of the PIN code associated with the card.

If your credit or debit card is lost or stolen, contact your card company immediately.

In order to ensure your card works overseas, it is worth contacting your bank or credit card provider in advance of travelling.

CURRENCY

Sweden's currency is the Swedish krona (plural kronor). The krona (abbreviated as SEK or kr) is divided into 100 öre. The smallest coin is 1 kr and the largest note is 1,000 kronor, which is not commonly used. If possible, it is advisable not to carry notes of more than 500 kr.

Many of Stockholm's larger shops and department stores will accept euros as payment for goods but to avoid disappointment, it is best to check with a shop employee that this is indeed the case before trying to purchase your goods.

20 kronor

50 kronor

100 kronor

500 kronor

1,000 kronor

Notes
Swedish currency notes are issued in denominations of 20, 50, 100, 500 and 1,000 kronor. They depict historic Swedish artists, authors, scientists and monarchs.

Coins
Coins are issued in values of 1, 5 and 10 kronor. The 1 kr coin depicts Sweden's monarch on the obverse side, while the 5 kr has his monogram on the reverse side.

1 krona

5 kronor

10 kronor

Communications and Media

Sweden has a top-ranking telecommunications industry, one of the most successful and innovative in the world, and high living standards have placed the Swedes among the world's biggest users of mobile telephones, and there is a very high level of Internet usage. Telephone cards – and usually credit or debit cards – can be used to make a call from a public telephone, while a mobile phone can be purchased at a relatively low price. With Internet access readily available, there is no risk of being cut off from the world here.

Logo of Telenor network provider

The major network providers in Sweden include **Telia**, **Telenor**, Tele2/Comviq and 3 Sweden. Inexpensive GSM mobile phones can be purchased at a number of stores, including **The Phone House**, Telia or Telenor, together with a pre-paid SIM card for local phone calls.

Within the Stockholm area, mobile users need to dial the area code 08 before a local number – the country code is not needed.

Computer terminals at Sidewalk Express in City Terminal, Central Station

INTERNATIONAL AND LOCAL TELEPHONE CALLS

The prefix for international calls from Sweden is 00 followed by the country code, the area code (omitting any initial 0) and the local number.

Public telephones are usually operated by phone card, which are sold at newspaper kiosks and shops. Normal credit cards and most international telephone cards can also be used, although the charge per minute is generally higher. It is possible to make reverse-charge (collect) calls and calls to the emergency number 112 (free of charge) from all phones. Coin-operated phones are becoming increasingly rare.

Local numbers can be obtained by ringing directory enquiries on 118 118, or on the Internet at Eniro (www.eniro.se) or at Hitta (www.hitta.se). Computer-to-computer phone calls allow visitors to call free of charge using the Internet. Popular service providers include Skype and Google Talk.

MOBILE PHONES

The number of telephone kiosks in Sweden has shown a marked decline in recent years because virtually every Swede has a mobile phone. Sweden's mobile network is based on GSM and most foreign visitors can use their GSM phones. However, visitors from North America should check with their service providers to ensure their phones are GSM-compatible.

A typical Swedish telephone kiosk

INTERNET FACILITIES

Most hotels offer guests fax, and email services. Furthermore, nearly all hotels and hostels in the Stockholm area offer Internet access, although they may charge a daily fee. Public computers are generally available at local libraries, such as the Stockholm City Library at Odengatan 63. Users may be asked to present some form of identification.

Sidewalk Express offers pay-per-minute Internet access from computer terminals at Arlanda Airport, Central Station, and a number of Pressbyrån and 7-Eleven stores throughout the city. The cost varies by location but usually ranges from 25–35 kr per hour.

Wireless Internet (Wi-Fi) access is widely available for visitors with their own computers. Most hotels, many cafés and all **Max Hamngatan** restaurants offer free Wi-Fi.

POSTAL SERVICES

The Swedish postal system – easily recognized by its blue and gold symbol – is based on a series of small postal kiosks located in local grocery stores, such as **Hemköp** which is one of the most central. These kiosks offer the most common

Pressbyrån kiosks, newsagent selling stamps

services and are open during normal shop hours. Some official post offices remain to handle more specialized services; one is located on Klarabergsvia-dukten 84 near Central Station and is open on weekdays from 8am to 6pm.

Stamps can be bought at post offices and postal kiosks, as well as at Pressbyrån kiosks and tourist information offices. It costs 6 kr to send a postcard or letter under 20g (0.04 lb) within Sweden and 12 kr to the rest of the world. Post boxes are painted in different colours: the yellow boxes are for national and inter-national mail and the blue boxes for letters destined for the Stockholm area (post codes starting with "1"). In some areas, there are only yellow boxes, which can then be used for local mail as well. Collection times vary and are always shown on the post box.

Most international courier services, including **DHL**, **UPS** and **FedEx**, are represented

Post Office logo

Yellow postbox for national and international, blue for local mail

in Stockholm. DHL and UPS services are available at **Mailboxes Etc.**, which is located in the city centre and open on week days from 8am to 7pm. In addition, special courier services are also offered through the Swedish post office.

TELEVISION AND RADIO

Virtually all hotel rooms have a TV with a range of national and foreign channels. The most common channels are the Swedish SVT1, SVT2, TV3, TV4 and Channel 5, as well as the international CNN, Sky News, MTV and Eurosport. SVT1 and 2 are State-run public-service channels. SVT2 and TV4 broadcast local programmes in the morning and evening, which include weather forecasts.

There are a number of local radio stations that broadcast a selection of international and Swedish music. P6, Stockholm International, broadcasts English- and German-language programmes on 89.6 MHz.

NEWSPAPERS AND MAGAZINES

Many foreign newspapers and magazines can be bought in Stockholm. For the broadest range, visit Press Stop, Press Center or Press Specialisten. Alternatively, the Pressbyrån kiosks and tourist information offices around the city stock a limited number of foreign publications. A wide variety

of foreign titles can be found at the Plattan Library at Kulturhuset, which is open Monday to Friday from 8am to 7pm, and Saturday to Sunday from 11am to 5pm.

DIRECTORY

MOBILE PHONES

Telenor Store
Drottninggatan 70.
Map 2 C4.
Tel 020-015 90 80.

Telia Store
Kungsgatan 36.
Map 2 C4.
Tel 08-696 96 80.

The Phone House
Gallerian, Hamngatan 37.
Map 2 D4.
Tel 077-199 10 00.

INTERNET FACILITIES

Café String
Nytorgsgatan 38.
Map 9 E3.
Tel 08-714 85 14.

Max Hamngatan
Kungsträdgårdsgatan 20.
Map 3 D4.
Tel 08-611 38 10.

Sidewalk Express
Located in Stockholm Central Station, Arlanda Airport, and 7-Eleven and Pressbyrån stores.

POSTAL SERVICES

DHL
Tel 077-134 53 45.

Federal Express (FedEx)
Arlanda Airport.
Tel 0200 252 252.

Hemköp
Mäster Samuelsgatan 57.
Map 2 C4.
Tel 020-23 22 21.

Mailboxes Etc.
Mäster Samuelsgatan 20.
Map 3 D4.
Tel 08-411 70 10.

Swedish Post
Klarabergsviadukten 84.
Map 2 B5.
Tel 08-781 20 42.

UPS
Tel 020-788 799.

GETTING TO STOCKHOLM

Stockholm's location at the centre of the Baltic region has made it an important transport hub. Direct, daily flights link the capital to most major European and North American cities. Arlanda Airport, served by about 60 international and domestic airlines, is one of the most efficient in the world. In addition, Sweden's infrastructure is constantly being improved, with new motorways under construction and the railway system being upgraded for high-speed trains. Car ferries operate between Stockholm and Finland and other points in the Baltic, and from Sweden's west and south coasts, the capital can be reached by high-speed trains and motorways in 6 hours. Sweden also has a direct link to the Continent via the Öresund bridge to Denmark in the south.

Aircraft of Scandinavian Airlines (SAS)

Duty free at Stockholm's Arlanda Airport

ARRIVING BY AIR

Most major European cities have direct flights to Stockholm. Many of the world's leading airlines, such as **British Airways**, serve Arlanda Airport, located about 40 km (25 miles) north of the city centre. Some Swedish domestic airlines also use Arlanda Airport, including **SAS** (Scandinavian Airlines).

Stockholm is also served by two other airports. Bromma, close to the city centre, is used by several of the smaller domestic airlines as well as Finnair and Brussels Airlines. Skavsta, about 100 km (62 miles) south of Stockholm, is used by **Ryanair** for flights to and from London Stansted Airport. A bus takes travellers into Stockholm.

Direct flights between Stockholm and North America are run by SAS, Delta and United.

AIR FARES AND TICKETS

Fare options are varied, particularly if you can be flexible about departure and arrival dates, or can book well in advance. SAS, for example, has low-cost fares, which must be booked at least seven days before departure and require a Saturday night stay at the destination. Bookings on this type of ticket cannot usually be changed.

Scheduled airlines generally maintain their basic fare structure throughout the year. However, special offers and last-minute online deals are frequently available.

CUSTOMS

Travellers arriving from within the EU are able to bring an unlimited amount of alcohol into the country for their own consumption, provided they are at least 20 years old, and an unlimited amount of tobacco for their own consumption, as long as they are at least 18 years of age. Travellers from outside the EU may only bring 1 litre of spirits or 2 litres of fortified wine, 4 litres of wine and 16 litres of beer, and 200 cigarettes or 50 cigars, all of which must be for personal use only.

Visitors from within the EU can bring any amount of food into Sweden, with the exception of fish, which is subject to an import restriction of 15 kg (33 lb). Those wishing to import fresh food from other areas must be in possession of a health certificate and understand that such food will be inspected at the border. Visitors from non-EU countries travelling by commercial airlines or ferries can take in goods, including beer and food, with a value of up to 4,300 kr.

Tax-free sales in Sweden are permitted only for travellers with a final destination outside the EU.

SAS logo

GETTING TO THE CITY FROM ARLANDA AIRPORT

There are several ways of getting to the city from Arlanda Airport. The "Flygbussarna" bus service, which operates every 10 minutes at peak times, takes 45 minutes to the City Terminal at Central Station and costs about 110 kr one way or 220 kr for a return ticket. Tickets can be cheaper if you bought online in advance. An onward journey by taxi can be booked on the bus. A taxi from the airport is quicker but more expensive.

Ferry from Finland on the way to its terminal at Stadsgården

Most taxi firms have a fixed charge of about 500 kr to the city centre. Use only authorized taxis waiting in the official taxi queues at Arlanda and agree on the fare with the driver before departure. The Arlanda Express train takes 20 minutes to Central Station and costs about 240 kr each way.

The Arlanda Express, linking Arlanda Airport with the city

ARRIVING BY TRAIN OR COACH

Rail and coach travel from the Continent to Stockholm is quick, inexpensive and comfortable. The opening of the Öresund bridge in 2000, which carries both rail and road traffic between Denmark and southern Sweden, significantly shortened travel times.

Within Sweden, the state-owned railway company **Statens Järnvägar (SJ)** operates most of the long-distance trains. Some routes are run by private companies, notably **Tågkompaniet** (Stockholm–northern Sweden). Air travel between Stockholm and Malmö or Gothenburg faces strong competition from SJ's X 2000 high-speed train. The lowest fares can usually be purchased 90 days in advance. The journey by train from Malmö to Stockholm is about 5 hours; from Gothenburg it is 3 hours.

The same routes are served by express coaches, most of which are run by **Swebus**. Journey times are longer (about 9 hours from Malmö and about 7 hours from Gothenburg), but fares are generally much lower and advance booking is not required.

ARRIVING BY FERRY

Large passenger/car ferries sail to Stockholm from Finland. Both **Viking Line** and **Tallink Silja Line** operate daily services and have their own terminals at Stadsgården near the city centre and Värtahamnen respectively. The journey from Helsinki takes about 15 hours, while it takes 11 hours from Turku. Both shipping lines offer excellent passenger facilities, including good food, entertainment and shopping. Tallink Silja Line operates daily from Tallinn in Estonia to the Värtahamnen terminal.

ARRIVING BY CAR

Visitors driving from Denmark can use the Öresund toll bridge between Copenhagen and Malmö. The toll costs around 375 kr for a normal passenger vehicle. On the Swedish side, the bridge connects with the E4, a 550-km (340-mile) motorway to Stockholm. Another option is the 20-minute car ferry from Helsingør in Denmark to Helsingborg in Sweden.

Car ferries to Gothenburg operate from Denmark (Frederikshavn) and Germany (Kiel), with an onward journey on

DIRECTORY

ARRIVING BY AIR

British Airways
Tel 0770 110 020.
Tel 0844 493 07 87 (UK).
www.britishairways.com

Ryanair
Tel 0900 100 0500.
Tel 0871 246 000 (UK).
www.ryanair.com

SAS
Tel 0770 727 727.
Tel 0871 521 60 00 (UK).
www.scandinavian.net

ARRIVING BY TRAIN OR COACH

Statens Järnvägar (SJ)
Tel 0771 757 575.
www.sj.se

Swebus
Tel 0200 218 218.
www.swebusexpress.se

Tågkompaniet
Tel 0771 444 111.
www.tagkompaniet.se

ARRIVING BY FERRY

Tallink Silja Line
Tel 08-666 33 30.
www.tallinksilja.com

Viking Line
Tel 08-452 40 00.
www.vikingline.se

the E3 of about 450 km (280 miles) to Stockholm. The fastest route from Germany to Sweden is the catamaran ferry from Rostock to Trelleborg in southern Sweden, then the E6 to Malmö and the E4 to Stockholm.

Speed limits are usually clearly signed. On Swedish motorways, the limit is typically 110 km/h (68 mph) or 120 km/h (75 mph). On other main roads, the limit is 90 km/h (56 mph), while it is 50 km/h (31 mph) in built-up areas. Take care when driving in the countryside, as elk and deer can suddenly appear on

Warning, elk on the road

the road. Accidents involving these animals must be reported to the police.

GETTING AROUND STOCKHOLM

Stockholm is a perfect city for pedestrians. Distances between sights are usually short and around every corner there is something interesting to explore. The capital extends across a large number of islands, offering eye-catching vistas and waterfront scenes. Public transport on buses, underground trains, trams and local trains is efficient and covers the entire city and surrounding region. Apart from the area of Gamla Stan, and during rush hours, driving in Stockholm is relatively easy and indoor parking facilities are adequate. However, the best way of exploring the city centre is on foot.

Pedestrian and cycle route

GREEN TRAVEL

In recent years, Stockholm has focused on encouraging travellers and inhabitants alike to move about the city in the most environmentally-friendly way possible. For tourists, day tickets on public transport are significantly cheaper than paid parking, and visitors arriving or travelling across the city by bus, Tunnelbana or train are not subject to the city's congestion tolls. Every major site in the city is easily accessible by public transport, and switching from one form of transport to another is easy.

A good alternative to public transport during the summer months is the Stockholm City Bikes system (see p205), through which visitors can borrow a bike and tour the city on their own. The cheapest method of getting around, however, is walking and doing so is easy because of Stockholm's compact city centre. Many roads are pedestrian friendly and, in most cases, it is easy to walk from one attraction to the next.

STOCKHOLM ON FOOT

While walking is the best way to see the sights in central Stockholm, there are regulations to be aware of. Pedestrians are not allowed to cross a road against a red light, and motorists must stop and give way to pedestrians at zebra crossings without traffic lights (always look carefully). Don't forget to press the pedestrian crossing button at intersections – otherwise you

Pedestrianised square in Gamla Stan, the city's Old Town

may wait a long time before the light changes to green.

The city's clear street signs make it easy to find your way around. There are sidewalks everywhere, as well as plenty of pedestrian streets and park areas.

Pedestrian crossing sign

Gamla Stan is a popular area for exploring on foot, and there is always something to see around Kungsträdgården. A stroll along the quayside opposite the Grand Hôtel and the Nationalmuseum can be followed by a walk around Skeppsholmen. Another delightful area is Djurgården, with a host of attractions set in a park environment a short distance from the city centre.

Those who like to walk along the waterfront can follow the quaysides from Stadshuset along Norr Mälarstrand or the Riddarfjärden bay. Fjällgatan (see p129) is also recommended, not least for its magnificent views of the city.

Guided walks are organized regularly, often with a special theme, such as architecture, history or parks. Sometimes they are available in different languages, especially during the summer months. Most walks take place in Gamla Stan, but there are a number of other routes. Ask at the **Stockholm Visitors Board** for details.

DRIVING IN STOCKHOLM

Driving around Stockholm is straightforward, except during rush hours (7:30–9:30am, noon–1pm and 3:30–6pm). It is also best to avoid driving in Gamla Stan, due to narrow one-way streets. However, cars are not necessary in the city centre given the short distances between sights and the excellent public transport system.

Fines for speeding are high, and you can lose your driving licence even if the limit is only slightly exceeded. Vehicle headlights must always be on, and drivers and passengers are required to wear seatbelts. Sweden's drink-drive laws are zero-tolerance: the maximum permitted blood alcohol level is 0.2 mg per mil. Motorists must give way to pedestrians at crossings without traffic lights. Visitors bringing their own car to Stockholm should have an international Green Card for insurance.

READING STREET SIGNS

Street name

Roslagsgatan

kv. Ingemar   **46-34**

Block

Street number range in block

Stockholm has introduced a congestion charge system. Road tolls must be paid by all private vehicles entering or leaving the city between 6:30am and 6:30pm Monday to Friday. The toll varies from 10 kr to 20 kr depending on the time of day, with the higher charges in effect during the morning and evening rush hours. Cars with foreign licence plates are not charged, but cars rented in Sweden are subject to the fee. Car rental agencies generally charge congestion fees back to the renter.

CAR RENTAL

A number of car-rental firms, including **Avis**, **Europcar** and **Hertz**, have offices in Stockholm or at Arlanda Airport. The larger hotels and the main tourist office at Vasagatan 14 *(see p191)* can arrange a car, which can be delivered at your convenience. A driving licence and a major credit card must be shown before signing a rental agreement. Some agencies have age restrictions for renters.

PARKING

There are plenty of parking spaces on the streets and in multistory car parks, but it can sometimes be difficult to find a vacant spot, particularly in the summer. If you plan to park on the street you need to familiarize yourself with the various road signs. In the city centre, it often costs 14 kr or more per hour for on-street parking and fees must be paid in advance at the blue and white parking meters marked with a "P". If paying with coins, place your coins in the slot and wait for the screen to display the time at which your paid parking will end. To pay with a credit card, swipe the card and

Parking zone

Parking charge 9am–5pm; free at other times

No parking on weekday night indicated, midnight–6am

use the 1 kr, 5 kr or 10 kr buttons to select the amount of money you wish to spend. Wait for the screen to display the time at which your paid parking will end. If you wish to add additional time, continue to use the currency buttons. Regardless of your payment method, you must press the green button when the desired end-time for your parking shows on the screen. Place the ticket on your dashboard so that it is clearly visible from the outside.

Parking on many streets is free on weekends, or between 5pm and 9am except on street-cleaning nights as indicated on road signs. Major attractions like museums often have their own car parks, which are subject to a charge.

The city's parking wardens are diligent. Any breach of regulations can involve a fine of 500 kr or more, and it costs at least 700 kr if a vehicle is parked within 10 m (33 ft) of a crossing. Valuables should not be left in the car.

GETTING AROUND BY TAXI

Given the short distances between places in the city centre, the demand for taxis is not as high as in other major cities. However, they are

DIRECTORY

STOCKHOLM ON FOOT

Stockholm Visitors Board
Vasagatan 14, 111 20 Stockholm.
Map 2 C5.
Tel 08-508 285 08.
www.stockholmtown.com
@ guides@stockholm.se

CAR RENTAL

Avis
Tel 0770 820 082.
www.avis.se

Europcar
Tel 0770 770 050.
www.europcar.se

Hertz
Tel 0771 211 212.
www.hertz.se

TAXIS

Taxi 020
Tel 020 20 20 20.
www.taxi020.se

Taxi Kurir
Tel 0771 860 000.
www.taxikurir.e

Taxi Stockholm
Tel 08-15 00 00.
www.taxistockholm.se

convenient and relatively cheap for brief journeys.

Taxi 020, **Taxi Kurir** and **Taxi Stockholm** are the three main companies that operate in the city. Tourists should be cautious when using other taxi firms as many are known to be very expensive.

There are usually plenty of taxis available, particularly at stations and sights, except during rush hours. Empty taxis, indicated by an illuminated sign on the roof, can also be hailed down. However, the best method is to order a taxi by telephone or book one in advance on the Internet. The initial charge is usually 40 kr, with an additional 85–185 kr for a journey within the central area but it is always worth enquiring what the fare is likely to be. Avoid using the unauthorized "black taxis", especially at night.

A Stockholm taxi

Getting Around by Public Transport

Stockholm Tunnelbana logo

Virtually all of Stockholm's sights and attractions can be reached easily by Tunnelbana (underground train) or by bus. The map below shows the Tunnelbana network, and a map of inner-city bus routes is on the inside back cover, as well as the pull-out map. SL is responsible for public transport by Tunnelbana, bus and local train. The various types of transport complement each other and cover Greater Stockholm.

A modern SL Tunnelbana train

TUNNELBANA

Work started on Stockholm's first underground railway, the Tunnelbana, in the late 1940s. Since then, the network has been extended and now has 100 stations on three routes – the green, red and blue lines – all run by **Storstockholms Lokaltrafik (SL)**. All three routes link up at T-Centralen, which adjoins Central Station, and 19 of the network's stations are located in the inner city.

The Tunnelbana provides a quick and efficient way to move around the city. Travellers can transfer from one Tunnelbana train to the next with relative ease, and Tunnelbana employees are usually happy to help anyone needing assistance.

The Tunnelbana operates from 5am until 3:30am from Sunday to Thursday, while on Friday and Saturday it runs until 4am. At other times, night bus services are available. Schedules may differ on national holidays.

The Tunnelbana stations display various works of art, making the network an attraction in itself. A guide to the art is available at tourist offices.

TUNNELBANA

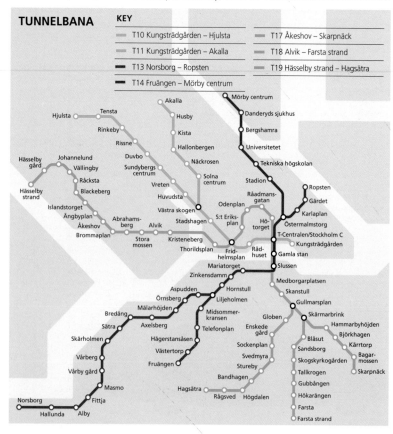

Restored vintage tram, a popular way of getting to Djurgården

BUSES

Stockholm's network of red city buses run on the main inner-city routs, and the blue "feeder" bus operate on the routes out to the suburbs. Many streets have special bus lanes, which make travel quick and easy. The buses are all modern and comfortable, with easy access for prams and wheelchairs, and they use environmentally friendly fuels like ethanol and natural gas.

The best routes for sight-seeing are 2, 3, 44, 47, 65 and 69, which cover most of the central area and stop near many sights. Routes 47 and 69, which can be boarded at Norrmalmstorg, are particularly useful for reaching sights not served by the Tunnelbana. Route 47 takes visitors to Djurgården, where they can visit Skansen, Gröna Lund, Vasamuseet and Nordiska museet. Route 69 goes to southern Gärdet with its four important museums and Kaknästornet before continuing to Blockhusudden at the easternmost tip of Djurgården.

Buses run every few minutes throughout the day and about 20 to 30 minutes in the late evening. There are also three night buses that operate hourly.

TRAMS

In 2010, Stockholm opened the first stage of the new tramline, Spårväg City. This line takes travellers from Sergels Torg to Waldemarsudde on a regular SL ticket. The trams run every 15 minutes from 5am to 1:30am Monday to Friday, from 6am to 1:30am on Saturday, and from 6:30am to 1:30am on Sunday. The tram system is scheduled for completion in 2014 when trams will run from Kungsholmen to Ropsten.

A charming way of travelling to Djurgården, particularly in the summer, is to take one of the lovingly restored vintage trams. **Djurgårdslinjen**, a voluntary organization of tram enthusiasts, run services on the former line 7 (now Line 7N) between Norrmalmstorg and Djurgården, where 14 trams are stabled. The vintage trams run approximately every 15 min-utes between 10am and 7pm daily from early July until late August. The rest of the year, they run on weekends and holidays only. Refreshments are served on some services.

Every year more than 300,000 passengers enjoy a trip using this popular method of travel. SL tickets cannot be used on the vintage trams but holders of a Stock-holm Card or SL Access card may ride for free.

LOCAL TRAINS

Stockholm's inner-city public transportation system is complemented by an extensive network of local trains *(pendel-tåg)*, many of which accept the same SL tickets used on the Tunnelbana system. Travellers can therefore easily visit a number of towns and villages around Stockholm, including Täby, Södertälje, Åkersberga, Nynäshamn and Kungsängen. While most regional trains leave from Central Station, the regional trains on the Roslagsbanen line leave from Östra Station, which is adjacent to the Tekniska Högskolan stop on the red Tunnelbana line.

TICKETS

A single ticket for travel on public transportation costs 30 kr and is generally valid for 60 minutes. Travel cards valid for 1 day (100 kr), 3 days (200 kr) or 7 days (260 kr) are also available. They are issued through the SL Access system and are valid for all zones. To use an SL Access card, hold it against the blue entry pad when entering a bus or a Tunnelbana station. Reduced-price tickets are available for children *(see p191)*, students and pensioners with a valid ID. Tickets and Access cards can be bought at Pressbyrån kiosks, the SL Central Ticket Office or at most stations. The Stockholm Card can also be used *(see p190)*.

DIRECTORY

PUBLIC TRANSPORT

Storstockholms Lokaltrafik (SL)
Central Ticket Office,
Central Station Lower Hall.
Map 2 C5. *Tel* 08-600 10 00.
www.sl.se

TRAMS

Djurgårdslinjen
www.sparvagssallskapet.se

Red city bus and blue "feeder" bus

Getting Around by Ferry and Boat

Waxholms-bolaget's logo

Stockholm's location between Lake Mälaren and the Baltic archipelago means that its waterways play an important role in city life. A large number of scheduled boat services, ferries and sightseeing tours offer visitors endless opportunities to enjoy Stockholm from the water. Note that from mid-August transport schedules are adjusted for winter, so always check the times.

Djurgården ferry in front of Nordiska museet

FERRIES

One of the best ways to visit Djurgården is to take a ferry from the city centre. Operated by **Waxholmsbolaget**, the ferry service links with bus and Tunnelbana routes, and is free for holders of SL's 1-3- or 7- day cards (the Stockholm Card is not valid). Single tickets cost 40 kr.

The ferry runs year-round from Slussen via Skeppsholmen to Allmänna Gränd near Gröna Lund, and operates from 7:30am until 7pm. From May to August there is a route from Nybroplan to Vasamuseet, Skeppsholmen and Gröna Lund from 10am to 6pm.

SIGHTSEEING BY BOAT

A pleasant way of enjoying Stockholm is to take one of the many sightseeing boat tours *(see maps below).*

Strömma offers several tours including a hop-on, hop-off tour that costs around 100 kr. Their "Historical Canal" tour departs hourly from the quayside near the City Hall and costs 150 kr. The "Under the Bridges of Stockholm" tour and "Royal Canal" tour depart from Strömkajen near the Grand Hôtel (passengers can also board at Nybroplan). The former tour operates from April to October between 10am and 8pm and costs about 200 kr. The latter operates from April to December between 10:30am and 6pm for about 145 kr. On all tours, guides speak English and Swedish.

Waxholmsbolaget operates a number of scheduled public transport boat services year-round. An excellent way of exploring the archipelago is to take one of the regular services from Strömkajen, which call at countless picturesque jetties along the way. The ferry company and tourist information offices can suggest suitable itineraries.

Organized excursions both in the archipelago and on Lake Mälaren are run by Strömma and other operators. You can, for instance, take a gastronomic evening cruise to Vaxholm. A number of sights that can be reached by fast passenger boats or traditional steamers are listed on pages 140–151.

HIRING BOATS AND CANOES

Enjoying the city from the water is an exciting experience. Rowboats, canoes, kayaks, pedalos and small boats with outboard motors can be hired near the Djurgården bridge at **Djurgårdsbrons Sjöcafé**. The gentle waters of the Djurgården Canal are ideal for rowing, paddle-boating or canoeing.

DIRECTORY

FERRIES

Waxholmsbolaget
Strömkajen. **Map** 3 D5.
Tel 08-679 58 30.
www.waxholmsbolaget.se

SIGHTSEEING BY BOAT

Strömma
Södra Blasieholmshamnen 11.
Map 3 D5.
Nybrokajen 9. **Map** 3 E4.
Tel 08-12 00 40 00.
www.stromma.se

HIRING BOATS

Djurgårdsbrons Sjöcafé
Galärvarvsvägen 2. **Map** 3 F5.
Tel 08-660 57 57.
www.sjocafet.se

KEY TO FERRY ROUTES

— Djurgårdsfärjan *(see inset map)*

— Under the Bridges of Stockholm Tour

— Historical Canal Tour (Jun–Aug)

— Royal Canal Tour (Apr–Dec)

— Drottningholm Tour (Jun–Aug)

KEY SÖDERMALM

····· Djurgården Ferry (May–Aug)

CITY
Nybroplan
Strömkajen
Stadshusbron
Vasa-varvet
SKEPPS-HOLMEN
GAMLA STAN
Allm. Gränd
Slussen

KUNGSHOLMEN
CITY
DJURGÅRDEN
Drottningholm
SÖDERMALM

0 kilometres 3
0 miles 2

Getting Around by Bicycle

Suggested bicycle tour

Stockholm and its surrounding area are tailor-made for cycling. The capital's network of bicycle tracks is increasing all the time and you do not need to be a very experienced city cyclist if you want to explore the central area from the saddle. Furthermore, anyone wanting to go out into the countryside and enjoy the fresh air and beautiful surroundings will not have to travel far from the city centre.

CYCLING IN STOCKHOLM

With over 700 km (435 miles) of bike lanes, and numerous bike paths in Djurgården and other parks, Stockholm is easily accessible to biking enthusiasts and casual bikers alike. In recent years, the city has significantly increased the number of bicycle lanes on major streets and run several campaigns to increase awareness of bicycles as an environmentally friendly alternative to automobiles.

Djurgården, with its gently graded cycle tracks and roads, that are mostly free of cars, is an excellent area for those wishing to explore by bike. Gärdet, Lilljanskogen and Hagaparken are other good areas for biking. It is also possible to cycle in parts of Ekoparken (see p121), which are virtually traffic-free.

Bicycle routes are clearly posted throughout much of Stockholm and there are marked routes that stretch further out from the city centre. Maps can be bought from **Kartbutiken** and in most bookstores and are also available from the tourist office.

A Stockholm City Bikes stand

Under Swedish law, all cyclists are required to wear helmets, and all bicycles must have electric lights after dusk. Cyclists generally do not have right of way at intersections and should watch for turning cars. Bike racks can be found almost everywhere and it is advisable to lock any bike left unattended to avoid the risk of theft.

There are numerous cycling tours available in the city. **Bikeguide Stockholm**, located outside Historiska museet, organize various tours that take in all the major sites as well as paths along the waterfront. Those who wish to find out more about cycling, or cycling tours in Stockholm and throughout Sweden, should contact **Cykelfrämjandet**.

DIRECTORY

CYCLING TOURS AND MAPS

Bikeguide Stockholm
Narvavägen 13. **Map** 3 F4.
Tel 07-330 956 26.
www.bikeguide-stockholm.se

Cykelfrämjandet
Tel 08-545 910 30.
www.cykelframjandet.se

Kartbutiken
Vasagatan 16. **Map** 2 C5.
Tel 08-20 23 03.
www.kartbutiken.se

BICYCLE RENTAL

Cykel & Mopeduthyrningen
Strandvägen, quay berth No. 24.
Map 3 F4. *Tel 08-660 79 59.*

Cykelstallet
Scheelegatan 15. **Map** 2 B5.
Tel 08-651 00 66.
www.cykelstallet.se

Djurgårdsbrons Sjöcafé
Galärvarvsvägen 2. **Map** 3 F5. *Tel 08-660 57 57.* www.sjocafet.se

Stockholm City Bikes
Tel 077-444 24 24.
www.citybikes.se/en

BICYCLE RENTAL

Stockholm City Bikes offers an excellent option for visitors wishing to explore the city by bike. Tourists can purchase a 3-day rental card for 125 kr at the Stockholm Visitors Board or at the main SL office at Central Station. After swiping the card at any one of the city's 80 bicycle stands, the renter can borrow a bike for up to 3 hours. Bikes can be returned to any stand, which creates a great deal of flexibility. Renters must have their own bicycle helmets to use this service.

Two rental firms, **Djurgårdsbrons Sjöcafé** and **Cykel & Mopeduthyrningen**, are located on Strandvägen near the Djurgården bridge. These companies offer bicycle rental by the day and also hire out rollerblades. **Cykelstallet** is the best place in town to go for mountain bike rental.

A bicycle rank on the waterfront

STOCKHOLM STREET FINDER

The map below shows the areas of Stockholm covered by the street map only. Gamla Stan (Old Town) is shown on a larger scale than the rest of the city. The map references listed in the guide for many sights, restaurants, hotels, shops and entertainment spots refer to the maps in this section. The first figure of the reference indicates the map page, while the letter and following figure shows its location on the map grid. All the more important sights are marked so that they are easier to find. The key below explains other symbols on the map, including post offices, tunnelbana stations and churches. An overview map of Stockholm is on pp12–13.

Japanese visitors

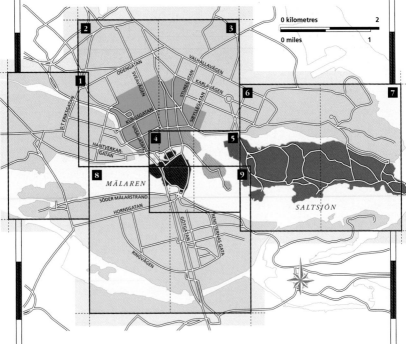

| 0 kilometres | | 2 |
| 0 miles | | 1 |

KEY TO STREET FINDER

	Major sight		Tourist information office
	Place of interest		Hospital with casualty unit
	Other building		Police station
	Train station		Church
	Tunnelbana station		Synagogue
	Main bus stop		Mosque
	Coach station		Post office
	Ferry boarding point		Viewpoint
	Tram stop		Railway line
	Car park		Pedestrian street

SCALE OF MAP PAGES
1–3 AND 6–9

| 0 metres | 200 |
| 0 yards | 200 |

SCALE OF MAP PAGES
4–5

| 0 metres | 200 |
| 0 yards | 200 |

Street name index on pp216–18

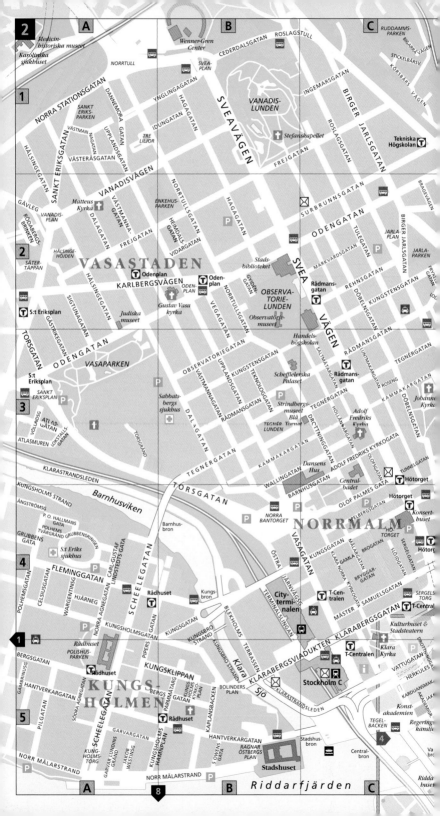

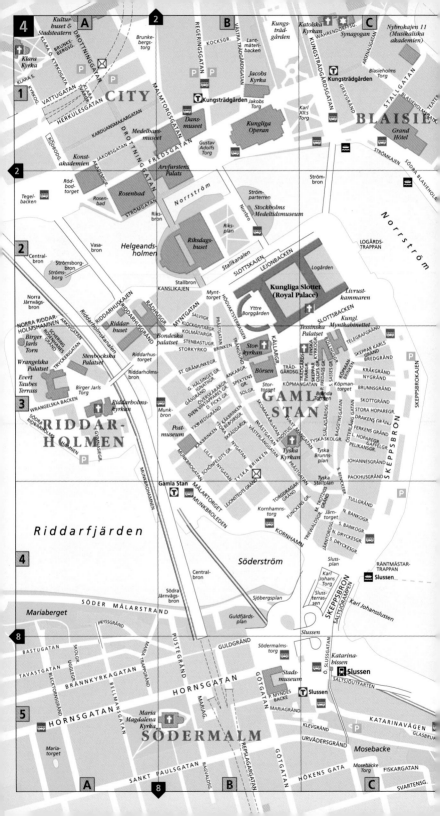

6

A   B   C

BRÄNTKÄRRS-GATAN
BANER-GATAN
WITTSTOCKS-GATAN
RIGAGATAN
BORG-VÄGEN
Filmhuset
LINDARÄNGSVÄGEN

1

GUSTAV ADOLFS-PARKEN
GYLLENSTIERNSGATAN
TAPTO-GATAN
OXENSTIERNSGATAN
VALHALLAVÄGEN
TV-huset

HAK-BERGET
GREVE VON ESSENS VÄG
Ladugårdsgärdet

LADUGÅRDSGÄRDET

3

LINNÉGATAN
Berwald-hallen
Sveriges Radio
GÄRDESGATAN
SKARPÖGATAN

ULRIKAGATAN
LÖVI SAG
STORG
STRANDVÄGEN
Engelska Kyrkan
LABORATORIE-GATAN
NOBELGATAN
DJURGÅRDSBRUNNSVÄGEN

2

NOBEL-PARKEN
Diplomatstaden
KRUTHUS-PLAN

Tekniska museet & Telemuseet
Sjö-historiska museet
FOLKE BERNADOTTES VÄG
MUSEIVÄGEN
Etnografiska museet

Djurgårdsbrunnsviken

KÄRLEKS-UDDEN
DE BESCHES VÄG

KLUSTHUS PORTEN
Nordiska Museet
SÖDRA VARVSPORTEN
ROSENDALSVÄGEN
SIRISHOVSVÄGEN
ROSENDALSTERRASSEN
Rosendals Slott & Trädgårdar

3

HAZELIUSPORTEN
Biologiska Museet
Vin- & Sp_rithistoriska museet
Liljevalchs Konsthall
HAZELIUSBACKEN
BOLLNÄS-TORGET
Skansen
ORANGERIVÄGEN

DJURGÅRDEN

FALKENBERGSG
ALLMÄNNA GRÄND
DJURGÅRDSSLÄTTEN
LÅNGA GATAN
BELLMANS VÄG

4

Gröna Lund
Allmänna gränd
BREDA G
ANDRI EG
NORDENSKIÖLDG
BECKHOLMSV
Djurgårds-staden
Beckholmssundet
Beckholms-bron
SOLLIDSBACKEN
SINGELBACKEN
AF PONTINS VÄG
DJURGÅRDSVÄGEN
BELLMANSRO
VARMDÖ BYVÄGEN
DJURGÅRDSVÄGEN
BERGSJÖLUNDSVÄGEN
RYSSVIKSVÄGEN
PRINS EUGENS VÄG
Ryssviken
FRISENS PARK

Beckholmen
Waldemarsviken
Waldemarsudde
BISKO

9

Saltsjön

5

ÖSTRA TEGELVIKSSLINGAN
LONDONVIADUKTEN
TEGELVIKS-PLAN
MASTHAMNEN
MASTHAMNEN
Danvikskanalen
Saltsjökvarn

A   *Fåfängan*   B   C
FÅFÄNGAN

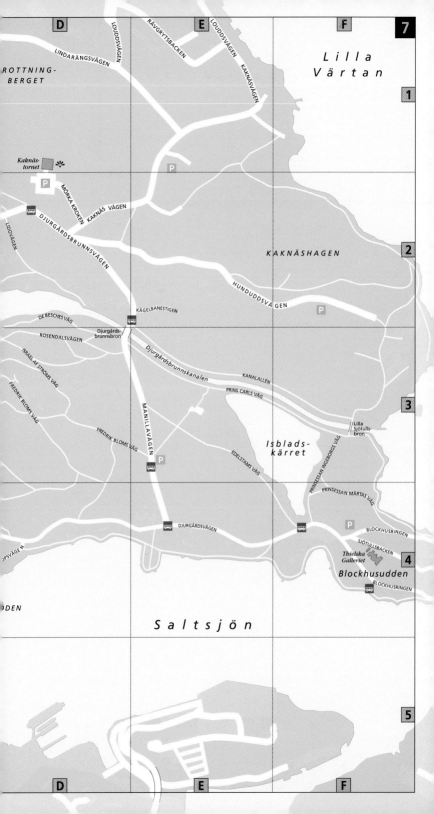

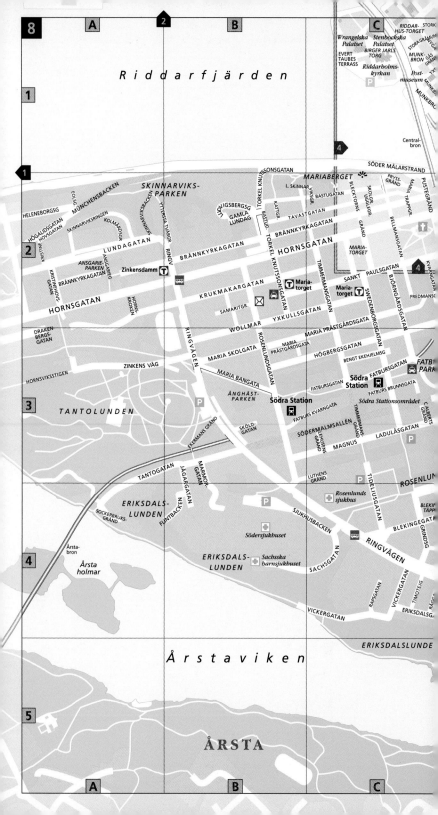

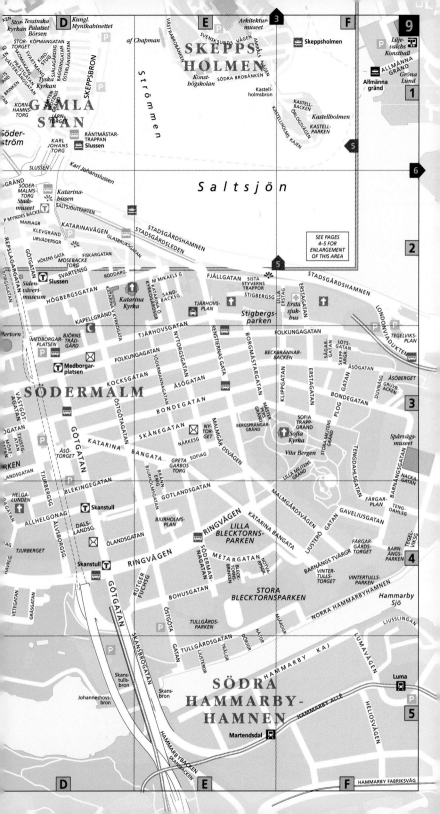

Street Finder Index

General Index

SPECIAL EDITIONS OF DK TRAVEL GUIDES

DK Travel Guides can be purchased in
bulk quantities at discounted prices for
use in promotions or as premiums.
We are also able to offer special editions
and personalized jackets, corporate
imprints, and excerpts from all of our
books, tailored specifically to meet
your own needs.

To find out more, please contact:
(in the United States) **SpecialSales@dk.com**
(in the UK) **TravelSpecialSales@uk.dk.com**
(in Canada) DK Special Sales at
general@tourmaline.ca
(in Australia)
business.development@pearson.com.au

Acknowledgments

Dorling Kindersley would like to thank the following people whose contributions and assistance have made the preparation of this book possible.

Main Contributor
Kaj Sandell began his career as a journalist, writing for the Swedish publishers Åhlén & Åkerlund and *Dagens Nyheter,* Sweden's largest daily newspaper, and has contributed to other guidebooks. For some decades, Kaj Sandell was the Head of Information at Scania Trucks and Busses and he has in recent years written several monographs on leading Swedish companies.

Additional Contributors
Anna Mosesson, Tina Pedersen, James Proctor, Kristin Prouty

Special Assistance
The Publisher would like to thank Stockholm Visitors Board (SVB) and their representatives Roland Berndt, Kjell Holmstrand, Charlotta Lorentz and all other SIS employees for their efforts and support throughout the project. Particular thanks are also due to: Irina Chiriboga, Dorothée Greitz (food and drink consultant), Olof Hultin (architectural consultant) Christina Sollenberg-Britton (Swedish design consultant).

Senior Managing Editor
Louise Bostock Lang.

Editorial Director
Vivien Crump.

Managing Director
Douglas Amrine.

English Translation
Philip Ray.

Editors, English Edition
Jane Hutchings, Caroline Radula-Scott.

Proofreader
Michelle Clark.

Factchecker
Sharon A. Bowker.

DTP, Design & Editorial Assistance, English Edition
Emma Anacootee, Liz Atherton, Marta Bescos Sanchez, Sonal Bhatt, Kathleen Blankenship Sauret, Lucinda Cooke, Karen Fitzpatrick, Lydia Halliday, Stuart James, Claire Jones, Priya Kukadia, Maite Lantaron, Alison McGill, Sam Merrell, Casper Morris, Viveka Mörk, Monica Nilsson, Vikki Nousiainen, Anna Ohlsson, Helen Peters, Marianne Petrou, Lee Redmond, Marisa Renzullo, Ellen Root, Simon Ryder, Sadie Smith.

Additional Illustrations
Jan Rojmar, Jane Bark.

Additional Photography
Neil Fletcher, Ian O'Leary, Ulf Svensson.

Artwork Reference
Svenska Aerobilder AB.

Photography Permission
Dorling Kindersley would like to thank all those who gave permission to photograph at various churches, museums, restaurants, hotels, shops and other sights that are too numerous to list individually. Particular thanks to the Guild of Museum Directors in Stockholm for permitting access to picture archives as well as making additional photographing of objects and exhibitions possible.

Picture Credits
a = above; b = below/bottom; c = centre; f = far; l = left; r = right; t = top.

The publisher would like to thank the following individuals, companies and picture libraries for permission to reproduce their photographs.

4CORNERS IMAGES: SIME/Anna Serrano 205bl; ALAMY IMAGES: Rolf Adlercreutz 196cla; Sten Andersson: 77tc; Marie-Louise Avery 162cl; Chad Ehlers 194cl; Peter Forsberg 163c; imagebroker/Thomas Schneider 205ca; Jon Arnold Images Ltd/Russell Young 200ca; Nicholas Pitt 163tl; pixonnet.com/Ingemar Edfalk 139cr; Sweden And Swedish 192cr; Anna Yu 193.

BERGIANSKA TRÄDGÅRDEN: Åsa Stjerna 124b.

CAMERA PRESS: Scanpix/Thure Wikberg 137tr; GUNNAR CYRÉN: © BUS 2000 184cl.

DANSMUSEUM: 35bc, 62tr; Drottningholm SLOTTSTEATER: Bengt Wanselius 149tr, 149bc.

FJÄRILS & FÅGELHUSET: 122cla. GETTY IMAGES: Sven Nackstrand 201bl; Grand Hôtel: 155tl. HALLWYLSKA MUSEET: 35tr; Sven Nilsson 73tc; S. Uhrdin 73c. IMS Bildbyrå: 25tl.

KUNGLIGA MYNTKABINETTET: 47crb, 68br; Jan Eve Olsson 48cl; KUNGLIGA BIBLIOTEKET: 18br, 19cr, 37tr, 70trc; KUNGLIGA HUSGERÅDSKAMMAREN: *Karl XI's Triumph,* Jacques Foucquet 19tl, 32bc, 50tl, 51tc, 51cr; Alexis Daflos 52tr, 52clb,

53tr, 123bl, 145tlc, 146cl, 146bl, 147tc 147bl, 148tr, 148clb; Håkan Lind 5cl, 50cra, 50crb, 50br, 52cla, 147cr; Kungliga Operan: Mats Bäcker 62bc, 65tl, 65cl.

Livrustkammaren: 19bl, 23br; Göran Schmidt 23cla, 34cla, 47tl; Nina Heins 48bl. Medical Products Agency: 193cl; Medicinhistoriska museet: 121br; Moderna museet: *Ivan by the Armchair*, Isaac Grünewald © Allan Grünewald 80tr; *Breakfast Outdoors*, Pablo Picasso 80tr; *Monogram*, Robert Rauschenberg © BUS 2000 80crb, *The Child's Brain*, Giorgio De Chirico ©BUS 2000 81cl; Per Anders Allsten 80br; Museum Tre Kronor: 53br.

Nationalmuseum: 38clb, 39tr, 51br, 82clb; *The Parhelion Painting*, Urban Målare 14; *The Entry of King Gustav Vasa of Sweden in Stockholm 1523*, Carl Larsson 16t; *Portrait of Erik XIV*, Steven van der Meulen 16c; *The Fire at the Royal Palace May 7th 1697*, Johan Fredrik Höckert 17tr, *Portrait of Queen Kristina*, David Beck 17cl; *The Death of Gustav II Adolf of Sweden at the Battle of Lützen*, Carl Wahlbom 18bl; *The Crossing of the Belt*, Johan Philip Lemke 18–19c; *Bringing Home the Body of King Karl XII of Sweden*, Gustaf Cederström 19br; *King Gustav III of Sweden*, Lorens Pasch the Younger. 20tl; *Portrait of the Bernadotte Family*, Fredrik Westin 20crb; *The Coronation of Gustav III of Sweden*, Carl Gustav Pilo 22cla; *The Battle at Svensksund*, J.T. Schoultz 22clb; *A Noisy Dinner*, Johan Tobias Sergel 22bc; *Conversation at Drottningholm*, Pehr Hilleström 22–23c; *The Murder of Gustav III*, A.W. Küssner 23tr; *Bacchanal on Andros*, Peter Paul Rubens 32clb *Flowers on the Windowsill*, Carl Larsson 38–39c; *The Conspiracy of the Batavians under Claudius Civilis*, Rembrandt 82cla; *David and Bathsheba* 82bl; *The Love Lesson*, Antoine Watteau 82tr; *The Lady with the Veil*, Alexander Roslin 83tl; *Amor and Psyche 1787*, Johan Tobias Sergel 83cb; Åsa Lundén 125br; Hans Thorwid 144tr; Naturhistoriska Riksmuseet: Staffan Waerndt 124tl, 124c; Peter Nordahl: 134tl, 135cl, 137br, 138tr; Nordiska museet: 33c, 91tl, 91tr; Peter Segemark 31tc; Birgit BrÅnvall 90tr; Mats Landin 90cl, 91cra; Sören Hallgren 90bc.

Postmuseum: 55clb; Pressbyran: 197tl; Pressens bild: 133br; Rolf Hamilton 25cr; Hans T. Dahlskog 25br; Jan Collsiöö 50bl, 70bl; Jan Delden 67bl; Hans Dahlskog 88br; Gunnar Seijbolds 109bc; Axel Malmström 117bl. Hans Rossel: 138bl; Riksarkivet: Kurt Eriksson 15tc; Richard Ryan: 9tr, 134cr.

Courtesy of SAS Group: 198tc; Sjöhistoriska museet: 33cra, 107tr, 107cl; Skansen: 96-97c; Marie Andersson 33bc, 97tc, 87bc, 97cra;

Skogskyrkogården: 133cl; Stadsbiblioteket: 117tr; Statens Historiska Museum: 34br, 104cla, 104clb, 104bl, 104br, 105tc, 105ca, 105cb, 105br, 105bl, 144cl, 144bl; Christer Åhlin 31cl, 33tr; Statens Museum für Världskultur: Etnografiska museet - Bo Gabrielsson 108bc, 108t; Medelhavsmuseet - Ove Kaneberg 62cla; Ostasiatiska museet - Erik Cornelius 76cla; Karl Zetterstorm 78bl; Steninge Slott: 145b; Stockholms Auktionsverk: 23bl; J. L. Sánchez, Hans Hedberg © BUS 2000 38tr, Sigurd Persson © BUS 2000 39tl; Stockholms Stadsbyggnadskontor: 110cl; Stockholms Stadshus: Jan Asplund 114br, 115tl; *The Mosaics in the Golden Hall*, Einar Forseth © BUS 2000 114tr; Stockholms Stadsmuseum: 24bl, 25clb; *The Three Crowns Castle*, Govert Camphuysen 18cl; Gustaf Carleman 21cb; *Newspaper Readers*, J. A. Cronstedt 21tl; *The Regicide Anckarström punished in front of the House of Nobility*, 23cr; Stockholms Universitet: Per Bergström 116b; Courtesy of Stockholm Visitors Board: 190cb, Frédéric Lindquist 190cra; Strindbergsmuseet: 138cl; Per Bergström 69br; Stromma Media Bank: 8br; Svenska Akademien: Leif Jansson 22tr; Svenska Handelsbanken AB: Bengt Wanselius 194bl; Sveriges Riksdag: Holger Staffansson 59tc. Telemuseum: Carl-Erik Viphammar 107br; Telenor Group: 196tr; Courtesy of TeliaSonera: 196; Thielska Galleriet: *Hornsgatan*, Eugène Jansson 99tr, Tidningen Svensk Polis. 192crb.

Vasamuseet: 94br; Hans Hammarskiöld 3ca, 4tr, 33br, 86cla, 92tr, 92cla, 92bl, 92br, 93tc, 93cra, 93crb, 93bc, 94cla, 94tr; Vin- & Sprithistoriska museet: 95c; Pia Wallén: © BUS 2000 184bl; Ingrid Vang Nyman: 86tr; Claes Westlin 38cla; Waxholmsbolaget: 204tl; Jeppe Wikström: 5tr, 8cl, 9cl, 9br, 15bc, 26cr, 26bl, 27cr, 29cr, 31cra, 36tr, 36cl, 38cl, 40tr, 40cl, 40clb, 40br, 42-43, 44, 55tr, 59tc, 60, 61tc, 62clb, 63bl, 63crb, 67t, 68tl, 72bc, 73tc, 73bl, 78br, 79c, 85tc, 87cr, 89t, 95tr, 98bl, 100, 101tc, 102bl, 114bl, 116tr, 121bl, 122clb, 126tr, 126bl, 127c, 127bl, 128tc, 129crb, 131tr, 134cl, 135tr, 136tr, 136bc, 138tl, 139tc.141cl, 141b, 142cl, 143br, 150cr, 151tr, 151bc, 160bl, 175tl, 180tc, 180cl, 180bl, 188-9, 199t.

Sheet Map front cover: Photolibrary: Berndt-Joel Gunnarsson.

JACKET
Front: Photolibrary: Berndt-Joel Gunnarsson; Back: 4Corners Images: SIME/Canali Pietro tl; Alamy Images: Jon Hicks cla, SCPhotos/Dallas and John Heaton bl; Corbis: Jean-Pierre Lescourret clb; Spine: Photolibrary: Berndt-Joel Gunnarsson t.

All other images © Dorling Kindersley.

For further information see: www.dkimages.com

Phrase Book

When reading the imitated pronunciation, stress the part which is underlined. Pronounce each syllable as if it formed part of an English word, and you will be understood sufficiently well. Remember the points below, and your pronunciation will be even closer to the correct Swedish.

ai:	as in 'fair' or 'stair'
ea:	as in 'ear' or 'hear'
ew:	like the sound in 'dew'
EW:	try to say 'ee' with your lips rounded
oo:	as in 'book' or 'soot'
OO:	as in 'spoon' or 'groom'
r:	should be strongly pronounced

Swedish Alpahbetical Order

In the list below we have followed Swedish alphabetical order. The following letters are listed after **z: å, ä, ö**.

You

There are two words for 'you': 'du' and 'ni'. 'Ni' is the polite form; 'du' is the familiar form. It is not impolite to address a complete stranger with the familiar form.

In an Emergency

Help!	**Hjälp!**	yelp
Stop!	**Stanna!**	stanna!
Call a doctor!	**Ring efter en doktor!**	ring efter ehn doktor
Call an ambulance!	**Ring efter en ambulans!**	ring efter ehn ambewlanss
Call the police!	**Ring polisen!**	ring poleesen
Call the fire brigade!	**Ring efter brandkåren!**	ring efter brandkawren
Where is the nearest telehone?	**Var finns närmaste telefon?**	vahr finnss nairmasteh telefawn
Where is the nearest hospital?	**Var finns närmaste sjukhus?**	vahr finnss- nairmasteh shewkhews

Communication Essentials

Yes	**Ja**	yah
No	**Nej**	nay
Please (offering)	**Varsågod**	vahrshawgOOd
Thank you	**Tack**	tack
Excuse me	**Ursäkta**	ewrshekta
Hello	**Hej**	hay
Goodbye	**Hej då/adjö**	haydaw/ahyur
Good night	**God natt**	goonutt
Morning	**Morgon**	morron
Afternoon	**Eftermiddag**	eftermiddahg
Evening	**Kväll**	kvell
Yesterday	**Igår**	ee gawr
Today	**Idag**	ee dahg
Tomorrow	**I morgon**	ee morron
Here	**Här**	hair
There	**Där**	dair
What?	**Vad?**	vah
When?	**När?**	nair
Why?	**Varför?**	vahrfurr
Where?	**Var?**	vahr

Useful Phrases

How are you?	**Hur mår du?**	hewr mawr dew
Very well, thank you.	**Mycket bra, tack.**	mewkeh brah, tack
Pleased to meet you.	**Trevligt att träffas.**	treavlit att trajffas
See you soon.	**Vi ses snart.**	vee seas snahrt
That's fine.	**Det går bra.**	dea gawr brah
Where is/are ...?	**Var finns ...?**	vahr finnss...
How far is it to ...?	**Hur långt är det till**	hewr lawngt ea dea till
Which way to ...?	**Hur kommer jag till ...?**	hewr kommer yah till ...
Do you speak English?	**Talar du/ni engelska?**	tahlar dew/nee engelska
I don't understand	**Jag förstår inte.**	yah furshtawr inteh
Could you speak more slowly, please?	**Kan du/ni tala lång- sammare, tack.**	kan dew/nee tahla lawng- ssamareh tack
I'm sorry.	**Förlåt.**	furrlawt

Useful Words

big	**stor**	stOOr
small	**liten**	leeten
hot	**varm**	varrm
cold	**kall**	kall
good	**bra**	brah
bad	**dålig**	dawleeg
enough	**tillräcklig**	tillraikleeg
open	**öppen**	urpen
closed	**stängd**	staingd
left	**vänster**	vainster
right	**höger**	hurger
straight on	**rakt fram**	rahkt fram
near	**nära**	naira
far	**långt**	lawngt
up/over	**upp/över**	ewp/urver
down/under	**ner/under**	near/ewnder
early	**tidig**	teedee
late	**sen**	sehn
entrance	**ingång**	ingawng
exit	**utgång**	ewtgawng
toilet	**toalett**	too-alett
more	**mer**	mehr
less	**mindre**	meendre

Shopping

How much - is this?	**Hur mycket - kostar den här?**	hewr mewkeh - kostar dehn hair
I would like ...	**Jag skulle vilja ...**	yah skewleh vilya
Do you have?	**Har du/ni ...?**	hahr dew/nee ...
I'm just looking	**Jag ser mig bara omkring**	yah sear may bahra omkring
Do you take credit cards?	**Tar du/ni kreditkort?**	tahr dew/nee kredeetkoort
What time do you open?	**När öppnar ni?**	nair urpnar nee
What time do you close?	**När stänger ni?**	nair stainger nee
This one.	**den här**	dehn hair
That one.	**den där**	dehn dair
expensive	**dyr**	dewr
cheap	**billig**	billig
size (clothes)	**storlek**	stOOrlek
white	**vit**	veet
black	**svart**	svart
red	**röd**	rurd
yellow	**gul**	gewl
green	**grön**	grurn
blue	**blå**	blaw
antique shop	**antikaffär**	anteek-affair
bakery	**bageri**	bahgeree
bank	**bank**	bank
book shop	**bokhandel**	bOOkhandel
butcher's	**slaktare**	slaktareh
cake shop	**konditori**	konditoree
chemist	**apotek**	apoteak
fishmonger	**fiskaffär**	fisk-affair
grocer	**speceriaffär**	spesseree-affair
hairdresser	**frisör**	frissurr
market	**marknad**	marrknad
newsagent	**tidningskiosk**	teednings-cheeosk
post office	**postkontor**	posstkontOOr
shoe shop	**skoaffär**	skOO-affair
supermarket	**snabbköp**	snabbchurp
tobacconist's	**tobakshandel**	tOObaks-handel
travel agency	**resebyrå**	reasseh-bewraw

Sightseeing

art gallery	**konstgalleri**	konnst-galleree
church	**kyrka**	chewrka
garden	**trädgård**	traidgawrd
house	**hus**	hews
library	**bibliotek**	beebleeotek
museum	**museum**	mewseum
square	**torg**	tohrj
street	**gata**	gahta
tourist information office	**turist- informations- kontor**	tureest- informashOOns- kontOOr
town hall	**stadshus**	statshews
closed for holiday	**stängt för semester**	staingt furr semester
bus station	**busstation**	bewss-stashOOn
railway station	**järnvägsstation**	yairnvaigs-stashOOn

Staying in a Hotel

Do you have any vacancies?	**Har ni några lediga rum?**	hahr nee negra leadiga rewm
double room wih double bed	**dubbelrum med dubbelsäng**	doobelrewm med doobel seng

twin room	dubbelrum	doobelrewm
	med två	med tvaw
	sängar	sengar
single room	enkelrum	enkelrewm
room with	rum med	rewm med
a bath	bad	bahd
shower	dusch	dewsh
key	nyckel	newckel
I have a	Jag har	yah hahr
reservation	beställt rum	bestellt rewm

Eating Out

Have you got a	Har ni ett	hahr nee ett
table for…	bord för…?	bOOrd furr …
I would like	Jag skulle vilja	yah skewleh vilya
to reserve	boka ett	bOOka ett
a table.	bord.	bOOrd
The bill, please.	Notan, tack.	nOOtan, tack
I am a	Jag är	yah är
vegetarian	vegetarian	vegetariahn
waitress	servitris	sairvitreess
waiter	servitör	sairviturr
menu	meny/	menew/
	matsedel	mahtseadel
fixed-price	meny med	menew med
menu	fast pris	fast prees
wine list	vinlista	veenlista
glass of water	ett glas	ett glahss
	vatten	vatten
glass of wine	ett glas vin	ett glahss veen
bottle	flaska	flaska
knife	kniv	k-neev
fork	gaffel	gaffel
spoon	sked	shead
breakfast	frukost	frewkost
lunch	lunch	lewnch
dinner	middag	middahg
main course	huvudrätt	hewvewdrett
starter	förrätt	furrett
dish of the day	dagens rätt	dahgens rett
coffee	kaffe	kaffeh
rare	blodig	blOOdee
medium	medium	medium
well done	välstekt	vailstehkt

Menu Decoder

abborre	abborreh	perch
ansjovis	anshOOvees	anchovies
apelsin	appelseen	orange
bakelse	bahkelse	cake, pastry, tart
banan	banahn	banana
biff	biff	beef
bröd	brurd	bread
bullar	bewllar	buns
choklad	shooklahd	chocolate
citron	sitrOOn	lemon
dessert	dessair	dessert
fisk	fisk	fish
fläsk	flaisk	pork
forell	fooraill	trout
frukt	fruckt	fruit
glass	glass	ice cream
gurka	gewrka	cucumber
grönsaksgryta	grurnsahks-grewta	vegetable stew
hummer	hummer	lobster
kallskuret	kall-skuret	cold meat
korv	koorv	sausages
kyckling	chewkling	chicken
kött	churtt	meat
lamm	lamm	lamb
lök	lurk	onion
mineralvatten	minerahl-vatten	mineral water
med/utan	mehd/ewtan	still/sparkling
kolsyra	kawlsewra	
mjölk	m-yurlk	milk
nötkött	nurtchurtt	beef
nötter	nurtter	nuts
ost	oost	cheese
olja	olya	oil
oliver	oleever	olives
paj/kaka	pa-y/kahka	pie/cake
potatis	potahtis	potatoes
peppar	peppar	pepper
ris	rees	rice
rostat bröd	rostat brurd	toast
räkor	raikoor	prawns
rökt skinka	rurkt sheenka	cured ham
rött vin	rurtt veen	red wine
saft	safft-	lemonade
sill	seell	herring

skaldjur	skahl-yewr	seafood
smör	smurr	butter
stekt	stehkt	fried
strömming	strurmming	baltic herring
salt	sallt	salt
socker	socker	sugar
soppa	soppa	soup
sås	saws	sauce
te	tea	tea
torr	torr	dry
ungsstekt	ewngs-stehkt	baked, roast
vinäger	vinaiger	vinegar
vispgrädde	veesp-graiddeh	whipped cream
vitlök	veet-lurk	garlic
vitt vin	veett veen	white wine
ägg	aigg	egg
älg	ail-y	elk
äpple	aippleh	apple
öl	url	beer

Numbers

0	noll	noll
1	ett	ett
2	två	tvaw
3	tre	trea
4	fyra	flewra
5	fem	fem
6	sex	sex
7	sju	shew
8	åtta	otta
9	nio	nee-oo
10	tio	tee-oo
11	elva	elva
12	tolv	tolv
13	tretton	tretton
14	fjorton	f-yoorton
15	femton	femton
16	sexton	sexton
17	sjutton	shewton
18	arton	ahrton
19	nitton	nitton
20	tjugo	chewgoo
21	tjugoett	chewgoo-ett
22	tjugotvå	chewgoo-tvaw
30	trettio	tretti
31	trettioett	tretti-ett
40	fyrtio	furrti
50	femtio	femti
60	sextio	sexti
70	sjuttio	shewti
80	åttio	otti
90	nittio	nitti
100	(ett) hundra	(ett) hewndra
101	etthundraett	ett-hewndra-ett
102	etthundratvå	ett-hewndra-tvaw
200	tvåhundra	tvawhewndra
300	trehundra	treahewndra
400	fyrahundra	fewrahewndra
500	femhundra	femhewndra
600	sexhundra	sexhewndra
700	sjuhundra	shewhewndra
800	åttahundra	ottahewndra
900	niohundra	nee-oohewndra
1 000	(ett) tusen	(ett) tewssen
1 001	etttusenett	ett-tewssen-ett
100 000	(ett) hundra-	(ett) hewndra-
	tusen	tewssen
1 000 000	en miljon	ehn milyOOn

Time

one minute	en minut	ehn meenewt
one hour	en timme	ehn timmeh
half an hour	en halvtimme	ehn halvtimmeh
ten past one	tio över ett	teeoo urver ett
quarter past one	kvart över ett	kvahrt urver ett
half past one	halv två	halv tvaw
twenty to two	tjugo i två	chewgoo ee tvaw
quarter to two	kvart i två	kvahrt ee tvaw
two o'clock	klockan två	klockan tvaw
13.00	klockan tretton	klockan tretton
16.30	sexton och trettio	sexton och tretti
noon	klockan tolv	klockan tolv
midnight	midnatt	meednatt
Monday	måndag	mawndahg
Tuesday	tisdag	teesdahg
Wednesday	onsdag	oonssdahg
Thursday	torsdag	toorsdahg
Friday	fredag	freadahg
Saturday	lördag	lurrdahg
Sunday	söndag	surndahg

Stockholm Transport Map